CONTROLLING ANGER

Comments on Suzette Heald's *Controlling Anger*

'Since Uganda became independent in 1962 Bagisu have had to come to grips with the uncertainties of life "in a situation approaching anarchy". This excellent and often moving book examines the ways in which ordinary people have coped with this crisis'. – Paul Baxter, in *The Times Literary Supplement*

'It is an utterly absorbing study for anybody concerned seriously with this part of Uganda, and most stimulating for the ideas it throws out regarding the Gisu'. – Michael Twaddle, in *Africa Journal*

'This masterly anthropological study of the Gisu (eastern Uganda) takes as its point of departure a rather unusual, but in this particular case very fruitful topic: internal violence and its control . . . the Gisu are in many ways rather atypical compared to the majority of African cultures, but . . . Heald turns this atypical situation into a virtue by using the unusual traits of Gisu culture in order to take issue with the ideas of some leading anthropologists: Evans-Pritchard on lineage theory, Fortes on the concept of self, morality and ancestors, and others on topics such as joking relationships or witch-cleansing cults. This makes her book of interest not only to the "happy few" who may have a passion for Gisu society, but for any anthropologist'. – Robert Buitenhuijs, in *Development and Change*

'Her prose is engaging and it is clear that she has made a novel and important contribution to the rural sociology of Africa . . . Heald's study truly invites a wide reading'. – John W. Burton, in *Anthropos*

'. . . this is an innovative monograph which . . . will help rejuvenate African anthropology'. – Wendy James, in *Man*

D0919995

Eastern African Studies

Revealing Prophets
Prophecy in Eastern
African History
Edited by DAVID M.
ANDERSON & DOUGLAS H.
JOHNSON

Religion & Politics in East Africa
The Period Since
Independence
Edited by HOLGER BERNT
HANSEN & MICHAEL
TWADDLE

Swahili Origins
Swahili Culture & the
Shungwaya Phenomenon
JAMES DE VERE ALLEN

Being Maasai
Ethnicity & Identity in
East Africa
Edited by THOMAS SPEAR
& RICHARD WALLER

*A History of Modern Ethiopia
1855–1974*
BAHRU ZEWDE

*Ethnicity & Conflict
in the Horn of Africa*
Edited by KATSUYOSHI
FUKUI & JOHN MARKAKIS

*Conflict, Age & Power
in North East Africa*
Age Systems in Transition
Edited by EISEI KURIMOTO
& SIMON SIMONSE

Jua Kali Kenya
Change & Development
in an Informal Economy
1970–95
KENNETH KING

*Control & Crisis in
Colonial Kenya*
The Dialectic of Domination
BRUCE BERMAN

Unhappy Valley
Book One: State & Class
Book Two: Violence &
Ethnicity
BRUCE BERMAN
& JOHN LONSDALE

Mau Mau from Below
GREET KERSHAW

*The Mau Mau War in
Perspective*
FRANK FUREDI

*Squatters & the Roots
of Mau Mau 1905–63*
TABITHA KANOGO

*Economic & Social Origins
of Mau Mau 1945–53*
DAVID THROUP

Multi-Party Politics in Kenya
The Kenyatta & Moi
States & the Triumph of
the System in the 1992
Election
DAVID W. THROUP
& CHARLES HORNSBY

*Decolonization & Independence
in Kenya 1940–93*
Edited by B.A. OGOT
& WILLIAM R. OCHIENG'

*Penetration & Protest in
Tanzania*
The Impact of the World
Economy on the Pare
1860–1960
ISARIA N. KIMAMBO

Custodians of the Land
Ecology & Culture
in the History of Tanzania
Edited by GREGORY
MADDOX, JAMES L. GIBLIN
& ISARIA N. KIMAMBO

*Education in the Development
of Tanzania 1919–1990*
LENE BUCHERT

*The Second Economy
in Tanzania*
T.L. MALIYAMKONO
& M.S.D. BAGACHWA

*Ecology Control &
Economic Development in
East African History*
The Case of Tanganyika
1850–1950
HELGE KJEKSHUS

Siaya
The Historical
Anthropology of an
African Landscape
DAVID WILLIAM COHEN
& E.S. ATIENO ODHIAMBO

*Uganda Now
Changing Uganda
Developing Uganda**
From Chaos to Order
Edited by HOLGER BERNT
HANSEN & MICHAEL
TWADDLE

*Kakungulu & the Creation
of Uganda 1868–1928*
MICHAEL TWADDLE

Controlling Anger
The Anthropology of Gisu
Violence
SUZETTE HEALD

Kampala Women Getting By
Wellbeing in the
Time of AIDS
SANDRA WALLMAN

*Slaves, Spices & Ivory
in Zanzibar*
Integration of an East
African Commercial
Empire into the
World Economy
ABDUL SHERIFF

Zanzibar Under Colonial Rule
Edited by ABDUL SHERIFF
& ED FERGUSON

*The History & Conservation of
Zanzibar Stone Town*
Edited by ABDUL SHERIFF

* forthcoming

CONTROLLING ANGER

THE ANTHROPOLOGY OF GISU VIOLENCE

Suzette Heald

James Currey
OXFORD

Fountain Publishers
KAMPALA

Ohio University Press
ATHENS

James Currey Ltd
73 Botley Road
Oxford
OX2 0BS

Fountain Publishers
PO Box 488
Kampala

Ohio University Press
Scott Quadrangle
Athens, Ohio 45701, USA

© Suzette Heald, 1998
First published by Manchester University Press
for the International African Institute,
in its African Library Series, 1989

1 2 3 4 5 01 02 00 99 98

British Library Cataloguing in Publication Data

Heald, Suzette
    Controlling anger : the anthropology of Gisu violence. –
    2nd ed. – (Eastern African Studies)
    1. Gisu (African People) 2. Violence – Research – Uganda
    3. Social conflict – Uganda – Sex differences
    I. Title
    303.6'09676

ISBN 0-85255-246-7 (James Currey Paper)

Library of Congress Cataloging-in-Publication Data is available

ISBN 0-8214-1215-9 (Ohio University Press Paper)

Printed in Great Britain
by Villiers Publications, London N3

CONTENTS

TABLES

FIGURES

PREFACE TO THE PAPERBACK EDITION

In 1989, when this book was first published, it was sub-titled, 'The sociology of Gisu violence'. At that time, this appeared as the most appropriate title as I felt that there was no distinctive anthropology of violence into which this book naturally fell. This is no longer the case. In so far as this relates to the endless outbreaks of hostilities around the world, it is to be regretted. However, it is to be welcomed in so far as it indicates a change of perception among anthropologists who no longer feel compelled to filter such events out of their vision or written accounts. I mention this because this book was conceived very much against such a tradition, and it largely explains the recourse to Hobbes rather than to Durkheim in my treatment of Gisu violence of the 1960s and my sometimes rather apologetic tone. The violence which I found was no symbolic violence, it was no mimicking device, no counter-statement to the regularity and order of ritual or everyday life. Nor was it predominantly a matter of inter-ethnic disputes and warfare. Rather, it related to interpersonal violence at the local level. With the national newspapers of Africa carrying their daily toll of violent crime, and with reports of self-help being increasingly resorted to in dealing with witches and thieves, the subjects of this book, far from being out-dated, appear all-too current.

A new edition of a book inevitably raises dilemmas for the author. The temptation is to rewrite the text, to develop the arguments to the point – since one's thinking has inevitably changed – that one can find oneself writing another. My sympathetic editors persuaded me that all that was needed was a short preface, answering some of the queries raised by the reviewers of the first edition, which mainly related to what had happened since I had left the area, particularly the trajectory of the new movements described in Part 4. Yet this request raises the whole question of the abrupt ending to my field-work among the Gisu, and why it has remained frozen in a particular period; a question which links the political to the personal.

Previous generations of anthropologists spoke of their experiences in terms of 'culture shock'. We of the current generation perhaps experience something more akin to survivors' guilt. When I left Bugisu in 1969, despite all the tragedies described in this book, there was a basic optimism; a place where people expected life to get better for both themselves and their children.

It was a wealthy agricultural area, people had not known serious famines for a generation or more. True, the troubles of the postcolonial state were apparent enough in the political jockeying for power on ethnic and religious lines, but there was no portent of the cataclysm that was to come a scarce 18 months later in the form of Amin. Later, in 1973, in the British press, I read of a massacre in Mbale and realised that letters from my friends in Bugisu had dried up. I took the hint, and also stopped writing and sending money. Perhaps one of the most telling experiences of a short return that I later made was to receive thanks from them for *not* writing. They had lived in dread of a letter that might well, in the climate of paranoid persecution, have spelt their death as 'foreign agents'.

For 10 years or more return was a well-nigh impossibility. When I did eventually go back in 1981, the circumstances were far from ideal. I took a one month's consultancy to advise on the water and sanitation problems in four Ugandan towns. This was in the aftermath of the Tanzanian-led 'Liberation War'; the country was quite literally shattered, civil peace tenuous and Obote's new regime contested. The state of fear was only a hair's breath away and 'talking politics' a risky matter. Uganda seemed largely to be ruled by rival warlords who, with their armed retinues, dominated most of the commerce. Indeed, the danger was to be brought home by the fact that three of the Ugandans involved in the water project were to be shot dead in the Kampala streets in the following two years. But, in 1981, the consultancy gave me the opportunity I had wanted for so long to return to Uganda. For ten days of that time I was based in Mbale, the administrative headquarters of Bugisu, but due to the lack of transport I was only able to make one visit to the places where I had lived, to the mountain ridges of Busano and to Nabumali in the foothills of Busoba. I arrived unannounced, disconcerting my former friends who thus had no way of welcoming me as they would have wished. But, even if announced, the situation for many would have been the same. This was no occasion for a joyful reunion.

Television bulletins have now made us familiar with circumstances in war-torn nations. Where a few survive and prosper, the great majority barely scrape a living. The Gisu countryside of 1981 now sported a few substantial permanent houses in European style amid the scatter of mud and wattle and, by now, rusting tin roofs, highlighting such differences in fortunes. After two years of drought, accompanied by a severe epidemic of rinderpest which had wiped out most of the cattle, I was shocked by the poverty of much of the area. True, the mountainous areas had come off relatively well, with their banana groves and their coffee, which could be smuggled over the border into Kenya to yield good profit. But, lower down the mountain, in the area that I had known best, around Nabumali, the soils, never good, now seemed exhausted. The millet harvests which my friends showed me seemed not enough to last a month, let alone a year. And, inevitably, many of my old friends, those with whom I had shared my youth, were dead. I speak of this not to dwell on the pathos of the occasion but because it exposes the gulf that separates the First and the Third world, a gulf in which anthropologists are deeply implicated and which lays them open to charges of bad faith. We go under and work under a guise of friendship but that friendship may be of precious little worth. It has been put to me that our job in such circumstances is to be there to witness and testify. Perhaps. But I felt that the very conditions of my working there again had disappeared. The gap had been too long; the people whose lives I had shared for 3 years had experienced so much I had now not shared. I could not simply pick up where I had left off.

Nevertheless, the visit did allow me to gather new information on the movements mentioned earlier and that information is incorporated into chapter 11. Then, both the vigilantes organisations and drinking companies had survived the turmoil of the Amin years; indeed, adapting to circumstance, they had perhaps formed a major strategy for survival, as described on pp 253-4. The indications that I have gathered since then, somewhat fortuitously to be sure, picked up in newspaper reports from times when I have been doing fieldwork in Kenya, indicate raised rather than lowered levels of violence in the area. There have been regular surges in inter-ethnic disputes, with the land-short Gisu who have migrated into neighbouring districts providing an on-going source of contention. Massacres have occurred and Gisu have been forced to flee both from Sebei to the north and from the south where they have spread into Kenya. Nor have the problems of 'witches' and 'thieves' disappeared within Bugisu itself. As recently as January 1995, a Ugandan newspaper reports the killing of 36 alleged sorcerers in Bulucheke sub-county of southern Bugisu. It reports that 'the victims, who were aged between 50 and 80 years, were hacked to death between January 16 and 22 by an angry mob of youths who accused them of witchcraft. They were also accused of practising sorcery which prevents the elite from getting employment and making youthful girls barren.'[1] Such an event, so much more excessive than any I describe for the 1960s, yet bearing such clear continuities with the analyses contained in these pages, leads me to believe that this book will provide a useful form of understanding both for the Gisu living through these troubled times as well as for social scientists trying to grapple with similar issues both in Uganda and elsewhere in Africa.

Suzette Heald
July 1997

[1] I am very grateful to David Mills for sending me this report.

ACKNOWLEDGEMENTS

Fieldwork was financed by grants from the Department of Education and Science, the Worshipful Company of Goldsmiths and the University of London. In Uganda, I was affiliated to the Department of Sociology at Makerere University and I also held a junior research fellowship at Makerere Institute of Social Research from 1968 to 1969. To all these bodies I wish to register my gratitude. Personal debts are more difficult to enumerate but in addition to my husband, Donald Heald, who shared the years in Bugisu and beyond, I would like to thank Raymond Apthorpe, Beverley Brock, Anne Sharman and Susan and Michael Whyte for the friendship they gave me in the field; Mary Douglas and Adam Kuper for bearing with me in the long and tedious process of writing up my thesis; Roy Barter, the chief magistrate in Mbale, who provided tea together with the court records and George Brown for his help with survey design. To Jean La Fontaine I owe a special debt. She was remembered in Bugisu with great affection – all knew of Nambozo – and to be credited with a tie of quasi-kinship with her was of immeasurable help during the early period of my fieldwork. Later debts proliferate in different directions and Paul Heelas, Ivan Karp, David Parkin, Audrey Richards and Jean Smith helped me at many and various points along the line while Talal Asad, Gillian Feeley-Harnik, Stephen Bunker and John Peel came to the rescue to comment on particular chapters. In addition, I am especially grateful to Ivan Karp, whose encouragement gave me the confidence, and to the Smithsonian Institution, which gave me the fellowship, which finally allowed me to prepare this manuscript for publication. The Press readers also gave valuable and constructive comments and I gratefully acknowledge the permission of the International African Institute to use material from my articles in Africa 52 (1982) and 56 (1986).

My greatest debt is to the Gisu for their great kindness and friendship towards me. I write with some trepidation in case my presentation of their experiences offends: but I write with respect, with admiration for the fortitude they never failed to display in the face of the many sadnesses of life and their knowledge of the darker side of human experience. So many people helped me, especially among the Basoba, Basiu, Basano and Bangokho, that it seems better to extend a collective appreciation, singling out only my assistant, Yovani Mataya, who shared so much with me and whose experiences are described at several points during this study. To the memory of our household in Bugisu – to Yovani, Wamboka, Mataki, Leya, Don and my daughter, Karen Khaitsa – I dedicate this study.

S.H.
November 1988

A NOTE ON THE PEOPLE AND LANGUAGE

In 1900 a Ganda general, Kakungulu, was directed by the British to subdue the peoples of what is now eastern Uganda. The Ganda used the name *Bageshu* to distinguish the Bantu-speaking people living on the western slopes of Mount Elgon from the other acephalous people of the mountains and plains. This name (sometimes written *Bagishu* or *Bagesu*) was adopted by the British administration, with the spelling changing to *Bagisu* in 1954. In the past it is probable that the people used *Bagisu* to refer only to the northern cluster of clans and this name can still be used with this more limited referrent today. The more inclusive name then becomes *Bamasaba*, people of Masaba, referring both to the eponymous ancestor from whom the Gisu claim descent and to Mount Elgon itself, which is considered to have been his birthplace. This name is the preferred usage when cultural identity is being stressed. Yet the term *Bagisu* is used more often and more widely and, since it has become the name by which they tend to be known outside the region, I will follow this usage, abbreviating the name to 'Gisu' by using the convention of deleting the plural personal prefix. However, for all other names I will keep the prefixes so that the following prefixes carry the same meaning throughout: *umu* is the singular personal prefix, *ba* is the plural and *bu* refers to the place. Thus Masaba is the name of a person, Umumasaba is a person of Masaba, Bamasaba are the people of Masaba, Bumasaba refers to the countryside where they live and, one might add, Lumasaba is the language they speak. Other prefixes will be explained in the text as they occur.

At the time of writing I am still unsure as to whether a common orthography has become accepted for Lugisu or Lumasaba. In the 1960s this was still the subject of much debate and I therefore transcribed the Gisu words I used according to spellings appropriate for the central dialect. Since then a linguist, B. Siertsema (1981), has published a dictionary and this is invaluable for those familiar with the language and the complexity of dialectic variation. However, the orthography used is less than ideal for the purposes of this book because it does not relate in many instances to the phonetic realisation of sounds in the central dialect and thus provides no guide here for the non-Gisu reader. My compromise solution is, firstly, to use official spellings for all the administrative divisions and terms. Secondly, to continue to use a central Lugisu transcription in the text but, thirdly, to list here those symbols that would differ if one were to use Siertsema's orthography based on the dialectic 'macro-phonemes'.

Central transcription	Siertsema's orthography	Phonetic realisation in Central dialect
x	kh	Velar fricative
c	kh	Palatal fricative as 's' in sugar
ts	z or nz	Alveolar affricative
ng	nk, ng, nkh	
nd	nt	
mb	mp	

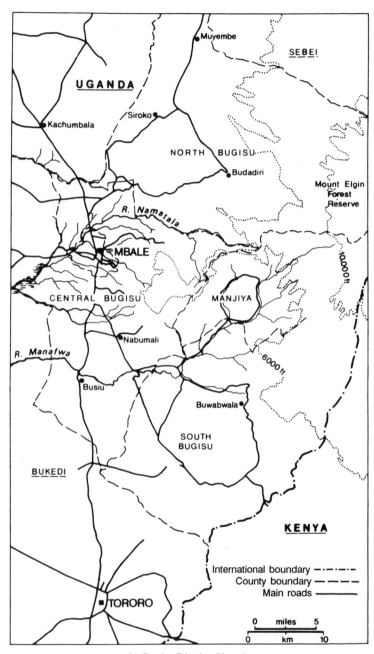

1 Bugisu District, Uganda

INTRODUCTION

'Mulembe'. Gisu greetings start with this avowal of 'peace' and, after an enquiry into the other's health, pose the question, 'Any bad news?' Perhaps this in itself is as revealing, as the conventional response of 'It is quiet' or 'It is well' was, as a formula, usually inaccurate. Every morning exposed the sadnesses and troubles of the night, bringing fresh news of illness, assault, threat, theft and murder. Violence and the fear and suspicion it bred were the main subjects of daily conversation. The initial response when I began field-work in the mid-1960s seemed pessimistic to the point of fatalism. 'The Gisu are just a bad people' was the plaint after every act of violence. 'What could one do?' The violence was seen to be out of control and the problem to lie in their own human nature. In fact, in the succeeding years the Gisu were to organise themselves into vigilante groups and drinking companies, initiatives they saw as establishing a distinctive 'Gisu Government' with new and effective sanctions to control violence.

These movements originated at a time, in the immediate post-colonial period in Uganda, when the administrative structures in the rural areas had been shattered by a succession of political initiatives, originating at both national and local levels. Yet the very pragmatism of the Gisu movements – one setting out to control beer-drinking, the most dangerous social activity, and the other to police and eradicate thieves and witches in their local areas – should not be seen only against a vacuum of political authority but in terms of their own distinctive ideologies of social relationship and the practicalities of their experience. This book is about the nature of that experience, of a people's attempt to come to grips with the uncertainties of life in a situation approaching anarchy.

Twentieth-century anthropologists have used the idea of anarchy to make points about order and, in so doing, they have ignored the study of 'disorder' as a contingent reality. Indeed, the assumption has been that the Hobbesian 'state of nature' is purely hypothetical and neither exists nor has existed. To take one quotation to represent many: 'It is well known that real wars of all against all, in which every man's hand is against his brother's, never happen' (Murphy, 1971: 67). Indeed, the discipline has rested on the presumption of order in society, alone allowing for the possibility of a rigorous sociology. In Britain, social structure was seen to be about the articulation of people into orderly patterns of relationship and behaviour while, in America, culture was defined in terms of consistency and described in terms of theme and pattern. Yet the 'order' thus discerned was often at a very high level of abstraction from everyday political realities.

Evans-Pritchard's (1940) classic study, *The Nuer*, is a type example here, showing how political processes presupposed a recognition of common rules. Thus, the feud was fought according to the recognition of degrees of kinship closeness, formulated in terms of the elaborate structuring of Nuer lineages, and the feud in turn maintained this structure. The idea of order was thus tied to reproduction, the existence of the system over time, and to a consistency produced by the recognition of common rules. Yet 'order' here did not mean either orderly, peaceful or cohesive. In textbooks of sociology and anthropology the Nuer became the prototype of an 'ordered anarchy', an exemplar of order without the state which systematically underplayed the extent of violence and the importance of force in Nuer life. Despite the recognition of rules and elaborate dispute procedures, as Evans-Pritchard writes, 'it is very rare for a man to obtain redress except by force or threat of force' (1940:162). This reliance on force, available equally to all men, invites a Hobbesian perspective as much as a Durkheimian one.

The present appeal of Hobbes is not to resurrect Leviathan but is to be found in his political realism and in his psychology which sees anarchy as a problem which man faces as a member of society and in the face of his fear of other men. Anarchy exists not necessarily in actual fighting but, as he writes, 'in the known disposition thereto, during all the time there is no assurance to the contrary' (1651/1968:185). His psychology shares the same realism; man's fears are an outcome of anarchy and of the lack of personal security it engenders. They are not a product of his 'nature' for he does not 'accuse man's nature in it' (1651/1968:187). Yet, if in a state of 'warre' man is ruled only by his reason, a reason which dictates self-interest and inevitable violence, it is also reason which leads him out of it. Fear of death, desire for good living and hope to obtain it provide for Hobbes the inclination to peace, an inclination which can be reached by man's reason and agreement with others. In the Hobbesian view man is thus 'both matter and the artisan of the political body' (Roy, 1984:8), and this prominence given to human agency makes Hobbes's political theories especially relevant to a concern with how men shape just as they are shaped by the forms of their society.

The Gisu have a strong concept of order as it should manifest itself in human life, a concept of order which they see as embedded in the restraints of kinship and in the rules and discipline which promote peaceful social existence. The

Gisu word for order, *lukoosi*, thus implies an acceptance of authority, of the submission of the self to moral rules. Yet this need for restraint is the counterpoint of an aggressive or violent individualism which (unlike many in Africa) does not recognise the limitations imposed by segmentary loyalties nor that of authority validated by ancestorhood. It is an individualism based on each man's control of his own household and land and of his ability to defend it by force. Further, the value of autonomous manhood is valorised in circumcision, the most important ritual of the Gisu, which adds the element of violence to the male constitution. From this arises some of the paradoxes as well as the distinctive character of the Gisu moral universe. Its individualistic stress may be said to highlight the problem of order. Where do the rights of the individual give way to the rights of the group? How far may the individual go in pursuing and defending his own interest? How is *lukoosi* to be achieved?

This book will attempt to address these problems. In aiming to document the distinctive ways in which violence is endemic in Gisu life it is not assumed that man's motivations are, in the Hobbesian way, necessarily utilitarian. Nor do I argue that Gisu society represents some kind of regression to an original 'state of nature'. Rather, Hobbes is relevant because he shares with the Gisu a concern with how civil peace may be obtained in a volatile political climate. And, particularly, it is the idea of fear which I see as a useful way of approaching the forms of Gisu life. The problem of 'violence' thus merges into that of fear. While my reasons for this emphasis arise from my particular understanding of Gisu life, this also avoids any problem arising from essentialist concerns with 'violence' or 'aggression' as inherent human capabilities. Fear implies an object and a motivating rationale, that is a cultural setting and situation, in the way that the concept of violence when conceived of as a basic human potentiality does not. It thus throws the emphasis immediately on to the social constructions of reality which affect motivation and social action. It is true that violence may also be treated as a semantic category to be deconstructed, free then to be reconstituted and reclothed. But this approach would take the study in other directions. Rather, the cultural depiction of fear, of how fear of others is articulated, acted upon and managed in the practices of everyday life is a starting point for analysis.

Thus one major approach in the book is to attempt a phenomenological understanding of aspects of Gisu life, particularly in relationship to kinship, the causes of misfortune and the concept of the 'self'. In this latter I most closely follow Hallowell, who uses the term to denote the inner world of the subject, an inner world that is nonetheless culturally constituted and thus as amenable to understanding and analysis as any other cultural category. This is important because 'the nature of the self as culturally defined becomes an integral part of the implicit assumptions that become the basis for the activities of the individual and his interpretation of his experience' (Hallowell, 1955: 81). It is thus the key to understanding the character of Gisu violence and how it is produced.

Yet actors' understandings are not the be-all and end-all of analysis. Socio-logy, as Giddens (1976) has argued, is involved in a double hermeneutic, and a more distanced style is adopted in order to engage in a dialogue with the sociological tradition of social anthropology in which I was trained and which has dominated our understanding of African cultures. It allows me to question some of these forms of understanding and to locate Gisu patterns and responses in relationship to others in Africa. Further, although I argue against uncritical use and reliance upon official statistics in chapter 2, I believe it is important to document, and document as fully as possible, things which are amenable to measurement and statistical enquiry. Where, as in this case, arguments deal with concepts and accusational patterns, linking these with poverty and land pressure, it is crucial to attempt to go beyond a suggestive hypothesis and search, if necessary through surveys and statistics, for further validation. The reasons here are partly internal to the study itself, addressing the question of the degree of reliance one can have in the relationships and arguments put forward. And they are also partly for reasons of comparison, giving sufficient information so that the patterns suggested may be compared in fairly exact terms with ethnographic studies elsewhere in East Africa. Ultimately, how-ever, the two forms of understanding, the more 'subjective' and the more 'objective', are not opposed in this book, nor presented as being in conflict, for if the sociological discussion takes us out of the world of the subject it does not invalidate or contradict Gisu understandings of their predicament. No hidden and determinist hand, to be identified in material conditions, human nature, structure or history, is advanced.

THE PLAN OF THE BOOK

Part 1 sets the scene. After a brief introduction to the Gisu we turn to an account of their reputation for violence and situate this historically, in the early colonial period, seeing this reputation as generated in part from the particular circumstances that surrounded the imposition of British administration. The second chapter, keeping still to an external view, examines the patterns of violence which are manifest in the court records of the 1960s. This takes a first look at the interactions between the Gisu and the apparatus of the modern Ugandan state, interactions which are fundamental to understanding the context and changing pattern of Gisu life. However, my concerns here are also methodological; for the collation of these statistics involved three divergent perspectives: that of the Gisu, that of the courts and that of the anthropologist. Examination of the statistics thus allows me also to consider my own role in their production, to reflect upon my own practice.

The statistics illustrate the fact that Gisu killing is largely a matter of self-help, predominantly involving men, with much of it justified on the grounds that the victim was a witch or a thief. The question of who is vulnerable to such accusations is thus critical to understanding Gisu homicide patterns and this leads the book through a series of linked arguments. Chapter 3 examines the way Gisu associate violence with manhood and anger. The ordeal of circumcision undertaken when boys are between eighteen and twenty-four years old is here seen as crucial to understanding both Gisu perceptions and experience, for the qualities that a boy has to develop in order to undergo the ordeal courageously are the same which might later lead him to violence. Indeed, there is a sense in which the ritual of circumcision can be regarded as anachronistic, creating warriors with no war to fight. Yet the problem is not so easy, for it is not only that circumcision is seen to create fearless men but that this fearlessness is not restrained by any submission in adult life to authority. The necessity for self-control, which the circumcision ritual stresses, thus receives no social support: it is seen to rest solely on a man's disposition.

It is in terms of their inherent disposition that witches and thieves are taken to differ from other people. Given the impasse in witchcraft studies in functionalist anthropology, the newer semantically-based anthropology in Britain (Crick, 1976; Parkin, 1982) has called for a renewed effort to explore the different dimensions of meaning involved. Instead of cutting Western-based analytic schemas across the subjectivities of agents, Crick, for example, calls for a 'recasting' of witchcraft which is capable of setting the problem in the context of differing cultural evaluations of human action and concepts of the person. This form of analysis could evidently embrace both witchcraft and theft. On both counts, I would argue, we need to widen our schemas of relevance.

The coupling together of theft and witchcraft is alien to a Western perspective. In terms of our basic ontological categories they are different kinds of phenomena, the one being 'natural' and the other 'supernatural' while, in terms of legal categories, one is a crime against property and the other a crime against the person. They thus appear as different types of offence. And so they have largely been seen by anthropologists. In contrast to the extensive literature on witchcraft beliefs and accusations, there is little comparable material on thieves and thieving. References here are tucked away in discussions of customary law and give little information on cultural stereotypes and patterns of accusation. For, by and large, theft has been treated as a self-evident category of offence, carrying with it the assumption of a direct relationship between delict and accusation. Prosecutions of thieves are assumed to be a matter of 'fact'; they have an evidential basis which is generally taken to be missing in witchcraft accusations, and it is this lack which has made us see witchcraft as a problematic offence.

Yet just as it has been argued that the distinction between natural and supernatural has no real meaning outside our own schemas (Evans-Pritchard, 1965), nor do the distinctions implied in Western law. It will be argued that there is no substantive difference between theft and witchcraft as these two types of offences manifest themselves in Gisu life and ideology. Both form part of a system of interpersonal aggression and vengeance which includes physical assault, crop-slashing, and arson. All may equally be regarded as offences against the person, to adopt this terminology, since the offence is considered to be motivated by personal ill-will and because it is considered that all such attacks carry the threat of death. Thus, for example, thieves are not unknown pilferers who rob simply for self-gain. They are both known to the victim and, it is assumed, motivated by a desire to harm him directly. Connected with this motivational schema, all physical attacks are seen to carry the threat of death. The image in Uganda of the *kondo* or bandit who will kill you as soon as rob you is thus germane to all theft. Nor does this apply solely to theft for the generic word for witchcraft, *bulosi*, is used also of violence and aggression.

However, the point I wish to make here is not only methodological. Thus, I argue that it is not just that the accusation 'thief' would benefit from the type of analysis which has been seen as appropriate for witchcraft but that in the specific context of Bugisu both forms of accusation must be treated together. Ideas about witchcraft thus should not and cannot be analysed as a self-contained explanatory system and analysed in isolation from other ideas about the sources of trouble and misfortune. Indeed, the processes of accusation are themselves linked; linked, not only by being generated by the same intra-familial conflicts, but also because witchcraft is deemed to be the causative agent in making a man turn to theft. The accusations form part of a single conceptual and accusational nexus.

An initial problem in the field was to understand how men gained the reputations which carried such fearful consequences. Here it is important to incorporate an economic dimension since Gisu fears of violence focus largely on the poor. Chapter 4 thus presents an outline of the inheritance system to show that it has the effect of creating classes of impoverished men at both ends of the adult life cycle – among the young, newly and not-so-newly circumcised, waiting to be allocated the basic items of wealth by their fathers, and among the old who have passed on their patrimony to their sons. Yet the *sine qua non* of adult male status is to be economically self-sufficient, and failure here threatens status, just as it breeds interpersonal conflict which is frequently expressed through violence. In the following chapter (5), the processes of accusation are followed through in some detail, especially those that involve bachelors (who are vulnerable to accusations of theft) and the old (who are seen to use their powers malevolently against their juniors through cursing and witchcraft). This chapter pairs with the methodological appendix, reporting the results of a survey of homicide I undertook in order to check whether the patterns I was inferring from case analysis were in fact borne out in a wider sample. They were.

La Fontaine has pointed to the distinctive features of the Gisu inheritance system which generate conflicts between father and son (La Fontaine, 1960b, 1967). Gisu boys come into at least part of their inheritance on their circumcision when their father should hand over part of his estate to meet their needs. Yet the father at this time may be a mature man in his early forties who is still fully capable of managing his acreage. A father thus sees in the circumcision of his sons the almost inevitable decline of his own position in the community. Thus many men attempt to delay such an allocation of their resources. On this basic feature of Gisu society and the intergenerational conflict it breeds I am in full agreement.[1] Further, we may see that it has implications not only for understanding accusational processes but for the nature of kinship itself.

Part 3 of the book then turns to kinship. Though Gisu kinship groups can be described in patrilineal terms as is common in Africa, they work in some distinctive ways. The very interdependence of patrikin, centred on the transmission of property, breeds a discord which is openly expressed in daily life and receives recognition in the norms and values associated with agnatic kin. When a man fathers a first-born son, this is not the occasion for unmitigated joy. On the contrary, he is told or may even announce that he has given birth to 'anger' (*lirima*). For such a son there will be no cattle from the marriage of an older sister to provide the bridewealth he will need to marry, nor the guarantee of any sister's cattle at all. He will have to wait to marry, a situation which is seen as breeding acrimony between father and son.

The recognition of conflict at the very heart of kinship, in the competition of father and son for basic resources, may be seen as a form of dialectic which ramifies throughout the sphere of kinship, with individual autonomy set against dependence, and hatred paired with friendship. This is true of neighbourhood as well as kinship relationships, so that every occasion which exists to assert commonality and goodwill is seen at the same time to contain its negative, the jealousy and enmity of others. The beer party is feared as the source of violent death and death from poisoning, just as witches are feared most active and indiscriminate at the collective feasts that celebrate events among kin.

Chapter 6 gives an account of the basic structure of kinship, dealing with the agnatic framework and the importance of affinal and matrilateral ties in its dynamics. From there, in chapter 7, the problem of the absence of retaliatory killings after deaths is broached from the point of view of what might be called 'classic lineage theory', as it was developed especially for Africa initially by Evans-Pritchard, in order to develop through contrast an argument about the lack of segmentary loyalties in Bugisu. The discussion leads to a consideration of the pre-colonial period, for the main part to assess whether there is any evidence that kin loyalties have broken down under a more individualistic order wrought by commodity production and colonialism, as is often surmised. In Bugisu, it is argued that this does not appear to have been the case. The establishment of an administrative system consolidated what was undoubtedly a fluid political system in a very short period of time. Yet far from breaking down the lineage framework, it tended to give it greater coherence by channelling loyalty to a territory and a chief with extensive powers to support his position. While at higher levels the administration represented a political integration which had never existed before, it also extended downwards to the locality where the chieftainships became a focus for lineage identity, each clan and lineage demanding its own chief. As a result of this process we may see the present formal resemblance of the Gisu lineage structure to segmentary forms described elsewhere in Africa as largely a function of the particular political history of Bugisu and one which has acted to disguise its basically unsegmentary form.

Chapter 8 turns to the management of hostilities in the neighbourhood at the present day. On the one hand, these may be characterised as strategies of impotence; lacking the ability to act concertedly against outsiders, Gisu kin groups can offer no protection to their members. On the other, individual autonomy is seen as basic, carrying with it the right to act in one's own interest and one's own defence. The point of intersection between individual right and community right is thus the cutting edge of the system. On the one hand, it breeds self-help; on the other, it breeds intolerance for those who are deemed to have gone beyond the pale, who are seen as having forfeited all rights. The 'troublemaker', whether an adulterer, thief, witch or slanderer, is one who in pursuing his own self-interest violates the interest of others. The main part of this chapter is taken up with an extended case study which details the reaction of people in a neighbourhood following a murder. The strategies which people use for limiting the repercussions of such events within the community are detailed in order to bring out the extreme importance of character assessment and the nature of Gisu morality.

The question of morality is taken further in the following chapter (9) when the discussion of kinship expands to include a cosmological dimension. In looking at beliefs about ancestors, a particular focus is on the nature of Gisu ancestor beliefs in a system which recognises neither segmentary loyalty nor the authority of elders. Some of this takes the form of a dialogue with Fortes (especially, 1959, 1969), against whom I argue that what is basic to Gisu kinship is not amity but rather a continuity which is ensured through ancestral transmission of a person's body, spirit and powers. More fundamentally, it is argued that kinship encodes an implicit philosophy of being and the final section of the chapter turns back to an unique form of peacemaking which was found in Bugisu. Here feuds were settled by contracting a joking relationship which combined the patterning of peace and hostility in a single relationship and in such a way as to demand an exploratory interpretation of its significance for the Gisu understanding of social relationships. Taken in conjunction with the avoidance relationship of son-in-law with mother-in-law, I interpret both these relationships as encoding contrasting dramas of self-denial, of sex in the one instance and violence in the other. Not simply about the regulation of behaviour, they may be taken also as parables, speaking to the kinds of restraint people must exercise over themselves in order to achieve lasting relationships in an egalitarian community.

In part the processes by which men come to be castigated as witches and thieves can be seen as triggered by the increasingly unfavourable economic squeeze in the district and land shortage. Accusations thus form the idiom for repudiating responsibility and denying resources. Yet the harshness of Gisu reactions to witches and thieves does not seem to have been a constant, nor to have grown gradually as one might suppose if we were to see the accusational process as fuelled solely by the increasing ecological constraints manifesting themselves in difficult problems of choice. On the contrary, there seems to have been a sudden, almost dramatic, hardening in attitude in the 1960s, a change that was to be accompanied by the rapid development of vigilante groups to further eradicate troublemakers from the community. This suggests that other factors were at work, and particularly the political changes involved in the passing of the colonial state.

This takes us back in the fourth section of the book more directly to the concept and problem of anarchy. The argument here is that the immediate effect of the new post-colonial state was its withdrawal from the locality: patterns of authority which had been established early in colonial times and remained more or less unchanged for forty years, were now rapidly disassembled in a way that left a vacuum of power at the local level. The problems of control in interpersonal settings now loomed large and the new Gisu movements set about programmatically reformulating norms and reconstituting the basis of the community, with concepts of order that were conceived in basically governmental terms. There are major differences between these Gisu movements and others reported in Africa at the time, as for example witch-finding cults. Chapter 11 goes back into the history of the Gisu relationship with the government administration in order to assess how particular aspects of this history might have affected the way protest was manifest.

Social anthropological work has its own time dimension, the intense period of fieldwork, making the 'synchronic' account its natural *métier*. Yet such accounts mask the complexity of process, of history and, since time does not stand still even if the anthropologist does, easily produce a complex overlay of custom belonging to different epochs even when presented as 'of one time'. As Marcus and Fischer point out, 'ethnographies have in fact rarely reported what the ethnographers actually see of the present in the field' (1986:96). The task then as they see it is not to 'do away with the synchronic ethnographic frame, but to exploit fully the historical within it' (1986:98). The observations which form the core of this book derive from observations made in the field between 1965 and 1969 and from Central Bugisu. But the problems they posed taught me to seek understanding in the past history of the Gisu – indeed, some problems are only problems in the light of this history. The Gisu presented no pristine tribal order but an order which had been profoundly shaped by its political history, by its incorporation firstly into the colonial state and secondly, and immediately prior to my period of fieldwork, into the post-colonial one.

The history with which I am concerned thus divides easily into three, according to its own distinctive political economies. Firstly, there is the 'traditional' or, less tendentiously, the pre-colonial, a period prior to around 1901. The history of this period is largely told in accounts of warfare and calamity that occurred in the time before the arrival of the Ganda and then the British. Some of these events are subject to a chronological ordering of some exactitude as they are codified in the names of circumcision periods; others are not. Nevertheless, my reconstruction of this era is best regarded as speculative, for the men who were alive in 1960s and from whose accounts and experiences I drew had been but children at the time and their memories of events as well as of custom inevitably tended to overlap with the turbulence associated with the imposition of colonial rule.

The second era, the period of colonial administration, can be dated fairly exactly at least with respect to its end, 1962, and documented with reference to archival sources. The imposition of colonial rule, the period from 1901 to about 1930, saw the most extensive changes in the pattern of life in the district, with the establishment of a chiefly hierarchy and of the cash crops on which the wealth of the district came to depend. The third period, as dramatic in its effects as the setting up of the colonial state, was its dismantling or partial dismantling with independence. These periods are dealt with at various places in the book but some attempt to keep a chronology has been made. Thus the first chapter deals with the imposition of British rule and touches on the nature of the pre-colonial political order which is then developed in chapter 7. The immediate post-colonial period is the time span for most observations in the book and the transition to this forms the subject of chapter 12.

FIELDWORK

The fieldwork on which this book is based was carried out in Central Bugisu where I lived for three years between August 1965 and June 1969. The way we are drawn to topics, drawn to make some observations the central problem for our analyses, is now seen as a central problem in interpretation. We can no longer escape our own subjectivity, our own responsibility for what we have seen and recorded. Yet the truism that 'we see what we want to see' fails to inform on the dynamics of perception, the features that shape our 'wants'. The Kwakiutl informant whom Boas brought to New York in the early years of the century remained stony-faced and apparently uninterested until confronted with the elaboratedly carved balustrade of a hotel stairway. Was this something in an otherwise bizarre and meaningless world which had direct and positive continuity with the material artefacts of the North-West Coast? Or was it something which, perhaps in so doing, shocked his sensibilities?

My original study had been planned as one in sociolinguistics among a Nilotic-speaking Ugandan people. In the event, another ethnographer was working in the area and I had to rethink my plans on arrival in Uganda. My husband, a teacher, had been posted to Bugisu, but I had no familiarity with the language and, since little linguistic work had been done on it, I did not initially consider it as a possibility. Instead, I began learning another Nilotic language, of a group that lived some thirty miles away, and visited the area a number of times. It was perhaps not until six weeks after my arrival and living in Bugisu that I began to think seriously about switching my study to Bugisu. With my original thesis plans in shreds because of the change of area I had in any case to rethink a study from scratch. For a while I still thought in terms of sociolinguistics but after about three months I realised that my focus had decisively changed. To study violence thus involved a double switch, a change of area and change of interest, and to this day it is difficult to decide what was 'push' and what was 'pull' in such a decision.

In any event, what appeared to me at the time as a breakthrough occurred after I had been in the field about two months. The conversation of the morning revolved around the ambush the previous night of a notorious witch who lived close to my house and the details of this were meticulously relayed to me. In the morning, about a week later, I ran into a party of local men armed with clubs and pangas. They explained that they were following the tracks of a thief who had stolen from a granary during the night and that the very least that such a thief should expect from them was a very sound thrashing. If he died, so well and good. Soon I began to realise that these were not exceptional events and that any analysis of Gisu life would have to take them into account, whether it chose to do it by a central or by a sideways focus.

To an extent, the Gisu themselves led me to a central focus. It was not until much later that I realised the significance of the fact that my first real access to 'current events' – as opposed to custom and norm – concerned attacks on a witch and a thief. Anything which concerned such people was a matter of public concern and hence open to public gossip and scrutiny. I soon discovered that all other matters of dispute were kept as closely guarded private concerns and were not open to the same extent for gossip and comment. My inclusion in the gossip of the public arena was at least a first step but it did not indicate quite the privileged position to which I aspired. What it did was to almost automatically direct my attention to the more violent side of Gisu life.

Thus it was not solely the drama of events nor yet the heuristic importance of 'trouble cases' that prompted my investigation into these issues. Rather, the way in which the Gisu applied the distinction between public and private meant that initially on the fate of the unrespectable and unregenerate I could get information but on the situation of the solid, respectable citizens I was able to learn very little. Thus I learnt first about all the categories of troublemakers in the community, running the gamut from witches and thieves to adulterers, slanderers and perpetually quarrelsome individuals. As a preliminary step towards a fuller inclusion in Gisu life I learnt first to identify those people towards whom the respectable thought it wise to be punctiliously polite and, at the same time and, as punctiliously, to avoid.

Yet although the above account of the genesis of this study is faithful to my memory it omits to record my own reactions. I present myself as a disinterested observer, being drawn – albeit under pressure of wanting acceptance and needing a thesis topic – to it by the nature of events outside of my volition. But, in these more reflexive times, it is incumbent on me to examine more critically my own role if not in the creation of Gisu violence at least in the creation of it as a problem for investigation.

Greenblatt (1982) has recently pointed out that one reaction which accompanied the rise of 'scientific' anthropology in the twentieth century was the suppression of revulsion; ethnographers not only refrained from articulating their own disgust, but very often refrained from describing events which might have elicited it in their readers. To some extent this was achieved by an act of distancing: people were subsumed into lineages and their actions into custom. And were they ever shocked, one might ask? If they were, very little comes through in their writings. The anthropologist as observer could give a detailed and clinical account of, for example, a circumcision operation but usually failed to to indicate how much it hurt or if indeed it hurt at all. Yet if the task of ethnography was accompanied by this enormous act of suppression, Greenblatt maintains that its effects remain: 'It is the ethnographer's nausea that gives him his particular discursive field' (1982:3), defining for him the problems that he must tackle interpretively.

A child of post-war Britain, reared in a middle-class world where personal security – barring the devastation of war – was taken as a natural given and then educated in the still predominantly functionalist anthropology, my early experiences with the Gisu challenged many – perhaps all – of my basic categories of living. And not in a way that was comfortable. The lure of anthropology, its tacit promise to reveal not only alternative but preferable ways of living, once more perhaps had failed the test. The anthropological task became not just to describe languages and lineages (as I had somewhat naively supposed in my twenty-two-year-old way) but to come to grips with human problems, with insecurities and hatreds, which I had but barely imagined. Twenty years later there is greater urgency in these topics for violence is no longer 'out there' but has 'come home' as the burgeoning literature on aggression attests. The Gisu experience of anarchy, of personal insecurity and risk, perhaps now will speak to a wider audience.

Yet my account is a partial one, a particular distillation of Gisu life. In the first place, because of the topic, it deals almost exclusively with the world of

Gisu men and not that of women. In this it is unfashionable and may further be accused of exaggerating the agonistic aspects of Gisu life, for women certainly carry more strongly than their menfolk the values of compassion and co-operation. This bias must be acknowledged. Secondly, the picture that we have inherited from functionalism puts the co-operative machinery of village life at the centre of rural life in Africa. If I did not find this nor did I find human beings who were absorbed in hatred. I found rather, in the complex life of a community, people who were struggling to create conditions in which they could survive and in which trust and mutuality could become a possibility. There was joy as well sorrow, laughter and rejoicing as well as dirges and laments. Yet this was against a life situation that was becoming increasingly difficult and against a definition of relationships which had danger built into them. As Mbiti has written of the paradoxical features of societies of rural Africa:

Within this intensely corporate type of society, there are endless manifestations of evil. These include murders, robberies, rape, adultery, lies, stealing, cruelty especially towards women, quarrels, bad words, disrespect to persons of a higher status, accusations of sorcery, magic and witchcraft, disobedience of children and the like. In this atmosphere, all is neither grim nor bright. It is hard to describe these things: one needs to participate or grow up in village life, to get an idea of the depth of evil and its consequences upon individuals and society. A visitor to the village will immediately be struck by African readiness to externalise the spontaneous feelings of joy, love, friendship and generosity. But this must be balanced by the fact that Africans are men, and there are many occasions when their feelings of hatred, strain, fear, jealousy and suspicion also become readily externalised. (1969:209–10)

Since there is no natural mechanism which ensures that the two sides are kept in balance, no apology should be necessary for portraying the more negative side of African life as it manifested itself in the life of one community in conditions of exceptional difficulty. As Geertz has written, 'the problems, being existential, are universal; their solutions, being human, are diverse' (1973:363).

NOTE

1 La Fontaine has written on many of the themes explored or touched upon in this book. Where my account differs in important respects from hers an effort has been made to indicate this in the text or in footnotes.

PART 1
The problem

1

A REPUTATION FOR VIOLENCE

Bugisu district lies on the western slopes of Mount Elgon in Eastern Uganda. To the west Mount Elgon falls sharply in a dramatic series of radial ridges undercut by steep mountain valleys. To the north-west this ridge pattern is broken up by irregular hills which extend down into the plains, the hills of Manjiya being distinctive and rising in a series of steps to the edge of the extinct volcanic caldera of Elgon itself. The spur of Elgon, Nkokonjeru, known as Wanale by the Gisu, is the most westward extension of the mountain and divides the district in half. Its heights command a view over the western plains reaching as far as Lake Kyoga, fifty miles away, while its precipitous cliffs dominate the landscape of Central Bugisu. The dispersed homesteads of the Gisu today stretch down from the line of the government forest reserve, running between 6,000 and 7,000 feet, to the plains lying just below 3,000 feet.

In pre-colonial times Gisu homesteads straddled the wavering mountain ridges at higher altitudes, while in the plains and lower foothills walled and fortified villages of between ten and 100 houses were common to protect the inhabitants from the marauding peoples of the plains who were vying with the Gisu for territory. Today, with a vastly increased population and with the need to congregate for such defence removed, Gisu homesteads stretch down the hillsides out into the valleys and across the irregular countryside of the lower foothills and plains. Settlement is both continuous and dispersed with no appreciable clusterings of houses. Gisu men recognise the right to build on any portion of their own land and homesteads are scattered among the plantations of plantains and between fallow and cultivated fields alike.

The rich volcanic soils of Bugisu support a numerous and dense population. In 1980, the population of the district numbered over 500,000, the great majority of whom claim Gisu descent.[1] People with other ethnic affiliations are found only where the district adjoins its neighbours, particularly in the plains' border zones. To the west of Bugisu lies Bukedi District, composed of several small groups, each of which maintains a separate ethnic identity (see figure 1). Several of these groups share a common border with Bugisu; the para-Nilotic

2   Gisu homestead surrounded by bananas

Teso to the north-west and south-west and, between these two branches of the
Teso, two small groups of Bantu-speaking people, the Gwere and Nyole. To
the north, Bugisu adjoins Sebei, composed of another para-Nilotic group,
though groups of Sebei-speaking people are also found to the south and above
the broad band of the forest reserve between 6,000 and 10,000 feet. These
groups are known to the Gisu by the generic term, Balwa, and many Gisu
traditions are said to derive from them. However, much closer cultural affinity
is claimed with the Bukusu of the adjacent Western Province in Kenya and the
same clans are represented in both the southern half of Bugisu and in Bukusu.
The present distinction between the two peoples would appear to have
developed from the partition of the clans by the colonial administration when
they established a border between Uganda and Kenya in 1904.

ON UNITY AND VARIATION

The pre-colonial history of the region would appear to have been one of an
intermingling of peoples through migration, warfare and intermarriage. As
Southall (1970) has said, the peoples of the area are both more and less than
'tribes'. More, in that the cultural practices which are taken as diacritical signs
of membership are in fact widely diffused and shared by neighbouring groups.
Less, in that they did not recognise an exclusive identity in the past. All the
peoples of the area were acephalous and the effective political units were much
smaller than the units recognised today. The present strong sense of ethnic
identity is thus a product of their more recent history and subsequent to their
being incorporated into the Ugandan state at the turn of the century (La

Fontaine, 1969; Twaddle, 1969).

Yet the present sense of identity and exclusiveness is not the less strong for that, and the Gisu claim a common cultural heritage with reference to descent, a common language and the practice of male circumcision. The cultural traditions which distinguish the Gisu from their neighbours are associated with Masaba, the name both for the Mount Elgon and the eponymous ancestor from whom all Gisu claim descent. Traditions vary as to the origin of Masaba himself; some say he emerged like a mushroom on the mountain, others that he crept out of one of the caves above the forest line and others that he climbed down a creeper from the sky. Today, some claim that the Gisu probably migrated to their present home from Abyssinia, a tradition which appears to derive from the missionary anthropologist, Roscoe (1924). Perryman (1937), who was District Commissioner in the area from 1911 to 1918, however, is emphatic in his claim that the Gisu are the only Ugandan people of which he knows who have no tradition of prior migration but claim to being auto-chthonous.[2]

Ancestry also provides a principle for internal segmentation. The Gisu are divided into a pyramidal structure of descent groups which, in decreasing order of magnitude, I propose to call sections, which divide into clans and these, in turn, divide into sub-clans. The sub-clans further divide into lineages and these are further segmented into lineage segments. While clans and sub-clans are associated with a definite territory with well-defined boundaries, the lineages and lineage segments tend to lack such territorial integrity and their members live scattered throughout the territory of the sub-clan. The higher-order descent groups can fairly readily be related together in terms of a genealogical charter whose apex is Masaba. Commonly, Masaba is said to have had three sons and these, Wanale, Mubuya and Mugisu, are said to be the founders of the three sections which take their names and which are associated with the administrative division into the counties of Central, South and North Bugisu respectively. The grandsons of Masaba in turn are usually cited as the eponymous ancestors of the clans and identified with administrative sub-counties.

While the principles of descent may be used as a fairly flexible idiom for expressing the relative status and interrelationships among groups, the implications of descent are, for the Gisu, immutable. Associated with and transmitted by descent and consanguinity are the ritual observances which constitute their heritage. It is through the practice of these ritual observances, known as *kimisambwa* – hallowed by the ancestral spirits, *basambwa* – that the Gisu express pride in their ancestry and its distinctiveness. By far the most important of these is the practice of male circumcision (*xuxwingila imbalu*) which boys undergo when they are between fourteen and twenty-two years old.

In the past, the Gisu appear not to have identified themselves simply as 'people' which, as Southall (1976) has pointed out, is by far the most common ethnic label in use around the world. Rather, they identified themselves by the much more specific idea of themselves as 'men'. Their sense of their collectivity is thus tied to their concept of manhood which, in turn, is indistinguishable from the practice of male circumcision. In 1909, Rev. J. B. Purvis, one of the first CMS missionaries in the area, wrote of the Gisu that they 'distinguish themselves as a race apart from others by the name Basani, i.e., men, whils't all men of uncircumcised nations are called Basinde, i.e., boys' (Purvis, 1909:271). In modern Uganda the idea of the Gisu as a nation of circumcised men remains as strong as ever, and serves to set the Gisu apart from all except the neighbouring Sebei, with whom they share the custom. Within Bugisu, it is the most valued of the ritual observances and believed to be the only such observance shared by all. The practice of circumcision is thus synonymous with the idea of a shared and distinctive ancestry for all Gisu.

The biennial circumcision ceremonies act as a focus for the sentiments of ethnic identity and as a dramatic display of its power. From the blowing of the horns which ushers in the circumcision year to the final aggregation ceremonies during the following December, the whole ritual cycle takes about a year. The actual operations are performed in August, in strict order of clan precedence, with the clan where the practice is believed to have originated cutting their boys first. The day after, the circumcisors move to the next clan territory and so on throughout Bugisu. At their height it would be no exaggeration to claim that the festivities involve the entire population of the district, some 500,000 people, from the young children, carried along with the circumcision dancing parties to the elderly who are visited as relatives of the novices, approached for guidance on ritual matters or who act as spectators. At the centre are the novices, with the ordeal of circumcision acting not only to validate their own claim to status as adult men but also to demonstrate the values of the entire community.

The elaborate rituals of circumcision vary in detail from area to area and these variations, together with the *kimisambwa* which are more limited in distribution, act in turn as a principle for cultural differentiation. The variations reflect to some extent the divisions into descent groups; with lineages, sub-clans and clans each associated with a specific constellation of *kimisambwa* in the form of totemic animals, rituals and powers. However, the coincidence can only ever be partial for the powers are inherited through both male and female lines. Thus some are scattered throughout Bugisu while others tend to be shared by people who are geographically contiguous but who do not form a distinct unit in the descent system.

Since ancestry divides as well as unites, it is worth considering briefly the concept of tradition which is here implied. Gisu society is marked by few myths which validate or set down a template for present action. On the contrary, there is a recognition of change and adaptation with the major myth relating to circumcision, for example, relating how the practice came in through the marriage of a Gisu man with a woman of Sebei origin and how it then came to spread throughout Bugisu in the same way. Further, there is the recognition of great geographical variation within Bugisu itself and the rituals are subject to extensive innovations year by year. Yet this is not contrary to the idea of 'tradition', for it is not only *what* is handed down but also *how* it is handed down which matters. It is believed that the *kimisambwa* perpetuate themselves by 'catching' the descendants of those people who have exercised that power and, in this way, they follow kinship and are an aspect of personal identity. The fact that Gisu boys still desire circumcision and have the courage to stand the pain of the operation is thus a sign for the Gisu that the power of the ancestors is still a force active in their lives. The unchanging nature of ancestral tradition derives from this: it is seen to continue down the generations with the same strength. But which ancestral powers people are subject to is variable and, to some extent contingent, for the constellation of kinship varies for all, over time and over space, and so too do the *kimisambwa*. Custom, understood in this way, is open and changeable and not static and fixed.

Linked to ancestry, variation is valued for its own sake. This is nowhere clearer than the Gisu attitude to their language. Within Bugisu it is variations in dialect which provide the main criteria for the perception of cultural difference. The Gisu have been said to speak the most archaic form of extant Bantu (Johnston, 1919; Doke, 1945). Following Guthrie (1948), it is usually classified along with the Nyanza group of Kenya and the languages of the intra-lacustrine Bantu. Nevertheless, a considerable range of dialects are recognised within Bugisu, going down to the minute level which distinguishes the speech of one sub-clan from another.

The Gisu draw lines between the main dialects in two ways. Firstly, following the lines of division between the tribal sections, in which case the corresponding dialects are called Lubuya, Lugisu and Luwanale. Or secondly by making a division into 'north' (all clans north of Mbale including the Bafumbo who are part of Central Bugisu County) and 'south' (all clans south of Mbale).[3] Mention has already been made of the division along the lines of the tribal sections but the opposition of north to south is also of significance. For example, even the most northern clans of the southern belt, the Bangokho and Basoba, identify southwards and not northwards. They both have traditions of alliance in war with the southern clans and stress that they never allied with those to the north. This memory of ancient cleavages has been overlaid by other patterns. When the Gisu migrate for both wage employment and settlement, the northerners favour Buganda, while southerners tend to look towards Kenya. Again, in the towns of East Africa two Gisu tribal associations are found and these likewise tend to draw their membership from the two separate areas. Cultural traditions and language therefore diverge here as well as along the lines of the present county divisions.

Modern factors, such as the consolidation of the clans under a single administration, the rivalry with other tribes over the border zones, and the opposition to the Protectorate government during the latter part of the colonial era have made the Gisu more aware of their unity (Twaddle, 1969). Nonetheless they are still conscious of the cleavages among themselves, and indeed value them. The fact that variations in ritual and dialect provide a way of expressing the distinctions between the various groups at any level helps to explain the resistance of the Gisu to agreeing on a common orthography for their language. For the Gisu a common orthography implies the submerging of difference or, even worse, the inevitable favouring of one dialect above the rest. As early as 1904, Rev. J. B. Purvis, stationed in Central Bugisu, produced a small grammar (1904) and later translated the Gospels into Lugisu. The orthography proved so unacceptable that the Gisu are said to have burnt most of the books and very few copies survived. The Bamasaba Historical Association formed in 1956 made the introduction of an orthography one of its major aims but, despite this, agreement could not be reached for many years.[4] The educated, as before, continued to write to each other in Luganda or English and the existence of these lingua franca was certainly a factor lessening the need to promote agreement on a Lugisu orthography. Many, perhaps most, Gisu are bilingual in Luganda. It was the local official language up to independence and thus used by the local government officials, and it was also the medium used for teaching in primary schools, as English was used for instruction only at secondary-school level.

Most of the ethnographic materials used in this book come from the sub-counties of Busoba, Busiu and Bukhiende. These sub-counties lie in the southern sector of Bugisu, and the inhabitants feel they have more in common culturally with the clans of South Bugisu than they do with those lying to the north of themselves, with the exception of their immediate northern neighbours, the Bangokho. Given the extent of variability within Bugisu there are thus more than the usual difficulties in using the collective 'Gisu'. However, since lengthy specification would be tedious, the reader is asked to bear in mind that particular aspects of practice and custom recorded refer primarily to Central Bugisu, and even here there are variations.

A REPUTATION FOR VIOLENCE

In a country which, since the rise of Amin in 1971, has become notorious for repressive state violence as well as for the ferocity of the inter-ethnic struggles for control within the army, the reputation of the Gisu for violence might well have become submerged. The 500,000 Gisu, outside the cleavages of power that have contributed to the recent bloody situation in Uganda, have played little part, either collectively or individually, in this violence. They have not been recruited into the army in any numbers nor have Gisu politicians been influential on the national scene. While the area has not escaped massacres and persecution, the Gisu attitude itself can be characterised as defensive. As far as possible they have sought to protect their areas from the arbitrary fiat of rulers and the incursions of a civil war prosecuted by others. Their reputation for violence predates these events, going back at least as far as the inception of colonial rule in 1900.

The earliest British explorers, administrators and missionaries presented the Gisu in terms of an almost prototype savagery, an image which invites interpretation of its political context. For, to a large extent, these attitudes may be seen not only as echoing the prejudices of the age but also as reflecting a perceived contrast with the Ganda and the circumstances of early colonial rule in Eastern Uganda. In the first place, British attitudes were forged by their experiences in Buganda, the administrative centre and starting-point for all journeys and careers in the Protectorate. As Apter writes, 'There grew up among the British a myth of Buganda as a knightly and feudal nation. Admired were the discipline and bureaucracy which flourished under a monarchic system of government. The institutions of the Buganda Kingdom appeared in sharp contrast to those of other African nations' (1961:63). Practically all of the British who came to Bugisu at the turn of the century came by way of Buganda and thus by way of a society that was not only centralised, with a highly effective state hierarchy, but had also shown itself open, even eager, for conversion to Christianity and education. Mission activity had started in Buganda a quarter-century before British controlled expeditionary forces were sent to Eastern Uganda to subdue the various acephalous groups of the region and bring them within the orbit of the newly-formed Uganda Protectorate. And the Ganda themselves were both agents and initiators of this process.

Serious attempts to establish an administration in Eastern Uganda did not begin until 1898 when a Ganda general, Semei Kakungulu, led his forces to the area.[5] In 1900 he moved towards the tribes to the west of Mount Elgon and by 1902, largely on his own initiative, he had carved himself out a kingdom in the area, establishing himself as *kabaka* (king) with a 'royal capital' at Budaka in what is now Bugwere. When the British in the person of the Collector followed in 1902, worried as he was at the personal empire being carved out by Kakungulu and his lieutenants, he was in no position to dispense with their services. The 'thin white line' of British imperialism was nowhere thinner (Kirk-Greene, 1980). Initially, as an interim measure, Ganda were given official positions, firstly as chiefs and then to assist and train local chiefs, as and when these were appointed. This 'interim' measure was to last a good thirty years, with the last Ganda official not retiring until 1935.[6]

The earliest descriptions of the Gisu may thus be seen as refractions produced through both English and Ganda eyes. They were not only 'inferior' as African was to English but as non-Ganda was to Ganda. Their acephalous political system with its egalitarian emphasis was seen not only as anarchic but barbaric. Sir Harry Johnston, in his report on the condition and prospects of the Uganda Protectorate, commented that 'They are perhaps the wildest

people to be found anywhere within the limits of the Uganda Protectorate'
(1902:724), an early judgement amplified by Sidney Ormsby, the first British
Collector in the then Bukedi District, a district which included the Bagisu
along with various other acephalous peoples who lived in the surrounding
plains to the east and south. He wrote:

Force alone appeals to them . . . They have respect neither for one another's lives nor
properties and among their intemperate habits, raiding and murder are frequent
occurrences. (March Report for Bukedi District, 1907)

He amplified in his annual report for the same year:

The Bagishu Hill Tribes . . . are and probably will remain for some time the only
disturbing elements in an otherwise peaceful district. When it is remembered that many
of these natives are cannibals, and none submit to parental authority, much less to the
Head of a Clan or Tribe, their behaviour up to date can hardly be considered extraordinary. (Annual Report for Bukedi District, 1907/8)

Such statements might well also reflect the frustrations of an understaffed
and underarmed British Collector subject to the vicissitudes of imposing an
administration on a mountain-dwelling people. At this time the administration
had barely extended beyond the plains and lower foothills. Higher up on
Mount Elgon, Gisu settlements on the high ridges and spurs were more easily
defended though, as the Gisu had learnt, retreat is often more effective than
defence. The caves with which Elgon is pitted traditionally served as places of
refuge. Hidden and inaccessible, the people could literally melt away before
the advance of an unwanted administrator or punitive force.

Here, as elsewhere in British Africa, the punitive force was the main
instrument of pacification; 'to thrash them first, conciliate them afterwards'
(Lugard, quoted in Low, 1973:22). Initially Kakungulu extended his rule
from a series of forts, leading his army first against the Bangokho, then against
the Bawalasi and Bafumbo to the north. From there he moved south to Busoba
and built a fort at Nabumali, known to the Ganda as Mpumude, 'I rested'.
With Nabumali as his base, he led forays to the mountainous areas of southern
Bugisu and in 1901 he created the county of Bubulo, to be parcelled out and
ruled by his lieutenants. While the British, following on the heels of
Kakungulu, sought to curb his personal power by 'retiring' him to Mbale in
1902, they continued to use his followers both as chiefs and police. The
punitive expeditions continued. Indeed, the argument was that pacification
could proceed in no other way.

The records of the district up to 1912 tell of frequent rebellions by the Gisu
against their Ganda overlords and their own chiefs. The clans did not unite to
fight but were subdued piecemeal, with one clan after another subject to the
punitive expeditions of the government forces. By 1911, the District Commissioner[7] reports that only about one-third of the tribe was under effective
administration, namely the clans of the more accessible foothills and plains

who had all 'learnt their lesson' and accepted the superior force of the British and Ganda. The mountain clans ensconced among their high ridges and deep valleys were more intractable, but with the punitive expedition of 1912 against the Balucheke of what is now Manjiya County, the region as a whole quietened down.

Yet what was the 'lesson' that the Gisu had learnt? By 1911, British sureties were waning. While the local District Officers still wrote in terms of the 'refractory disposition of the natives', political opinion at the centre seemed to be conceding that the influence of the Ganda agents was not 'civilising' but a source – even the main source – of atrocities. Whose barbarism became a moot point: that of the Gisu who ambushed (usually isolated) Ganda agents or burnt down the houses they had been coerced to build? Or that of the Ganda, effectively mercenaries, armed with guns, collecting tax on a percentage basis and extorting other tributary rights? Or, that of the British themselves who, in pursuing a policy of collective punishment, laid waste to whole villages? The issue fired opinion at the time, with sharp divisions appearing within the administration. There was a vigorous correspondence on this issue between Jackson, then Acting Chief Secretary of the Protectorate, and the local District Commissioner in 1911, a correspondence which allows us to infer some of the political context which lay behind many of the negative opinions that the British expressed of the Gisu at the time.

For example, in responding to a proposal that the Ganda agents in the area be withdrawn, the District Officer, arguing the need to impose an administration, writes that the Bagisu were 'still steeped in the lowest form of superstition, sodden with native liquor and addicted to cannibalism. Until our advent they had no political system of any description. Family feuds dating back for several generations were relentlessly pursued and fights between clans were of common occurrence.' He adds that the 'remarkable progress of the District was almost entirely due to the Agents' (Mbale District Records, letter 1.6.11). Jackson replies that after consulting the monthly reports of the number of killings both by the Gisu of their own chiefs as well as Ganda agents and the retaliatory killings by the government police, he 'considers that the system of employing Agents, with armed but unpaid followers, is to be condemned as unsound, obsolete and a totally wrong method of administration.' And, after considering the argument that the Ganda might be necessary in a supervisory and teaching role, he concludes that he was 'doubtful if it would not have been better to leave people to occasionally kill each other rather than employ aliens who are admittedly difficult to control and cannot owing to the shortage of D.O.s be properly supervised' (Mbale District Records, letter, 26.6.11). The District Officer's defence takes now a more pragmatic turn and he argues that he cannot increase the extent of European supervision because of the spreading plague and owing to 'the mountainous nature of the country in which they live and their very primitive characteristics, the Bagishu are more than ordinarily difficult people to administer'.

From Entebbe, the administration could consider that the Ganda had sufficiently served their purpose and give vent to what had indeed been a long-standing reluctance to entrust the administration to them. The policy of employing agents had always been justified as an unfortunate necessity and never as an explicit policy and, as early as 1904, following a government inspection of the region, specific instructions forbidding the use of Ganda were sent to Mbale. These were only waived after vigorous representations from the then District Collector. And so it was in 1911; the policy of withdrawal was to be embarked on but slowly.

However, other voices now were stronger in condemnation. Perhaps the most moving is that of Rev. J. B. Purvis, who concludes his book on his experiences in Uganda with an epilogue addressing the effects of the administration:

One of the greatest difficulties that we have had to contend with in the work at Masaba was the unsettling of the native mind and mode of life by the incoming of Government administration . . . after some four years' residence in the district I am bound to say, having earnestly and carefully weighed the seriousness of the statement, that during the years of my residence which mark the introduction of law into Masaba there seems to me to have been less peace, less security of property, and more, very much more, bloodshed than during the period I lived there without direct British administration . . .

My memories of the troubles between the Administration and the people of Masaba are altogether painful, for in almost every instance my sympathies are with the native, as I am sure would be those of any man who had been asked by the men of a clan to beg back the women who had been taken prisoners; to console the relatives and friends of a dead woman whom they had deposited at my door, and said to have been one of four, besides men, shot that day by the native police; and obliged to turn the vestry into a hospital for the wounded, shot by native hut-tax collectors and their men without any provocation whatever.

These armed Baganda hut-tax collectors, many of them of the very worst type, distributed throughout the district and working on the percentage system, could be no other than a menace to peace and prosperity. (Purvis, 1909: 359-60)

Barbarism is a two-way mirror. And, if the British were from then on to become more sympathetic to the complaints of the Gisu against their Ganda overlords, the policy of withdrawal was to be long drawn out. Ganda chiefs were to be dismissed only to be replaced by Ganda agents, who were to take on overall executive control and at the same time train and supervise Gisu chiefs as and when these were appointed.[8] And the system was indeed foreign to the Gisu who were now reorganised into a hierarchic series of administrative units, a modified form of that used in Buganda and introduced to the prerogatives of a new chiefly elite, prerogatives which the Gisu chiefs as well as the Ganda were to claim. In this way, 'Uganda came to comprise a congerie of little Bagandas' (Low and Pratt, 1960:229).

Labour tribute seems to have sparked off the greatest resentment, with Gisu chiefs following the Ganda in levying forced labour for public work on roads and buildings but also to work their own fields. They also claimed produce; a leg from every animal slaughtered and a calabash of beer from every brew. From time to time, efforts were made to regularise these demands but, as late as 1925, 'tribal obligations' are recorded as thirty days per annum *luwalo* labour (free labour for government projects) plus road-sweeping of earth or gravelled roads, plus fifty-two days' 'Saturday labour', that is for work on the chiefs' own crops and buildings. At the same time the chiefs continued to receive a rebate on poll tax and beer tribute. In 1927, a salary scheme was brought in for the chiefs and labour for the chiefs was reduced to twelve days a year. And perhaps none too soon, for the extortion of labour was one of the main causes of unrest in the district and contributed to the vast tide of emigration from the district from 1911 onwards.

The desperate poverty of the district also contributed to this exodus. In a way that has become familiar in the literature on early colonial contact, the area was struck by a series of epidemics and famines. Plague is reported as endemic in 1909, with rinderpest threatening the cattle population of the district the following year. Plague continued to be a problem and a virulent epidemic of smallpox spread throughout the area between 1917 and 1920, coinciding with the severe famine of 1919–20. Further, Bugisu had its own special problems. The severity of land pressure in many areas was an early cause of administrative concern and led to the opening-up of the Sirokho valley north of Mbale in 1911, an area which then had to be closed because of the prevalence of sleeping-sickness. In 1918 it was reopened and attracted settlement mainly from the densely settled areas of central and southern Bugisu. At the same time, Gisu living in the north had begun to extend their cultivation not only upwards into the forest zones that covered the mountain but northwards into the territory of the Sebei. Nevertheless, these measures appear to have done little initially to stem the flow of out-migration. In 1918 it was estimated that 1,300 taxpayers (adult men) had left the district for temporary employment elsewhere and in 1929, the number of men absent rose to the astronomic figure of 16,868. The majority of these came from the populous southern county, where over half the taxpayers were estimated to have left (Annual Report for Bugishu District, 1929). Even as labour migrants the Gisu are reported to have been stubbornly anti-official, spurning the official recruitment agencies and preferring instead to contract themselves independently, in Kenya and in Buganda.

Yet despite this record of disaster and the brutality that accompanied the early colonial occupation, what stands out in retrospect is the very rapidity with which the system became accepted after 1920. Here as elsewhere there was a *pax Britannica*, cash crops were developed, and the chieftainships established amidst such turmoil were to form the framework of the administration for the next forty years.

The establishment of suitable cash crops was an early priority in the district.

As early as 1911 experiments were made with both wheat and coffee at higher altitudes, but neither proved successful. Cotton in the plains was more successful and, after an initial hostile reaction, acreages increased yearly. This initial prosperity of the plains-dwellers was not matched by those in the mountains until much later. In the 1920s, the establishment of government nurseries to raise the delicate coffee seedlings, together with the gradual appointment of agricultural field staff, led to an increase in coffee planting and production. By 1930, this had risen to 260 tons of coffee parchment a year.[9]

The period up to 1930 thus saw the development of the crops on which the wealth of the district was to depend, just as it saw the formation of a hierarchic administrative system and the consolidation of the powers of the chiefs. The Gisu chiefs who had no precedent in the traditional political organisation became the all-purpose authorities typical of British local administration throughout Africa. As the system was brought more firmly under British control, the Ganda agents were withdrawn, the worst abuses of the tribute system were stopped and the chiefs were incorporated into an official bureaucracy, directed and disciplined by higher ranks whose authority was directly sanctioned by the District Commissioner. In 1927 the chieftainships became secure posts, salaried and, at higher levels, pensionable. A chiefs' council was established to discuss administrative affairs in 1920 and in 1925, the year after Bugisu had been created as a separate district, authorised to pass minor legislation. The chiefs also controlled their own courts, their jurisdiction being defined in the Ordinances of 1919 and 1925. In addition they had powers of arrest for all criminal offences under both Protectorate and customary law and were responsible for enforcing the decisions of the courts.

And here, as elsewhere, the distinction between 'traditional' leaders and the new chiefs was to become hazy. The foreignness of the chieftainships was in the 1960s marked only by the use of Ganda loan-words to refer to the chief and many of his duties, words which were by then part of normal Gisu usage. The units of the administration were known by the Ganda terms, *saza* for county, *gombolola* for sub-county, *muluka* for parish, *butongole* for the village divisions of the parish and *mutala* for further sub-divisions. And with few old men retaining any memories of the time before the coming of the Ganda, the transition from 'elders', *baxulu*, or 'notables', *bakosi*, who 'led', *xurangisa*, to 'chiefs', *babami*, with 'authority', *buuli*, who 'ruled', *xufuka*, received little comment. Indeed, stories of past leaders frequently turned out to be stories of the great *bakasya* (rich men) who were elevated to positions of chieftainship by the British at the turn of the century, a feature which again tends to mask the enormous transformation in power which occurred.

That the Gisu chiefs initially had no authority on their own account was frequently reiterated by the officials stationed in Mbale and, indeed, provided the main justification for retaining the Ganda as agents. There were no hereditary posts of authority among the Gisu though there were many men of some prestige who gained respect through a variety of abilities, as peace-makers, war leaders or even as sorcerers. The influence that such men exerted was confined primarily to their own 'ridge' which was for the most part an autonomous political unit though united by clanship with adjacent ridges. The administrative officers of the time emphasise the extremely small-scale nature of the political unit.[10] Nevertheless, the administrative system was created and crystallised around the more powerful of these men. Perryman reports that at first each chief had to be given equal status and allowed to exercise independent command whether he had a following of 500 or 5,000.[11] These first 'sub-chiefs' were each assisted by a Ganda agent and his unpaid (but armed) followers and were subsumed into counties with a Ganda agent as county chief. By 1924 the number of sub-counties had been considerably reduced and two definite grades of chief recognised below that of the sub-county, that of the parish and village. Yet by 1929, even with the rationalisation of such units (usually by amalgamation of units on the death of a chief), the sub-counties varied in size from 500 to over 3,000 adult men and the parishes from 200 to 500. The villages were all of between 100 and 150 men.[12]

In the process, the initially almost despotic powers of the chiefs were moderated until they became by the 1920s part of a regulated district bureau-cracy. As Lord Hailey says generally of chiefs in Uganda, 'the basis of their authority lies not in their traditional status but in the place they occupy as part of an official or semi-offficial organisation, the District Native Administration' (1950:28). The rule of law had begun. Certainly from 1925 onwards, both the chiefs' council and the courts appeared to achieve legitimacy. Following an initial period when the courts were spurned, the records seem to demonstrate a remarkable aptitude for litigation with no fewer than 17,485 cases – one to every two taxpayers – registered in the Native Courts in the year 1924 (Bukedi District Annual Report for 1924). And the chiefs' council set about enthusias-
· tically formulating and codifying customary law, dealing with marriage, abduction, bridewealth, divorce, circumcision and land – decisions which, once made, were to vary little in the coming years.

The acceptance of the new forms of administration was matched by an abeyance of interclan and intertribal fighting and also, apparently, a rapid decrease in killing of all kinds. Murder as a problem is hardly commented upon in the archives after about 1915 and, although few statistics could be found, those that do present a consistent picture. In February 1911, the District Commissioner reports that there had been only three spearing affrays during the month, all occurring at beer parties and that in the administered areas, 'deliberate murders formerly so common were now practically extinct' (Monthly Report for Bukedi District, 1911). In 1920 only fourteen murders were prosecuted in the courts and in 1929 the District Commissioner comments that while acts of violence were still common, very few seem to have a fatal outcome with only four murders investigated by the police in Bugisu

(Annual Reports for Bukedi District, 1920 and 1929).[13]

Yet the legacy of the early colonial period may perhaps be seen in the reputation for violence which the Gisu have retained in East Africa. Throughout Kenya the Gisu are proverbially thought of as cannibals, the term itself being synonymous with them, and speculation as to whether or not it is true is a source of endless fascination. In Uganda, they are more feared because of their personal aggressiveness. In the 1950s A. I. Richards indicated the attitude of the Ganda towards those Gisu who had taken up settlement in Buganda: 'Ganda just steal but Gishu come with knives to kill you' (Richards, 1956:116).

The imputation of cannibalism can certainly be traced to the earliest colonial writings on the area, in the reports and letters of missionaries and administrators. But it was Roscoe, the missionary anthropologist, who was to give it greater specificity and thus credence. In his earlier book (1915), Roscoe heads the chapters on the Gisu by calling them a cannibal tribe, though it was not until 1924 that he chose to give any details of such practice. In that he reports that the Gisu ate their dead, the time of the wake being also the time when the relatives dismembered the body and feasted secretly on the corpse. Roscoe states that this practice was common to all the Gisu clans. The truth or otherwise of this statement is now beyond verification. Certainly, at the time the British arrived the Gisu did not bury their dead but consigned the corpse to the bush at sunset, there to be consumed by scavenging hyenas, leopards and vultures. Later the skull would be recovered and placed together with other skulls of the dead in a repository. Evidently, such practices allowed for both the repute and the possible activity of human scavengers also, and, while most Gisu today deny it vehemently others believe it true, for there are resonances with other Gisu beliefs.

Firstly, there is the idea of mutilating the corpse and thus destroying the power of the shade to wreck vengeance on living murderers. In the past, too, it is said that attempts would be made to destroy the skulls of enemies so that they could not be placed in the repository with the result that any children named after that person would die. Secondly, certain ritual properties are associated with some organs of the body, particularly the arm or finger, which are said to be used in the preparation of beer in some areas as a potent source of fertility. Such reports always have the ring of defamatory myth, associated, as they are, not with our people but the clan in the next valley or over the other side of the mountain. However, many Gisu firmly believe that such things are practised as ancestral observances by some clans, and the Bakhiende of Central Bugisu are often cited here. Such clans, of course, are also likely to harbour witches but, unlike other peoples in East Africa, necrophilia is not inevitably associated with witchcraft. Nevertheless, rumour abounds and stories are told of people who become 'spoilt' and take to eating their kin, and at least once a year the report of sinister events sends a *frisson* of fear through the rural communities.

Given such beliefs on the part of the Gisu, it is not altogether surprising that such stories are also widely believed by non-Gisu and give a sensational value to their reputation in East Africa. With regard to their reputation for violence in colonial Uganda, again there is an element of factual corroboration. In a volume of essays on African homicide and suicide, edited by Paul Bohannan (1960), the average annual rate of death from homicide between the years 1945 and 1954 was calculated at 8.2 per 100,000 people (Southall, 1960: 228). This was the fourth in the Ugandan league table, higher than that of any other Bantu-speaking group but lower than that of the neighbouring Teso and Sebei.

Levels of violence of this magnitude would not necessarily be notable and one could probably dismiss the reputation for dangerousness as a matter of negative outsider definitions deriving, as outlined, from the particular circumstances of colonial contact. In the 1960s the situation was, arguably, different with a dramatic increase in the homicide rate. In 1960 the rate of death from homicide in Mbale Police District was 27.4 per 100,000 (table 1), almost twice

Table 1 *Ugandan homicide rates, 1960 and 1963: rate of death from homicide per 100,000 of the population by police districts*

District	1960	1963	District	1960	1963
Karamoja	33.4	46.4	Busoga	5.1	12.6
Mbale	27.4	28.4	Bunyoro	5.6	11.6
Teso	14.9	20.6	Ankole	4.8	4.4
Acholi	11.2	15.1	West Nile	3.9	3.4
Toro	7.2	8.2	Kigezi	2.8	4.7
Bukedi	5.1	1.9	Lango	1.9	3.7
	Uganda			9.7	12.9

Sources: Rates calculated by R. E. Turner from police statistics and reproduced in Wallace, Belshaw and Brock, 1973: 118. Rates for Kampala and Buganda are not included because of computational difficulties but the rate was estimated to fall between that of Teso and Acholi.

that of any other comparable settled agricultural people, with the rate for Teso being only 14.9. Only Karamoja had a higher rate, due to the upsurge of cattle-raiding in this northern and only partially administered area of Uganda. And during the 1960s this rate was to remain uniformly high in Bugisu, with an average annual rate of death from homicide of 32 per 100,000 for the years between 1964 and 1968. Some idea of the magnitude of this figure is evident when placed alongside the highest recorded rates in the world at that time, e.g. Colombia with 34 per 100,000 in 1960 and Mexico with 31.1 per 100,000 in 1958. The next chapter examines the court statistics on homicide in the 1960s in order to delineate the forms and character of this violence.

NOTES

1   The census of 1980 records the population of Bugisu District as 529,202, a figure

which excludes Mbale, the administrative town of the district. This gives an intercensal rise of 33% in the population since the census of 1969. Ethnic composition was not recorded in either of these censuses, but according to the figures of the 1959 census approximately 95% of the population claimed to be Gisu.

2   For further discussion of origin myths, see G. S. Were, 1977-78, 1982.

3   Both of these classifications have been endorsed recently by two linguists who have studied Lugisu. Siertsema (1981) divides the dialects into three groups following the lines of the county divisions, with a fourth for Bukusu, and Brown (1968) distinguishes between north and south Lugisu, with each dialect having three sub-divisions.

4   A new translation of the New Testament, entitled *Indagana Impya*, was not published until 1977.

5   There are a number of detailed studies of Kakungulu's activities both as freebooter and British agent and of the historical circumstances which gave rise to the distinctive political compromise between Ganda and British interests in Eastern Uganda. In particular: Thomas, 1939; Gray, 1963; Twaddle, 1966: Roberts, 1962; Vincent, 1982, esp. ch. 2.

6   Kakungulu himself chose to 'retire' from the services of the government. He applied for and was given a grant of land in recognition of his past services. He chose to settle in Mbale and 1902 saw him and 5,500 followers building the first houses in what was to be Mbale township (Twaddle, 1966).

7   Mbale District Archives. Letter 1.6.11 from the D.C. Mbale to Jackson, Acting Chief Secretary to the Protectorate.

8   The policy was to withdraw the Ganda agents as the Gisu chiefs were deemed to have gained competence. By 1914 most agents at the sub-county level had been withdrawn, but the Ganda continued in executive control of the counties, with the last Ganda agent who was acting as a county advisor withdrawn in 1935.

9   History of the Bugisu Coffee Scheme, Department of Agriculture, Mbale.

10   An especially full account is provided in Mr Cubitt's report on the causes of the murders of the Baganda by the Bagishu, 26.11.07. Entebbe Secretariat Archives, 1572/07.

11   Perryman, The Development of the Native Courts in Bukedi. Entebbe Secretariat Archives, B10.

12   Report on Chiefs' Salaries, 1925. Entebbe Secretariat Archives, Cg 6025.

13   During the period of the colonial administration in the area (1904–62) administrative boundaries changed several times. Initially Bugisu was included within Bukedi District, becoming a separate district only in 1924. With the financial stringency of the years preceding and during the Second World War, Bugisu was again amalgamated with Bugwere and Bunyole. In 1936 this district was known as Central District and later the Padhola or Dama were added and the name changed to Mbale District, the Teso to the north being administered separately. In 1954 Bugisu was again created as a separate district and the areas based around other groups again united with the Teso into a reformed Bukedi District. Throughout this period Sebei was included in the same district as the Gisu but with independence in 1962, Sebei was granted separate district status. Bugisu, since then, has comprised four counties, namely, North, Central, South and Manjiya. Manjiya is the county of most recent origin, being formed out of a division of the old South Bugisu county in 1959. Counties are in turn divided into sub-counties and these into parishes.

2
DIFFERING STANDARDS: HOMICIDE STATISTICS AND METHODOLOGICAL IMPLICATIONS

Gisu men are expected to stand up for their rights in everyday life and all grievances thus carry with them the threat of retaliation. Some such threats are expressed openly in the formulas of *kono ubone* (you will see) or *ulinde* (just you wait). Not all such threats lead to killing, with personal retaliation also taken by forms of physical assault, theft, arson, crop-slashing and certain forms of witchcraft. Gisu murder is thus a matter of interpersonal violence and retribution and, while killing is regarded as bad (*bubi*) and is deplored, at the same time it is held that 'if someone is troubling you then it is up to you to do something about it'. Killing an adulterer caught *in flagrante delicto* is an obvious instance, but other situations of dispute or ill-will may summon an equivalent response and predictably so, from the Gisu point of view. Yet the clearest pattern in Gisu killing during the 1960s is not one produced from such essentially private disputes, but produced by killings which are justified in terms of the public good with the victim being accused as a thief or a witch.

Four key features of Gisu killing emerge from the above. Firstly, that Gisu killing is a matter of individual self-help and that this is seen as a male prerogative. Secondly, that killing is not only a right but also seen as a legitimate form of retribution. Thirdly, that this retribution is exercised by individuals acting on their own behalf and not controlled by kinship groups: there is no feud. And fourthly, a dominant pattern is of the Gisu adopting these measures of self-help against thieves and witches in their midst. These patterns form the backcloth against which all discussion in this book is set. They also emerge clearly from an examination of the court statistics for the area during the 1960s. A natural starting place is thus with these, not simply because they allow a degree of specification of the murder patterns in the district, but because they take us immediately to a major dynamic in the context of murder; the contact between the Gisu and the local administration, particularly the official system of police and courts. Examination of the statistics thus allows us to take a first look at the interactions between Gisu and the apparatus of the Ugandan state, interactions which have implications for both action and perception. However, my concerns here are also methodological, for the collection of such statistics involved three divergent perspectives; that of the Gisu, that of the courts and that of the anthropologist. Examination of the statistics thus produced allows me also to consider my own role in their production, to reflect upon my own practice.

The last thirty years have seen dramatic changes in the sociological study of crime and deviance. Before 1965, Durkheim's (1952) study of suicide remained the dominant paradigm for studying crime; official figures for crimes were seen as objective social facts, as true indices of the social trends or problems to be explained. Through his access to such rates the sociologist saw himself as having access to a scientific knowledge inaccessible to ordinary members of the society. And the more it might be at variance with common understandings, the more its 'scientific' status was assured. The way was open, then, for the correlation of one rate with another and the construction of deductive theories to explain any coincidence found. Such a positivistic approach came under heavy challenge in the 1960s. R. K. Merton was one of the first to raise doubts about the validity of official statistics, evidencing not only the number of unreported crimes but the differential treatment accorded to those apprehended by the police. 'Before social facts can be explained, it is advisable to ensure that they actually are facts' (Merton, 1957: xiii). This critique was taken further by those who became known as 'interactionists', who argued that crime rates were largely the product of the way that social definitions were applied, and thus of the perceptions of those involved in law enforcement.[1] Crime was seen in its political aspects, a product of the inter-action of powerful 'labellers' and less powerful 'labelled'.

Rates can no longer then be seen as innocent social facts. They are social products, produced as a result of complex social processes which are institu-tionally organised. In elucidating the way rates are organisationally produced the task of the sociologist becomes essentially different. Rather than the rate itself, it is the nature of the categorisation process which comes under scrutiny (Kitsuse and Cicourel, 1963). The nature of the common understandings that inform action or the act of definition, together with the nature of the social constraints and incentives that operate at every level of decision-making, become of prime importance. If rates are to have their uses it is not as brute indices of some social fact but largely in an understanding of how they are produced. Later commentators have demurred from two opposed positions. On the one hand, the ethnomethodologists have argued that symbolic inter-actionists do not go far enough in uncovering the largely tacit bases for judgement. On the other hand, the response of the more orthodox criminolo-gists has been that the interactionist approach, in seeming to deny the fact of crime, its reality independent of any societal reaction to it, has deflected interest away from it as a phenomenon which demands sociological under-standing in its own terms. Rates, it is argued, are not conjured up out of thin air: offences are committed (Taylor, Walton and Young, 1973). Between the polemics on each side the anthropologist can steer a middle course. Indeed there is no option. Working in a situation where the law and legal institutions are largely a foreign imposition, any officially produced figures can only be treated with caution and their validity assessed only from a knowledge of the way they have been processed. Yet they cannot be ignored either. The fact of arrest and prosecution for certain offences is part of the context for action, and the particular nature of the sample that ends up in court gives insight into the nature of local as well as legal social processes. Further, on the more actuarial and demographic aspects, they may give information which can be gained in no other way.

SOURCES OF OFFICIAL DATA

The official procedures followed in cases of suspicious – that is, generally violent – death were introduced during the colonial era, together with the rest of Ugandan law, and follow the general pattern of those in England. Thus such deaths should be reported to the police who take the body in for a *post-mortem* examination and investigate the case. A Death Enquiry Report (DER) is then filed with the court, in this case, the District Court sited in Mbale, the administrative capital of the region. Any further action depends on the nature of the case. Suicides and accidental deaths are investigated by the Coroner's Court while homicides are subject to prosecution through the Courts. In cases of prosecution, the accused were arraigned initially before the Chief Magistrate, who held a Preliminary Enquiry to decide if the evidence was sufficient to commit the case for trial before the High Court. In the 1960s, the High Court based in Kampala sat in Mbale two or three times a year. Here the procedure differed from that in England because there was no trial by jury but instead a High Court judge, most of whom were still British, who tried cases with the help of two African Assessors.

For the anthropologist there were thus a number of possible sources of official data – the police, the Coroner's Court, the Magistrates' Court and the High Court. It is never, however, a matter of simple choice and where official permission must be sought access is inevitably constrained.[2] I did ultimately gain permission to see the police figures, though only their figures. I had no access to their files nor even to their daily registers. The figures by themselves posed problems of interpretation that were insoluble and I was eventually forced (and with great regret given the time I had spent in getting them and the amount of trouble taken by the police to get them to me) to decide not to pursue them. To give some idea of the problems involved, Mbale Police District included an area far wider than the one that I was interested in as it included Bugisu along with the separate district of Sebei and two counties of Bukedi. With the main body of the police stationed in Mbale and responsible for all policing there, the figures were also biased towards crimes committed within the township. In the rural areas minor offences were not normally reported to the police but to the relevant sub-county headquarters and investigated by the chiefs and not by the police. They thus formed no part of the police statistics and thus obviously the police statistics could not be taken as representative of levels of crime in the rural areas. With homicide the situation was different for, as mentioned above, all such crimes should be reported to the police. Before I could use these, however, I needed a breakdown of the figures by district and, with great kindness, the police agreed to do this specifically for me, on both a monthly and annual basis. Unfortunately, these figures showed such a degree of divergence from the figures I was able to collate myself from the Death Enquiry Reports that I decided not to use them. Nor were they internally consistent. Uncovering the basis for such divergence appeared like a research project in itself and, without access to the sources of primary data, not one that could prove fruitful.

The District Court provided a far more useful source of data. Through the good offices of the then Chief Magistrate, Roy Barter, I was able to collate my own statistics from the Death Enquiry Reports (DERs) and from case records. In compiling statistics there is a definite, if infuriating, satisfaction in knowing that when the totals fail to add up correctly it is due solely to one's own carelessness. There were other reasons also for preferring the court as the main source of data. The material was rich and allowed for a direct comparison with the figures collected by Jean la Fontaine (1960b) in the early 1950s since she had relied on this also. It also allowed me to follow up and cross-reference with the cases I came across in the field and, with a few cases, to extend a case study begun in the field by attending the court hearings.

THE STATISTICAL BASE

The Death Enquiry Reports (DERs) contain the basic actuarial facts about the deceased; age, sex, tribe, place and time of death and usually some idea as to the cause of death. The DERs for the five-year period from 1964 to 1968 provided a record on some 578 homicide victims, and these were used as the basis for calculating the annual incidence of death from homicide in Bugisu as well as the incidence by sex and age. My main interest here was to produce a statistical profile of violent death that would be comparable with homicide statistics elsewhere, and particularly with those compiled by Bohannan and others in their pioneering studies of homicide in East Africa in the early 1950s. Thus suspected 'poisonings' were not included as homicide; only deaths from the effects of strangulation or more commonly from the effects of wounds where the police indicated that there were definite causes for suspicion.

The rates calculated err on the low side for other reasons also. The files themselves were not complete and while they could be supplemented by comparison with the court case records, even after this procedure some 9% of the records were still missing. However, I decided to make no adjustment to

Table 2 *The statistical base*

cases	
1948–54 court case records and Death Enquiry Reports	99
Court case records, 1960–66	375
victims	392
accused	636
Death Enquiry Reports, 1964–68	578
percentage prosecuted	48%

Table 3 *Mean annual rate of death from homicide in rural Bugisu by age and sex per 100,000 people*, 1964–68 %

Children (14 years and under)	3.6
Adult women (15 years and over)	15.8
Adult men (15 years and over)	91.8
Bugisu District	32
Adult men: 15–29	46.7
30–44	80.5
45 and over	132.8

take account of this because the only evidence of any systematic bias suggested that this would affect cases other than homicide. The current files most likely to be missing were those where an inquest was being held and it seemed probable that it would be these files which went astray thereafter. In the 1960s, the Coroner's Court investigated only accidental deaths (largely traffic accidents) and suicides, with unsolved homicides not investigated due to the pressure of other court work. Thus it did not appear that error in the filing system alone would seriously distort the distribution of homicide by age and sex. With regard to the overall incidence of homicide I thought it preferable to err on the low rather than on the high side.

The average annual rate of death from homicide in Bugisu given in table 3 for the years between 1964 and 1968 of thirty-two victims per 100,000 of the population is therefore a conservative estimate. It is certainly lower than one computed from police figures. Before leaving this subject some other possible sources of error and underestimation should be mentioned. Firstly, there is the possibility of non-reporting of cases. I do not think that this was a major problem in Bugisu. I came across very few suspected or rumoured cases of murder which were not reported to the police, and these were a very definite category of killing where a miscreant was put to death secretly with the approval of the community. Even here non-reporting was rare as the local authority chiefs tended to pursue their duties zealously in this area. Non-reporting was really only an option where the body was hidden or the killing disguised in some other way. I did not get the impression that it was any easier to do this in Bugisu than it would be, say, in England. Bugisu is densely settled and it is difficult to do anything without there being a witness of some kind around. Further, bodies tend to turn up. Occasionally, the records indicate that a body was uncovered during digging or after heavy rain. One was discovered in a latrine. More usually they were washed up. A favourite way of disposing of a corpse was to throw it in the river. The Manafwa, the largest river of southern Bugisu, became known as the river of blood in the late 1960s because of the number of corpses found in it. On one occasion while I was in the field I was told that seven bodies had been washed up, caught where a railway bridge crossed the river down on the plains. But if bodies tended to turn up, deciding then what kind of an offence had been committed posed a very definite problem for the police. Was it misadventure, suicide or homicide? A similar problem arose where bodies were found incinerated in their houses. Such sources of ambiguity are inevitable and I followed the police judgements – or misjudgements – in so far as these themselves were clear in categorising cases.

On balance, I don't think that these judgements or misjudgements dramatically affected the overall statistics on homicide because of the overwhelming number of cases where the victim had died from the effects of wounding. Gisu murder appears largely as a matter of assault and battery. Very few people are killed without recourse to a weapon or, more precisely, an implement of some type or other, as can be seen from table 4. Yet the traditional weapons of war

Table 4 *Weapons used in 375 homicide cases, 1960–66*

Weapon	Cases	%
Stick or club	115	30.7
Panga	71	18.9
Knife	54	15.4
Spear	28	7.5
Axe	11	2.9
Arrow	10	2.7
Stone	10	2.7
Walking stick/pestle	7	1.9
Hoe	6	1.6
Metal rod	4	1.1
Slasher	1	0.3
Gun	1	0.3
Strangulation	5	1.3
Blow with fist	3	0.8
Kick	3	0.8
Push off hill	3	0.8
Arson associated with murder	13	3.5
Unknown	30	8.0
Total	375	100

enter into murders comparatively infrequently and in only about 10% were spears or bows and arrows mentioned in the record. Much more common were sticks or clubs, 30.7%, pangas, 18.9%, or knives, 15.4%. Such weapons are usually to hand and in these terms Gisu men are rarely completely unarmed. In the morning people carry their hoes and pangas with them into the fields, the all-purpose panga with its broad blade being a lethal weapon. At night each man picks up a stick, knobkerrie or again, a panga to brave the dark since it is then that attacks from enemies are most feared. Even during the day as men go about their affairs or attend beer parties they are a rarely completely unarmed, it being usual to carry a stick or to have a small knife secreted in a pocket.

However, it is another matter when one turns to suicide. Unlike murder, suicide is regarded not only as bad but as utterly polluting (*imbixo*), bringing danger and misfortune to the suicide's kin. There can be no normal burial but instead the kin of the dead must pay outsiders to come and cut down the body and destroy the tree or the house where the suicide has died. It is an act which incites horror and fear. It nevertheless occurs though, at 3.6 per 100,000 per year, at a rate which is only about one-tenth of that of homicide (see table 5). But, in saying this, one has to be clear what one means by suicide. The Gisu verb used is *xuxwikoka*, 'to strangle' or 'hang oneself', and it is only this form of self-killing which attracts odium.[3] Other forms of 'suicide' are not ritual offences of the same kind and hanging is probably the only form of suicide which is regularly reported as such. This issue obviously raises the whole question of the cultural definition of offences. Paradoxically perhaps, the figures taken from the Death Enquiry Reports can probably be regarded as representative of suicide in the specific Gisu sense but, by the same token, they probably underestimate it in the English legal sense of intentional self-slaughter. Drowning, the other obvious alternative here, did occur and formed a proportion (6%) of the cases found reported in the records, but it was not invariably so reported. For example, following the death by drowning of a local man I visited his two widows. At the time, only two days after the death, it was rumoured that he might have been killed and I asked them about this. They agreed that it was possible but thought that it was unlikely. More probably, in their view, he had killed himself. He was an old man who had been ill for some considerable time and recently been in great pain. He had intimated to both of them his desire to put an end to his suffering. Preparations for a normal burial were going ahead. This death was recorded in the records as misadventure, reflecting, I suspect, the cultural as well as the physical indeterminateness of the situation. The question of definitions and of the cultural biases operating to produce a given set of statistics will be raised again in later discussion with respect to the idea of murder.

To return to homicide, other information on patterns of Gisu murder was collected by going through the court case records for the years from 1960 to 1966. The information contained in these records varied widely depending on

Table 5 *Comparative homicide statistics*, 1948–54 and 1960–68

	1948–54	1960–68
Annual rate of death from homicide per 100,000	7	32★
Annual rate of death from suicide per 100,000		3.6
Victims of homicide by sex		
Percentage of male victims	82	81.7★
Percentage of female victims	18	16.7★
Percentage of child victims	0	1.5★
Sample size	100	578★
Accused of homicide by sex		
Percentage of men	93.4	96.4†
Percentage of women	6.6	3.6†
Sample size	137	636†
Sex of accused in relation to sex of victim (%)		
Male killed by male(s)	76	79.6†
Female killed by male(s)	15	15.3†
Child killed by male(s)	0	1.0†
Male killed by female(s)	6	2.8†
Female killed by female(s)	3	0.5†
Child killed by female(s)	0	0.8†
Total victims	100	392†

Figures for 1948–54 calculated from Appendix: Gisu Case Charts, in P. Bohannan (ed.), *Gisu Homicide and Suicide*, 1960.
★ Figure calculated from Death Enquiry Reports, 1964–68
† Figure calculated from court records, 1960–66.

how far the case had progressed through the courts. Where the case had been withdrawn by the police or discharged by the Magistrate the files frequently contained no more than the charge sheet. Others contained a transcript of the preliminary enquiry held by the Magistrate and, where he committed the accused for trial, a copy of the High Court judgement. In these latter cases the Magistrate heard the main evidence for the prosecution but the defence was reserved for the High Court proceedings and filed in Kampala. Evidence for the defence was only included in the files where the accused pleaded guilty and elected for a summary trial. The magistrate then heard all the evidence and committed the case to the High Court only for sentencing.

Whereas the DERs may be said to contain a relatively good actuarial record of violent death with respect to homicide – at least, one that is as good as one can get in these circumstances – the same cannot be said of the court case records. This is despite the relatively large sample for which I collected information: 375 cases, containing data on 392 victims and 636 accused (see table 2). But one cannot have any confidence that these are representative of patterns of Gisu murder in a statistical sense. The skewing effect of prosecution is all the more evident when the rate of prosecution was as low as it was in Bugisu at this time, only some 48% of cases. Of these, a further 17% were withdrawn or discharged early in the proceedings.

At the local level it thus appears that registering cases was one thing but prosecution another. The reasons for this may be sought both with the police and with the villagers. On the police side, one may evidence the tremendous burden of work implied in high rates of homicide and violent crime. Further, they were almost completely reliant on the statements of eye-witnesses to achieve a prosecution since, without sophisticated forensic proof, circumstantial evidence alone was unacceptable in the courts. The only forensic evidence usually available was that contained in the *post-mortem* report. Added to which, they were unused to working in the villages and could only operate effectively here with the full co-operation of the local chiefs. And the chiefs, local men as well as officials, tended to hold the same opinions as their fellow villagers. They would thus tend to push for a prosecution only where the matter was self-evident or there was some local demand for it. This implies also that there were people willing to give evidence and evidence that would stand up in court. Compliance with official dictates and the police only went so far.

BIAS IN THE RECORDS

Some idea of the kind of general bias present in the records may now be attempted. In the first place it would appear that the cases most easily prosecuted were those that occurred where there were many eye-witnesses, that is at social gatherings or where crowds gathered, as at thief-beatings. On the other hand, killings which took place at night with few if any eye-witnesses would be difficult to prosecute, even where the killers were known locally. Since the former situation is more typical of essentially unpremeditated killings and the latter of premeditated, the court sample is likely to be biased towards unpremeditated killings, that is, generally manslaughter rather than murder in legal terms. This is indeed exactly what is found. Of the cases taken to court, only 52% resulted in a conviction for either murder or manslaughter and, of these, 86% were sentenced for manslaughter (table 6).

This raises a very interesting issue since it touches on basic differences in judgement between English-derived law and Gisu attitudes to killing. There is coincidence only at some points and where there is such coincidence it derives from basically different postulates. The Gisu do not distinguish morally between premeditated and unpremeditated killings. This is a subject which must be explored further elsewhere but the example of thief-killings may be cited here to illustrate the point. A large proportion of the court cases, some 23%, involved the killing of thieves. In over half these cases (54%), the victim was said to have been actually caught stealing and killed on the spot by the man or men involved. Thief-killings also occurred at other times. It is a common sight in Bugisu to see a party of men on the tracks of a thief and, once captured, such men can expect extremely harsh treatment, being roped and beaten, with every passer-by lending a hand. Killings by lynch mobs of this kind formed a further 26% of the court sample. There remains a sizeable percentage (20%) of thieves killed some time after the alleged offence, not always, it appeared, with any tangible evidence against them. The Gisu do not distinguish morally between these different categories of thief-killing. For them what is important is that the man killed was a thief. The killers are then held to be justified in their actions, and it does not reflect upon their moral worth except in so far as it may indicate a predisposition to use violence. The courts take a different attitude but, nevertheless, the judges, while deploring the abrogation of law involved, tended to deal leniently with thief-killers. Only two thief-killers were found guilty of murder (out of fifty-eight cases where the decision of the courts was known) and over 80% of those convicted for manslaughter were sentenced to less than three years in prison (table 6).

Table 6 *Court sentences*, 1960–66

Court sentence	Thief-killings		Other homicide		All homicide	
Total convictions for murder or manslaughter	58	59.80%	137	49.63%	195	52.00%
Case withdrawn/discharged/ *nolle prosequi*	10	10.31%	54	19.57%	64	17.07%
Acquitted	3	3.09%	35	12.68%	38	10.13%
Change of charge, i.e. grievous harm, infanticide, insane	0	0%	17	6.16%	17	4.53%
Unknown	26	26.80%	35	11.96%	61	16.26%
Total	97	100.00%	278	100.00%	375	100.00%
Sentences for the convicted *Murder* (death or life imprisonment)	2	2.06%	26	9.42%	28	7.47%
Manslaughter total	56	57.74%	111	40.21%	167	44.53%
0–6 months	16	16.50%	14	5.07%	30	8.00%
7 months–3 years	29	29.90%	47	17.02%	76	20.26%
3–6 years	8	8.25%	30	10.87%	38	10.13%
7 years and over	3	3.09%	20	7.25%	23	6.14%

In these particular cases, the standards of the Gisu and the courts do not work out too differently in practice. The same cannot be said of other kinds of cases. Witch-killings, also held to be justifiable by the Gisu, are almost always committed in situations which suggest premeditation. There was one case in the court records where a man of twenty-one caught his father's sister cursing him on his father's grave, took out his knife and stabbed her to death. But, by the nature of such cases, catching a witch *in flagrante delicto* is the exception. More typically such attacks are planned and the witch is ambushed at night, or the thatch of the house is fired and the witch is speared as he or she tries to escape. This last method is held to serve dual duty, destroying both the witch and any medicines that might be secreted in the home. Very few of these cases reach the courts and where they do, allegations of witchcraft are often withheld. In fact only seventeen cases out of a total of 375 or 4.5% of the court cases could be classified as witch-killings. In contrast, out of the thirty-seven cases of murder that I investigated in depth occurring in the area where I was working in Central Bugisu, some six of the victims were considered witches (16%) while eighteen were considered thieves (49%) (see appendix 1).

Different factors therefore conspire to make one category of offence rather than another salient in the court records. The Gisu are well aware of the standards of judgement used by the courts and the court's attitude undoubtedly has an effect both on the type of cases prosecuted and on the evidence then presented. In thief-killings, many of the accused plead guilty. However, even this may be not as self-evident as it sounds as it is possible, of course, that the evidence of theft was sometimes rigged. The judge, in fact, suspected this in a few instances since it is easy enough after a killing has been committed to lop down a bunch of bananas to impute theft. The court situation is extremely complex, with many different strategies operating. Given the stakes involved – and the death penalty was in force for murder – fabrication of all kinds is one of the more obvious.

PATTERNS OF GISU MURDER

Despite the limitations of the records they do reveal some dominant patterns in Gisu homicide and these can be briefly summarised here. In the first place by far the greatest proportion of both the victims and accused in homicide cases are men. In the 1960s sample, 81.7% of the victims were men, 16.7% were women and only 1.5% were children (table 5). The rate of death from homicide per 100,000 (table 3) emphasises this differential, being only 3.6 for children under the age of fifteen, 15.8 for women but 91.8 for men. And men are even more likely to be accused of homicide with only 3.6% of the accused being women. There was only one accused who was under fifteen and that was a boy in his early teens who killed another boy of the same age in a fight. The dominant pattern is thus of men killing men. Eighty per cent of cases were of this kind, with men killing women in a further 15% of cases and women killing men in only 2.8% (table 5). The killing of women by women is extremely rare: there being only two cases in the 1960s sample, giving a percentage of 0.5%. The killing of children is also infrequent and, apart from infanticide, usually appears to have been accidental, typically occurring when the child has become mixed up in a brawl and catches a blow meant for another.

There is a wide difference in Gisu attitudes to the killing of men and the killing of women and children. The former is very often considered justifiable: the latter rarely is. Moreover, this pattern appears to be stable over time. Comparing the 1960s sample with that collected by La Fontaine (1960b) based on court cases and death enquiry reports from the period 1948 to 1954, we find that despite the huge increase in the overall rate of death from homicide in the 1960s, the sex distribution is identical. This is a surprising concordance and is found on almost every count: thus (table 5) the proportion of male victims is 82% in both the 1954 and 1966 samples; of male accused, 93.4% in 1954 and 96.4% in 1966, and men killed men in 76% of cases in 1954 compared with 79.6% in 1966. Moreover, the difference apparent with respect to the killing of men and women is reflected not only in the relative frequencies of the offences but in the pleas and justifications made to the court (table 6). A plea of insanity is made more frequently in cases where women or children are killed, for example, in five out of the fifty-seven cases as compared with only two out of the 306 cases where men killed men. Moreover, there are very many more pleas of accidental killings in such instances. Indeed, as will be explored later, the killing of women is usually regarded as a senseless act. At this juncture it is sufficient to say that it is strongly felt that a man has no reason to fear a woman except in the instance where she is a witch. Further, where the woman killed is his wife, as is the most common case, then the killing is regarded as doubly senseless for, in destroying the basis of his household and family, a man is effectively destroying himself. With the killing of children attitudes are even stronger and child-killing is regarded as an abomination.

The linkage of gender with violence applies not only to killing but also to some other forms of crime, particularly theft. Thieves, *babifi*, in Bugisu are always men. While women are occasionally accused of theft, most usually by their husbands, brothers or lovers, I never came across an instance where a woman was reputed to be a 'thief ' nor was there a single case in the court records where a woman was killed for stealing. In contrast, male thieves accounted for almost one-third of the cases where men killed men (table 7). The term carries a symbolic load which associates it with violent troublemak-ing and thus with men and not women. In the court records, the witches killed were also mainly men (thirteen men to four women), and this also reflects a difference in the relative 'dangerousness' of male and female witchcraft.

These harsh attitudes to witches and thieves also have a historic dimension. In the past, it appears both that the offences were bracketed together much as they are today and that offenders were killed. Repeated offence is said, in both cases, to have invited death. An elder in Central Bugisu summarises the attitude like this:

Long ago when a thief stole, on the first two occasions they made him pay a fine but on being caught the third time he was killed. The kin of his mother and those of his father said, 'So take him away outside and kill him', and they took him out into the bush and beat him with sticks until he was dead. No one avenged the death of the thief for it is said that you do not avenge a wastrel: for that one there is nothing. No one spoke of the death for all had agreed.

Alternatively, the kin might take it upon themselves to kill a delinquent member. Here, the task would be delegated to the mother's brothers who would entrap their sister's son by calling him to a feast. As he stepped over the threshold, a noose would be tightened around his neck. Similarly with witches.

They too were denounced by their kindred, though it is said that attempts were made first to placate them by offering them a cow. If they accepted such a gift this was tantamount to an admission of guilt and they would then blow beer over the victim to demonstrate their goodwill and share meat to affirm friendship. But any further witchcraft would be punished by death.

The killing of witches and thieves remains the dominant rationale for killing in Bugisu and is central to the arguments developed in this book. If one looks at table 7, which summarises the motives attributed in 308 killings where men killed men, no other clear pattern of other dispute emerges. Land, property and adultery are mentioned in about the same number of cases but the proportion is small in each case.[4] Beer-party brawling – categorised as such only when no other motive was mentioned – emerges as the most frequent situation for death after thief killing. Yet this does not indicate a lack of 'motive' – still less that the Gisu kill blindly in their cups – but that the procedure used was inadequate and insufficiently attuned to Gisu practice. To a large extent the killing of witches and thieves is paradigmatic for wider attitudes to killing with individual self-help being justified in terms of the necessity to take action against a ne'er-do-well. As will be seen in later discussion, character evaluations rather than the particular situation, pretext or grievance thus are critical aspects of homicide. This is something which cannot be inferred from the court statistics which, taken on their own, remain opaque and open to misinterpretation.

Nevertheless this tabulation does reveal a pattern that is significant by its very rarity; the obvious lack of retaliatory killing. In only eight of 308 cases where men killed men was the killing rationalised in terms of revenge for a previous death. This lack of kin-mobilisation forms the main topic of later chapters but intertribal fighting also forms a small part of the statistics and this may be dealt with here. In the first place, it must be emphasised that these statistics relate to Bugisu District itself, that is to the rural areas excluding both Mbale township and the surrounding districts covered by the police figures. However, rivalry over the district borders has been serious in the area during both colonial and post-colonial times and has led to affrays between people of the rival districts. A particularly sensitive zone is the Lwaboba area of South Bugisu where both Teso and Gisu live together in the same parish and where violence has flared up periodically throughout the contemporary period. The three cases recorded in the list in table 6 are from this area.

However, inter-ethnic rivalries in the neighbouring areas, outside Bugisu itself, have led to more serious outbreaks of fighting, particularly in Sebei. There have been three large-scale uprisings of the Sebei against the Gisu; in 1964, in 1980 following the liberation war, and in 1986–87. In all the Gisu have been forced to flee from the area and, while little is known of the latter periods, the context for fighting in 1964 may be outlined briefly. Throughout the colonial era the Sebei were included in the same district as the Gisu, but with

Table 7 Attributed motives in 308 court cases where men killed men, 1960–66

Dispute	Cases	%
1. Theft	104	33.8
2. Witchcraft	13	4.2
3. Land/bridewealth	13	4.2
4. Other property and debt	15	4.9
5. Adultery	16	5.2
6. Other disputes involving women	10	3.2
7. Slander	10	3.2
8. Vengeance murder	8	2.6
9. Assault	7	2.3
10. Accused lost court case	6	1.95
11. Intervention in quarrel	6	1.95
12. Accidental	4	1.3
13. Inter-tribal fight	3	1.0
14. Beer party brawl	25	8.1
15. Miscellaneous	11	3.6
16. None proffered	19	6.2
17. No information	38	12.3
Total	308	100

Notes on categories
Cases were only categorised once and, except for 15, 16, and 17, where more than one cause for dispute was mentioned in the record, disputes were categorised according to the rank order indicated above.
1 includes all cases where the victim was attributed with theft and 7 cases where the thief was alleged to have killed a member of the arresting party.
2 includes all cases where witchcraft was mentioned as a source of grievance.
3 includes disputes over the division, boundary and debts.
4 includes crop damage by domestic animals.
5 includes 13 cases where a man killed his wife's lover and 3 where the lover killed the husband.
6 includes cases where adultery was alleged by person other than wife's husband.
8 does not include vengeance following deaths attributed to witchcraft.
13 only includes cases of retaliatory killing following, for example, boundary disputes among rival groups and not cases where the men were of different tribes but the motives given were personal.
14 is a residual category. Other killings occurring at beer parties will have been categorised above.

independence the Sebei desire for autonomy was recognised by the Sebei being granted separate district status in 1962. The Sebei desire to handle the marketing of their own coffee crop was delayed until 1964 with the formation of the Sebei–Elgon Coffee Union. For the Gisu, the marketing and control of their own coffee crop was the most powerful way in which their desire for self-determination was demonstrated in the colonial era and has powerful affective implications (Bunker, 1987). The 13,000 Gisu living in Sebei, at that time approximately one-quarter of the population but growing most of the coffee crop, resisted selling through the new union and continued as before to market through the Bugisu Cooperative Union. It was this that appears to have sparked off hostilities which developed into what has been called the 'coffee war'. In the first four months of 1965 over 200 cases of arson, threatening violence, crop-slashing, theft of livestock or murder were reported to the police in Sebei. The presence of the Special Force, a para-military branch of the police, eventually brought the situation under control, but fighting continued until 1966 and resulted in a mass exodus of Gisu from Sebei.[5]

Intertribal fighting of this kind is associated with particular intransigence and retaliatory killings are here the norm rather than the exception. The proverb – *numwira umumia urao kukundu* – 'if you kill a Mumia another corpse will follow' is still apt. The term *Bamia* is used of the Teso but the same principle applies with other non-Gisu groups. Further, it is associated with atrocities such as the killing of children, found washing by streams or out herding, killings that are almost unknown within Bugisu itself.

STATISTICS, VALIDITY AND THE QUESTION OF POISONING

At the more actuarial level the statistics demonstrate patterns which can be demonstrated in no other way and which in the instances outlined above have clear resonance with Gisu belief and attitudes. Yet there are limits to their usefulness and reliability as an index of Gisu practice when we come to aspects more closely related to issues of evaluation and court procedures. For example, the high proportion of cases prosecuted for manslaughter cannot be used as evidence for a general lack of premeditation. In contrast to the courts, the Gisu see probably the majority of killing as premeditated in one way or another. To refer again to the information collected in the rural situation on cases in Central Bugisu, the evidence suggested that as many as twenty-one out of thirty-seven were planned in advance and in many of these the word that a man was likely to be killed was abroad before the event. This applied equally to thief-killings so that even here the court case material, if used without due caution, can be misleading.

I am perhaps overlabouring this point. The idea that statistics are 'created', are a product of the classificatory grid used by the observer, is well accepted. Nor are the problems unique to statistics; they are implicit in any use of the comparative method. Whenever we seek to organise our material into uniform categories for the purposes of comparison *pari passu* we risk imposing inappropriate and misleading standards. Nor is there any obvious way out of this dilemma. One may counsel oneself to be aware of likely sources of distortion, but the process operates in many ways, some more subtle than others, so that merely engaging in the exercise commits us to an external view, which may not be 'correctable'. This takes us to a fundamental issue, for in merely deciding to investigate death through the category of homicide, and in pursuing enquiry through the court statistics, I have committed myself already to the view that this is a meaningful category of death, and meaningful largely in the terms that English law has defined. But this is not at all self-evident in a situation such as that in Bugisu where all death is seen as a form of murder. Clearly, I must now look at my own practice and examine whether and in what way it is valid to make a distinction between murder and non-murder in the Gisu context.

The statistics here cannot help me since they simply reinforce our own cultural preconceptions. This foreclosure effect can be illustrated with reference to the Death Enquiry Reports which, as I have said, form a more reliable source of information on violent death in Bugisu than do the court case records. What emerges from these – as it does also from the court cases – is that Gisu murder is primarily a matter of armed assault and battery. A weapon of some kind is usually used, most frequently, a club, a panga or a knife. But, as I also said, in order that my tabulations would be comparable with others, from the beginning not only did I exclude all other forms of non-reportable death but I also excluded suspected poisonings from the Death Enquiry statistics. Nor at the time did I have many misgivings about doing this – the numbers were relatively small in any case. It is only in retrospect that it becomes clear how easily the category of 'murder' was reduced from 'all death' to the sub-category of 'violent death by the hand of another' and from there to 'deaths from a direct physical assault' alone. Further, in classifying poison out, I think I too began to think of it as 'not murder' and thus was less alert than I might have been to certain problems posed by this very interesting kind of death.

The first interesting thing to note is the fact that deaths from suspected poisoning were reported at all, albeit not many (about six a year). Such deaths were therefore being treated by the Gisu as possible murder. The fact remained, however, that government pathologists did not find any traces of poison in the stomach contents. In some cases the cause of death was attributed to alcohol poisoning, most commonly due to methyl present in *waragi*, the raw spirit distilled locally. In other cases no medical cause of death was established. At the time I was fairly satisfied with these judgements: Gisu 'poisoning' could be seen as a largely imaginary category, with particular instances occurring either because of drunkenness or because of, presumably, the inadvertent contamination of alcohol. I was later less sanguine about such a conclusion. In the first place, it was rarely less than a week before the government pathologists in Entebbe had the opportunity of examining the stomach contents. It is therefore possible that traces of poison might have disappeared in the interim. Further, it appears more than likely that the Gisu, or rather, some Gisu, with their extensive knowledge of herbal properties, did know and use actual poisons. Elsewhere in East Africa, poisons are widely manufactured for use in tipping the arrowheads used for both hunting and warfare. It now seems unrealistic to suppose, as I think I did then following the standard line of all anthropological accounts following Evans-Pritchard's (1937) analysis of Zande witchcraft, that all that goes under the heading of sorcery or witchcraft constitutes magic rather than medicine. It might well be both.

The category of 'poison' might be magic at one level but it was medicine at another. It was clearly on the cusp. And this is how it appeared in practice. The Gisu believe that practically all deaths are brought about by other people, either – and most commonly – through witchcraft (*bulosi*) or through physical violence. Thus, of any death, it might be said, '*bamwira*', 'they have killed him or her', a phrase which was always used in the plural. Only rarely are deaths laid at the door of the ancestral spirits or to the action of death, *luufu*, alone. The Gisu say that it is possible to die from natural causes, either from sheer age or from the effects of a fatal disease, the latter being 'divined', so to speak, today by doctors trained in Western medicine. But, even where such ideas are entertained, there are few cases where witchcraft is not simultaneously rumoured. Such rumours are usually confined to the close kin of the dead and rarely result in an open accusation. Nevertheless, every death is in a sense a murder. The question which is then posed is what makes physical assault different from witchcraft? Today, different procedures apply; only offences which fall into the Western category of murder are investigated as such by the police. But were the two types of offence so clearly distinguished in the past? It seems possible that they were – compensation was often payable after a killing but not usually after sorcery. Since blood compensation is no longer offered at the present time, this practice could not be used to distinguish between these forms of killing. But, in any case, the fact that different forms of redress were sought after sorcery does not necessarily prove the case either way. It might simply be due to the differing degrees of certitude one can have as to the identity of the culprit or culprits. It is here that the category 'poison', clearly on the divide between one kind of killing and another, promises to hold important clues as to the nature of Gisu perception.

The poison cases reported to the police fall into the category of sorcery known as *kumusala*. In the first place, one could say that this form of sorcery is seen by the Gisu as similar to direct murder because it causes almost instantaneous death and not the lingering illnesses typical of most other forms of witchcraft. *Kumusala* in fact means lethal medicine, with the root of the word derived from the verb *xusala*, to slaughter, used of killing animals by slitting the throat, and so on. Nevertheless, not all forms of *kumusala* overlap with the Western category of poison. Some 'catch' the victim by touch, others when he steps over it. Only some are administered orally, and it is only this form which ends up in the police records. The symptoms, typically violent vomiting, followed by collapse and death, also suggest organic poisoning. However, despite this overlap in categories, as I have said, the evidence is never sufficient for prosecution and so one is left with a paradox. If prosecutions never follow and the report received back denies the fact of poison, why do the Gisu persist in reporting these cases? Clearly, there is more here than simply official compliance. In focusing on this question I also then become aware that it is only a small proportion of 'poisoning' cases that are reported anyway. Not every case of vomiting followed by death is reported. In fact, with very few exceptions, the only cases that are reported are those where the death occurred at a beer party or very soon thereafter.

The beer party is in fact the place where murder of all kinds is most feared. Not only do brawls develop under the influence of alcohol but the Gisu also fear conspiracies and plots with, for example, a drunken victim being set upon as he finds his way home in the dark. Poisoning fears enter here, the poison believed to be inserted in the mouth of the tube used to suck the beer out of a collective pot, inserted perhaps when the victim left the room. In this way it attacks the individual and not the group. The fact that the beer party is seen as a situation of violent death undoubtedly influences the reporting of cases of poisoning that occur here.

A return can now be made to the problem of distinguishing 'direct murder' – for lack of a better tag – from all murder, that is, all death including that from witchcraft. One critical point to be made here is that murder tends to incite a different social reaction from other death. It is an affair in the public arena and there is far greater pressure to identify the murderers even when, as is common, no further action is taken against them. I don't think this can be attributed solely to the modern legal process, nor to the different nature of the causation in itself. At one rather basic level witchcraft and physical attack simply present a choice in the weapons available. A person may seek retaliation or redress against another through the many varieties of witchcraft or through physical attack, by theft, arson, assault, and so on. For both purposes he may hire others to do the job for him and either may, according to the circumstances, be considered justifiable. However, it could be argued that the urgency of the kinds of inquest that occur after a violent death occur simply because it is sudden and unexpected. In the case of serious illness, diviners would have been consulted probably many times prior to death to determine the malignant agency. But, in itself, this does not explain the apparent lack of any general feeling against the 'killers' in these instances and the fact that open accusations are, in my experience, rarely made. After much thought, I think that the key difference lies in the degree of overtness of the offence.

Witchcraft is, by its nature, usually covert and its actions hidden. With a witchcraft death there is always ambiguity; there could have been another agency just as there could be several, possibly independent, witches at work. Murder, on the other hand, is an open event which demands a public reaction; the identity of the killers can, in practice, be known with a certitude not available in witchcraft cases. However, one can go further than this, for the distinction between public and private events is crucial for understanding a number of different aspects of Gisu morality. For example, incest is described in general terms as polluting and carries a dire supernatural penalty. But both the pollution and the penalty only follow where the offence becomes known. The consequences are contingent on public awareness and thus on the way offences affect relationships in the community. Nor is this kind of supernatural pragmatism unique to the Gisu. Mbiti has written that 'the essence of African morality is that it is more "societary" than "spiritual": it is a morality of "conduct" rather than a morality of "being"' (1969: 214). The evilness of acts exists not in themselves but in their social effects, which in turn depend on the degree to which they are open and known. Murder is pre-eminently an open offence and, in having repercussions on social relationships, it demands a public response. This, I think, is the main way in which murder differs from witchcraft death.

The nature of the morality in question here will be returned to in a later chapter. Here it is sufficient to reiterate that the argument with respect to murder and witchcraft does not hinge on any supposed difference between 'natural' and 'supernatural' events or imply that there are different kinds of causative theory at work, as in Evans-Pritchard's (1937) analysis of Zande beliefs. Rather, the distinction hinges on the implicit morality of everyday life. From here a return must be made to the question of statistics and their relevance for anthropology.

ANTHROPOLOGY AND STATISTICS: AN ASSESSMENT

There have been relatively few anthropological studies of crime and even fewer which have used official statistics in any systematic way. In his pioneering study, Bohannan's (1960) interest in homicide was inspired by his realisation that the court records contained valuable ethnographic data of a kind not usually available to the anthropologist. With a group of associates at Makerere, he aimed to develop a comparative approach to the topic by focusing on 'culture patterns', that is, the 'concatenations of social relationships and the accompanying idiom of culture which are associated with homicide and suicide in different human groups' (1960: 28). In so doing he broke with the ethnocentric position so evident in sociological studies of homicide at the time where the accused, the 'murderer', was seen as the problematic figure whose behaviour must be explained. Instead, he extended the actuarial approach of Von Hentig (1948) and Wolfgang (1958), both of whom had looked at the social relationships between the victim and accused, insisting that any anthropological study must take as its starting point the idea that this relationship is, in itself, interlocked with others. Homicide, from this anthropological perspective, must thus be seen as a meaningful act, occurring within a specific social context, and not merely enumerated as an aberration or statistical digit.

In applauding such aims the reservation remains as to whether the use of court data as the primary source of case material can ever be anything other than misleading. As I have tried to show in this chapter, the distorting effect of the case records is hard to evade. The bias imposed by court procedures, legal definitions and the concept of relevance filters much out. Further, we would be unwise to assume that this is any simple filtering process, giving access to at least some 'pure' cases. The situation is more complex than this. Even where the standards of the court and those of the people are variant, the people are likely to be cognisant with court procedures and indeed have a sophisticated understanding of them. Certainly this was so of the Gisu, and the knowledge both of the stringency of proof needed for conviction as well as the types of homicide judged less culpable by the courts all entered into the courtroom situation and affected the statements and pleas made. Many Gisu, it seemed to me, in presenting their own cases were as skilled as any advocate, quick to make play with any inadequacies or discrepancies in the evidence against them.

Court data tends to provide a straitjacket on analysis in other ways too. The 'case' is inevitably the unit of analysis and even where the research goes beyond an interest in the accused to the relationship between the accused and his victim, it is difficult in fact to proceed beyond this. Despite Bohannan's initial aims, his comparative examination of homicide falls back upon a discussion of the dyadic relationships between victims and accused. Here, one faces in relief the problems of bias in the court-case samples. For example, to give an idea of just how misleading it might be to draw conclusions about Gisu murder on the basis of such evidence, I might be drawn to the conclusion that, since the relative frequency of parricide in Bugisu appears to have fallen, from 7.1% of the cases tabulated by Jean la Fontaine in 1950–54, to only 2.6% in the 1960s, there has therefore been some amelioration in the tensions between fathers and sons. Or, that since disputes over the allocation of bridewealth or land were mentioned in only thirteen of the 308 killings between men (table 7), that conflicts over property are a relatively insignificant factor in Gisu murder. In fact I will be drawing diametrically opposed conclusions, for these factors are of utmost importance to an understanding of Gisu murder. The statistics here mask the complexity of social process and indicate only that the situation which eventually prompts a killing may be at one or several steps removed from the basic conflicts which might equally be said to prompt it.

These provisos do not only apply to case analysis in court records. A further methodological question, of what exactly should be taken to constitute a 'case', has been fully discussed in the literature on witchcraft (see Douglas, 1967). As those who have advocated an 'extended case method' have argued, it is only when events are placed in the interactive setting, and not abstracted from the ongoing flow of social life, that their significance can be unravelled. Yet these remarks are not intended to totally negate the use of either official statistics or the collecting of quantitive data. But their use for the anthropologist can only be to *extend the inferences made from case analysis in natural settings*. The court statistics contain useful data but Jean la Fontaine is surely right when she uses them 'mainly in illustration' (1960b:118), and the overall value of the studies of Bohannan and his collaborators comes from their ability to extrapolate from the case records the relevant features of the social structure and values of the groups studied. The bare bones of homicide statistics must be clothed by the knowledge and intuitions of the fieldworker.

Notes

1   For example, Cohen, 1971; Erikson, 1962; Lemert, 1967.

2   Researchers' access to official records was a highly political issue in Uganda in the mid-sixties, with justifiable official suspicion over the uses later made of such data sometimes carried to the point of paranoia. At least this was the view of a researcher, waving her *bona fides,* to often very little effect. Not only did the gaining of official permission take time, a time that had often to be counted in years rather than months, but separate permission had to be obtained from each Ministry to obtain access to the annual reports produced by the various government departments operating in the district. Yet this is not intended as a complaint but rather as an oblique way of registering gratitude. Without the support of many local officials, and their willingness to help in informal ways, research would have proved extremely difficult, if not impossible.

3   It is relevant to note that suicide by hanging carries the implication of self-sacrifice, for traditionally animals were sacrificed without bloodshed, by strangulation or stunning.

4   This is despite the fact that the procedure used to classify cases here by prioritising them in the order listed was designed to produce as high a frequency as possible for those 'motives' first selected. Initially, cases were also classified according to whether the reason was given as an underlying source of grievance or a precipitating cause to make them comparable to the listings given by La Fontaine (1960b). However, this revealed no patterns of significance and the two kinds of rationale have been amalgamated in this table. But it is relevant to note that this procedure also selected for land and property disputes.

5   Later outbreaks of fighting appear to have taken a roughly similar form. Gisu were driven by Sebei from their homes in Sebei in 1980 following the Tanzanian liberation war which ousted Amin, and were again forced to flee in 1986. In November of that year the Kenyan papers reported that 1,600 Gisu had fled and sought sanctuary at Suam over the Kenyan border and the hostilities continued, with Sebei firing Gisu houses, with over 200 reported destroyed in one night in December.

PART 2
The accusational nexus

3

ON BEING A MAN:
THE NATURE OF GISU EXPERIENCE

Early in my fieldwork I suggested in conversation that much of the killing was essentially unintentional in nature, a product of the use of excessive force. After all, I argued, it is difficult to control the extent of injury if one strikes another with the broad-bladed panga. But did that mean that a man meant to kill? Or again, many Gisu had enlarged spleens due to repeated attacks of malaria, and blows to the stomach were thus sometimes fatal. Yes, it was agreed, such things happened, but the problem did not lie here. They, as Gisu men, had no fear of acting violently and killing. There was no reluctance, for one does not act violently by half-measures. If one was a circumcisor one had to cut; not make a stab at it. It was the same for boys undergoing circumcision. Violence and killing did not happen by default but were an expression of male purpose. These statements were not made with any pride; they were not vainglorious but meant as a factual comment and one which, in the circumstances of increasing violence, was a source of disquiet.

The Gisu, indeed, see violence as specifically a male problem. Only men have the capacity for it, or at least for the kind of violence which is a danger to others. Women categorically do not and, while the facts of daily life might lead one to challenge such a totally unaggressive stereotype, it is nevertheless powerful in shaping judgements about events. A man is held never to have just cause to fear a woman and this affects the way the use of physical violence against women is judged. Women, one is told, are like the slow-worm, *namakanda*, which looks like a snake but is in fact harmless. Other imagery used for women also reflects their essentially benevolent role as help-mates and the bearers of children. Women are like the castor-oil tree, frail but fertile, which spreads its seeds widely. Or they are like the bullfrog whose croaking warns of the passage of an enemy, as a woman warns her husband of the rumours she has heard which might threaten his life.

Further, the picture is consistent throughout, so that the violence of men in its anti-social aspects may be contrasted with the kindheartedness of women. Women are said to have compassion (*cisa*), a compassion which is signified in their gathering to attend the funerals in the neighbourhood. Indeed, women play the role of mourners; it is they who beat the bounds announcing the death, they who sing the laments, and they who dance in distress and defiant anger at the burial. Yet since men dig the graves and take charge of the burial itself, the contrast is not of participation as such but the type of participation. Men's attendance at the funerals of their close kin and neighbours is an obligation, just as is the giving of financial and other assistance. But women's sympathies are held to be more widely and generously aroused. They attend not only through obligation but through pity and, identifying with the bereaved, they attend a far greater number of funerals than do their husbands. Further, women's feelings and compassion with the mourners are linked to their fear of death. Men, it is maintained, do not fear death and this points, for the Gisu, to a critical difference in the potentialities of the sexes.

Yet women must endure the pains of childbirth and survive. In this they must be tough. But, though in many ways parallel, the equivalent ordeal for men, that of circumcision, is believed to attest to a courageousness of a different order. The courage of men comes from their capacity to experience some emotions more strongly than women. If women may be aroused to feel sympathy keenly, they are not deemed capable of experiencing the same emotional responses and passions as men. This is given in the contrast *libuba/ lirima*, both of which refer to 'anger' but indicate a different intensity of response. Women and children are believed to be capable only of the weaker form of emotional arousal as given in *libuba*, while men are subject to that of *lirima*.

Lirima is pre-eminently a manly quality. While there is no easy English equivalent, one might start with the idea that it refers to violent emotion and many ways in which the Gisu talk about it suggest that such emotion is also experienced as overwhelming and even out of control. Lirima is spoken of as 'catching' a man and as 'bubbling-up' in him, though 'boiling over' might be more accurate here, as the usual simile is used with the boiling of milk or water. While in this state of possession, *lirima* is seen to dictate a man's attitudes and actions; he is filled with *lirima*, it gives force to his motivations and impels him to action. Further, *lirima* is linked to the negative emotions, to jealousy, hatred, resentment and shame. One could add, though tentatively, and bearing in mind the difficulties of directly linking emotion to physiological stimuli (Schacter and Singer, 1962), that the situations in which it is adduced and its breadth of reference make it tempting to associate *lirima* with a state of sympathetic arousal of the nervous system. It is an equation made the more plausible by the fact that the Gisu associate *lirima* and indeed sometimes define it with the sensation of having a lump in the throat. Such a symptom could well be produced by the release of adrenalin and the subsequent contraction of the muscles of the throat. While this parallel might help to conceptualise the breadth of the Gisu concept one must be wary of assuming any easy equation.

It is not just the indeterminacy of the physiological input to the experience of emotion which is at issue but the cognitive associations which set the Western and Gisu models at variance.

For us such extreme affect tends to suggest the overriding of reason by passion, a lack of self-control. For the Gisu, who do not think of reason and emotion as opposed modalities embattled within the personality, *lirima* can not only be volitional but an aspect of the control a man should assert over himself and over the world, a quality or capacity to be mustered by the individual to achieve or serve his purposes. If a man can be in the grip of *lirima* he can use it to steel himself too. In this way *lirima* not only has negative but also forceful and positive connotations, the force behind that strength of character which makes men courageous and determined. In this way, and through the experience of circumcision, all the positive aspects of manhood, autonomy, self-mastery, virility and power, can be related to *lirima*. That *lirima* bestows such affirmative powers, and is the capacity of men and only men, gives overall poignancy to its more usual associations with violence.

My purpose in this chapter is to outline the basic standards of judgement as they apply to human action; standards of judgement which rest on the basic motivational schemas of Gisu male society. This calls for an enquiry into Gisu concepts of their own experience, of their understanding of the psychological process and the nature of the self. One way of probing this area is to look more closely at the rituals of circumcision. For most Gisu men circumcision is undoubtedly the most formative experience of their lives and the subject arouses deep emotions. Further, the rites can be seen to have a direct psychological purpose. a transformational aim, not merely marking the divide between boyhood and manhood but in a very direct way creating the proper capacities and dispositions of manhood. What these are, their cognitive associations, as well as clues as to how they are experienced, may thus be explored through examining the themes and symbolism of the ritual.

They are all crucially concerned with the triad *kamani*, *buwangafu* and *lirima*. *Kamani* refers primarily to physical strength. *Buwangafu*, on the other hand, implies 'toughness'. However, since the Gisu do not rigidly distinguish between qualities of mind and qualities of body, *kamani* is used with the wider meaning of a 'strong man' and *buwangafu* implies toughness of mind as much as of body, singleness of purpose as much as physical strength. Deriving from the verb *xuwangala*, it combines the connotations of ageing and bravery. Thus one set of meanings relate directly to the fact of age, being translatable according to context as 'to come of age', 'to last long', 'to survive', to 'endure'. The other connotations make this a masculine rather than a feminine quality, with the ability to endure identified with courage, boldness and bravery. Thus the term *umuwangafu* may be used to describe an old and worthy or, alternatively, a man with a reputation for bravery. Used as a form of address it is the praise term *par excellence*. Yet male power of this kind rests ultimately on *lirima*, the power of men that allows for forceful and determined action. *Buwangafu* thus cannot escape some of the negative connotations that go with *lirima*. The things which last long, that are toughest, are also the most dangerous to others, just as the most bitter medicines are the most potent.

What must be stressed is that for the Gisu the ambivalence of *lirima* is a basic fact of life and regarded as inherent in the nature of men. It is central to the transformational purpose of circumcision since this is the first time that the boy is expected to display the emotion. Thereafter it is as much a part of his manhood as the circumcision cuts themselves. Moreover, in the context of circumcision *lirima* is accorded a positive and essential role. It is for the Gisu the key to the complete identification of the boy with the ordeal he faces. As the ordeal gets closer it is *lirima* which is seen to drive him on and to dominate his thoughts and his feelings. It is *lirima* which allows him to overcome his fear. The induction of *lirima* thus appears both as a technique of the ritual, developed in the boy to allow him to stand the ordeal and also as its aim, to turn him into a man with the capacity thereafter to experience *lirima*.[1]

THE CIRCUMCISION RITUAL

Throughout most of Bugisu boys are circumcised when they are between the ages of eighteen and twenty-four and, in so becoming a 'man', assume a status of equality with all other men. They now gain the all-important rights to marry, to inherit land and to enjoy such other privileges of adult life as drinking beer. They are effectively emancipated in a society of free and autonomous men, each economically independent, with his own household and land. Such status and such rights are seen as achieved through undergoing the ordeal of circumcision.

The values of circumcision may be explored in terms of the personal qualities looked for and ultimately tested by the ordeal itself. Circumcision is conceived of as a personal test, a test of bravery which is publicly witnessed. The boy stands for the operation in the courtyard of his father or other senior relative, and must stand absolutely still while first his foreskin is cut and then stripped from around the *glans penis*. He is required to display total fortitude under the knife, betraying no signs of fear, and even what might be regarded as involuntary twitches and tremblings, such as the blinking of the eyes, are evaluated negatively. The degree of pain is never underplayed, the most commonly used descriptive adjectives being 'fierce', 'bitter' and 'terrifying'. Only those who have faced this fact and overcome their fear can undergo the ordeal successfully. Success, however, is triumphantly celebrated: the watching men roar in unison while the women rush forward, ululating as they dance. The boy is then allowed to sit down and the onlookers come forward one by one to call him by the honorific term *umusani*, usually reserved for men who have themselves circumcised sons, and to thank him by presenting him with gifts.

Initially, the most important prerequisite for circumcision is seen to lie in the boy's physical maturity and age. Gisu boys are not considered ready for *imbalu* until well past puberty, with boys throughout most of Bugisu being circumcised in the age range eighteen to twenty-four. In the first instance, then, the strength (*kamani*) to undergo the ordeal is related to physical maturity. Later it is assessed in terms of how the boy dances in the build-up to the operation. It is important to note here that the word 'strong' implies more than just physical power, but also what we would call strength of purpose. The boy is continually exhorted: *samba imbalu ni kamani* – dance *imbalu* with strength – and *amba imbalu ni kamani* – hold on to *imbalu* with strength. The expressions are interchangeable, just as firmness (*xuwangala*) of intent will ultimately be manifested in the firmness of his body when he actually stands for the operation. Then he is told that he must breathe normally and let his stomach muscles relax; there must be no trembling, no giveaway involuntary movements of his body which betoken fear. The commitment required of the boy is total, evidenced by his complete command of his body at the time of the operation.

The sources of this commitment are twofold; in the first place it is thought of as volitional; in the second it depends on the build-up of *lirima* in the boy. To begin with the volitional component, there is constant stress throughout the rituals by the boy himself, his kinsmen and those officiating that the desire for *imbalu* can come from the boy alone. He himself chooses the year in which he will be circumcised and he is repeatedly told that no one is putting any pressure on him. The plain fact is that the Gisu take some pride in not tolerating uncircumcised men and those considered old enough are clearly faced with the choice of going through the operation 'voluntarily', fleeing the District or facing the prospect of being circumcised by force. I witnessed a number of these when local feeling was running high against a few boys and they were literally seized while tending their fields or along the wayside, marched to their father's houses and unceremoniously cut. The denial of coercion in the ritual context should not however be taken as some simple ritual reversal of 'truth': it exists in an inevitable dialectic with it. The ritual may be said to assert two things, firstly, that circumcision is the first act of self-assertion of a Gisu man, an act which will emancipate him from parental controls. Secondly, it stresses the fact that social pressure is ultimately irrelevant: a boy cannot be forced to undergo the ordeal courageously. Success attends those who feel impelled against the end themselves. Yet, in so far as the ritual presents the boy as being totally responsible for his own fate it systematically underplays the role of others and this will be returned to in later discussion.

The element of self-determination comes out clearly in the following extract from a conversation between a boy who had decided to take *imbalu* and was explaining his feelings to another who was clearly wavering:

It is as they tell you. It comes from your heart itself. You don't sleep but think only of *imbalu* and that if it means that I will die then I must die. You cannot say, well just let me try, for it is your heart. It is the heart itself. It is my heart which is speaking now. Every time I hear the sound of other boys' bells I want to run and see them and my stomach trembles like that of a circumcisor.

This desire to take *imbalu* is thought of as spiritually inspired. Boys are said to be 'caught' by the *kumusambwa kw'imbalu*, the ancestral power of *imbalu*. *Imbalu* is the most important of the Gisu ancestral powers since it is the only one believed to be shared by all, a product of their ancestry. The ancestral power of *imbalu* is said to seize the boys with the desire to dance. Yet, as with all the powers, this is not conceived solely as an external force which possesses the boys but rather as a potentiality now made manifest. It is an aspect of their identity, a discovering of their potential. Thus, while there are elements of what we might call possession in the sense of abnormal or special states of consciousness and feeling, the desire is seen as coming directly from the heart. The act of dancing *imbalu* is thus seen as the ultimate volitional act, the boy freely making manifest the powers to which his ancestry makes him heir.

The emphasis on self-determination gives a distinctive form to what in Van Gennep's scheme would be referred to as the rites of separation. For example, a pattern common in the ethnographic literature is for such separation to be achieved by the abrupt and sometimes violent removal of the boy from the domestic setting to sacred initiation sites in the bush, there to face unknown dangers. In such situations the novices appear relatively passive, submitting to the authority of the elders and being initiated by them. Gisu separation rites display none of these features: the boys remain the central actors, presented as freely choosing the ordeal and ultimately, too, being tested in a public open ceremony. Indeed, the dangers which the boys face are known only too well and involve no secret or esoteric knowledge. Nor, since the operations are performed in the domestic compound, is there any spatial separation of the candidate from his family and neighbours. Ritual separation is achieved rather though a succession of graduated stages which mark changes in the boy's commitment and identification with the ordeal he faces. Significantly, each is inaugurated by the boy himself. The main stages can be outlined here.

The circumcision year is ushered in during late January by the blowing of horns. From May until July individual candidates announce their intentions of going though the ordeal by dressing in the special regalia and beginning to dance. The full regalia is elaborate and flamboyant, with a head-dress made from the skin of the black and white Colobus monkey, and long tails decorated with cowrie shells which hang down the boy's back and swirl in the dance. What items of costume a boy wears depends, however, on what he is lent by his kin or can hire or buy from others. The essentials are the metal thigh bells, two to three to each leg, and strings of beads crossed over his chest. The individual items of costume are given no particular significance: it is the overall effect which is important. The costume is said to make the boy look 'wild'.

At this stage small groups of boys usually dance together, dancing along the paths and through the compounds of their neighbourhood, sometimes to assemble and perform a display on an open space. The dancing at this time has a distinctive name and takes a stamping form unaccompanied by song. It is also sporadic. The period as a whole is known as *xuwetsa imbalu* – searching for *imbalu* – implying the gradual awakening of intent in the boy and its provisional nature. A boy may drop out at this stage without any disgrace.

The second phase begins in July, two or three weeks before the actual operation. It is marked by the boy threshing the millet which will be used to brew the beer which is offered to the ancestors and to visitors on his circumcision day. It is accompanied by the sacrifice of a chicken and the inspection of the entrails. This is the first time that augurs are consulted for the boy. Thereafter the dancing is known as *xusamba imbalu*, dancing *imbalu*, and is accompanied by song. Younger men and women, as well as boys and girls, now identify with particular candidates and accompany them on their travels. These are now more purposeful, since a boy must now visit all his close relatives and elicit their permission for the operation; that is, he must demonstrate his fortitude through the vigour of his dancing. These visits take a set form. The boy and his group dance into the compound and a close relative then comes forward to address the boy, warn him of the ordeal he faces and urge that he dance with determination. One repeated theme of these speeches is that the boy must not confuse the glamour of his costume and the dance with *imbalu* itself. *Imbalu*, he is told, depends not on the costume but upon the person. Circumcision is not a game. He must think only of the ordeal he faces. The boy must remain silent under these often violently expressed tirades and he is then exhorted to show his worth by jumping. These jumps are regarded as extremely important as they are taken as indicative of his determination and of how he will perform under the knife. Indeed, they can be seen as a direct rehearsal of the final jump the boy must make in the circumcision enclosure to show his readiness to face the knife.

The third phase which leads directly on to the operation is again linked to the brewing of the circumcision beer. Two days before circumcision the boy pours water on the prepared millet and is then himself smeared from head to toe with millet yeast. From now until the operation in the afternoon of the third day are concentrated all the important rituals to ensure the boy's protection. Sacrifices are offered for him by his mother's brother, his father's sister and on the compound where he will undergo the operation. For himself, his followers and his close kin the rites now move towards a crescendo of activity and involvement.

Circumcision involves everybody and the atmosphere is charged with excitement. The boy himself dances more or less non-stop, the dances continuing often throughout the night as well as during the day. Emotions are running extremely high and the circumcision parties give way to no one, with unwary passers-by risking getting a lash from the sticks they carry. For the boy the

3 Early display dancing, accompanied by a dance leader on the left (Manjiya)

normal rules of conduct can appear suspended; his absorption in the dancing and thus in *imbalu* should be so total that the normal courtesies of everyday life are irrelevant. The energy put into the dancing and the aggressiveness of the circumcision parties are revealing of other important pyschological and symbolic themes. Throughout the circumcision period the penis is referred to as *isolo*, the wild animal, and the overall effect of the boy's costume, as already mentioned, is to make him 'look wild'. Such wildness brings together the idea of strength with that of *lirima*.

The rituals of the three days that culminate in the operation itself are concerned primarily with this symbolic theme, the boy being smeared with millet yeast, chyme and black swamp mud, all substances seen to be transforming by their very nature, fermenting like beer with bitter *lirima*. The yeast-smearing rite is first performed after the boy has poured water on the millet for his circumcision beer, that is on the morning of the third day before circumcision. Later that day his mother will add millet yeast to the brew, thus beginning the final fermentation. But first the boy is smeared from head to toe with some of this yeast made into a thick paste, so that his body is thickly encrusted. This rite is repeated on each of the three days leading up to the operation. In addition to the yeast the boy is usually smeared twice with chyme from sacrificial goats, firstly by his mother's brother and secondly on the morning of his circumcision, in the compound where he will stand for the operation. This, in the most usual case, is his father's compound but it could be the compound of another senior agnate or even that of his mother's brother as it is customary to honour matrikin by sending at least one of a set of brothers to undergo circumcision there.

Unlike the yeast and chyme, the smearing with mud does not take place in the domestic setting but at special mudding swamps associated with the *kumusambwa kw'imbalu* and reserved for this purpose alone. The elders of the swamp literally prepare the ground by stamping on it until it forms a foaming mire. Typically, in the southern areas where these rituals are still held, the boys leave their compounds around mid-morning on the circumcision day, smeared with yeast and chyme, and begin a last round of visits to their close kin. By mid-afternoon the boys and their parties will assemble together on the communal dancing-ground. From there the parties set off first for the ancestral grove where they will be blessed by the elders of the area by the blowing of beer over them. From there they proceed to the swamps. Here the elder of the swamp blesses each individually with beer and then, depending on the depth of the swamp, they either jump in or stand on the edge while the elder smears them all over with the black mud. The boys then return directly back to their separate compounds for the operation.

If one asks about the importance of these smearing substances, a major strand of the Gisu exegetical tradition puts the emphasis on their power to impress the boy yet again with the nature of his undertaking. To give an extract

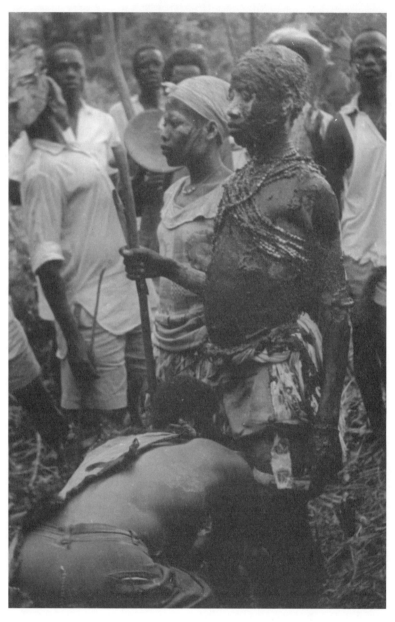

4   Sister stands with her brother as he is smeared with mud (Central Bugisu)

from one such account which I recorded from an elder of Bungokho, an elder who was articulate and knowledgeable, but by no means a ritual expert:

They smear the boy with all these things to see if he is intent on circumcision. They make his whole body cold so that he shivers and is covered with goose-pimples . . . They show him that *imbalu* is tough and he goes knowing that *imbalu* is tough . . . Circumcision is fierce and these things . . . give him strength. They are done for the strength of the ancestral power of *imbalu*. People do these things in order to change him into a very fierce person, different from others. He is like another person. He has only the intention to think about *imbalu* . . . And when they make him jump they encourage him, saying '*ingi, ingi, ingi!*' And when he jumps high and low with vigour it shows that he is really fierce. You go to war and fight with all your strength. You must make yourself see that you have enough strength to overcome another man's strength. So these things are like being prepared for war.

The power of these substances to show a boy 'toughness' and to change him into a 'very fierce person, different from others' is, however, also held to derive from their associations with beer. The same elder went on to explain:

These things, mud, chyme, yeast and beer, are all mixed up and in this they are alike. They are like the mud in that it is the soil which they have stamped on and walked on so they have mixed it with water from below to form mud, When it bubbles it erupts like porridge. They say the ancestral power of *imbalu* is there, for even if it is dry the mud there bubbles by itself without rain and looks as through someone has brewed his beer. That mud is its beer and when it bubbles they say it has fermented. And the boys must jump in that mud and return to be circumcised. They have jumped in the beer of the ancestral power of *imbalu*.

Here is an extended metaphor which rests on the significance of fermentation, of an induced change – a mixing-up – which sets in train a fundamental reaction, changing the nature of substance. The volatility of beer fermentation is clearly here the model for change, and since the rituals draw a symbolic equation between the boy, the process of fermentation and the ancestral powers, the significance of the circumcision beer can be looked at more closely.

The prestigious finger-millet beer, *busera*, is used for all rituals and takes two to three weeks to make, involving two distinct periods of fermentation. The first fermentation is used to give colour and flavour to the beer and is achieved by dampening millet flour with water and leaving it covered in a dark place for about a week. Any alcohol and yeast is then driven off by roasting this millet porridge over a fierce heat. Water and fresh millet yeast (made from germinated millet seed) is then added to produce a second fermentation, with the beer drunk on the third day. At circumcision the boy initiates both these fermentations, the first by threshing the millet and the second by pouring water on the roasted porridge. As beer is regarded as essential for all rituals many of them are geared to the second three-day brewing cycle, but in no other is the person at the centre involved in its preparation. The participation of the boy draws attention to and effectively synchronises two processes: the growth of his determination and the fermentation of beer. Thus the beer-brewing

5   Boy stands facing the circumcisor for the operation

cycle is doing far more than simply orchestrating the sequence of the rites; it reflects in a fundamental way on the nature of the boy's commitment. Hence it is crucial that the second fermentation be quick and active, the brew clearly 'bubbling up' (*xutubana*). This fermentation is always associated with the ancestors and is likewise indicative of *lirima*. The boy and the beer are thus similarly held to be imbued with ancestral power and *lirima*.

In the course of the smearing rites the boy is brought into relationship and progressively identified with the ancestral powers and other potent things 'fermenting' with *lirima*. All the substances gain their significance through their association with beer: the yeast as the initiator of fermentation, the chyme and the mud because of their eruptive qualities. The smearing rites thus encapsulate and advance the process of change in which the boy is involved. If we take the metaphorical associations seriously here then we can see that it is a very special kind of change. *Lirima* and fermentation are thus seen to share a number of characteristics: both are volatile, strong, bitter, potent and transforming in themselves. Moreover, where previously *lirima* was described in conjunction with the emotions it now seems more appropriate to see it as a type of power or aspect of creative energy. Indeed, through its association with fermentation it is presented as one of the creative processes in the cosmos, on a par with human procreation.

The model used by the Gisu to understand human fertility is not taken from analogy with seeds and vegetable fertility but is rather the process of fermentation. In procreation it is believed that the 'white blood' (semen) of a man mixes together with the 'red blood' ('placental') of a woman to form a child. The substance of the child is thus deemed to be equally formed from male and female fluids, and frequent intercourse during the first six months of pregnancy is thought necessary to develop a healthy foetus. As in beer fermentation, the 'bloods' inside a woman are said to 'bubble up' and this volatility of gestation is thought likely to spill over and affect the woman emotionally. Again, 'bubbling up' carries the overtones of *lirima*, and the fermentation model is used to explain a number of the characteristics of pregnancy. For women it is seen as a time of heightened emotion, of irritability and bad temper. Further, in terms of the parallelism with fermentation, gestation also has a spiritual counterpart, indicative of the presence of the ancestral spirits, with the child inheriting at birth the life force of someone of his kindred who has recently died.

And here it is important to reiterate the creative power of the circumcision ritual. Circumcision, in its task to create men out of boys, has a real and not just a formal dimension. A boy does not just take on the mantle and responsibilities of adulthood but becomes a man, with the distinctive capacities of a man. Before circumcision boys are held to be incapable of *lirima*, and for this reason their misdemeanours are usually discounted. Revealing of Gisu attitudes on this score is an exceptional case, where there was a strong body of local feeling that a youth of about eighteen who had gained a reputation for aggressive anti-social troublemaking should be killed (see p. 240). Many others held equally firmly that the killing of children was a senseless act, since by definition the weaker powers of a child could pose no serious threat to adult interests. In such terms child-killing is an abomination. The counter argument was, however, that evidence of such an anti-social disposition in one so young boded extremely ill for the future. After circumcision this tendency could only be intensified and his *lirima* put to ever more violent ends.

THE PARADOX OF THE RITUAL

This brings us to a consideration of the paradoxical character of the ritual. At one fairly evident level circumcision seems designed to produce 'fierce' men, but 'fierce' men for whom the society has little use. Ordeals of this kind, linked to warfare, can be seen as a form of training for the bravery and stoicism of the warrior. Elsewhere in East Africa this association holds, and the evidence is well summarised by Ocaya-Lakidi (1979). The ideal tribal virtue of manly excellence, he writes, was strongly connected to warfare and 'led the Eastern African societies to place undue emphasis on masculinity and manliness, the one to be tested sexually and the other in hot combat' (1979:152). Ultimately, however, the two tests were one and, taking the Kikuyu as an example, he elaborates, 'the lengthy initiation rites gave ample opportunity for gauging a man's masculinity, while the supreme pain of circumcision tested his manliness and suitability for warriorhood. That is why becoming a man meant access to physical sex and warriorhood at the same time' (1979:152).

In a large number of East African societies, male gender identity linked to circumcision has therefore a strong military accent. Yet for the majority of these societies the warfare and raiding patterns with which it was associated are no longer relevant. Some seventy years after colonial pacification this is certainly the case for the Gisu, just as it is for the Kikuyu. In the Gisu case, all that remains of the association is the idea that the fortitude required of the circumcision candidate is akin to the courage of a warrior. An analogy is drawn: a boy must have faith in his powers and strength in the same way. To succeed at standing *imbalu* without flinching, as the elder said, the boy must make himself see that he has 'enough strength to overcome another man's strength'. But I never heard it suggested that the ritual either would or should make him into a good fighter. Such, indeed, is definitely not the aim. Significantly, of the objects of adult life handed to him in the cleansing rite after the operation, a spear is not included. It is perhaps notable by its absence. The boy receives food, fire, a panga, a hoe and a drinking-tube, but no spear. Further, the individual is admonished to use these objects properly and not for destructive purposes.

Comparisons may serve to make this problem sharper. As indicated above, many East African societies similarly extol martial virtues, but in the modern era not all of these have feared male violence in the same way. The Kikuyu are a case in point and, as a related Bantu-speaking people, their concepts bear direct comparison with those of the Gisu. For the Kikuyu, the cardinal virtues of the warrior combine fierceness with restraint. *Urume*, the quality *par excellence* of the warrior (*injamba*), has evident affinities with the Gisu *lirima*, implying bravery, determination in the face of adversity and violent forceful action. Men may shake with *urume*, a physical manifestation which is widely recognised among both the Bantu and para-Nilotic peoples of Kenya as a sign of courage and, more especially, battle-readiness. At the same time the Kikuyu warrior was expected to display the virtues of identification and loyalty to his age set, and obedience and submission to the authority of seniors. Disciplined self-control thus emerges as a major theme in Kikuyu life, with a man expected to exercise restraint both in his use of violence and, indeed, in sex (Kenyatta, 1938). In this gerontocratic social order warriorhood was only part of a process of individual self-development, orchestrated by age-group status, and circumcision marked only the beginning of the achievement of the full potentialities of adulthood. Speaking of the Meru, closely related to the Kikuyu, Fadiman notes that the process of 'hardening' for a Meru warrior involved a whole series of ordeals and beatings where the true warrior 'was expected to show neither weakness in the face of pain, nor resistance to those who applied it' (1982: 49). Indeed, he writes that most of the pain that a warrior was expected to bear was inflicted by members of his own community. As with the Kikuyu, the warrior was part of a disciplined fighting force which came under the direction of elders.

In so far as these historically forged attitudes persist we may perhaps find clues as to the different perceptions of the capacity of men for violence. From the previous discussion what emerges as a significant shaper of attitudes is age-set organisation, traditionally absent in Bugisu. Among the Gisu named age sets were formed to include boys circumcised at the same time, generally every two years, and such men were held to have special bonds with each other, a comradeship developed in the months of healing, and presumably tested in subsequent fighting. But such sets did not form standing corps of warriors, nor did they collectively progress through a series of set ranks based on age status. Thus, while self-discipline is a valued quality, it is not stressed to any great degree and receives little institutional support. Indeed, once he is circumcised and has established his own homestead, the Gisu man is freed even from parental control. In Bugisu, rather than to age status and the submission of the group to its leaders, the greater weight is given to the essential equality of all men, won on a kind of once-and-for-all basis through the ordeal of circumcision.[2]

Gisu manhood is therefore achieved; achieved by undergoing an ordeal by which the individual simultaneously proves himself and proves himself equal to all those who have gone before him. At the most evident level, then, the rites dramatically assert the unity of male experience. Boys are initiated and become men in exactly the same way as their seniors and are heirs to the same status in the community. 'Let the son resemble his father' is the chorus line of one of the most popular circumcision songs. From this perspective it is the aspect of continuity which comes to the fore, a continuity which is deemed to rest with ancestry and the powers of the *kumusambwa kw'imbalu* which catches boys with the desire to dance. The potency of *imbalu* as a cultural symbol rests on this aspect: the linked ancestry of all Gisu and the continuation of the powers which go with it.

THE QUALITIES OF MANHOOD

This leads to another point of contrast in Gisu concepts of manhood. The Gisu, unlike the societies with age sets briefly mentioned – and many others – do not polarise the qualities of youth and age, in terms of, for example, violence versus restraint, physical power versus knowledge and social power, 'hot hearts' and 'cool heads'. Gisu youths after circumcision are not released into a warrior corps, thus socially removed from society and serving protective and other tasks. They become adults in the same way as their seniors: householders and cultivators. They are also seen to have the same capacities, and the social development that is envisaged is not one of different and contrasting roles but of an overall increase in capacity and power (*bunyali*) in accordance with age. All a person's capacities and dispositions are seen to develop with age, increasing not only a man's wisdom but also his *lirima*, which is thus a characteristic feared alike in young and old men. Nevertheless, the aggressive potentialities of youth and age differ for while the young are feared for their use of physical violence, the old have access also to witchcraft. Aggression is thus not seen as a prerogative of one section of the society but as an option open to all. Indeed, the generic word for witchcraft, *bulosi*, is used more widely to refer to all uses of violence and physical aggression.

With the possibility of anger available to all, a man's character and disposition are seen to be of utmost importance to the way he controls his *lirima*. A good man, one is told, controls his anger, a bad man does not. *Lirima* operates as a dispositional characteristic. It is both a capacity which may be called into existence and also, of some men, a more permanent characteristic. As the Gisu say, *lirima* is in their hearts. The heart (*kumwoyo*) is regarded as the strongest organ of the body and is associated with the essential nature of the individual. Thus, on the one hand, it is associated with their strength and, on the other, the idea of a good or bad heart carries the same range of moral implications that it does in English. The heart is seen as the centre of the intentions and dispositions, of thoughts and wishes. It is linked to the lungs and associated with breath and speech. In the case of a sacrifice, the heart, together with the top ribs and lungs of a goat are offered to the ancestors to show that the whole of the goat – its life, its strength and its dispositions – have been given. To say of a man that he 'speaks well' is thus not a comment on his oratorial skills but a phrase which sums up all that is desirable in his bearing. It is not an aesthetic judgement but a moral one. A good man – one who speaks well – shows no disparagement in his bearing and attitude to others. Further, he is slow to anger, acting not in the heat of the moment but only after careful consideration. Such judicious behaviour implies the control of *lirima*.

In this context the first washing of the boy by the circumcisor on the morning following the operation is revealing. This is the only occasion on which the boy is given any formal teaching or instruction on his new role and he is bound here solely by moral injunctions. The boy receives a panga, a hoe, the circumcision knife, a firestick and a drinking-tube and he is told to use these objects properly, in a socially productive way, and not for violence and disruption. The circumcisor cleanses both the boy and the younger sister who accompanied him in the final three days and who is also smeared with him. Circumcision also acts as a rite of passage for girls, binding them to their brothers, whose ritual 'wife' they become, just as their bridewealth will be used to provide wives for their brothers. Extracts from one such speech may serve to make the point.

The first object that the circumcisor handed the boy was a panga, saying as he did so:

I give you this knife and say 'Build a house, do not just roam around. I have given you this knife that you might cut down trees and build a house, cut down bananas and banana stems to plant so that you will have your own food. Let me give you this knife for you to do this work. Let me not have given it to you so that you go and cut your neighbours. Nor have I given it to you to go and steal the cows of your neighbours and cut them up'.

The last object he handed the boy was a piece of smouldering firewood:

Kindle this piece of firewood and as you kindle it I say, 'Do not go and burn down the houses of your neighbours. I have made you kindle it so that your wife can cook for you. But if your wife is out digging then you yourself can make fire and drink tea. Do not just wait for your wife. While you are healing you can heat water for yourself to wash.'

And in the way of a final statement, he turned once more to the boy and said:

Hold firm to digging, to paying taxes and to your relatives.

This final injunction – reiterating the values of civil society everywhere – to support oneself, to be a responsible citizen, to be a loyal and dutiful kinsman, comes with particular force after the dramatic recital of the abuses which the privileges and responsibilities of adulthood equally invite. The context makes it clear that this is not only a form of teaching through contrasts – though it is this – but is linked to very real fears. The Gisu boy is entering a world of relatively free competition with other men. *Lirima* might be essential on the one hand for the independent assertiveness required of Gisu men but, on the other, it has its natural outlet in violent retributive action. Further, that the individual is admonished in this way highlights the fact that there are seen to be few other checks on violence. Its use is a matter of personal disposition.

However, patterns of violence in Gisu society are not random nor are accusations of violent troublemaking. Thus one needs at this point to turn to the ways personal disposition and character are judged and to the existential notions which underlie such judgements.

THE BASIS OF JUDGEMENT

Circumcision is a very clear turning-point in adult life and this brings us to a consideration of the nature of judgement and of the things which may go wrong with human development. At one level, just as self-determination is the keynote of the circumcision ceremonies, so it is in life thereafter. The strength to endure the operation with courage must come from the boy himself; if his heart is not in it then no one can help him. The boys' songs in the weeks before the operation glory in the independence of their choice and their own determination to face 'death'. As an adult man the same values hold; the emphasis is on the individual qualities which allow some men to succeed where others fail. This attitude has a cosmological dimension.

Gisu ontology is deeply anthropocentric: man is the centre and the measure of all things (Douglas, 1966; Mbiti, 1969; Tempels, 1959; Zahan, 1970). There is no good and no evil which is not first and foremost the good and evil in human life. The powers which matter are not only those which affect life but which, like the ancestors, are in real measure dependent upon it: the world of the flesh and the world of the spirit are symbiotically linked and, to this extent, indivisible. Thus a person is a product of his ancestors in the sense that he is subject to their influence in his very being and in the course of his life, yet at the same time his own life attests to ancestral power and ensures its continuation. While spiritual forces, beyond sensory observation, are to some extent hidden and unpredictable in their effects, they are at another level manifest. Their power can be assessed from their direct effects on those they are held to influence.

There is a sense in which the same may be said for the person. A man is what he does. His actions and his success attest to his nature and his powers. A man's worth is thus publicly accessible in a way that allows no conflict between virtue and reward. That life is unpredictable and men vulnerable to a multiplicity of misfortunes is self-evident. Luck, as the Gisu say, is not for everyone. But a man's luck bespeaks his character. The strong may withstand misfortune, repel forces that would lay others low. Vitality and strength thus appear as prime values upon which all else depends.

Vitality may be rendered simply as life (*bulamu*). During life, a person's body, *kumubili*, and 'life force', *cisimu*, are indivisible so that the words *bulamu* and *cisimu* may be used interchangeably in many contexts to indicate the relative vitality of the person. For the purposes of exposition different aspects of this vitality can be usefully distinguished. The first is the literal 'life- giving' aspect, the fact of being alive, sentient, active. The second relates to the qualitative aspects of this vitality, its variability and differential strength. The *cisimu* is the key to both these aspects: it comes to the child at birth and leaves the body at death. During life it takes the form of the penumbra around a person's shadow and its visible manifestation thus allows not only the correlation of life and death with its presence or absence but also with the diurnal rhythm of life. The clarity of the *cisimu* in the morning is contrasted with its appearance towards evening when it is said the *cisimu* weakens (*cisimu ciwengana*), taking an enervated and unstable form. During sleep the *cisimu* fades and is no longer distinguishable. In other respects, too, the *cisimu* can be seen to mirror the physical and mental state of the person; if a man is drunk, so too is his *cisimu*. The state of the *cisimu* is thus diagnostic of the state of the person and this relates also to the life cycle. In general terms the *cisimu* is believed to grow in strength with age. The *cisimu* of a child is as yet undeveloped and weak; that of an adult is prominent, attesting to his strength in warding off and surviving dangers to his health and vitality.

The *cisimu*, then, is variable in its intensity, weakening during the evening and night and according to the manifest qualities of the person. A powerful man has by definition a strong *cisimu*, a child or an invalid a weak one. The generic vitality of the *cisimu* thus equates with the essence of being. To attack the *cisimu* of a person is to weaken his disposition, his ability and strength of purpose. Thus a common technique of diviners in dealing with suspected witches is to 'draw out their *cisimu*', with the aim thus to weaken their resolve and intent on vengeance through the use of witchcraft.

The *cisimu* attests to a person's strength, his *buwangafu*. A man who builds up a considerable stock of wealth in land or cattle and who has many children and even grandchildren is praised in such a way. His 'toughness' is evidenced by the facts: for such a man is seen to have come unscathed through the perils of life. He has withstood the attempts of his enemies to whittle away his strength through witchcraft and has protected his descendants in the same way. On his death the mourning ceremonies will be more protracted, for his power fades slowly and his descendants must be careful to honour him lest his vengeful spirit attacks them from beyond the grave. Many children will be named after such a person, his *cisimu* becoming their life force, *bulamu*.

For those that die childless there is no such ceremony and their spirits do not go to the home of the dead, *imakombe*, but are doomed to wander perpetually in the bush. They become the *kiwele*, the evil spirits of the streams, bush and paths. Whereas the spirits of the fertile are seen as life-giving, those of the childless are evil and bring death to anyone who inadvertently sees them. The names of the childless are not handed on. Their corpses are tightly bound and shrouded to prevent the escape of the *cisimu*. The attainments of men are thus believed to live on after them, echoing their evaluation during life.

If we turn briefly to consider the implications of such a cosmology for the concept of the person, we can note that it implies that a person's very being is subject to outside influence whether from ancestral powers or the malignant force of others. Yet this is not to deny the fact of individuality, the phenomenological discreteness of the person. The idea of the individual, and individual autonomy, going along with a recognition of discreteness, and even peculiarity in character, is strongly emphasised among the Gisu. Everyone has their way (*isambo*), just as communities have theirs. Yet one could say the individualistic tendencies in Gisu life are without individualism. Ultimately the person makes no distinctive marks, leaves no distinctive trace either in this world or after death. His fortunes and his virtues, stripped of their peculiarity are, so to speak, reabsorbed back into his kindred. His heritage lies in the living bodies of his descendants and in the powers they might have directly or indirectly inherited from him, from his part in the living tradition. Ultimately, there is no fame and no honour beyond this.

There thus appears at a rather basic level to be no room for the heroic virtues, or for true individualism, since ultimately no value is placed on the individual and his uniqueness. One may contrast this with the Greek yearning after 'immortal fame', entailing a courageous risk to life, and where a man strove to make his mark (see the discussions in Arendt, 1958 and MacIntyre, 1981, ch. 10). Indeed, from this perspective the individual is anonymous and uncelebrated. One is struck by this in Bugisu. The dead are very shadowy and even the leaders of the past, while their exploits may be recounted on request, come across as wise and judicious men but not as folk-heroes. They are virtuous but not charismatic figures. One hears nothing of the dead in the normal course of life, unless their shade is suspected of causing damage to the living or to explain some usually disagreeable characteristic that someone might have inherited. The value of an individual lies therefore in his part in the ongoing flow of specifically Gisu life. What counts is the individual's tenacity in keeping to life's purposes and these purposes tie together into one single schema for living.

This, a productive life, rests on having children. Indeed, the basic template for the adult life course is for a man to marry, set up his own household, have children and grandchildren. It is a schema which rests upon vitality, on fertility, on health, but it also rests on the possession of basic economic resources. Failure thus has a real – indeed a tangible – dimension and threatens a man on many fronts; his wife might leave him, he and his family might sicken and thus be unable to work, or his children may die. All such events may have a calamitous effect on his fortunes and indeed on his very self, for to fail in this task is to fail not only in the main but the only motivational schema of Gisu society. And fault is held to lie in character. Poverty, as riches, is seen to be the result of individual qualities, and indigence is judged harshly. The feckless wander around instead of cultivating, spend their money on beer instead of caring for their family. For such men there is only contempt.

Circumcision also plays a role here for, though it qualifies a boy for manhood, it is manhood that he does not really attain until he has established his own household independent of his father. Only then is he 'fully grown' or 'mature', as the Gisu say. Manhood thus has important economic correlates. After circumcision a father should provide his son with the resources necessary to make him economically independent: land and the cattle necessary for bridewealth. The allocation of these resources forms the basis of the young man's wealth and he must thereafter expand such resources largely through his own efforts and those of his wife. Indeed the evaluation accorded to individuals is largely indistinguishable from their wealth and manifest success.

Here as elsewhere in Gisu life, the onus is upon the individual. Gisu individualism, like individualism everywhere, systematically underplays the dependence of people upon each other. Yet this is a society which is based upon kinship, on 'status', as Maine would put it, and not on 'contract'. The values of Gisu individualism thus inevitably run against other values embedded in kinship dependence and herein lie some of the key dilemmas of Gisu society. If Gisu male society sees itself as a society of self-determining autonomous individuals there are also other currents which, if they do not invalidate this conception, run counter to it. As is the case with the exception which proves the rule, the challenge posed by the recognition of contradiction can be denied by an assertive restatement of the official view, a view which holds the individual responsible for his own fate.

This can be seen most clearly in the values of *imbalu* which, in the very forcefulness with which they are propounded, create a threefold double-bind. In the first place, as has been commented upon, the ritual process can be seen to create warriors with no war to fight. The ambivalent connotations of *lirima* point to the difficulties all Gisu men face in controlling their anger and their potential for violence in civil society. In the second place, *imbalu* qualifies a man for adulthood; it grants formal licence to the status but does not of itself bequeath it. It remains for a man to win economic independence from his father. The third point relates to this. The ritual, in extolling the boy's self-determination, tends to mask the fact that his fate rests also with others. Ideas of independence and of equality thus tend to run up against the very real dependence of a boy upon his kinsmen, and particularly upon his seniors.

Autonomy and self-reliance is thus only one side of the story. A man's chances of success in life, of achieving indeed the basic qualifications for manhood, depend crucially upon his place in the kinship structure, on his relationship with his father and upon his father's relative wealth. The Gisu lack of toleration for failure must thus be set in the context not only of a set ideological vision but in the context of competition for basic economic resources, a competition which pits brother against brother and father against son. The next chapter serves to outline the nature of the Gisu economic system, of wealth, inheritance and marriage, which set the parameters for the bitter struggles among Gisu men for control over the basic resources for livelihood and status. We will then be in a position to turn again to the nature of judgement and to the fears and accusational patterns which dominate Gisu life.

NOTES

1 This treatment of ritual requires a definite shift away from the sociological frame of analysis which, stemming from Durkheim, tends to emphasise its regulatory aspects. I am not concerned here with how ritual may represent an abstracted moral order nor with how it might symbolise social relationships or principles of social structure. Rather, I am concerned to see how it may be seen to create patterns of psychological response in the individual. From this perspective, rites achieve purposes; purposes which may be linked with the motivations of the person. No polarity is thus set up between 'instrumental' and 'expressive' aspects of ritual, between purpose and meaning, participants' and observers' views of the ritual process (see Beattie, 1970). Rather, ritual is seen as a formative process in the construction of the self, structuring the psychological field in which the person acts and is made capable of acting. Ritual, then, does not just enact a theatre of forms but engages the person in that theatre, moulding his aspirations and his self-understandings (see further, Heald 1982a; Asad, 1987). We may also see how in the Gisu case this involves a fairly coherent vernacular psychology.

2 This interpretation runs against the tenor of that advanced by La Fontaine, 1977. There she valuably exploited the idea of 'experience', and experience which 'cannot be communicated – it can only be undergone' (1977:433). I am less happy with her corollary that undergoing this experience is then the source of the 'power of rights' (1977:434). Deriving from a structuralist concern with social classification she argues that the rituals should be seen as a way of maintaining discrete social divisions; achieved through the establishment of an opposition between youths and elders, power predicated on physical strength versus authority predicated on knowledge. Disagreement rests on a different assessment of the power of elders. Her argument depends on seeing it in terms of authority, validated in terms of their nearness to the ancestors, in turn, presented as all-knowing. Here I am more in sympathy with her earlier writings (1962, 1969) which stressed the tenuousness of authority in this egalitarian system (see further, chapters 5 and 9).

4

SOME SOURCES OF TENSION: WORK, WEALTH AND REPUTATION

Mwayafu was a troublesome youth and never wanted to settle down to anything or to cultivate. I gave him land but he just sold it and then I refused him, saying how could I give him more land just to sell? He only wanted to drink beer with his friends and everyone complained of little things missing from their compounds. He took everything: chickens, money, blankets. I said to him 'Papa, why do you do these things and make your kin angry?' but he disregarded me and began to abuse me until we quarrelled and he cut me with his knife.

Soon afterwards we were all mourning at a funeral when a man came from another area, saying that he had traced the footsteps of the thief who had stolen all his clothes to our place. People were very angry and went to Mwayafu's house and tied him up and began to beat him.

This account was given by Mwayafu's father's brother who had reared Mwayafu since his real father had died fifteen years previously. Mwayafu was twenty-four years old when he was beaten to death in this way in 1967 and apart from the man who reported the theft, the four others accused in the ensuing court case were related to Mwayafu. Three were lineage brothers and the other a father's sister's son. Kinship has little moderating effect on the attitude adopted to such offenders.

The portrayal of Mwayafu's character falls into a conventional pattern. The Gisu see the position of such men as largely self-induced; it is a man's own actions which precipitate the harsh action later meted out to him. Such men are deemed oblivious to the reasonable arguments of their kin and may turn even on those who have cared for them. Such men manifestly do not hold firm to digging, to paying taxes and their kin, as the circumcisor admonishes them. Yet what stands out from case histories such as that of Mwayafu is that the individual concerned was in an extremely unpropitious position to gain his initial allocation of land and bridewealth. Mwayafu was an orphan, destined to rely solely on the magnanimity of his kin and, with no sisters, he had no automatic rights to bridewealth cattle. Without the resources necessary to establish himself as an independent householder, Mwayafu had little chance of demonstrating the normal responsibilities and capabilities of manhood.

The problem of deviance in such instances can be seen as a facet of poverty. Indeed Gisu fears of theft to a large extent focus on the landless and particularly on wifeless men. The roots of this attitude lie in the fact that a man without a wife cannot maintain a household successfully; he is forced either to demean himself with 'women's work' or to rely on another household for food, a cause of considerable resentment, usually on both sides. While it is no longer considered polluting for a man to cook his own food, it is the subject of jest and disparagement. As one man graphically put it, bachelors are like dogs wandering around in search of scraps of food. And such scavenging is seen to carry threat. Indeed, bachelors tend to be regarded as general nuisances, *batambisi*, the noun deriving from the verb, *xutambisa*, 'to make trouble/ to be a nuisance', being an elaboration from the basic form of *xutamba*, 'to be without'. This is not to say that all bachelors get accused of serious offences and that no one else does, but that the system of evaluation encourages this. This relates simply to plausibility, so that any sign of *lirima* draws unfavourable attention. With no household to maintain, they wander around, and their thievery relates to the fact that they have no visible means of subsistence, their adultery to their lack of a wife.

The nature of these character-assessments and the interpersonal context for accusation must be left until the next chapter for further discussion. This chapter will approach the problem of attribution from a different angle by contextualising it in terms of the severity of the economic constraints operative in Bugisu in the 1960s. These were such as to threaten increasing numbers of Gisu men with inadequate means for supporting themselves and thus, as has been indicated, to fundamentally threaten their position in the community.

The Gisu stress the values of individual enterprise and industry. Gisu men see themselves as not only independent economically, each in control of his own household productive unit, but also as essentially self-made. People start off poor and end up rich, one is told. Indeed, individual enterprise is in many ways decisive to a man's fortune. In the past, young men from the densely settled mountains of southern Bugisu pioneered land in the more open foothills and plains, while those in the north extended their settlements around the mountains, penetrating into the territory of the Sebei. Today, with such options no longer open, many take to migrant labour in the towns of East Africa and a good proportion have settled outside Bugisu. In the 1950s and 1960s buoyant commodity production based on arabica coffee and cotton also created possibilities for local employment and a plethora of trade specialisations in the area.

Yet access to such wealth is not uniform and is determined by two major sets of constraints, one traditional and the other modern. In the first place, the Gisu inheritance system creates its own typical profile of wealth, just as it inevitably favours some against others. In the second, the modern-sector opportunities offered to those whose educational level qualifies them for professional or other well-paid employment have created dramatic variations in patterns of and access to wealth. Taken together, these constraints have a decisive effect on an individual's chances not only of achieving exceptional wealth but of maintaining a foothold in the area at all. For underwriting the entire system of independent agricultural smallholdings is land, land which is becoming increasingly scarce in the district as a whole.

In the 1960s the rural area was one of the most densely settled in the whole of Uganda. In 1959, Bugisu district (excluding Mbale township) had a population density of 329 to the square mile, a figure only approached by Kigezi and Bukedi districts, which had densities of 260 and 254 respectively.[1] Within Bugisu itself densities varied considerably, generally rising with altitude. Thus two sub-counties in 1959 had densities of over 1,000 to the square mile (this was only matched by eight other sub-counties in Uganda, all of which were urban or peri-urban areas). A further fourteen of the remaining twenty-three sub-counties had densities of between 400 and 999 people (*Uganda Atlas*, 2nd edition, 1967). Over the next ten years the population of the district rose by a further 30%, making it likely that many of the more fertile mountainous regions had densities in excess of 1,500 to the square mile in 1969.[2] With no new areas within the district being opened up for settlement, the land on which the Gisu depended for both subsistence and a cash income was subject to increasing pressure.

Land pressure is the backcloth against which all discussion of the economy and, as will be seen, of the conflicts among men must be set. Gisu society is unusual for the individual nature of the land rights held. Land is held by the individual and not by the community or lineage. It follows that membership of a Gisu community or lineage in itself confers no right to use or 'own' land. If a man does not inherit from his own father or other close relative, he must perforce purchase the land he needs for subsistence. This fact has two important implications. In the first place, it is apparent that no mechanism exists for the redistribution of rights to the poorer members of the community or to compensate for landlessness. In the second place, it makes the lineage the place for the most intense competition over the most important economic resource.

The question of inheritance centres on the father and son relationship and, with a Gisu boy coming into at least part of his inheritance on his circumcision, a father sees in the circumcision of his sons the almost inevitable decline of his own wealth and position in the community (La Fontaine, 1967). Thus many attempt to delay such an allocation of their resources. If this may be regarded as a basic dynamic of Gisu society, this chapter and the next set out to describe it and to document its ramifications, both in terms of the situations which are likely to exacerbate conflict and the way in which it is expressed in Gisu thought and action.[3] As was seen in chapter 2 when the court statistics were examined, in relatively few cases was the ostensible cause for murder an issue of land or inheritance. That it nevertheless underlies much violence in Gisu society is unquestionable. for these issues breed discord; discord which, refracted through the cultural repertoire of fear, transmutes these conflicts into other terms. It is here indeed that the pervasive fears of witchcraft and theft belong.

This chapter seeks to provide an overview of the economic system operative in Bugisu in the 1960s and the emerging patterns of stratification. Thus it begins with a description of the farming system and of the nature of the wealth produced with the success of commodity production. It goes on to detail the nature of Gisu land tenure, the dynamics of the inheritance system and thus the factors which affect a man's life chances. The concern is to identify those most at risk of losing their rights, seeing this as part of a regular process, integral and distinctive to the Gisu political economy. In the patrilineal system of the Gisu these issues involve men to the exclusion of women and it is male competition over these resources which is a dominant feature of Gisu society. Yet the reliance of men upon women, in an agricultural system based upon the conjugal family, has important ramifications. A man's ability to productively use his estate depends upon marriage and the labour of his wife. Yet Gisu marriage is markedly unstable, and this adds to the insecurity of Gisu men who fear the loss of a wife just as it adds to the competition among men over women. The final section of the chapter deals with marriage and divorce and the position of women in Gisu society. In so doing it acts to document further the insecurity over issues of basic livelihood which affect the mass of rural house-holders.

ECOLOGY AND ECONOMY

Situated on the slopes of Mount Elgon, Bugisu as a whole is characterised by rich soils of volcanic origin and a bimodal distribution of rainfall which allows for two cultivation seasons a year, one long and one short. However, ecologically the region varies greatly and this affects the types of crops grown and the crop/cattle mix. The most important ecological division today is that which determines the range of the two major cash crops, namely arabica coffee and cotton. Arabica coffee, by far the more valuable of the two crops, can only be successfully grown above approximately 4,500 feet, which marks at the same time the effective upper limit for cotton.

In the 1960s these crops were diversified with a variety of food crops. Traditionally the Gisu appear to have cultivated only a limited range of food crops, the major ones being plantains and millet. These crops can be grown throughout the different zones although the varieties differ. There are at least twenty varieties of plantain and the particular variety cultivated depends on both personal preference and ecological suitability. Of the millets, finger millet (*bulo*) is grown mainly at lower altitudes, with sorghum millet of different varieties predominating higher up. Plantains and millet remain staples; the plantain is normally steamed and served with a vegetable or meat sauce while most of the millet harvest is brewed into beer. Other introduced food crops add variety to the diet, particularly sweet potatoes, groundnuts and pumpkins. Cassava is also cultivated as an insurance against famine and beans are grown in preference to the indigenous cow peas. Yams and colocassia both have a more localised distribution and are found at higher altitudes where they are inter-planted with plantains or coffee, as are 'exotic' European vegetables – potatoes, onions, cabbages, carrots and tomatoes.

At first sight many of the hillsides in the mountains appear to be terraced, as the plots of land are separated by border plants and scrub. True terracing, however, is not found; the scrub being sufficient for the most part to protect the topsoil from serious erosion or landslip. In the steeper areas, however, landslides are a hazard during the wet season and take a yearly toll of life. Above 5,000 feet the greater proportion of the land is under permanent plantations of coffee and plantain, with rather less set aside for the annual food crops. Lower down most of the land is used for the cultivation of annual crops and there is greater need to leave land aside for fallow. The cotton cash crop is here grown in rotation with the finger millet or maize, which are in turn followed by beans or sweet potatoes.

In the 1960s, the wealth of the district depended primarily on the cultivation of coffee. The majority of Gisu farmers are coffee-growers, the *Uganda Census of Agriculture*, 1963–64 estimating that 71.2% of the landowners in Bugisu and Sebei produced coffee while only 32.8% produced cotton. Rising world prices in the 1940s and 1950s gave impetus to the industry and in good years in the 1960s over 10,000 tons of coffee parchment were produced (the crop is subject to biennial fluctuations in yield). The growers marketed their crop through a series of primary co-operative societies acting on behalf of the Bugisu Cooperative Union which then auctioned the crop on the world market at Nairobi. The proceeds provided between two-thirds and three-fifths of the recorded annual cash income for the district. The recorded cash value of the cotton crop was only about one-seventh of that for coffee; for the years between 1963 and 1968, the average annual amount paid to the cotton growers was £274,000 compared with £1,647,000 to the coffee growers (Annual Reports of Cooperative Department, Mbale).

The prosperity of the district in the 1960s was thus highly dependent on the world prices of these commodities, and these were decreasing. In 1955–56 a peak coffee price of 2.95s per pound was paid to the growers but this had fallen to 1.50s per pound by 1967–68. Similarly, the price paid for the highest grade of cotton fell and was only 45c per pound by 1969 (*Uganda Statistical Abstracts*, 1960–66). Despite price falls coffee still remained a valuable crop in the 1960s and acreages continued to increase, although slowly, rising from 24,000 acres during the period 1960 to 1964 to 27,000 acres in 1966. Acreages under cotton, an annual crop, were more sensitive to price, and there were considerable annual fluctuations in the acreage grown. However, taking the mean income over several years, it has been estimated that the average cash income per annum, taking into account income from non-agricultural sources, fell from £7.26 per capita in the years between 1955 and 1959 to £6.16 between 1960 and 1964 (Wallace, Belshaw and Brock, 1973).

ECONOMIC ACTIVITY

The smallholding economy of Bugisu is particular for being organised around the conjugal family. In fact a man and wife between them are responsible for virtually all of the agricultural labour. Children, of any age, are fairly marginal to economic endeavour; young boys may be set to herd and girls to help their mother both with household chores and cultivation. However, the basic division of labour is that between man and wife, who jointly undertake the cultivation of their fields. Only for certain rather specific tasks is help required outside the household, and these involve the need for male labour. Building and thatching are two such tasks. Another is the weeding and harvesting of millet, which is also regarded as men's work. By and large, women do not participate in such large working parties, offering help and collective labour less in agriculture than in the cooking and preparing of feasts for their neighbours and kinsfolk. The reliance on the banana as the staple food crop allows for a system that is land- but not labour-intensive.

Apart from millet and plantains, where again men have specific tasks, there are few specific rules governing the division of labour in cultivation. Both husband and wife, jointly or singly, may clear the fields, sow, weed and harvest. Cultivation is still based on hand-tilling; small acreages and mountainous terrain combine to deter the use of ox-ploughing except in the more open plains areas. The responsibility for providing a cash income is seen to lie with the husband and cash crops join millet as his province, though the wife is usually expected to labour on these fields too. Other crops are the sphere of the wife, particularly the vegetables, sweet potatoes and beans which go to make the relishes served with the banana staple. The particular organisation of household production varies from household to household, depending in part on any outside or non-agricultural occupation of the husband. In general, however, the burden of cultivation is not onerous, with both men and women rising before dawn to work on their fields until about 9.00 a.m. At certain points of the year, particularly during the millet cycle and the harvesting of the cash crops, more time might be spent in the fields, but it is rare at any time of the year to see people working after midday. More usually, women leave their fields in the early morning and return home to make breakfast, spending much of the rest of their day in domestic chores and activities around their house, though they too may join their husband at a beer party in the afternoon. After taking breakfast, men generally leave the home to 'go about their own affairs'.

The successors to the first carpenters and builders trained in the mission schools were legion by the 1960s. Almost every man has some skill or knowledge which he can turn into a marketable commodity and, with the thorough commercialisation of the economy which has derived from the success of cash-cropping, all services between men are offered on a cash basis. Building is a focus for many of these trades. While adolescent boys still build their houses together most mature men, who cannot look to their neighbours for free assistance, must perforce hire labour. Each man has here his own speciality; one sells thatching grass. another is a thatcher, a third erects the framework of poles while a fourth fills in the walls with clay. Fitted doors and windows are made by local carpenters, and others specialise in building the rectangular houses to be roofed with metal sheets and internally divided into rooms. Apart from those engaged in building there are also in every rural area other skilled artisans from bicycle mechanics and tailors to traditional potters and smiths, although the latter are relatively rare today. Others take to trade, some setting up as butchers or grocers, operating from small shops, while those with less capital may take to more itinerant forms of trade, for example, bringing dried fish back from the shores of Lake Victoria for sale. Ritual specialists, from curers and diviners to circumcisors and rainmakers, also expect remuneration for their services. And a man with no special acquired skill develops a middleman business, seeking buyers for someone's surplus of millet or negotiating sales of livestock, while the very poorest may collect firewood for sale. Everyone, then, has some way of raising small amounts of money, and for many the amount they can earn is considerable.

Central to the rural economy is the institution of the beer party. Beer is offered in exchange for labour, a man feasting his neighbours and friends who have responded to his call for a morning's work on his fields. The main need for such work parties is for weeding and harvesting of the millet crop, though parties may also be called together for other tasks. By the mid-sixties, few of the old reciprocal labour organisations survived in rural Bugisu and most such parties were mobilised on an *ad hoc* basis. Labour/beer exchanges were, however, a basic feature of the economy and formed a fixed rate of exchange. Thus an alternative to offering beer for labour is to pay each man 1s, the price of drinking all afternoon from a shared pot of beer. This form of casual labour is known as *legelege* and is extremely popular among the poorer sections of the community who are thus able to participate in the daily beer parties in the neighbourhood. But beer-making also offers ways of making considerably more money. In every rural area some premises are licensed for the sale of local beers – of millet, maize and banana – all of which are brewed locally. However, apart from sales through such venues most households also regularly bought a single licence and brewed for themselves, offering such beer to their neighbours at the rate of 1s.[4] Small outlays here brought relatively large returns and provided one of the main ways for the poor to raise the relatively large sum of money required to pay their taxes.

The money which is circulated in the community in this way derives primarily from cash-cropping and employment in modern-sector business. Every householder aims to be able to spare some land to grow a crop specifically for sale. Of the major cash crops, coffee is by far the more valuable both in terms of the total wealth it brings the district and in yield per acre. For tax assessment purposes, coffee was in the mid-sixties valued at 400s an acre and cotton at only 100s. These figures, as expected averages, do not take into account individual or annual fluctuations in yield or the fluctuations in the world price of these commodities. Nevertheless they underline the major ecological divide between the coffee-growing mountain areas and the lower-lying cotton-producing areas. However, average per capita incomes probably do not vary greatly from region to region, for large rewards from coffee are restricted by the greater densities of settlement in the mountain areas. Indeed, overall, the rates of assessed income for taxation vary little from area to area with 94.5% of adult men having an assessed annual income of less than 1400s.

The poor returns from cotton are also compensated for by larger acreages and by incomes from livestock which are more numerous in the plains. Cattle are held in great esteem but their significance in the Gisu economy has declined steadily since the turn of the century, due firstly to the depletion of the herds in the successive epidemics of rinderpest in the years up to 1920 and thereafter with the success of cash-cropping. The number of livestock in the district continued to decrease in the 1950s and 1960s as further acreages were planted with cash crops and grazing land decreased. To some extent this was offset in the mountainous region by zero-grazing on the stems of plantains. Nevertheless, in such areas a man rarely possesses more than one or two head of cattle and a similar number of goats, and their ownership tends to be transient as cattle are continually circulated as bridewealth payments. In the more open countryside of the plains exceptional men still possess herds of thirty to fifty head of cattle.

During the ten years prior to independence the amount of employment in the district also rose steadily, in line with the development of the locally-controlled co-operative societies, the proliferation of government agencies serving the area and the increasing local participation in the Asian-dominated commercial life of Mbale. Initially a predominantly Asian settlement, between 1959 and 1969 the population of the town increased from 14,000 to 23,529 with the African population rising to some 60% of the total in 1959 (Uganda Statistical Abstracts, 1960–70). Access to different kinds and grades of employment is here highly dependent on educational standard and, with educational opportunity limited both by competition and cost, few are eligible for the highly-paid professional occupations.

The patterns of income and stratification by income which result from a combination of these factors of ecological area, access to centres of employment and educational standard can be illustrated by turning to a small random sample designed to assess sources and variations of income in Busoba. This is given in some detail because of importance of the patterns it illustrates.

RURAL STRATIFICATION

The Busoba region of central Bugisu is ecologically variable since it stretches from the mountains down to the plains, and coffee gives way to cotton as the major cash crop at approximately 4,300 feet. Poorer soils as well as less reliable rainfall characterise the lower altitudes. However, this poorer agricultural potential is to some extent compensated for by the access of this area to Mbale township, some ten miles away, and for the opportunities for local employment provided by the existence of two large schools, one a secondary school and the other a teachers' training college. The heavy reliance on wage employment in the area probably disqualifies it from being considered typical. Nevertheless the patterns it demonstrates clearly point to the main structural features of the Gisu economy and the nature of the constraints, particularly those posed by land pressure.

The sampling area covered five square miles of Busoba sub-county, lying between 4,400 feet and 3,000 feet in the foothills.[5] This area fell into an intermediate ecological zone where neither cotton nor coffee grew particularly well. Relatively high densities of about 600 people to the square mile and a heavy red clay soil that was not particularly fertile combined to discourage over-reliance on either cotton or coffee. Indeed, proceeds from cash crops were extremely low, though the majority of men (35 out of 44) grew some cotton. Of these, fifteen earned less than 50s in the 1965–66 season and the average income per grower was only 117s. Only one man earned more than 250s and he was a Protestant clergyman who farmed land belonging to the church and had receipts totalling over 600s. Of the six men who grew coffee, the average income was again very low (109s) but this was largely because four of the six had only a few bushes. The other two earned between 200s and 300s from their crop. Plantain and vegetable sales earned rather more on average for three men who specialised in them. Incomes from livestock were for most men too small to be counted and only fifteen of the men in the sample had any cattle at all. However, two men, with ten head of cattle each, made a good and regular income from the sale of milk, averaging 500s per year each.

Beer-brewing and distilling *waragi* also gave high returns. Incomes from beer-brewing were only included where a man regularly brewed for sale, selling either from his own home or to a licensed beer club. The question of licensing with waragi was rather different as stills tended to circulate around a group of neighbours. Like beer, *waragi*-making was regarded as exceptionally profitable, producing good returns for a relatively small outlay of either money or labour. In 1964, the government had attempted to sponsor local industry through establishing a company to market *waragi* nationally. To this end it had licensed some individuals in the rural areas to distil the spirit and provided

Table 8 *Sources of regular income for 44 men of Busoba sub-county, 1966*

Source of Income	Men with income from this source (%)		Total value (s)	Average income per producer (s)
Crop sales				
Cotton	35	79.5	4,111	117
Millet	18	40.9	1,056	59
Coffee	6	13.6	654	109
Plantain	2	4.5	330	165
Vegetables	1	2.3	200	200
Others	4	9.1	105	26
Produce sales				
Beer	3	6.8	1,500	500
Waragi	2	4.5	500	250
Milk	2	4.5	1,000	500
Eggs	1	2.3	60	60
Dried fish	1	2.3	70	70
Employment				
Professional	4	9.1	18,280	4,570
Skilled	6	13.6	13,212	2,202
Unskilled	8	18.2	7,544	943
Co-operative secretary	2	4.5	1,200	600
Employed by fellow villagers	3	6.8	1,560	520
Total	44	100	51,372	1,168

	Income from all sources	
Income range (s)	Men	%
0–100	9	20.45
101–800	14	31.8
801–1600	10	22.7
1,601–2,400	5	11.1
2,401–3,200	2	4.5
3,201–4,000	2	4.5
4,001–4,800	0	0
4,801–5,600	0	0
5,601–6,400	0	0
6,401–7,200	1	2.3
7,201–15,000	1	2.3

them with large stills for this purpose. The scheme soon faltered as the price the government company was willing to pay was considerably less than the local going rate (39s a tin compared with 60s). Meanwhile the stills remained, ensuring not only regular supplies in the rural areas but good profits for the distillers. Indeed, *waragi*-making at this time set the effective rates of interest charged on loans by one villager to another; these being calculated on what the money was worth if it were to be used to buy the sugar and maize meal used to distil into *waragi*, i.e. 25% per month (or 100% after one year).

In general contrast to the rewards from agriculture and petty trade are the rewards from employment. There was a strong bias towards wage employment in the sample because of the presence of two major schools in the area. As a result over half the men (twenty-three out of forty-four) had a regular monthly wage.[6] Thirteen were employed either directly or indirectly by the schools – two teachers, a painter, a builder and an office boy and eight worked as labourers or cooks in the school fields or kitchens or those of the teachers. Of the rest, one man was a carpenter who worked in another school, some ten miles to the south, and two other men (a hotel cook and a driver) worked in Mbale, about the same distance away to the north. The remaining seven men all worked locally, two as secretaries to the locally-run primary co-operative societies, one in a butcher's shop which provided meat two or three times a week, and two as servants to fellow villagers. The other two were both professional men working in the area, a clergyman and an agricultural assistant.

If one looks at the distribution of incomes from all sources the range is considerable. In all, nine men earned less than 100s, many of these being old men who paid tax at the partially exempted rate, and over half the men in the sample had incomes less than 800s. At the other end of the scale about one-fifth of the men earned amounts in excess of 2000s. Such high incomes were all for men who had regular employment and, while six of the wage earners received less than 800s, only three who relied entirely on farming or trade had incomes in excess of this amount. The richest farmer earned 1500s and he sold milk from his cattle and had a profitable sideline in *waragi*-distilling. Above this level, all were employed and the figures show even greater individual variation. Five earned more than 2400s; a skilled carpenter earned 3000s and four professional people had incomes on a different scale altogether.

Here one encounters the pattern of dramatic disparities in wealth, associated with modern-sector employment. which has become increasingly prominent in East Africa. The wealth of the highly-educated professional men is far beyond the expectations of most villagers. Moreover, their work is secure, salaried and pensionable and, even when they live in the rural areas, they form a distinct elite whose standard of living and interests distinguish them sharply from their neighbours. This is not the case with the less highly-educated workers who seek employment primarily to establish their position in the rural areas and whose peers are the other peasant farmers. Nevertheless, a three-tier occupational structure emerges from the tabulation given in table 8, with professional salaries averaging 4500s per year, skilled artisans commanding half this amount at 2202s, and their less skilled but employed neighbours averaging 793s.

Education was until 1967 divided into three main types; primary, junior secondary and secondary, entry to the latter being restricted by competitive examinations. During the 1960s probably the majority of Gisu tried to send at least one of their children to primary school and there were 26,000 children attending local government primary schools in 1965, while many others attended the privately-run sub-grade schools, many of which were supported by the churches.[7] The fees at such schools, of between 20s and 40s a year, were well within the means of the majority of people. Very few, however, could afford the fees for secondary schools which rose to over 800s a year, and the total of eleven years' schooling necessary to reach school certificate. Beyond this level some scholarships were available both for higher school certificate and for entry to Makerere University College. In the 1960s the educational take-up had improved greatly, with very many more Gisu achieving senior or junior secondary education, which qualifies for the middle-rung professional occupations such as primary school teaching, agricultural assistantships, local government chieftainships and secretarial and clerical jobs of all descriptions. More too were achieving a university education, something that was extremely rare in the 1950s. Even so, educational standards remained relatively low in the district with under 50% of pupils gaining a pass in the primary leaving examinations and the proportion gaining places at senior secondary schools running below the national average (Wallace, Belshaw and Brock, 1973: 110).[8]

For only a tiny fraction of the population, therefore, was education the gateway to social advancement and to non-agricultural occupations. While some of these people returned to work in Bugisu, their work usually took them to the large towns of East Africa and they returned only for vacations, though a number established a home in the area, employed porters to work on their fields and sometimes left their wife to manage their estate. Yet even though the wealth of the educated elite is way beyond the expectations of most villagers, all categories of wage-earners have innumerable advantages in everyday life, their relative wealth buttressing them against droughts and other misfortunes which seriously affect the man reliant entirely upon his crops. The illness of a wife or a death in the family with the subsequent taboos on cultivation may bring the indigent to the point of ruin, forcing him to raise money on his only asset, his land. On the other hand, the man with money available may not only be able to employ labour on his land but may be able to easily capitalise on the misfortunes of others to increase his own landholdings.

LAND

Gisu society is unusual for the individualistic nature of the land rights held.[9] While the agnatic lineage has a proprietal interest in the land of its members, ownership is held by the individual man and gives him full rights to its usufruct and disposal. Nor can this system be seen to be the result of a breakdown of a more communal system following the introduction of commodity production in the colonial era. Writing at the turn of the century, Purvis is adamant that 'each male has an independent right over his own land, and no chief may turn him away' (1909: 273).

Indeed, the advent of colonial rule served to sharpen this issue, as the introduction of Ganda practice together with Ganda concepts of chieftainship posed threats to the system of tenure. The British awarded *mailo* (freehold) estates to Kakungulu, the Ganda general who opened up the region and to the Christian missions which followed him. These acted not only to dispossess the Gisu of their land but reduce them to tenants who were expected to perform labour service for their new landlords. Such estates were few but have served to crystallise fears of government claims to 'own' the land ever since. More directly threatening to the mass of Gisu were the powers of the new chiefly hierarchy created by the British. As was described earlier, the poverty and disease which plagued the district in the early years of colonial rule led to a mass emigration of Gisu from the district in search of employment elsewhere (an emigration that was inspired possibly also to evade the irksome new rule of the chiefs). This problem was seen as particularly acute after the famine and pestilence which followed the First World War and, in a district that was already recognised to be experiencing a severe problem of land shortage, led to apparently abandoned *shambas*. In 1921, the newly-formed council of chiefs empowered the sub-county chiefs to reallocate these plots, a reallocation that the chiefs used largely to extend their own estates. In the face of a massive popular outcry – insisting on individual ownership rights irrespective of usufruct – this resolution was repealed, but the last outstanding land case was not settled until the 1940s.

The issue of land tenure thus became an early focus for Gisu opposition to the Protectorate government and led to the appointment of a Commission of Enquiry into the system of land tenure under the chairmanship of a district officer, Charles Gayer, in the 1930s. With the delays occasioned by the Second World War the report of this Commission was not to be finally published until 1957. This came out firmly in favour of the view that individual rights were traditional in Bugisu, and Gayer speculated that such a system might have originated in the great labour necessary to clear the heavy forest which once covered Elgon, a labour that was achieved with very simple tools. Whether or not this was so, it is certainly congruent with the self-sufficient base of the agricultural system, with the conjugal family providing for its own subsistence.

This individual system of tenure led early to a developing market in land. Purvis is also of the opinion that selling land was a norm in the early years of the century. He writes, 'No land is exchanged, but any individual may sell his land and often does sell a portion of it' (1909: 271). However, it is unlikely that land was fully commoditised until well into the 1930s. By this time the Sirokho/ Kachumbala areas of North Bugisu had been opened up for settlement and many men from the densely-settled areas of Southern and Central Bugisu migrated there for free land, sometimes selling plots in their home areas for token payments of chickens and goats. Since then there has been no such free land available in Bugisu itself and the price has been rising sharply over recent years. The price paid per acre varied in the 1960s in line with demand; in the coffee-growing areas often for as much as 1500s an acre, in Busoba for between 500s and 800s and, in the still relatively lightly-populated areas of Sirokho, for around 200s an acre.

In fact, land sales are extremely frequent since all men hope to augment the land they inherit by purchase. Over three-quarters of the men in the sample just mentioned had bought land at some time and most also had sold some. Land becomes available as the poorer men migrate or are forced to raise money on their land to settle an urgent debt, or to pay taxes, bridewealth, funeral expenses or even to pay for food in times of shortage. Sometimes they try to pledge their land as security for a loan, but usually they are forced to sell outright as it is justifiably feared that such land will become the subject of litigation in the future. Probably, most such men sell the land in the hope that they will be able to recoup the loss at a more fortunate time.

Detailed investigations into the transactions of one family segment, a group of fifteen landowning men in Busoba, showed that they had been involved in twenty-eight distinct land sales involving about twenty acres of land in the period between 1950 and 1968. Since the total amount of land possessed by this family segment in 1968 was forty-five acres, this gives a fairly good idea of just how rapidly rights to particular plots of land change hands by sale alone. The lineage retains nominal control over the land owned by its members and can exercise some rights with regard to sale. Land should first be offered to an agnate and only afterwards to another kinsman or neighbour. However, in practice it often appears as if land goes to the highest bidder for no price concessions are offered on the basis of lineage membership. The transaction of the family segment mentioned above revealed that about one-third of the land involved had been sold between non-agnates. In some cases this caused acrimony within the lineage but this, in itself, did not usually affect the sale unless an agnate was prepared to cap the original bid. A rich man thus has little difficulty in obtaining land.

Further, while the family segment gained as much land as it alienated in their transactions, whereas in 1950 only eleven circumcised men had claims to it, in 1968 this had risen to sixteen. The available acreages per landholding man had consequently dropped by 25%, from about four acres to less than three acres each. Moreover, the distribution of this land among the members of the family segment was markedly uneven, with the three men of the senior generation holding twenty-one of the forty-five acres, while of the men of the junior generation, four had less than an acre and one, a boy circumcised in 1968, had yet to be allocated land.

On a wider scale the distribution of landholdings can be seen to correlate closely with age. In a survey (described in appendix 1) men were asked to compare their acreages with those of their neighbours. As can be seen in table

9, the men who estimated their holdings to be the smallest were, as would be expected, those in their twenties, and 27.4% of men between the ages of seventeen and twenty-nine were still waiting for land from their fathers. The wealthiest landowners were men between forty-five and fifty-nine, and 72.7% of these men reckoned that they had the same or more land than the average, while none were completely landless. For men older than this – more advanced in the process of dispersing their assets to their sons – there was greater variation, with half claiming good acreages while 8.3% had no land at all. The distribution of wives in the population shows the same trend, with many younger men forced into a prolonged period of bachelorhood while the highest proportion of polygamists are found in the age group 45–59 (see table 10).

This pattern might tend to support the Gisu theory that any man can get rich even if he starts out poor. It is said that in the early years of the century, younger sons or those of the impoverished would be sent off down the mountain to help their relatives stake out claims to land in the plains. A similar spirit of enterprise sent many Gisu travelling the roads of East Africa in search of employment almost as soon as the colonial administration touched Bugisu District. However, in the 1960s, there was not the same equality of opportunity for the poorer sections of the community.

In general, sons of poor fathers are unlikely to receive much in the way of direct help with land or bridewealth unless they have sisters of marriageable

Table 9 *Distribution of land by age*[1]

Age group	Same or more (%)	Less (%)	None (%)	Total number
17–29[2]	29.6	43	27.4	44
30–44	53.7	37.3	9	67
45–59	72.7	27.3	0	33
60+	54.2	37.5	8.3	24
Total	52.2	35.9	11.9	168

Table 10 *Distribution of wives by age*

Age group	Polygamous (%)	One wife[3]	No wife (%)	Total number
17–29	2	62	36	47
20–44	13	68	19	69
45–59	26	68	6	34
60+	4	71	25	24
Total	11.5	66.7	21.8	174

Notes

For further details on this sample see appendix 1.

1 It was not possible to obtain an accurate assessment of individual landholdings and thus each respondent was asked to estimate how his landholdings compared with other men's in the area.

2 Includes only men of this age who were circumcised.

3 Full or part bridewealth paid.

age. They are expected, as in the past, to make their own way in the world. Yet such boys are unlikely to be educated and are thus inevitably penalised in the system, having neither the means of subsistence nor access to the more remunerative forms of employment. Many leave the district in search of employment elsewhere but their chances of earning sufficient money to return to buy either land or bridewealth in Bugisu are not high. Over the years, permanent settlements of Gisu both in Buganda and Kenya have developed and temporary migration in search of work runs at a high level. Figures are not available for the 1960s but the censuses of both 1949 and 1959 showed that as many as 12% of Gisu were living outside their home district. However, the cost of living in the towns prevents poorly-paid labourers accumulating much in the way of savings and many probably never return to Bugisu. Such migration is thus usually seen only as a last resort and most young men attempt firstly to put as much pressure as possible on their agnates in order to gain help.

This brings me to an important point. Overall, young men are probably more reliant on their agnatic kin today than in the past. Not only is there now no opportunity for men to lay claim to uncultivated land but the chances of gaining land from a mother's brother or brother-in-law have decreased. Rev. Purvis, whose testimony tends to be reliable, says that boys in the past had the choice of inheriting land from either side (Purvis, 1909). This was probably always more true in the open foothills where Purvis was stationed than in the mountain zones. The need for allies lower down the mountain put a premium on attracting supporters. In the present situation there is no such advantage in offering land to a sister's son and while land is loaned and sold between matrilateral kin, gifts are usually restricted to those boys who are circumcised on their mother's brother's compound. In general, men are increasingly unwilling to recognise any economic obligation to their sister's sons. Thus, competition for resources is played out almost entirely within the lineage context.

INHERITANCE

The father's wealth is the single most decisive factor in determining the chances of a man marrying and acquiring sufficient land to support his family. The obligation to provide for a son following his circumcision rests with his father, and it is only in exceptional cases where the father is dead or extremely poor that any assistance can be expected from other agnates. A father making such an allocation calls his agnates together to witness the distribution and to signify that he has bequeathed full rights over the plot or plots concerned to his son, who may thereafter sell them if he so wishes with the consent of his lineage. A father is not obliged to allocate any further land to this son during his lifetime, although as the father's strength and that of his wives decrease, his sons tend to gradually appropriate more of the estate.

The Gisu inherit through a variant of the house-property complex with a boy claiming a right to that land cultivated by his mother in a polygamous house-hold.[10] In such households each wife is allocated her own fields and the husband usually retains a portion over which he alone has rights. In monoga-mous households, too, land is also often divided between husband and wife. However, circumstances may upset any regular division of land along these lines. For example, after divorce fields are allocated successively to different women, and thus their sons must compete for the same land. In addition, the head of the household always retains the right to reallocate his fields among his wives, although he risks alienating his wives and sons by so doing.

While it is expected that a father will attempt to divide his land fairly among his sons, his authority in such matters is absolute and cannot be challenged during his lifetime. This is not so much by virtue of his genealogical seniority as by virtue of his right as a householder. The division of land is considered a domestic matter under the jurisdiction of the head of household alone and, although a dissatisfied son may call upon his relatives to approach the father on his behalf, they have no powers to actively intervene. Nor is the division of land a matter which can be taken to arbitration by the son to any court. A man, therefore, may divide his land as and when he wishes among his sons, favouring one against the others. Here it is often said that the eldest and youngest sons, who mark important stages in the father's life cycle, are most favoured.

A man, prior to his death, may divide all his land among his sons but more commonly the land is divided among the sons on the father's death, with senior agnates acting as mediators in the various claims of the sons. Such claims depend on factors such as the fields cultivated by the mother, any claims of usufruct established during the father's lifetime and the son's present needs. One important aspect of Gisu land claims is that they are based on principles of equity which relate to perceived need. Thus a man with a wife and young family can exert a greater moral pressure on his father than his unmarried brothers.

The presence of a wife thus has a tangible effect on a man's fortunes both in terms of everyday subsistence and in terms of his long-term expectations. Yet many men are either unable to marry because they lack the bridewealth or lose their wife through divorce. Marriage in Bugisu, especially in the early years, is notably unstable. The sources of this instability require an examination of the position of women in Gisu society and it is to this that we now turn.

MARRIAGE AND DIVORCE

Theoretically, women in Bugisu remain jural minors throughout their lives, coming firstly under their fathers' authority and secondly under that of their husbands. However, in practice, the freedom granted to men to manage their own affairs is granted also to women. A woman has a recognised right to choose her own spouse and invariably the initiative in divorce comes also from her.

Such freedom of choice is considered fair; within bounds, for women who drift around, unwilling to commit themselves to a marriage, are disapproved of. In part, also, this freedom follows practice rather than principle, for it is more the case that women ultimately cannot be forced than that men do not attempt to constrain their choices. For a woman, unlike a man, is not inevitably committed to building up a single home and lineage.

There are three ways to marry in Bugisu; by formal alliance (*buxwale*), by elopement (*bubela*) and by widow inheritance (*xurela namelexwa*). All are equally valid once the bridewealth has been paid and all give the husband the same rights over his wife's person; rights to her labour, control over her movements and sexual rights. However, the payment of bridewealth does not bequeath automatic rights of paternity, which are seen to rest with the genitor.

With *buxwale* the marriage is formally arranged by the fathers of the couple and solemnised only after the payment of the bridewealth. The importance of the alliance which the marriage creates is given recognition in the elaborate and lengthy marriage ceremonials which honour the bride and dramatise her change in status. Her reluctance to move from home and make the transition from a daughter who may sit around and eat, secure in the affection of her kindred, to a wife who must prove her industry, is played out in ritual form. While all are eating at her marriage feast, she must fast; while all are drinking beer, she and her female companions are set tasks specially contrived by the groom's family. In the 1960s, the traditional ceremonies, often combined with a church wedding, were largely associated with the wealthy and educated elite who tended to marry among themselves (see further, La Fontaine, 1962). For the poorer families this prestigious and expensive form of marriage has no intrinsic advantages and is contracted only in the special case where two men wish to cement an existing friendship by the marriage of their children.

The overwhelming majority of marriages are therefore by elopement or widow inheritance, which involve only the minimum of ceremony. For a poor man, widow inheritance has the advantage that only a small gift (one or two goats) in recognition of the new marriage needs to be given to the woman's father. Widow inheritance is not a despised form of marriage and available widows are often the subject of fierce competition. Inevitably, though, such marriages are limited by the availability of a widow in a man's own lineage or that of his mother and are also subject to the widow's agreement. A widow is free to choose a new husband from among her husband's kin of the same generation but she is also free to choose to marry elsewhere, in which case the bridewealth is returned by her kin as if she were divorcing.

Most men therefore marry by elopement and, for young men, this is often seen as the only way to force a reluctant father to provide the bridewealth, which is then negotiated after the event.[11] Such a marriage may be the culmination of a clandestine love affair with an unmarried girl of the area but marriages by elopement also grow out of casual unions. A man might meet his future wife (usually in such cases a divorcee) at a beer party, perhaps when she is visiting kin in the area. In some cases she may only stay a few nights but, if the situation remains congenial after a few months and the man has the necessary cattle, bridewealth negotiations may be undertaken to legitimise the marriage. Whether or not bridewealth is paid during the time she remains in his house she is referred to as his 'wife' and performs the normal duties of a wife. Any children born or conceived during this time also belong to her lover, for biological paternity in Bugisu is absolute and inalienable. A man cannot repudiate such children. Illegitimacy occurs only where the woman refuses to name the father of her children, and they then become the responsibility of her brother.

Bridewealth is negotiated at a feast given by the groom's father to which the girl's senior kinsmen are invited. The amount of bridewealth is regulated by a Local Authority by-law and stood in the 1960s at not more than three head of cattle and three goats, or 900s.[12] However, the amount actually paid for any one marriage varies according to the type of marriage, the wealth of the groom's family and the status of the bride and the number of her previous marriages. Higher bridewealth is usual for *buxwale* and often exceeds the stipulated maximum, a reflection not only of the relative wealth of the families marrying in this way but also of the greater prior commitment of both sides to the marriage. The bargaining after an elopement is dominated by more mercenary considerations. Both sides attempt to secure a deal to their own advantage; the husband's side by pleading poverty, the wife's by threatening to take their daughter away if their demands are not met.

Yet it is to the advantage of both sides to secure a speedy agreement. The shadow of divorce hangs over all Gisu marriages and, once a woman leaves her husband, her kin forfeit all right to the cattle they might have used in the interim. Thus the wife's party are unlikely to hold out for three head of cattle if they are offered an immediate down-payment of two. The groom's family usually attempt to make the payments as soon as possible for the wife's kin are likely to continually harass their son-in-law, threatening to remove their daughter as long as more than a goat or two remains outstanding. The possibility of divorce also affects the bargaining more directly so that the amount paid tends to reflect the number of a woman's previous marriages. Higher payments are usual for a girl's first marriage, the marriage which marks her change in status from daughter to wife and which binds her ritually to the match, despite divorce. With successive divorces, however, the amount paid tends to decrease as the woman is considered, with reason, to be an insecure investment. The kin of a woman known to stay only a short time with a man, even where they know her whereabouts, rarely attempt to claim bridewealth, which will only involve them in future litigation.

However, a woman can generally rely on the support of her kin and if she remains unmoved by their remonstrances she is usually allowed to divorce and remarry. Indeed, it is often feared that a woman will resort to desperate measures if refused a divorce, so that suicide, running away or even cursing herself are often threatened by women who meet with initial resistance from their kin.[13] The high rate of divorce, despite a relatively high bridewealth payment, is thus strongly associated with the strength of the sibling bond and a woman's attachment to her own lineage. On marriage she gains a new identification, addressed as 'wife' by her husband's relatives of his generation, as 'daughter' by those of the senior generation and as 'mother' by those of the junior generation. If she dies while living with her husband she is buried at the edge of his compound by her husband's relatives. Yet this association with the lineage into which she marries never detracts from her membership of her own. Her own relatives have continuing responsibilities both to her and her children and close contact is maintained by visiting, often facilitated by marriage in the vicinity. While they may not interfere directly in the affairs of her marital home, her kin remain for a woman arbiters to ensure that she is treated fairly by her husband. If her marriage breaks down, it is their homes she falls back upon.

However, in the early years of marriage a woman has little stake in her husband's affairs and this is true even after her young children are born. In a sample of 118 marriages contracted by the living members of five lineage segments in Busoba almost 45% of marriages ended in divorce and over a quarter ended in the first three years.[14] The marriages tabulated included only those where at least part of the bridewealth had been paid and did not include casual unions, although in some of these cases women had lived with their lover as long as three years. With first marriages such divorces are often attributed to the immaturity of the spouses, unused to the give-and-take of married life. The husband is over-assertive, beating his wife harshly for small signs of disrespect to himself, while the young wife may well find her husband's authority more irksome than her father's. Such marital squabbling is not regarded with much tolerance by older people better adjusted to the proprieties of married life, and they dismiss such couples as merely 'playing with marriage'.

A woman may go through two or three such marriages before eventually settling down with a husband, a state some women never achieve. It is relevant to note here that the rights of a wife are to a considerable extent negotiable, and the success of a marriage therefore depends primarily on mutual adjustment in the areas where conflict is most likely. In particular, the use of the household resources is at stake in many quarrels. All the wealth of the household, land, cattle and money income from cash-cropping or wage-employment, is at the absolute disposal of the husband. Nevertheless, the wife expects to share fairly in her husband's prosperity both with regard to household items and with rights of usufruct over his land, which will determine the inheritance of her sons.

Polygamy is thus a threat to her position and, although it still remains an ambition for some men, others denounce it for the trouble it causes. The scrupulous fairness demanded of the husband in these marriages is difficult to achieve, and quarrels between co-wives jealous of the favours bestowed on the other are endemic. Such quarrels lead to accusations by one wife that the other is using love charms to entice away the husband's affections or bewitching her children. Such quarrelling reflects badly not only on the wives but also on the husband and, in fact, it is often he who is blamed by neighbours for the troubles in the household. The Gisu say that it takes a 'strong' man to control two women, and a younger man who attempts it often has his fingers burnt and finds himself with no wife at all. Indeed, only the richer men tend to achieve stable polygamous unions since they can offer both wives a relatively high standard of living and provide sufficient land for their use. Serial polygamy is far more common, though even here women have to face 'rivals' (and the claims of their sons) in the persons of previous or future wives, all of whom are referred to as 'co-wife' or 'rival'.

Yet divorce has different meanings for husband and wife. A woman, unlike a man, is never committed to one particular household for either livelihood or status. Whereas on divorce a man loses his housekeeper, the mother of his children and his partner in economic matters, and may have great difficulty in finding a substitute, there are no such penalties for women. La Fontaine reports a common saying that 'A woman can always find a husband but a man who cannot keep a wife is indeed unfortunate' (1960b:115). A woman loses her share of the household property to which she has over the years contributed but she may fairly easily find another protector and another household in which to rear her children. A woman's status and rights with regard to her children may be little affected by such behaviour, for her children automatically belong to the genitor and she has similar rights to them in wedlock or divorce. On divorce a woman usually takes her young children with her and older children are usually given some choice as to where they will reside, with their father, mother, mother's brother or other close relative. She cannot be refused access to them. While continual divorce is likely to infuriate her kin while she is still a young woman and her brothers are still dependent on her bridewealth, as she becomes mature and her sons adult, she might obtain a relatively secure position, with her household on her son's or brother's land becoming the centre for her children from several different marriages.

The man who loses his wife is however always placed in a disadvantageous position, and on this hinges the attitudes of the Gisu towards adultery and the constant anxieties of men that their wives will be seduced away by others. The rules regarding the return of the bridewealth on divorce are clear-cut and advantageous to the man. If his wife leaves by her own volition, whatever the reason, then her father or brothers must repay all the stipulated items of the bridewealth, irrespective of how long she has lived with her husband or the number of children born to the union. Bridewealth gives rights over the woman's person and is clearly not a payment for rights in genetrix. Barring his wife's death or his own dismissal of her – an act so manifestly foolish in Bugisu that it strikes men as all but inconceivable – a man cannot in the normal run of things lose control over his bridewealth. Nevertheless repayment is usually more tardy than payment, the woman's kin usually having to wait until she is remarried before they can find the necessary cattle. Further, in cases where the woman simply 'disappears', her father is under no obligation to repay it until she is 'found', as jural responsibility is held to remain with the husband. This literal escape clause was subject to obvious and frequent abuse.[15] Thus men do sometimes lose their bridewealth or have to wait a considerable number of years before they are able to recover it.

On divorce men suffer, in addition, an abrupt loss of status for divorce always reflects badly on them. A man whose wife deserts him is usually considered to blame for, it is argued, he should have looked after her properly. He may become the butt of jokes; the whisper goes around that he is an inveterate drinker who likes his beer too much to know how to treat a woman. The loss of a wife is thus often traumatic for a man. In one case of attempted suicide investigated by the court in 1964, the man said he was prompted by his intolerable position during the three years since his wife had left him. During this time he had become a laughing stock, particularly because his wife had left him for a patrilateral cousin who already had three wives. The family gave evidence in court that the man drank a lot and quarrelled with them all the time. The court commented that the individual clearly had been suffering from acute mental distress.

The relative rarity of wife-killing has its place here, as do the types of plea made to the court when they are killed. The killing of wives accounted for some twenty-one of the fifty-three cases where men killed women and in a further seven cases men killed their lovers. These killings rarely appear premeditated; the majority occurring during quarrels at beer parties or after having returned home from drinking. Eight of the cases fell into the category which one judge described as a 'senseless marital squabble'. Other cases more clearly reflect a man's fear that his wife will abscond; six wives were killed after they had either threatened divorce or already left their husband. In three other cases they were killed over suspicions of adultery, although in two of these the husband claimed that he had killed the woman by accident and had meant instead to kill the lover. In four of the cases where a man killed his lover, similar reasons were presented to the court, usually that the woman had refused to marry him and was leaving his home. Yet more significant is the avowed remorse of the men in these cases, a remorse which would seem genuine. Suicide following murder appears to be extremely rare in Bugisu. I only came across four such cases in the Death Enquiry Reports for the years 1964 to 1968, but in all of them the suicide had followed the killing of a wife.

Men are held never to have reason to fear a woman and thus have no justifiable motive for using violence against them. As was described in the last chapter, the imagery used for women stresses this fact and they are deemed incapable of the violent affect which makes men dangerous to each other. Further, such attitudes towards women would appear to have a long history in Bugisu. Purvis, for example, writes of women's safety in times of war: 'No clans would dream of molesting a woman belonging to the opposing force. She might with perfect safety walk between the combatants, and is even allowed to pass in safety through the enemy's territory, taking her husband's goats or other possessions to some place of safety' (1909:285).

One important corollary to this is that violence against women is not even sanctioned within marriage. Men do indeed beat their wives, but this is not seen as in a number of African societies either as an inevitable fact of nature nor as an inalienable right of the husband. Far from it, the facts of its occurrence draw widespread disapproval, both in general and in particular instances. A woman may indeed take a case to court against her husband, a procedure which in fact many follow where the beating has been severe. More commonly, they take the dispute to the neighbourhood elders who invariably impose a fine of a fowl on the offending husband, a fowl which forms part of the ceremony of reconciliation. Yet women are not entirely passive recipients of male violence: they are capable at times of defending themselves. Every neighbourhood has a man whom others ridicule because his wife beats him and women occasionally resort to more desperate measures and kill their husbands.

Nevertheless, their freedom to divorce is perhaps their strongest sanction in their relationship to their husbands. Even if a wife runs back to her parents' home this places the husband in an invidious position in marital disputes for the husband must then go to her as a suppliant to beg for her return. Unable to approach the house directly because of the avoidance relationship which exists between himself and his mother-in-law, he must perforce use others as inter-mediaries, thus drawing attention to the quarrels within his household and allowing the wife to air her grievances in a setting in which she rather than he may expect support. Thus, while jurally women have few rights in marriage, and on leaving their husband must leave all the property which has accrued to the marriage and even the crops which they have helped to cultivate (they may have some rights to these if they have provided the seed), the subservience of women is in many ways more formal than real. The authoritarian bias of marital relationships is thus often mediated in practice by a man's fear of offending his wife.

To repeat the problem that faces a Gisu man. His hope of maintaining a household, let alone developing his estate, rests on obtaining and then keeping a wife. Yet this is by no means an easy task, given the high bridewealth required right at the onset of adult life and the freedom of Gisu women to divorce thereafter. Many can be deemed to fail. To return to tables 10 and 11, 22% of men in this rural area were bachelors. A further 12% were landless:

high percentages in a society which insists that men be economically independent.

The household development cycle in Bugisu is extremely short, with a rapid turnover of personnel and assets. The normal process of accumulation begins with a man's marriage in his late teens or early twenties and his first allocation of land by his father. This estate he augments by his own efforts and those of his wife, gaining more land both by purchase and on the eventual death of his father. Yet the process of dispersal also begins early, as he himself must begin to divide his estate when he is in his early forties as his sons in turn reach adulthood. This system of inheritance produces a distinctive patterning in the distribution of assets, with landlessness occurring not only among young men but also at the other end of the life cycle among the old (table 9). Marriage likewise follows this profile, with the highest proportion of polygamists found in the age group 45–60 and the highest proportions of bachelors in the age groups 17–29 and again among men over sixty-one years old (table 10). Wealth is thus to a large extent an attribute of age, with poverty occurring at the two extreme ends of the adult life cycle.

If this may be regarded as the regular patterning of wealth produced by the traditional economic system, modern economic realities give it a cutting edge. Possibilities exist now as they did not in the past for the wealthy to accumulate resources well beyond their own labour power, and to pass on these advantages to their children both in the form of land and by providing them with the education necessary to professional employment. The Gisu elite have from the beginning of the colonial era used their wealth to educate their sons. Indeed, La Fontaine writes of the 1950s that economic changes 'have created a class structure which appears to be more rigid in recruitment and sharper in wealth differences than that of the traditional system' (1962:114). In the 1960s, in the situation of increasing pressure on the land, the other side of this pattern was the possibility that the poor would lose access to their means of livelihood. Not only did landlessness occur, but the effects of the rapid household development cycle and partible inheritance meant that the land was becoming increasingly fragmented, with many having less than met their needs.

Land pressure is a notoriously difficult thing to assess. Nevertheless, the overall density in Bugisu, together with a 30% increase in population between the censuses of 1959 and 1969, attest to its probable severity. In line with this the average density per square mile in Bugisu increased from 329 in 1959 to 441 in 1969, the highest in Uganda. With densities in the more fertile mountain areas soaring to 1,500 to the square mile, the settlement pattern in Bugisu as a whole is like that of a peri-urban area. Wallace, Belshaw and Brock (1973: 33–5), estimate the availability of cultivated land per head for Bugisu and Sebei in 1962 at 1.5 acres and available land at 1.9 acres. This gives a ratio of available land to cultivated land of 1.3:1. This – together with the neighbouring district of Bukedi – was the lowest in Uganda. Even so, the figure for Bugisu is inflated as Bugisu is here again included with the more sparsely populated district of Sebei. They conclude 'that there is a marked tendency to an intense and rapidly worsening population pressure in Bugisu' (1973:34).

Landlessness – or effective landlessness, with men having insufficient acreage to produce a livelihood, perhaps little more than a house site – was thus becoming a major problem in Bugisu in the 1960s. While, as described in this chapter, there have been some compensating developments in commerce and employment in the district, these have not been of the kind to guarantee livelihood to those most at risk of impoverishment. Growing land shortage is thus strongly associated with insecurity of tenure for the poorer sections of the community whose chances of obtaining land or holding on to a small plot are diminishing over time.

This harsh economic reality provides the backcloth for the equally harsh attitudes the Gisu take towards the poor. The basic system of evaluation, with its equation of worth with wealth and the pervasive fears of the Gisu of the misuse of male violence, was outlined in the previous chapter. Fears of male violence centre on theft and witchcraft. We need at this point to ask who is vulnerable to the accusation of being a witch or a thief. In fact, in Bugisu, both accusations are associated with the jealousies and resentments of the poor: a product of their anger (*lirima*). It is to the dynamics of the accusational process, set as it is in the context of the struggle for resources within the family, to which we now turn.

NOTES

1 Kigezi District in South-West Uganda resembles Bugisu in covering a fertile mountain area and Bukedi lies on the plains adjoining Bugisu. The population density in Uganda as a whole was eighty-six to the square mile in 1959.

2 The percentage increase in population between the censuses of 1959 and 1969 was 31.1%. The average density per square mile in Bugisu increased from 329 in 1959 to 441 in 1969.

3 My overall interpretation differs from that of La Fontaine. In her writing on parricide (1967) she relates the intensity of competition over property to the desire of both father and son to further their political careers in a society where power depends on wealth. Thus she sees the conflict between father and son as being more intense in the richer families. In my data, twelve years later and from a different area of Bugisu, the opposite pattern is more apparent, with impoverishment rather than a desire to build up exceptional riches as the issue. Additionally, I see this conflict over inheritance as having more far-reaching implications, leading not only to direct hostilities between fathers and sons but also to the creation of effective outcasts; adult men with little access to resources.

4 There was parity between the Ugandan pound and the pound sterling at this time and twenty Ugandan shillings made one pound.

5 The area was mapped and a random sample of forty-four household heads was selected, each being interviewed once in September 1966 and asked for details of his

income over the preceding twelve months. The interview was conducted in private and while there was often no way of checking the accuracy of particular receipts, the variations recorded corresponded fairly well with the patterns I had learnt to recognise from more detailed investigations. The survey had fairly modest aims and concentrated on estimating the major sources of regular income rather than a detailed assessment of income from all sources, for which a more sophisticated survey technique would have had to be designed. Thus the figures do not include *legelege* payments nor with any form of casual or intermittent labour for which the respondent had difficulty in estimating his income in the last year. For many of the men, the income earned in this way may well have added 100s to the recorded income.

6   This must be considered high though no figures are available for the district as a whole. Unfortunately, the Uganda Census of Agriculture taken in 1965 includes Bugisu along with Sebei, more remote from the centres of employment, thus inevitably depressing the percentage of those with an occupation in addition to farming, which it gives as 18% of the landowners in Bugisu and Sebei.

7   The District Education Officer estimated that between 40% and 50% of children of primary-school age attended local authority schools, a take-up figure that was restricted to some extent by the shortage of places (Wallace, Belshaw and Brock, 1973: 108).

8   The report on the Bugisu coffee industry states the situation thus: 'Of the boys who completed Primary 6 in Bugisu in 1963, only 40 per cent went on to Junior Secondary School. Of those who completed Junior Secondary School in Bugisu in 1964, at the very best, only one in four would have been able to get into a Senior Secondary School – the gateway to white-collar prestige jobs' (Wallace, Belshaw and Brock, 1973: 114).

9   Discussions of Gisu land rights can be found in Gayer, 1957; Brock, 1968; Wallace, Belshaw and Brock, 1973; La Fontaine, 1979.10.

10   In the Gisu variant of the house-property complex only land is heritable by house. Cattle are of the home and thus a girl's bridewealth may be used by both full and half brothers and, although in practice full brothers may exert a greater claim to it, all brothers may expect a share.

11   A man is expected to write to the girl's father to inform him of her whereabouts and to pay a fine for abduction, usually from between 10s and 30s.

12   In the plains and foothills bridewealth still tends to be paid in cattle, primarily because the premium put on cattle make it the cheaper method. Thus it is quite common for men to buy cattle specifically for a marriage and in this way save up to 200s. In the mountains where cattle are scarcer the payment is often entirely in money.

13   Though women occasionally do have a violent response, sometimes beating and even killing their husbands, the violence most feared in such situations is that of suicide. While the inquest files reveal that men commit suicide (as well as murder) more frequently than women, with 70% of the suicides recorded being those of men, a woman tempted to violence is more likely to commit suicide than murder. La Fontaine's figures (1960b: 127) show that over twice as many women commit suicide as murder (whereas men committed murder in 141 cases as compared with forty suicides). The situation in the 1960s was much the same and threats of suicide by women are hard for men to counter or ignore. Of the nineteen cases where women were accused of homicide in the court cases of the 1960s, seven killed their husband, two another male affine, two a male thief, two a child, one a co-wife, two another woman and for two it was unknown.

14   The Barnes (1967) ratio A (the number of marriages ended in divorce as a percentage of all marriages in the sample) is 44.9%. This would seem to be high for this area. Indeed Gisu women have a reputation for their freedom in neighbouring Kenya and figures both for divorce and polygamy differentiate the Gisu sharply from their

nearest cultural neighbours, the Bukusu, with whom they share a common language and ancestry. On polygamy my figures from Central Bugisu for the 1960s show that 14.7% of men had more than one wife, the same proportion as the 15% of marriages recorded by La Fontaine (1962) for an area of North Bugisu some fifteen years previously. In contrast, for the Bukusu, de Wolf (1977: 40) gives a range of figures based on a number of different surveys taken in the late 1960s, all of which indicate rates well over 40%. This high polygamy rate goes along with a low rate of divorce, which taking Barnes's ratio A is 20.2%, less than half that of the Gisu.

15   The Bugisu District Council revised the customary law on this issue in the late 1960s, making the father liable in cases where it was felt that the family was taking undue advantage of this loophole in the law.

5

WITCHES AND WASTRELS

The way in which a man controls his violence is basic to character judgements, marking for the Gisu the critical zone between the autonomy of the individual and his power to infringe the autonomy of others. The concept of 'troublemakers' is indicative here as it includes the whole gamut of offenders from adulterers, thieves and witches to slanderers and perpetually abusive individuals. Yet the argument has been made that perception of offence is directed by factors other than that of behaviour alone, for the nature of character is also a function of a person's place in the society. With relatively simple schemas as to what constitutes the desirable, motivation can largely be deduced, or attributed, according to the life situation of the individual. Most situations speak for themselves: success or failure can be assessed in terms of the outward facts of a man's life and from this can be read his likely attitude towards others. And it is failure in pursuing an adequate life course which is seen to generate resentment and hostility towards others. Thus accusations – at least those which stick – tend to be aimed at the poor as the Gisu concept of 'troublemaking' itself implies, deriving as it does from the verb *xutamba*, 'to be without'.

In this, theft and witchcraft are analogous offences and the accusational processes involved may be regarded as equally problematic. Even on the question of evidence, the question which made witchcraft in sixteenth-century English law clearly a *crimen exceptum*, there is arguably little difference in the Gisu context (see Larner, 1984). There are two sides to this; both that material evidence is often forthcoming in witchcraft cases and that often it is not there in cases of theft. An acceptance of the reality of witchcraft generates its own evidence; not only is sickness and death a continual reminder of the fact of witchcraft, but people are found in circumstances which suggest cursing or bewitching. They may indeed admit to it but this is extremely rare in Bugisu. However, there is material evidence in the form of sorcery substances, uncovered not only by professional witchcraft-finders who are brought into the compound to 'search it out', but sometimes discovered independently in the

thatch of the house or after a heavy storm in the mud of the compound outside.
Yet the concentration on material evidence is perhaps misleading. The point
to be made is that frequently there is as little objective evidence to link a
particular person with a theft in Bugisu, as is generally assumed by anthropologists in the discussion of witchcraft. I do not mean to imply by this that nobody
steals – indeed, petty pilfering is rife – but that the culpability of a particular
individual is by no means always obvious. The density of settlement, together
with the rather amorphous nature of social life, ensure that whenever something goes missing, the culprit must be sought among a large number of
people. The analysis of who gets accused of theft, of how the reputation is
imputed and acquired, is thus as critical here as it is with witchcraft, and
likewise might be expected to take us to central features of the society in
question.

As has been said, it is the poor who tend to be accused. Further, economic
factors are not only significant in the perception of violence but also crucial for
an understanding of the accusational process. The last chapter provided a basic
outline of the competing interests of fathers and sons over the division of the
patrimonial estate. The problem now is to see how such conflicts motivate
accusation. Since Mitchell's (1956) insight into the part played by witchcraft
accusations in the segmentation of Yao villages, the setting of witchcraft
accusations in the context of struggles for power and inherent conflicts of
interest has been developed particularly by Turner (1957), Middleton (1960)
and Marwick (1965). Their analyses have concentrated on the non-random
relationship between accused and accuser and on the effects of accusation in
accelerating structural processes, especially those involved in competition for
the headships of villages. Thus the 'witches' have been seen as 'made' by the
working-out of the development cycle in these residential groups, caught in an
inevitable political process, unable to achieve power or unable to maintain it.
Turner likens the process to the 'Fates', with the 'Fates' being seen as the
'necessities of the social process' (1957: 94). Similarly, in Bugisu, I see both
'witches' and 'thieves' as the failures or casualties of the system. However, I
argue that these accusations are not associated with the development cycle of
groups but related to the life cycle of individuals and to the underlying
competition for resources. At certain points in their life Gisu men become
vulnerable to accusation and liable to be killed as a consequence if they fail to
gain or maintain control over sufficient resources to establish their position.
This is most likely to happen at the two extreme ends of the adult life cycle.

The vulnerability of the old and the young to being killed is apparent in the
homicide statistics for the region and a summary of these may be presented at
this juncture. In terms of absolute numbers more young men are killed, with
the percentage of male victims in each five-year age group rising steadily from
15–19 upwards, to reach a peak of 14% in the age group 30–34 (see table 11).
The percentage then decreases but rises again for men over fifty-five years old.

Table 11 *Distribution of male homicide victims and accused by 5-year age groups* (%)

Age group	Population	Victims	Accused
0–9	31.8	1.0	0
10–14	10.8	1.0	0.2
15–19	9.7	2.3	7.7
20–24	7.95	8.0	13.8
25–29	7.4	14.4	24.3
30–34	6.25	14.1	16.9
35–39	5.7	12.2	12.0
40–44	5.1	10.0	9.6
45–49	4.5	7.4	7.3
50–54	11.4	10.0	3.4
55+		19.6	4.8
Totals	100	100	100

Sources: Percentage population taken from Uganda Population Census for 1959 and the rates for victims and accused calculated from the Death Enquiry Reports and Court records, respectively.

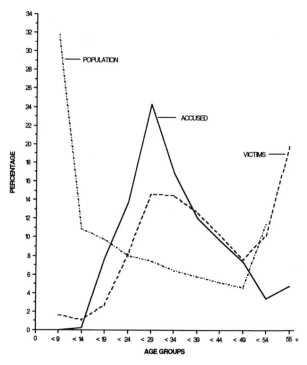

6   **Profiles of male victims** and accused by age

Table 12 *Rate per 100,000 for male victims and accused of homicide in Bugisu district*

Age	Victims	Accused
15–29	46.7	119
30–44	80.5	131
45+	132.8	67
Total, 15+	91.8	

Source: Death Enquiry Reports, 1964–68; court case records, 1960–66.
Note: The rates for the victims and accused in homicide are obviously not comparable. The first, as outlined in chapter 2, may be taken as a fairly accurate indication of the proportion of victims in the population as the rate is calculated from the Death Enquiry Reports. The rates for accused on the other hand include only cases where prosecution occurred, less than 50%, and are given here only for the indication they give on relative age.

This distribution is influenced by the age structure of the population and, if one allows for this by converting the percentages into rates per 100,000, then a very different pattern becomes clear. A man's chances of being a victim of homicide in fact increase dramatically with age, viz. 46.7 per 100,000 for men between fifteen and twenty-nine, 80.5 for men between thirty and forty-four but 132.8 for men older than this (table 12).

For offenders the picture is different. The proportion of accused again rises

Table 13 *Relationship by generation of victims to accused where both men, 1960–66*

	Kin		Affines			
Generation	Elementary family	Classi-ficatory	Wife's family	Classi-ficatory	Total	%
2nd ascending		3			3	2.3
1st ascending	8	37	4	2	51	38.6
Same	21	36	2	13	72	54.5
1st descending	2	3			5	3.8
2nd descending		1			1	.75
Total	31	80	6	15	132	100
Percentages	23.5	60.6	4.5	11.4	100	

Source: Court case records, 1960–66.
Note: This table enumerates data from the 110 cases where a kinship relationship could be established out of the total of 308 cases where men killed men. It includes all relationships of the victim to the accused, a total of 132.

abruptly after the age of fifteen to a peak in the age 25–29 age group, one-quarter of all accused being of this age. Thereafter, the percentage decreases with equal abruptness. Thus while the chances of being killed in Bugisu increase with age, that of being an offender would seem greatest in the active middle years between twenty-five and forty. If again, one converts these percentages into rates, then the rate for offenders is 119 per 100,000 for those between fifteen and twenty-nine, 131 per 100,000 for those between thirty and forty-four but only sixty-seven per 100,000 for those older than this. And this pattern is apparent also if one looks at the relationship between killers and victims (table 13). This table tabulates 132 cases where the relationship between male victims and accused could be ascertained with some certainty and shows that in the overwhelming majority of cases men killed others of the same or the first ascending generation. Despite the fact, as it appears from the case histories, that violence is frequently threatened on both sides, it would appear that the younger generation is in fact far more likely to resort to it. Juniors killed seniors in 41% of cases but seniors only killed juniors in 4.6%.

But if the resort to physical violence is associated particularly with the young, witchcraft is the prerogative of the old, and theft and witchcraft accusations reflect this bi-polar differentiation. It is the younger men who are accused of theft and the older of witchcraft. The court figures are again indicative of this pattern, with 78% of the men killed as thieves being between twenty and thirty-nine, whereas all the witches killed were over forty. This pattern of accusation bears clear signs of intergenerational conflict, conflict which, as has been indicated in the last chapter, revolves around basic inheritance. This chapter now turns to the way this conflict is imaged in Gisu beliefs and to the dynamics of the accusational processes themselves.

FATHER AND SON

La Fontaine and Turner are undoubtedly correct in seeing the father and son relationship at the crucial intersection of, on the one hand, the ideals of competitive equality among adults and, on the other, genealogically ascribed authority and patrilineal transmission of property (La Fontaine, 1960b, 1967; Turner, 1969). In Bugisu, the inherent conflict of interests in the relationship and the ambivalence of sentiment this generates are not bounded by an absolute stress on filial piety supported by the symbols of the father's ritual authority. Nor are the roles of father and son separated by ritual avoidance, as is found in some societies where, as in Bugisu, the son may be seen to arrogate his father's wealth and position. Rather the ideal is one of mutuality, the father nurturing his son, preparing the way for his safe and successful circumcision and providing him with property thereafter. In return, the son should be respectful and obedient, honouring his father. Nevertheless it is recognised that the relationship frequently falls short of the ideal, developing into a polarisation of mutually hostile interests. The dangers resulting from such alienation are readily drawn, as the following from an elder in Central Bugisu shows:

If the child is troublesome and disregards his father's words then he belittles any gift his father makes, saying it is not enough. He wants to get everything from his father and cares nothing for him. His father may say, 'Why do you quarrel like this with me all the time when I have given you land and cattle to marry a wife?' But such fathers and sons keep on fighting, for the son is after his father's last cow and for that they kill. Or the son wants the land which the father's old wife is still cultivating and for that they kill. But if the father makes friends with his son then he will be thanked for any gift he makes, whether a small plot of land or a single cow. Then the father is pleased and says, 'Help yourself, don't trouble to ask me again for what you need', for they are friends. And they act always as friends, drinking beer together from the same pot. If one is late, then the other keeps his share of beer aside, the father saying, 'Leave a little for my son so he can share it with his friends when he arrives.' They drink together like this and there is peace between parents and children in their lineage segment.

Yet such friendships are often hard to achieve as fathers procrastinate in order to preserve their wealth and position in the community for a few more years, and sons press their claims with growing impatience. For while common sense and the weight of approved customary behaviour require that a boy should bide his time, obey his father and fulfil his role as a dutiful son, many pressures militate against such a subservient position from adolescence onwards.

The aggressive independence of adult Gisu is fostered at an early age. At seven or eight boys begin to eat with their father, separate from their mother, and begin to be set small tasks by their father. Even at this early age boys are often concerned with the beginnings of their own personal wealth. When they herd their fathers' cattle they expect some reward for their services, usually a calf of their own. Or they may beg a kinsman to allow them to look after a hen or a nanny-goat so as to be eligible for at least one of the progeny. From such small beginnings, more frequently today with the help of a little money they have earned, they might, as do adults, begin to exchange one type of livestock with another of a more valuable kind. Such enterprise is encouraged, for it bodes well for the future. Yet while he remains in his father's household, he possesses personal wealth only with the indulgence of his father, who may appropriate it for his own use. Gisu boys are unlikely to sanction the use of their property without argument. Purvis, talking about the spirit of independence of the Gisu before 1910, stresses this: 'A child will defend with its own life its own small property, perhaps a single fowl, and dare his father to use it for himself' (Purvis, 1909: 286).

At adolescence the boy takes a further step towards his eventual independence, moving out of his father's house to build his own nearby or share with a friend. He can now freely entertain his friends and his comings and goings are no longer closely scrutinised by his parents. It is at this stage that the boy's obedience may become questionable and lead to open rebellion. Boys refuse to herd their fathers' cattle, escaping to live in a friend's house, or take the opportunity to visit their mother's brother or grandparents, refusing to return as long as demands are made upon their labour. Where the mother is divorced and has remarried they may go to live with her. Where the father and mother cohabit, a definite schism may appear in the household between the mother and son on the one hand and the father on the other. Frequently a mother rises in defence of her son, seeking to protect his eventual rights to property, while the son sides with his mother if she is reprimanded, or her position threatened by the father favouring a co-wife.

The seeds of hostility between father and son are thus often sown early, and the disobedience of the boy may well prejudice his later fortunes. Yet it is not usually until the son is circumcised that the relationship deteriorates and may have a violent outcome. Before circumcision few demands are made on the youths, who are allowed to wander freely and seek friendship and companionship with those of the same age. Once circumcised, however, a son is obliged to go as a suppliant to his father. If the father then refuses his assistance, the son remains his dependant, continuing to rely on the father's household for food. In such situations the resentment of the son, together with his awareness of his ignominious position, makes violence a real possibility.

While the actual number of parricides in the court sample was low (eight cases and a further two where a father killed his son), they may be said to represent the extreme outcome of tension between fathers and sons (see further, La Fontaine, 1967). In all but one of these ten cases (where a young man killed his father after the latter had intervened to prevent the son from beating his young wife), the sons were unmarried. In all cases, too, the witnesses testified to the ill-feeling and, in some cases, violent quarrels between the father and son on the question of inheritance. If we summarise the factors which have a crucial effect on the chances of a son claiming his inheritance, it is apparent that a son's chances are highest where (1) he is one of few male siblings together with an equal number of sisters, and (2) his father is monogamous and both his parents remain alive. They are correspondingly decreased where (a) he is one of a large number of male siblings with few sisters, (b) his father is a polygamist and his own mother is dead or divorced, or (c) where the father himself is dead. To a certain extent these factors are echoed in the court sample, for in the cases where the marital status of the fathers could be ascertained, three out of the ten were married to a woman who was not the son's mother, and in a further two the father himself was unmarried.

In neither of these situations does the son have a mother willing to intercede on his behalf. With the division of the estate being entirely at the father's discretion, a son's exasperation may reach a peak where he is tempted to resort to physical violence to demonstrate to outsiders the seriousness of affairs within the household. In some cases it would appear that a boy purposefully resorts to acts of violence or abuse merely to get the attention of the elders, in the hope that they will adjudicate. This strategy rarely brings results and may well mean the son is castigated as dangerous. The way such evaluation works can be illustrated by the fortunes of Wepuxulu, son of Masaba.

Case 1: Troublesome Sons   (Busoba)
Masaba had six sons, all adult, three by his first wife who was still alive and three by his second who had died some ten years previously. Wepuxulu was the eldest son of the second wife and the only one of the sons of this wife who still lived near his father and his half-brothers. His two full brothers had migrated to Buganda some years previously. Wepuxulu himself was about 30 and unmarried, but he had a considerable amount of land, by virtue of his brothers' migration. Masaba had previously divided his land into three parts, one part each to the sons of each wife and one part which he continued to cultivate with his first wife. The main bone of contention between Wepuxulu and his father arose from this division, for the portion allotted to him and his brothers had been smaller than that going to the sons of the elder wife. Partly this was because Masaba had in fact withheld some of the second wife's plots for his own use. It was over these latter plots that the dispute arose early in 1966.

   In February, Wepuxulu went as a suppliant to his father. asking that the rest of the land should be allocated to him. Masaba agreed to this request but insisted on retaining a large plantation of plantain which he needed to feed himself and his wife. Wepuxulu demanded this plantation also and, according to the evidence later presented to the elders, turned on his step-mother saying, 'You are a big head. Did you plant those plantains which you now eat? No, my mother planted them!' He then picked up a stick to attack his step-mother, but Masaba intervened, snatched the stick and threatened Wepuxulu with it. Wepuxulu rushed away, yelling abusively. Later that day Masaba found that twenty of his plantains had been cut down and ran to fetch the headman. Wepuxulu admitted to having cut down eight of the stems but accused his step-mother of cutting down the rest in order to incriminate him further. The headman, brought in to arbitrate, asked Masaba if he would agree to the land issue being discussed in conjunction. Masaba agreed to this and the case went against Wepuxulu, the chiefs deciding that the land should eventually go to his full brothers in Buganda, but would remain with Masaba for as long as he needed it.

Wepuxulu's intemperate behaviour was in all likelihood occasioned by the severe illness of Masaba, from which he was expected to die. The urgency of Wepuxulu's demands can thus be seen as an attempt to gain control over the land before his father's death, since afterwards he would stand little chance, in the face of the rights of a widow to continue farming her husband's land as well as the competition from his brothers. However, his actions only told further against him.

A few days after the case the parish chief issued a summons for Wepuxulu's arrest on the grounds that he had failed to pay his tax the previous year. Now it is unusual for chief to take such prompt action against a tax defaulter, a recognised principle in the village being that the chief defers for at least two years. Indeed the summons was interpreted as a possible change of procedure by some and prompted some ill-feeling against the chief. The chief, however, was acting on a report from the headman that Wepuxulu had rejected their rulings and was again pestering his father and step-mother. The summons had the desired effect and Wepuxulu left hurriedly for Buganda to join his brothers. They, like him, had left following quarrels with Masaba, and all three were unmarried. Likewise, all three were regarded as troublesome young men whom nobody wished to see return.

Violence in such situations is thus not only likely to meet with implacable opposition from the father, but the son's reputation also suffers with outsiders, as he becomes known as a man who cannot keep his temper and who will resort to extreme means to achieve his ends. This is effectively a no-win situation. A man may be tempted to step up a dispute by flouting the avoidance and respect rules, or by a direct resort to violence, in order to get outsiders involved in any dispute he might have with his father over land. But such action rarely operates to his advantage. Wepuxulu's position certainly worsened considerably as a result of forcing the issue over the land, since he not only lost outright any claims to it but in addition was forced to migrate. This, in turn, was interpreted to his detriment, confirming an impression that he was footloose and unlikely ever to farm his lands successfully. Taken together such behaviour may act as an effective disqualifier, for no man is obliged to allocate resources to a wastrel.

Thus, it is not just violence in the familial setting which is at issue in such cases, for bad relationships here may have repercussions that get the individual a bad reputation with others. And this is crucial to understanding patterns of accusation and killing; what might begin between father and son is taken further elsewhere and both may rebound on the individual's life chances in a literal way. In losing his patrimony a man also risks losing his character. The association of troublemaking with bachelors was briefly indicated in the last chapter. The nature of the judgements involved here may now be discussed further.

BACHELOR WASTRELS

In the case just described, conflict over inheritance leading to physical violence serves to make manifest the characters of the participants. Yet even where no such violence occurs, the presumption of bad character tends to remain with bachelors. A bachelor clearly cannot maintain himself as an independent and self-reliant master of his own affairs and, in so far as he cannot, it is likely to be thought that he is 'spoilt'. Thus the fault is seen to lie in the psychological make-up of the person. His actions are made explicable by evoking the concept of *tsinje*, an inherent quality which manifests itself in acts which are not only self-defeating but make him a danger to those around him. He is thought of as having little concern with orderly ways of behaviour and social relationships; he may indiscriminately seduce other men's wives, commit incest, quarrel, fight or be abusive. Above all, he may take to thieving. His *lirima* is seen to be directed not towards the normal activities of manhood but against himself and ultimately, too, against the community at large. As has been noted, this attitude in turn justifies repudiation by his close kin just as it absolves them of

any moral responsibility for the predicament of the individual. No man is held
at fault for denying resources to a wastrel son.

The idea of 'spoiling' (*xuxwonaka*) here is clearly more than a metaphor and
one that is worth exploring further, for both Gisu fears and the harshness of
their judgements rest largely upon this concept. The things which are spoilt
have been changed in their essential nature in a way that may be for good or
bad. For example, in the ritual context, three events are marked by the
shout that they are spoilt. As the boy pours water on the prepared millet to
make his circumcision beer, the shout goes up, 'You have spoilt it.' When he is
circumcised, again the cry is, 'They have spoilt you', and lastly, when a girl is
deflowered on her wedding night, the expression again is, 'He has spoilt you.'
The linking idea here would seem to be that in order to become fully potent, to
come to maturity, substance must be changed. An original state of integrity
must be destroyed in order to release true generative potential. And, as related
earlier, such potential is seen in terms of a fermentation model. Indeed, the
other word used for spoiling, *xululuxa*, is the passive voice of the verb *xulula*,
used for fermenting beer, which combines the idea of bitterness (*bululu*) with
change and transformation. For things may also be spoilt and ruined, like an
addled egg, and again the verb *xululuxa* is used. People too may be spoilt in this
way, their nature perverted so they take to deviant practices and are unable to
persevere in the proper ways of adulthood.

All those attributed with violent troublemaking tend to be regarded as spoilt
but the idea particularly clings to the feckless. There are a large number of
descriptive terms which are used to describe behaviour here – all of which
hinge on roaming around. For example, *xukubakuba*, 'to wander around
aimlessly', *xubikia*, 'to restlessly wander', *xukendakendatsaka*, 'to walk around all
the time', *xumoyana*, 'to be thriftless and behave in an uncontrolled way'. Such
behaviour defying rational explanation bespeaks *tsinje*, which may be glossed
as inherent deviance. Extending the semantic field here we can also note that
the fermentation idiom provides a linkage also to the idea of confusion. In
order to ferment, substances are mixed up, *butumbafu*, a word which is also
used to apply to ignorance. *Tsinje* carries this overtone; it is manifested in
senseless, foolish and ignorant behaviour.

To be a bachelor is necessarily to be deviant in Gisu terms, a challenge to
what the Gisu regard as not only the ideal but the only state of manhood.
Failure to gain or to keep a wife is often taken as symptomatic that the
individual concerned is spoilt, unable to set his mind to the normal pursuits of
adulthood and likely instead to be a wastrel. The Gisu proverb, 'The thing
which is spoilt goes on spoiling itself', is indeed prophetic when applied to the
fate of many bachelors and underlines the reaction to them. Outside, and
indeed adrift from, the mainstream of society not only are they penalised in the
normal processes of accumulation but every action they take to press their
cause and advance their interests may be interpreted, as has been seen, to their

detriment. It can now be noted, with reference to the homicide survey, that the longer a man remains unmarried the less likely he is ever to marry.

Of the 73% of the men in this survey who were married within eight years of being circumcised, 95% were still married (though not necessarily to the same wife) at the time of the survey. In contrast, of the 27% of men who had not managed to marry within eight years of their circumcision only 46.5% had managed to marry thereafter. This distribution is due not only to the lack of

Table 14 *The effects of wifelessness on eventual marriage chances*

		Percentage married at the time of survey
Percentage of reference group married within eight years of circumcision	73	95
Percentage of reference group not married within eight years of circumcision	27	46.5

For notes on this survey see appendix 1. The men of the reference group included for the purposes of this table were those aged thirty and above, a total of 127.

initial bridewealth but to the reputation that such men gain which then prejudices their chances of ever gaining bridewealth, just as it deters any woman from choosing them for a husband. A woman's grinding song serves notice of the attitude here:

The man who does not dig, look, how he quarrels with you
The man who has no job, look, he eats like an ass
The man with a job, look, he eats only enough.

Indeed, the point can be made that there are no acceptable roles for a wifeless man. Those that are tolerated in the community achieve adaptations to their position which are in themselves deviant but which define them as more or less harmless. This can be illustrated with reference to Maboni.

Case 2: Maboni: the recluse   Busoba
In 1969 Maboni, who was thirty-six, lived in a makeshift shelter of plantain leaves, going out each day to cut down firewood which he sold to buy the maize meal on which he lived. He had constructed for himself a rickety ladder which enabled him to climb into the tallest trees and lop off those branches which the women (who are in any case forbidden to climb trees) would in the normal run of things be unable to reach. Apart from that, he was rarely seen around the neighbourhood for he lived as a recluse, neither visiting nor visited by the fifteen members of his lineage segment near whom he lived. For the most part he stayed around his shelter or wandered off into another neighbourhood when he had enough money to buy beer.

His kinsmen called him by the nick-name Walele, which means literally one who is silent or talks nonsense. This in part was related to Maboni's speech, for his voice was thick and slurred and for the most part hardly intelligible. Yet his kin thought the name equally apt for other reasons; his wild and rugged appearance, dressed in rags with uncombed hair, and his neglect of all personal cleanliness, for he never washed himself or cleaned his shelter. Nor did he care to do any of the normal work of a man, for he made no attempt to cultivate his small plot of land nor did he chase after women. People said that he had never shown any interest in women and was probably impotent.

Maboni was regarded in 1968 as inherently aberrant, but his life history would seem to suggest that his personal characteristics were, at least in part, adaptational responses to the situation in which he found himself. For while his kin maintained that he had from his earliest youth been a wastrel, eschewing work, on closer enquiry they admitted that his speech defect had at one time not been so severe and until fairly recently he had been sociable, drinking with his kinsmen. Indeed when I first met Maboni in 1965, he was occasionally still to be seen at drinking parties in the area.

Maboni's history must be put in the context of the situation in which he and his three brothers found themselves when their father died in 1951, with their mother dying also the year after. The sibling group of four brothers (no sisters) then split up, each going to different relatives. The two elder brothers, Mungoma and Matsitsi, were at that time already circumcised and Mungoma was married. Both stayed on their father's land. The two younger brothers, Wekesa and Maboni, went to live in the house of Samusoni, their father's younger brother. After being circumcised in 1954, Maboni left Samusoni's house to join his father's sister who was married at a small trading centre some seven miles away. There he worked for some time in a shop, returning – or so his kin said – to his natal area only for a brief period each year to avoid paying his taxes. However, in 1963, an accusation of theft forced his return to the area.

While Wandera had left land for his sons, their chances of marrying were remote since they had neither sisters nor cattle. Samusoni claimed that he had always been ready to help Maboni but the boy's own thriftlessness and laziness had deterred him. He said that while Maboni had not been a troublesome youth in other respects, when he was asked to help out with the farming he suddenly became violent and refused. For these reasons he had lost sympathy with his cause. However, the failure of the other two bachelor brothers in this respect would point to more pervasive features in the situation of orphans, forced to rely on the magnanimity of their agnatic kinsmen. Indeed Wekesa, the youngest brother, was hard-working and sober, yet he had had as little success in persuading his relatives to help him. He brought a wife to live with him in 1962 and apart from the one cow he had bought himself, received no offer of animals to make up the requisite number from his kin. His claim to such cattle was weak when set against the claims of the six sons of Samusoni himself and the three sons of Wandera's other full brother. Indeed, cattle were scarce in the family segment as a whole due to the preponderance of young men over girls; in 1968 there were eleven adult members of the junior generation as compared with only four adult women in the entire family segment. The scarcity of bridewealth created a situation where only four of these men had completed their bridewealth payments, with two others (one being Wekesa) having a wife but being unable to complete the payments. The other five were bachelors. The problems here clearly were extreme.

In the case of Maboni, his strange behaviour provided ample justification for the refusal to allocate him cattle, but it becomes interesting to speculate about how far Maboni's own idiosyncracies may have developed as a way of avoiding competition with his brothers and other men of his generation in the lineage segment. Conflicts over property are evidently not confined to inter-generational relationships; men also enter into direct competition with their contemporaries. The history of Maboni's elder brothers, men who did not give up the struggle to establish themselves as householders in the area, gives some idea of the varied nature of such conflicts.

Matsitsi, the second brother, got a reputation early on among his kin as a troublemaker and thief, forever getting into fights and abusing his agnates. In 1958, Matsitsi died suddenly when staying with his mother's brothers in a neighbouring sub-county. The body was returned for burial and showed fresh cuts on the back and marks of a noose around the neck, which was badly swollen. The swelling of a corpse is for the Gisu a sign of witchcraft, but in this case the localised swellings suggested strangulation. His agnates suspected the mother's brothers of utilising their tradi-tional prerogative of killing a profligate sister's son. The standard procedure here is for the mother's brothers to invite the ne'er-do-well to drink beer with them, stationing one man behind the door ready to slip a noose over his head the moment he enters. This certainly was what was believed and no murder case was reported to the police.

Soon after, other misfortunes hit the remaining brothers. In 1960 Mungoma's wife divorced him and in 1962 he became seriously ill, having prolonged fainting fits and behaving as though he were mad. According to accounts, he became a complete nuisance, speaking wildly and making rash accusations. It was commonly believed that Mungoma's illness was caused by the *cisimu* (spirit/shadow) of Matsitsi since his body had been carried back over water and paths without the necessary purification ceremonies. It seems probable that at the time many other avenues of blame were also explored but in 1963 Mungoma sold off some of his land to pay for the ceremony to placate his brother's angry spirit.

During his illness, Mungoma moved to Wekesa's house to be looked after. At that time the two brothers lived next door to Wekesa's age mate and matrilateral relative, Waxoli. In 1963 they quarrelled with Waxoli over a piece of land, they claiming they had bought it from him and Waxoli denying any sale. Since they had no witnesses they were forced to move. They rebuilt their houses together on a portion of their father's land, very near the house of a reputed witch, Masinde, a man unrelated to them. Soon they quarrelled with him too. The source of these quarrels was Mungo-ma's wife's divorce, for she had absconded with the diviner whom Masinde had hired to perform curative rituals for his daughter. Living in proximity was too much for the hatred this had aroused. Every time a chicken or goat wandered across the boundaries between their land, the old enmities returned and accusations that the animals were despoiling the crops were soon transformed into accusations of witchcraft. Wekesa and Mungoma gave up their new houses and moved yet again, this time to a piece of their father's land as distant from the house of Masinde as from that of Waxoli.

Maboni, returning to Busoba in 1963, witnessed first the quarrels with Waxoli and later those with Masinde. When his two brothers moved away from that spot he stayed on, living in one of their houses until it fell about his ears for lack of repair. He then moved across the valley to join them, sleeping in one of their kitchens. Soon the brothers got tired of him, complaining that all he did was to bring jigger fleas into their compound, and expelled him. Mungoma allotted him a small piece of land nearby and told him to go away and live there.

There he lived quietly, if uncomfortably, but he was in that way isolated from the kinds of situations and troubles in which his brothers had become embroiled. He did not quarrel and took refuge in his incomprehensible speech and off-putting appearance. By turning his back on any kind of ambition or normal behaviour he escaped the acrimony arising from his competition with other young men of the lineage segment and vicinage. There were other men of this type too. Some lived with relatives as dependants, some as servants to richer men in the area. Some, it was said, were homosexual, and thus posed no threat to the married men of the area. Many also, like Maboni, did not drink in public. Some said that this was because they were afraid of their own aggressive responses when drunk as much as of arousing animosity in others.

The life style of men such as Maboni seems to revolve around the avoidance of all situations in which they might be regarded as competitors for basic resources, or where they may run the risk of acrimony from their kin and neighbours. Such life styles have fundamental consequences for those concerned, for to be convincing they must be absolute – absolute in their rejection of the basic values associated with manhood and any chance of achieving the resources which could improve their status in the area. Nevertheless, they still run the risk of becoming convenient scapegoats for minor misfortunes and when bunches of plantains went missing it was often Maboni who was suspected. Indeed, in 1968, he was brought up before the local vigilantes on this charge (see p. 238). However, his life was in much less danger than those whose frustrations with their position led them to open violence against those they blamed for their misfortunes.

THE CURSERS

Conflicts over the allocation of property within the family segment do not only generate accusations against the young but also against the senior generation. Whereas the younger generation are feared for their tendency to resort to physical violence and theft, the senior generation are feared for their malevolent use of supernatural power. Moreover, the two types of accusations are directly related for the aberrations of the young are invariably attributed to the work of witches.

The Gisu recognise the importance of both nature and nurture in determining personal qualities. They are fond of pointing to similarities in behaviour or appearance which derive from a person's namesake, though this view is not in any sense deterministic for it is not considered that men necessarily resemble the ancestor after whom they were named. In other cases the influence of family environment is considered paramount. Sons are believed to take after their fathers, and for this reason it is often feared that the sons of a troublesome man will likewise be aggressive. Yet for the types of personal failing which the Gisu regard as evidence that a man is 'spoilt', an explanation is usually sought in witchcraft and especially in cursing. Indeed, cursing holds the key to a wide variety of personal failings which are for the Gisu so intimately linked: infertility, failure to get or keep a wife, lingering illness, indolence, theft and violent behaviour. It strikes at the roots of motivation, destroying through one means or other the ability of a person to succeed in life. Indeed, cursing is believed to 'change a man's heart', and thus his attitude to the world; turning an industrious man into a drunkard, a clever schoolboy into a feckless youth, a married man into a wastrel, unable to persevere any longer in the pursuits of adulthood.

The Gisu believe that there are a great many powers available to the nefarious in their midst. All of these are termed *bulosi* and the user *umulosi*. The term covers a range from the use of certain medicines (varieties of *kamalesi*) to the manipulation of less material powers and to cursing by invoking the ancestral shades. *Bulosi* may be graded according to potency, an important classification since it determines who has access to them. Witchcraft beliefs are to a large extent consistent with the differential ability (*bunyali*) attributed on the basis of sex and age. No child or young adult is believed to have the necessary ability to use witchcraft, and women's powers in this respect, as in others, are inferior to those of men. Women are believed to have neither the power nor the motivation, as given by *lirima*, to utilise the more fatal forms of witchcraft. Irrespective of sex, ability is believed to increase more or less steadily with age, with thirty-five to forty believed to be about the earliest that people may resort to such powers. The more fatal forms of witchcraft are thus the prerogative of men, particularly old men.

In contrast to some other African societies where cursing or 'invoking' the ancestors is seen in at least certain circumstances as the legitimate prerogative of the old, in Bugisu it is regarded as the most heinous use of supernatural power, *bulosi*. Far from supporting the authority of the old, inducing obedience and respect, belief in their supernatural power tends to underline the structural hostility between the generations, with the old seen as ever tempted to abuse their ritual powers and bring destruction to their line, for cursing is believed to bring infertility and death.

Only the senior generation have the ability to curse, *xutsuba*, and, in so doing, are believed to put themselves in league with the dead against the living; they invoke the ghosts of the recently dead, *bamakombe*, to come to their aid and wreak vengeance upon the junior generation. There are, however, many ways of cursing, from the formal situation where an elder invokes over his parents' grave or incants naked over his threshold to merely wishing another harm. This latter form of cursing is difficult to separate from simple abuse. Indeed the boundary between them is vague and the power of abusive words is included in the same category, *citsubo*, although as such it is not tied to specific kinship relationships. Where cursing is imputed among kin, however, the curser's motivations are closely associated with those of the *bamakombe*. The *bamakombe* are regarded as both malevolent and capricious; they do not act to punish those who transgress kinship norms but strike because of slights to their own memory. They attack because they 'want to eat', appearing in dreams to state their demands only after having smitten their descendants with barrenness, enervating illness or death. Their motive is always greed and cursers, too, are considered to be 'greedy', cursing when someone has refused or merely forgotten to give them a present. In fact, beliefs about cursing closely mirror the conflicts among kin over property. The archetypal situation is where the mother's brother or father's sister have been refused their rightful share of the bridewealth of a girl. Cursing fears, however, permeate all senior–junior generational relationships with the exception of that of mother and child, although I did come across one case where a man believed his own mother had cursed him. Fears are not merely concerned with customary gifts, for those who resort to curses are suspected of taking umbrage at the slightest thing, perhaps only that the chicken prepared for them at a feast was too small. Indeed, children are persistently warned of the dangers from cursing and urged to give their last cent to a senior person who asks for it.

Yet it is at the time when a boy stands on the threshold of adult life that such dangers are most acute. Circumcision presents particular dangers for the initiate, for while his success is considered a product of personal bravery, he is susceptible to dangers beyond his control. The beliefs emphasise the boy's dependence on the senior generation on whom he must rely for protection but they also reiterate their potential malevolence. The ambiguity surrounding intergenerational relationships is thrown into relief during this transitional period when the boy is thus poised on the verge of adulthood, asserting his right to equality and to independence, usually in the very compound of his father. Before circumcision the good and bad luck he has experienced are a product of the forces aimed at his parents and their ability to protect him. Thereafter he will be a target for such forces in his own right and responsible for defending his own dependants. What befalls him at the time of his circumcision, however, depends both on his own qualities and on those of the senior generation, particularly the father, who is responsible for his ritual protection.

The unresolved tension in Gisu thought between the importance of the personal qualities of the boy and the power of others becomes a factor in the ritual situation of *imbalu* during the last three days leading up to the operation. Then, the boy's mystically vulnerable state lays him open to the influence of others, whether emanating from other people or from the ancestors. The duality in the locus of control between self and others is echoed in the interpretation given to various ritual actions. For example, one strand in Gisu exegesis puts the stress on the boy identifying himself with circumcision, so that it is said that the yeast gripping his skin shows him the idea of fierceness and what it means to be tough. In an alternative version, the yeast is deemed to be efficacious in itself in strengthening the boy's will (Heald, 1982a). Taking this line of interpretation, the boy is seen as only one agent in a field of interacting forces, each of them powerful, without the boy's conscious identification with them. The rites of the last three days have then a dual aim; to augment his fortitude and to protect him from evil influences.

In sharp contrast to the fears of ill-will translating itself into witchcraft at this time are the situations of positive transference of power. These involve three people alone, all of whom are seen as directly imparting bravery to the youth. Firstly, there is the smearing elder who is always chosen for the bravery he displayed at his own circumcision. Secondly, there is the mother who, while her son is being cut, goes inside her house and, clasping the centre pole, takes up the attitude she used in giving birth. This act of symbolic identification in this context would seem to have less to do with any idea of 'rebirth' of her son than with demonstrating her fortitude, a fortitude she now wishes for her son. Giving birth is seen as an equivalent – if lesser – ordeal. Lastly, there is the boy's sister, who is smeared with him and is now addressed as his 'wife', for it is her bridewealth that he will use to marry. During the last three days she accompanies her brother and submits to the same smearings, adopting also the mien of fortitude. Yet if a man's allies in the struggle of life are given such recognition in the rituals, so too are his opponents: the men of the senior generation.

A boy must obtain the permission of all his close relatives before he undergoes circumcision, both to forestall their curses, since reparation can be made if there is ill-will in the family, and so they may sacrifice to their ancestors. The mother's brother and father's sister in particular must make such sacrifices and cleanse the graves of the recently dead. Nevertheless the onus is upon the father to prepare the way for his son's circumcision. He should settle debts with his kinsmen so they are not tempted to curse the boy in retaliation, choose a trusted man to act as the boy's guardian throughout the ritual period and provide his age mates with gifts. Yet this very protective role gives access to the forces for destruction. At the time of circumcision itself the main fears are of cursing from the father's age mates and witchcraft from the boy's ritual guardian. Age mates have the power to curse one of their number's sons if they have been refused the customary gift. In the past a man was expected to slaughter a cow for his age mates but the practice came into such disrepute, inciting so many threats of cursing and violence that in 1954 the local government passed a by-law forbidding it (La Fontaine, 1959:42). The slaughtering has now been replaced by gifts of money. The ritual guardian in many cases is the boy's father himself, although another senior relative may be chosen. The guardian is responsible for protecting the compound from witchcraft, sacrificing to the ancestors, choosing a circumcisor and ensuring the correct performance of the cleansing rites. It is mandatory that he be an old and trusted man for he has complete power over the boy's safety and sole access to the boy's foreskin – the most potent of witchcraft substances – which he is responsible for safely burying.

Any of these varied means of attack may destroy the boy's chances of success in later life. When, after circumcision, a man fails to marry, his children die, he himself becomes weak and ill, or takes to wandering or even theft, then it is frequently in the maleficent powers of those who claimed to be protecting him at the time of his circumcision that both he and others will seek the cause of his misfortune. This does not exonerate individual failings but it does mean that accusations emanate from such men just as accusations of a different type are aimed at them.

It is difficult to assess the frequency of accusations against specific relatives. In my experience, the curses of the mother's brother and the father's sister were fairly frequently evoked to explain misfortunes, and the fact that the requisite cattle are rarely paid immediately after the marriage of a daughter, payment perhaps being delayed for many years until all the sons have married, makes them likely culprits in many cases. However such curses rarely appear to lead to murder. There was one case in the court records where a man killed his father's sister whom he found actually invoking on her father's grave, and another I heard of in Central Bugisu where two young boys were suspected of having a hand in the murder of their mother's brother, whose curses they believed were responsible for their inability to find wives. Rather than such violent action being taken against such cursers (killing is of itself believed to neutralise the curse), they are usually appeased. After the opinion of three independent diviners, *bafumu*, has confirmed the identity of the curser, a gift is made to him. Thus placated, he is expected formally to withdraw his curse by blowing beer over his victim. It is pertinent to mention here that no direct confession is necessary, for the accused can interpret the act of beer-blowing innocently since it has significance in many different ritual situations.

As against this, the murder of cursers (or witches of other kinds) is fairly frequent within the lineage. In fact, of the court cases, one of the eight fathers killed was accused of witchcraft by his son as was the case in nine of the twenty cases where a father's real brother was killed. Here the motive is not necessarily related to a specific issue where a member of the senior generation has been refused a rightful gift, but to the more intangible situations where a man feels that his chances of achieving a successful adult life are hindered not only by the meanness of a member of the senior generation but by their attempts to subvert the course of his life through supernatural means as well.

Case 3: Mutsonga: the notorious curser   Busoba
Homicide survey 1[1]
One night in October 1965 a group of men broke into Mutsonga's house while his wife was staying at her parents, and badly wounded him by slashing his arms and legs. This attack was greeted with much excitement in the area, for Mutsonga was a notorious curser. Indeed there was some speculation as to why the attackers had only wounded him, and one story had it that in the dark the attackers had mistaken his legs for his head. His eldest son, Deo, was suspected of being behind the attack, probably with the help of hired assassins, and symptomatic of the general approbation, was the fact that the attack was never reported to the police. Even the parish chief who lived barely half a mile away turned a blind eye. Mutsonga's misdeeds

were indeed household knowledge, everyone repeating that he wilfully bewitched his kin so that their children died or young men became mad or impotent. However, for the most part, I was unable to obtain much information about these cases and it began to appear that his reputation stemmed largely from his poor relationship with his eldest son, Deo.

In 1965 Mutsonga was a hale man in his late fifties or early sixties and lived with his wife and three sons, Deo, the eldest, being about thirty. Mutsonga himself, although far from rich, had by saving and working three days a week at a local butcher's shop managed to educate all his three sons. Deo had completed junior secondary school and spent one year in senior secondary, the second son was at a teachers' training college and the third still at a primary school.

The quarrels between father and son dated from 1961 when Deo abruptly left school in defiance of his father's wishes. Leaving school in this way is often a sign of youthful rebellion, indicating a desire to be initiated and to marry. It would seem especially likely that these were the major factors in Deo's case, given the fact that he was already in his mid-twenties. Indeed, in the same year as leaving school he brought two women to live with him and was circumcised the year after. However, at this point, Mutsonga refused to provide him with either land or bridewealth, a position which he justified on the grounds that the money spent on education constituted an alternative patrimony. This indeed is a growing sentiment among the educated elite who expect their sons to get well-paid work and thus provide for their own bridewealth and land. Customary obligations, however, cannot always be set aside so easily. Locally, the majority of people felt Mutsonga to be in the wrong despite the fact that he had very little land and what money he had went on the education of the two younger sons.

Perhaps if Deo had proved more successful the relationship between the two would not have deteriorated so quickly. As it was, Mutsonga's stand was reinforced both by Deo's growing hostility towards him and as what he interpreted as Deo's own improvident behaviour. Bringing two women home at one time was indeed presumptuous on the part of a young man, especially one not yet circumcised and with no bridewealth. Inevitably – as the Gisu see it – both women left him, the first in 1963 and the second in 1965. With the desertion of the first woman, Deo became embroiled in further dispute, not about bridewealth payments but because he refused liability for the 'feeding' of his two young children living with their mother's parents. Soon after the second woman left Deo himself was taken seriously ill, and spent a month in hospital and several months recuperating in the village from intermittent fever. At this point, because he was unable to work, he also lost his well-paid job as a carpenter at a local school.

Such a series of misfortunes is indicative of cursing and, since his illness had followed a quarrel where he had refused his father money, this was taken as the final proof that it was his father who was cursing him. Much else of Deo's behaviour could also be interpreted in the same light, including his abrupt refusal to continue at school and his behaviour towards his two young wives. Not only had he not saved his money towards bridewealth but he had neglected his wives, spending his money on beer and not on household items to keep them happy. Moreover, both his brothers and father maintained that he frequently beat them when he was drunk. Such self-defeating behaviour is, as previously described, pre-eminently a sign for the Gisu that a man has been cursed.

Although Deo recovered from his illness following the attack on the father (a sign that the curser's power had been broken), the problems remained unsolved. For Mutsonga also recovered, and he and his son continued as before to occupy contiguous houses barely twenty yards from each other. For three years after this they lived together quietly. In the meantime Deo took to poorly-paid itinerant work and found no other woman to come and keep house for him. Also he complained frequently that his strength was leaving him and he was thus unable to work. This complaint obviously irked Mutsonga, perhaps as it suggested that Deo was still under the influence of his curses. However, it appeared he was also angered by the fact that he was still supporting Deo. Early in 1969 violent quarrels blew up again between them and a report of one such quarrel circulated quickly through the area.

> One night Deo returned home late at night from drinking beer and asked his mother for food. Mutsonga appeared at that moment and, angered by his son's demands, taunted Deo, 'Perhaps I should marry you together with your mother, both of you will then be my wives. You are just like a big woman and will never marry a wife for you are a woman yourself!' Both men went for their spears and knives but the younger sons prevented them from fighting, though it was said that neither slept that night for fear of the other.
>
> Barely a month later another quarrel occurred. After this incident Mutsonga was arrested and kept for a week in the sub-county gaol. Since his wife brought him no food he went without. On his release he called at my home, to the consternation of my neighbours, whose fear showed in the ripples of nervous laughter we could hear from inside. In his account to me, Mutsonga claimed that he and his wife had started to quarrel over a cigarette which she had just begged from Deo. His wife, in a temper, shouted at him, 'Those who attacked you only half did the job, they only played with you!' Infuriated, he had given her a shove and unfortunately she fell on a metal bedstead which had been placed in the courtyard, thus cutting her arm. An elder present during this recital broke in derisively to let Mutsonga know that no one else believed this unlikely tale, and all believed Deo's version (supported by the wife) that he had slashed his wife's arm with a panga. In any event it was Deo who had that night run to fetch the vigilantes who were at that time operating in the area and it was they who had arrested Mutsonga and taken him to the sub-county gaol. Mutsonga did not return home after this, preferring to take refuge with his father's sister's grandchild in a neighbouring area.

Cursing with its power to destroy a man's heart and motivation provides a plausible explanation for the fate of many unfortunate young men, even if it does not in turn exonerate them. By 1969 Deo was as ill-liked as his father, although for different reasons. And here one might enquire further into the question of plausibility. In Mutsonga's case one may adduce several factors. In the first place he already had a reputation for violence. He had killed a thief in 1961 and while this act was considered justified – he received a nominal sentence of one day – violence of any kind is often in speech likened to witchcraft, being termed *bulosi*, both being emanations of the same emotion, *lirima*. Violence and witchcraft are straight alternatives. Added to this, he was also renowned for his knowledge of ritual matters (see further, case 11). Given this background, cursing his son in anger could indeed be seen as an understandable response. Nor at first, while he still had a well-paid job and a woman to keep house for him, did Deo's reputation suffer to the extent that he was defined as a 'danger' to others. Only when Deo lost his wives and then his job did people begin to comment unfavourably on his drunkenness.

Cursing for the Gisu is always a motivated act. Yet not all witchcraft is of this type, and where it is seen as motiveless it can be equally damaging to the reputation of the person accused.

WITCHES AND WITCHCRAFT

The Gisu have an elaborate aetiology of disease and each category of *bulosi* is related to specific symptoms. The three most fatal forms of witchcraft are *kumusala*, *iyatso* and *kamarolo*, all of which are believed capable of killing adults. All three take many forms but are material substances collected by the witch. *Kumusala* (literally, 'fatal medicine') may be used to trap a known enemy or may have the power to search out unknown enemies, perhaps a thief by placing it in the spot from which he has stolen. Most typically, *kumusala* is placed in the food or drink of the victim or buried to 'catch' him as he steps over it. The diagnostic mark of *kumusala* is sudden death, though *iyatso* too may have a similar effect. More usually, however, *iyatso* is invoked as the cause of illnesses which weaken the victim's constitution and send him slowly and painfully to the grave. *Iyatso* involves the making of medicines from the tendons of snakes, each species said to produce different effects. For example, the tendons of a puff-adder are believed to make the victim waste away, making him a complete liability to his kin who will openly wish him dead; that from another species will make him go mad, and so on. *Iyatso* is sometimes said to be combined with *kamarolo* where the bodily waste matter of the victim – nail-parings, shaved hair, excrement, half-eaten food or indeed any substance with which he has been in contact, including the earth from his footsteps – is collected together and tied into a ball to be hidden in the house, usually the thatch. As it rots so will the victim sicken and die, mirroring stage by stage the putrefaction in the *kamarolo*.

Access to different forms of witchcraft depends on relative power, which is sex-linked and motivation, which is not. All the types of witchcraft so far mentioned are regarded as predominantly male powers since only men have the necessary *bunyali*, though women are often suspected of attempting *kamarolo* since they have easy access to the necessary materials. However, in cases of serious illness women tend to be cited only as the accomplices of male witches and not as the principals themselves. Women's witchcraft from the point of view of potency is of a more minor order and is associated with *kumukamba* and *ifumu*. The first is believed to cause the acute stomach upsets common in children and adults alike, the difference being that in children they frequently prove fatal. This is the sphere of the *umumomoli*, the 'drawer-out', who extracts the noxious substances causing the problem directly from the stomach. Divination to establish the identity of the witch is rarely held to be necessary in such cases, and the same is true of the other typical form of women's witchcraft, *ifumu*. This is achieved simply by the witch blinking at her victim, usually a child, and the symptoms here suggest scabies or nutritional disorders. Accusations against women are thus in a sense less serious since they do not necessarily impute murder and further divination, with the intention of placating or countering the witch, is rarely held to be important towards achieving a cure. But the relative fatality of witchcraft forms is only one dimension. Rarely, for example, is women's witchcraft held to be justifiable and seen as just revenge. Indeed, in contrast to male witchcraft, it is perceived of as of a different ilk, both more pervasive in everyday terms and more accessible to those women with the necessary powers. Indeed, women witches tend to become known as people with *liloko*.

The Gisu have two category words for witchcraft: *bulosi* and *liloko*. Both are general enough to be used as synonyms but they carry different implications. *Bulosi* connotes aggression, to the extent that any act of violent hostility may be termed *bulosi*. *Liloko*, on the other hand, implies 'oddness', so that various forms of deviant peculiarity are held to imply *liloko*, from incest and cannibalism to more minor forms of aberrant and shocking behaviour. Since many acts of witchcraft are seen to involve both aggression and oddness, they may be referred to, alternatively, as *bulosi* or *liloko*. Nevertheless, the words distinguish two different tendencies or motivations which may be inherent in the resort to witchcraft, and certain forms of witchcraft are more indicative of one than of the other. Sorcery techniques such as *kumusala* and *iyatso* are conscious, motivated acts of revenge, usually seen as arising out of specific quarrels and aimed at specific enemies. The word *bulosi* is usually used of such acts, as it is of cursing, the most heinous use of witchcraft. The symbolic form such acts take is also indicative of conscious inversion. For example, cursing does not only violate accepted norms but explicitly turns them on their head. Cursers set out to destroy kinship values; they invoke the malevolence of the ghosts to bring destruction on their kin and their progeny. The man who killed his father's sister whom he found invoking on her father's grave reported that she cursed him as follows:

Let that child not get a wife
but if he gets a wife let him not get a child
and if he gets a child let that child die
let his wife never see the birth of children
and afterwards, let him be like his father,
alone, living like a wild animal in the bush
and last, let him die like his father, without anything.

Frequently, too, the linguistic form used in cursing is that of a counter factual, for example, as a man might curse his brother's son, 'If I am not the one who followed Samusoni, let his child stand *imbalu* well.' Action in the curse may also be inverted. A typical way of cursing is for the curser to remove his clothes and wrap them in a bundle and place these on the threshold. The curser then hops backwards over them, from inside to out and outside to in, invoking as he does so. The curser thus is explicitly disregarding convention and adopting the forbidden violating behaviour of *bumasala* (avoidance) to serve his ends.

Liloko carries a different symbolic load. Whereas the motive behind *bulosi* is usually detailed as anger, greed, envy or revenge, the imputation of *liloko* places such witches in a different motivational category; their use of witchcraft is more a product of their inherent disposition, a disposition which is seen as perverted. In part such an appellation is a matter of degree, for some people take umbrage more easily than others. But, in its ultimate form, it implies that their actions are not susceptible to rational interpretation. In terms of the normal range of emotions people feel they are 'motiveless'. They violate for the sake of violating; they harm others simply because they are witches. Unlike the cursers, who put themselves in league with the ghosts of the dead, those with *liloko* are believed to enter into a compact with the spirits of the unincorporated dead – with the *were*, the spirits of the childless, the hunchbacked and the crippled, whose life forces are not inherited but which are doomed to haunt the bush and whose manifestations spell death to any who inadvertently sees them.

Liloko, then, denotes inherent and deviant peculiarity rather than conscious inversion. Someone 'with *liloko*' is not so much transgressing the rules but has gone so far along the path that his actions are indiscriminate: all is confusion. They operate outside the normal schemas of society, both in action and in motivational terms. My first recognition of this fact came when a local woman, in bringing a witchcraft accusation against her husband's father's brother's wife, described how this woman had attempted to initiate her into witchcraft when she had first married in the area, some fifteen years previously. Her husband at that time was in jail and this mother-in-law had befriended her. Seeing her poverty, the mother-in-law had firstly suggested that the woman save all her head-shavings and give them to her. When she had enough they would take them to an Indian to sell and in that way get money to buy a cloth. Then the mother-in-law had enlisted her support in brewing millet beer, but insisted that she grind the millet naked. Then when she went to fetch the water she was instructed to go with her left eye closed, hopping on one leg. The mother-in-law then brewed the beer in a hole in the ground covered with banana stems as if it were banana beer. Finally, when it was ready, they drank the beer alone, turning away people who called. Meanwhile, the mother-in-law had also enlisted her support in more direct acts of witchcraft, giving her a *kamarolo* bundle which she instructed her to bring out after her real mother-in-law had visited her and, as the sun was setting, turn it in the direction the mother-in-law had taken when returning home. On another occasion she asked her to cut pieces of material out of the clothes of the mother-in-law and father-in-law, from the armpits of the mother-in-law's dress and from the crotch of the father-in-law's shorts.

These actions are all shocking, in a deep way, since they transgress the framework of social rules whose unquestioned acceptance ensures the possibility of orderly social interaction. Yet while some of these actions incite strong feelings of abomination, not all do; they are just odd and out of line; essentially unmotivated actions. This is true also of the enmities involved since no rationale for the hatreds of the suspected witch was ever given. She was a witch and therefore she hated.

Liloko thus implies odd, subversive, unmotivated and even indiscriminate action. In so far as witches represent inversions of human moral actions, the Gisu beliefs give notice of two possibilities. Firstly, there is the self-conscious negation of clear-cut values as in cursing or retaliatory sorcery. Secondly, there is the indiscriminate subversion of those with *liloko* whose behaviour is subversive not to any particular rules but to the idea of rules. The Gisu do not believe that witches with *liloko* are in general anthropophagous nor that they necessarily commit incest. But such behaviour is only thought possible of a witch; perverted natures have perverted outcomes. *Liloko* as an idea thus tends to shade into the idea of madness, *bukwatsole*, and stupidity. But whereas the mad and the foolish are confused without knowing it, those with *liloko* revel in their peculiarity. They delight in startling others and in shocking the sensibilities of their fellows. Yet although this possibility is defined, and thus by implication limited by identifying such action as witchcraft, at the same time it is seen as ubiquitous, with such deviation seen as an immanent possibility for all; suggested in every misfortune, in every feeling of anger.

THE NIGHT DANCERS

In men, *liloko* takes a typical form, manifesting itself as *bubini* or night-dancing. This is a unique category of male witchcraft in several ways. The night dancer (*umubini*) is not believed to deal in medicines, but harms others simply by the act of dancing. These men, who are always old, are believed to take off their clothes and together with their familiars, owls and wild cats which make the sinister noises so typical of the night, go out to dance around their neighbours' houses. They also have their own song, a song which every child can repeat, giggling as he does so.

I am a night dancer, night dancer
Do I mend it, do I spoil it?
aa   aa   aa.

The very words of this song suggest the ambivalent attitude to this category of witch. On the one hand it is believed that these night dancers only wish to frighten others and the complaints they cause are never of a very serious nature. Indeed during the daylight hours the idea of such witches holds little terror. An adult man will scoff at them, inviting the night dancers to come and dance outside his home, for at least they will frighten away the thieves and all he will have in the morning are aching joints or perhaps a slight fever. When two friends bend down to kindle the embers of a fire at the same time, they may joke: 'We have met together, may you meet the thief and I the witch.' The meaning here is that whereas the thief will in all likelihood kill you, the night dancer will run away. Night dancers are easily dealt with. Whereas, in order to prevent the actions of other witches proving fatal, ritual specialists must be consulted to combat the witch and remove the evil power, the night dancers can be dealt with by the individual. A good beating is considered sufficient to deter them. Yet just as the night dancers are the only really fantastic figures in Gisu witchcraft mythology, so too are their punishments. First one must catch the night dancer. This is fairly easy, for they dance with their buttocks bumping against the door. All that is necessary is to quietly undo the hinges and, hey presto, in he falls. Then the night dancer may be speared up the anus (or down the throat) with a young banana leaf shoot; he will then go away and quietly die. Night dancers are believed never to admit their actions nor their punishment for fear that all their children will die. When old men die it is often rumoured that they have been killed in this way.

Indeed, there is a sense in which all old men carry the presumption of *bubini* in much the same way as bachelors do of theft. The old are definitionally powerful, but this power is not that of active manhood, which slips away through their disposal of their resources as well as by infirmity or illness, reducing them once more to a state of dependence. The old gain little respect as elders; their power, their *bunyali*, lies in their control of knowledge, *kamaxura*, a knowledge which implies witchcraft. Housed and fed on sufferance, their every complaint is seen to carry a threat. It is in terms of this pervasive fear that the attitudes to night dancers have their place. Despite the apparent ease of ritual murder, the sentiment that night dancers should be killed outright is uppermost. The following case study indicates the salient characteristics of one night dancer and the different contexts of and motivations attributed to various forms of witchcraft.

Case 4: The man who lived too long   Busoba
Nalukumu's imminent return to Busoba in 1966 was discussed by his kindred with great dread. Nalukumu was said to have *liloko* which led him to attack his kin by cursing or night dancing. His relatives maintained that such a tendency had been noticeable at even an early age. As a youth Nalukumu had behaved strangely, delighting in startling his friends by springing out at them while they quietly herded their cattle, or even urinating in front of them. As it was, few who had known him as a youth remained alive for in 1966 Nalukumu was at least eighty (having been circumcised in 1905), and was the last of his generation.

About forty adult men of Nalukumu's lineage segment lived near one another in Busoba. Nalukumu himself had, however, only one child, Masaba, who was estranged from him and lived near Mbale where he worked. When Nalukumu returned, the only shelter that was offered to him was the disused kitchen of a classificatory great-grandchild. He presented a bedraggled picture, dressed in what had once been a policeman's khaki uniform, now worn and tattered and, since he had no wife and was himself too feeble to cultivate, he relied completely on the generosity of his kin for food. Yet he seemed harmless enough and, in a sense, this was supported by his kin since they agreed that he never quarrelled with anyone. Nevertheless, his life had been plagued with accusations.

With one exception these accusations had been of cursing and night dancing. However, in 1952, he had been suspected of *iyatso* and this, unlike all the other accusations, arose following a specific quarrel. Two years prior to this he had fought over a land boundary with a classificatory grandchild who had kicked him severely in the kidneys. Soon afterwards the grandchild Lazalo began to sicken and when no medicine, either European or simplistic, could halt the steady wasting of his body, diviners were consulted. Lazalo's father called Nalukumu to a feast, slaughtered a goat and demanded that Nalukumu should withdraw his witchcraft on pain of death. Nalukumu acquiesced, smeared Lazalo with the chyme and blew beer over him. Lazalo recovered after this, but Nalukumu was forced to migrate because of his kin's hostility. This was the first time he was forced to flee, yet accusations against him went back to 1945, and followed him throughout the fifties and early sixties. The suspicions that he was responsible for illness among children were so pervasive that women of his kindred hurried back from Kenya or Buganda when their children sickened so they could seek Nalukumu out and placate him with presents. Yet the particular reason given for his kin's hatred was the ill-luck which befell all the youths who were circumcised on his compound. In all, four boys had been circumcised under his protection as senior man between 1952 and 1962 and, in contrast to the men of this age group circumcised under their own father's protection, all had found difficulty finding or keeping wives and three still had no children by 1965.

During much of this time he could be said to be someone with no fixed abode, wandering from place to place, but to the despair of his kindred he kept returning to Busoba. Each time further accusations forced him away again. In 1965, he stayed a little under a year with his kinsmen. During this time accusations mounted steadily. People reported that they had seen him night dancing and finally, Wasikye, a neighbour whose mother had married into the lineage segment, reported that he had seen pots of *kamaloko* (witchcraft substance)[2] in Nalukumu's shelter. Members of the lineage met that night and burnt the kitchen down; the *kamaloko* was said to have crowed like a cockerel. Nalukumu himself escaped, fleeing to his granddaughter who lived in another sub-county. Six months later he died.

Nalukumu, in spite of (and because of) his longevity, had by any standards been unlucky. By 1920, twelve children had been born to him by his first wife but she died in that year and all but one of the children had followed her, dying before 1940. Since his wife's death his liaisons with women had been of a temporary nature and none had produced children. When his son, Masaba migrated away from Busoba in 1945, Nalukumu had been reduced to poverty, selling off plot after plot of his land to keep himself alive. He sold his last plot soon after his return to Busoba in 1965. Nalukumu had thus reached the height of his career in the 1920s and then, as a relatively young man with a flourishing family, had been chosen as a circumcision guardian for the first time. Since then his fortunes declined steadily and he was not asked to act as circumcision guardian again until 1952 when all the other senior men were dead.

The fate of Nalukumu is not untypical. Old people are notorious for their grumblings; the meanness of their children, the grandchildren who never bring them water and even the lack of salt to make life bearable. All such complaints are seen to carry a threat of witchcraft, just as they also point to the actual neglect which the old suffer. The old and senile are housed and fed only under sufferance, and where they have no real children whose moral obligation to care for them is greater, their fate often resembles that of Nalukumu.

CONCLUSION

Of all the varieties of human evil the idea of witchcraft has posed the clearest problems of interpretation for a rationalistic Western anthropology, unable to believe the reality it portrays. Seen as an imaginative construct, its symbolic role as a refraction of the social order has been most widely developed in interpretation. Thus the beliefs have been seen to dramatise evil and in so doing to reiterate the righteousness of conventional morality. Or they have been seen to mirror conflicts, thus allowing for the expression of otherwise hidden tensions. Yet where witch beliefs are a dominant form of explicatory idiom, they appear as anything but 'mere ideas' and give a frighteningly tangible dimension to human hostilities and fears. Their clearest message is that people are dangerous to each other and the pervasive misfortunes of everyday life keep that message in constant view.

The Gisu tend to talk about witches as if they were different from ordinary people. The implications of the cosmology point, however, in another direction. Everyone has some power and power gives access to witchcraft. Further, all are susceptible to the temptation. The beliefs then seem to reiterate the fact that the possibility of evil is in all. Lienhardt has written that among the Dinka 'the night witch is an outlaw because he embodies those appetites and passions in every man which, if ungoverned, would destroy any moral law' (1951:318). Among the Gisu witchcraft is an acquired skill but it is not so much one one has to search after but one that one must refrain from acquiring. The same goes for theft. The emphasis is thrown on self-control. Responsible social life requires explicit self-ruling, discipline and control. As the circumcisor instructs the initiand to refrain from the temptations of violence, so the old must restrain themselves from the temptation of witchcraft. But the reality, linked as it is to a particular theory of motivation, seems to be that they cannot.

The insecurity that comes from the fear of others is manifested in many ways in Gisu life. For example, 'good' and 'bad' are possibly the most frequent words in use as the acceptability and non-acceptability of actions and events is constantly being monitored. One needs to know whether it is a 'good' time to go and pay a debt; whether it would be 'good', or at least 'not bad' to offer a certain kind of present to a friend; whether the people one intends to visit are 'good' and thus safe. Indeed *bulayi*, 'goodness', covers a range of connotative significance from moral righteousness and straight dealing, to cleanliness, beauty and safety. 'Badness', on the other hand, always implies danger. Moral discourse of this kind is about practical action and predominantly it is about practical action which hinges on the nature of people. As has been discussed, there is a transparent quality to character. On the one hand it is evident in a person's actions and transgressions which speak of his attitude to others. As one man explained when identifying the person whom he believed was bewitching him, 'Even when you have quarrelled with many people when you get ill it is the person who does not visit you that you suspect. For not all who quarrel with you bear you hatred: it is the one who avoids you who hates.' Yet, despite the situational nature of such suspicion, witchcraft allegations only tend to stick when the objective conditions identified in the life situation of a person make the accusation plausible. It is from this that a person's ultimate disposition and motivations can be deduced. Indeed, the linking of festering resentment to poverty is so strong that it is probably impossible in Bugisu for a rich person to be considered a witch or a thief. The essential motivations are seen simply as lacking.

To summarise the arguments of this chapter, the value the Gisu place on male independence and the definition of this in terms of control of a household, together with a system of early partible inheritance, create a distinctive pattern of intergenerational tension and of vulnerability to accusation. This tension is transfigured in beliefs about witchcraft and theft, poverty and character and leads, as has been seen, to a series of cross-allegations, with seniors accusing juniors of theft and juniors accusing seniors of witchcraft. La Fontaine has written that in Bugisu, 'inegalities are the more glaring for the ideal of equality' (1963:216). Yet, it is not inequality in itself which I see as at issue but the insistence on a specific model of manhood, an irreducible basis, which requires material independence. A man definitionally possesses the capability for *lirima* which, as a legitimate mode of self-assertion, can only be exercised by an autonomous man who, in defending his own rights, has no reason to envy others. Where this ceases to be the case the individual may sharply lose social credibility; his motivation becomes suspect and his powers feared. Those at the two ends of the adult life cycle, the young and the old, are particularly vulnerable here but it also places any who in the course of life meet with ill-luck or disease in a situation where all is risked.

As Radcliffe-Brown (1940b) pointed out the crime at issue is not the commission of a single offence but that of being a 'bad lot', as he termed it. In this chapter the more important concepts – *lirima*, *tsinje*, *liloko* – which inform and comprise such evaluation of character have been indicated. What is significant is that they are seen as dispositional attributes which, as such, are seen as inherent, unalterable and therefore irremedial. Reform in such cases then ceases to be a possibility. It is not that killing is justified because the offence in itself is great, but it is justified because the individual is regarded as a degenerate who has turned his back on normality and for whom there is no other remedy. It is only in such terms that killing over the theft of a bunch of bananas or a single root of cassava becomes as likely as killing over the theft of cattle. *Tsinje* is a critical idea here and it is used in contexts that oppose it to respect and order, *lukoosi*, the mode of harmonious and proper living as a member of a community.

The development cycle in groups or villages, as Victor Turner (1964) argued, is only one form of process that may be relevant to the understanding of witchcraft accusation. This chapter has sought to relate the accusational process not to community or wider kinship structures but rather to the family and life course. Nor, I argue, are these wider processes relevant to the understanding of the direction of accusations in themselves. Where the structuring of kinship and community becomes relevant is in an understanding of the sheer speed of the process whereby an individual may lose social credibility and be killed as a consequence. Part 3 of this book now takes up that theme, setting it in the context of a discussion of the lack of segmentary loyalties in the Gisu lineage system.

NOTES

1   These numbers refer to the listing of cases given in Appendix 1.

2   *Liloko* has the following cognates: *kamaloko*, 'witchcraft substances'; *xuloko*, 'to bewitch'; *buloki*, 'acts of witchcraft'.

PART 3
Kinship, community and cosmology

6

THE AGNATIC CHARTER

The Gisu sometimes suggest that 'if they are angry' the relatives of the dead may take revenge on the killers. Revenge (*xuxwiliasa*) thus emerges as a possibility but not as an obligation. And, in fact, in only seven of the 375 court cases enumerated did the record reveal any suggestion of a connection between the case and a previous killing. This figure does not include cases where witches were killed, although some of these witches were believed to have used their powers to kill. However, it does include one case where a man avenged his son whom he believed had died of poison after drinking beer with his classificatory brother. Three of the seven retaliatory killings were committed in hot blood, at the same time or on the same day as the original murder. The other four occurred at varying times afterwards. In all cases it was an immediate member of the victim's patrifamily, his brother, father or son, who took vengeance on the murderer who was in three of these cases also a relative.

Thus what emerges from the record is an extremely low rate of vengeance murder. Before proceeding it is necessary to ask if the court-case record is likely to be reliable on this issue. Some sources of possible bias suggest themselves. For example, except in cases of immediate retaliatory action, many years might elapse between an original murder and any sequel. In such circumstances the previous killing might no longer be considered relevant by either the court or the witnesses as other disputes have occurred in the interim. Alternatively, the witnesses may be reluctant to mention it and thus perhaps prejudice the case against the accused. This appears to have happened in the clearest case of revenge murder that I came across and one which, for reasons that will become clear, is not included in the seven cases of vengeance murder tabulated from the court records.

Case 5: Revenge   Busiu, 1960
homicide survey 11

At 3.00 a.m. one morning Katenya, a man in his early thirties, and his wife awoke to find their house ablaze. Both got out and while his wife rescued the children and raised the alarm Katenya gave chase to the incendiary. A little later he was found seriously bleeding from a spear wound in a nearby cassava plantation. He was taken to the hospital in Mbale some ten miles away and in a dying statement made to the police indicted Napokoli, a neighbour who lived some 400 yards from him. Some three months prior to this event, Napokoli's house had been burnt down and he had filed a charge against Katenya. However, Katenya was acquitted the week before the incident which led to his death.

I have compiled this brief synopsis from the statements made to the police by Katenya and by neighbours immediately after the attack. A few months later, however, when the case came up before the Magistrate (and even later at the trial itself), only Katenya's wife continued to give evidence which implicated Napokoli. The other witnesses called denied knowledge of their being any further grievance between the two men after the case of arson had been settled. Napokoli was acquitted on the grounds that the only evidence against him was Katenya's statement, which the presiding judge ruled as suspect because of Katenya's motive for indicting Napokoli.

A rather different account was given to me when I asked about this murder some seven years later in 1967. I was told of a long history of grievance between the families of the two men which went back to the murder in 1940 of a woman from Katenya's lineage. This woman was killed by her husband – the father of Napokoli – when, it was said, she wanted a divorce and her death was avenged by one of her brothers. A state of hatred, *cixonde*, had existed between the two families since these murders, and these feelings had not lessened when members of both families – including Katenya and Napokoli – migrated down from their mountain homeland to the plains area of Busiu, where again they took up residence in close proximity. The arson and later murder of 1960 were thus put in context as the most recent manifestation of hatred.

This case history initially raises the question of how far court procedures are seen as an alternative to direct vengeance; to be taken only when the court processes fail to convict. For example, this case could be seen as a record of judicial 'failure', at least as far as some participants are concerned, as it reveals four situations where the courts failed to convict a suspect. In both of the original murders of 1940 the suspects were said to have been arrested initially but later released. The arson case of 1960 again produced an acquittal as did the homicide case which followed against Napokoli. However, while judicial failures prompting self-help must be considered a factor in a situation of fear, the low rate of prosecutions and convictions would seem to belie that vengeance is being systematically pursued through the courts. If this had been so one would expect a rather more consistent pattern with people ready, willing and even eager to stand up in courts to indict their enemies. This is precisely what we do not find. Katenya's relatives, although initially ready to give evidence against Napokoli, seemed to think better of their actions once he was arrested and – with the notable exception of his wife – withdrew any such testimony at the formal judicial hearings. The question is why, why this apparently accommodating attitude to murder?

Such a question arises from the perspective of what might be called classic lineage theory as it was developed specifically for Africa following Evans-Pritchard's work on the Nuer (1940). Vengeance is the essence of the system. In broad outline, the theory goes that lineage groups exist in a dynamic tension, internally divided yet externally solid. Such solidarity is most apparent – and indeed often only apparent – in vengeance and feuding situations where the group temporarily rises above its own internal dissensions to mobilise against another group. Further, the dominant perspective for understanding reactions to homicide has come from those segmentary societies where the overriding emphasis is on 'balance' between the two groups concerned and *lex talionis* is the overriding principle. A man's loss must be made good, either by vengeance or by compensation; it being possible, at least in principle, to reckon a man's worth in cattle or the equivalent. However, it is recognised that it is only in a very few societies that this principle reaches its full expression and the 'true feud', in the sense of perpetual hostility between families and lineages is allowed to run full rein (Peters, 1967; Black–Michaud, 1975). Feuding, it is here argued, represents a type of social structure, an outcome of (often ecological) competition between mutually discrete interest groups.

Elsewhere, even where lineages are well-defined in Africa, the desire for vengeance has been seen as tempered to a greater or lesser extent by the desire to avoid a general escalation of disputes within the community, by the desire that is to keep a more general 'peace'. Interest groups are less clear-cut and 'balance' between lineages or descent groups here becomes a less appropriate concept with which to understand the actual processes of warfare and peace-making. One of the best known examples here is Elizabeth Colson's analysis of the Plateau Tonga where the obligation to pursue vengeance on behalf of an unilineal kinsman is set against the equally imperative necessity to maintain relationships with non-unilineal kin and neighbours. Compromise is here the keynote. Both Colson (1962) and Gluckman (1956, 1963) have argued that conflicting cross-cutting allegiances exert a pressure towards reconciliation and early settlement of blood disputes by the payment of compensation. The threat of retaliation remains here only until compensation is paid with the payments, in compensating for loss of life, serving also to effect a genuine reconciliation. In so doing there is a general contrast with feuding societies where the payment of compensation is but a temporary palliative and one which may, by keeping alive the memory of the debt and thus dishonour, foster future retaliation.

Given the evident lack of the feud in Bugisu, the question is whether it is useful to analyse the structural set in terms of lineages plus cognatic and affinal cross-cutting ties? I will argue that it is only up to a point, for one can visualise a scale with feuding societies at one end, the Plateau Tonga somewhere in the middle, and at the other end, societies where the corporateness of the unilineal descent group is so diluted by the personal extra-group affiliations of its members that 'balance' between lineage groups ceases to be a meaningful principle at all. Here there is not only no possibility of feud but even the threat of blood vengeance is remote, at least within local communities. As will be seen, the strategies used in dealing with murder at the present time in Bugisu all tend in a single direction, a direction which acts to limit the social repercussions of such an event by acting to counteract any perception of it in terms which might suggest that it is a lineage rather than a purely individual matter.

This theme is pursued in the following three chapters. This chapter sets the scene by giving a brief description of the kinship system, starting with the framework of descent. The lack of vengeance in Gisu life is then broached in chapter 7 by setting the problem in the context of past patterns of warfare and fighting while chapter 8 considers the praxis of relationships within the neighbourhood during the 1960s. The lack of group loyalties is here shown to have important implications for the patterns of Gisu violence and for the nature of moral judgement. Not only do lineage judgements of individuals tend to be in line with community ones but the lineage, far from supporting a member in trouble, may feel under particular pressure to disown him. A political analysis of the Gisu kinship system thus reinforces the points made in the previous section. Not only are the most serious conflicts in Gisu life generated within the family and lineage but membership of such groups provides no countervailing set of loyalties which operate to give protection to the individual. Put another way, Gisu lineages are divided both from within and from without. With the individual left standing alone, there are few checks on the speed of the process whereby certain individuals lose social credibility and are in danger of being killed as a result.

THE AGNATIC CHARTER

The Gisu visualise their society in terms of a series of progressively more inclusive patrilineal descent groups, from the smallest lineage segment to the category of all the descendants of Masaba, the Gisu. The major divisions of the descent system – the lineage, the sub-clan and clan – are all referred to by the word *cikuka* (pl. *bikuka*), which means literally, 'of the grandfather'. They are known commonly but not exclusively by ancestral names, the group being named after the apical ancestor and making the personal plural prefix *ba*, 'people of'. Together with the strong territorial associations of the descent groups above the level of the lineage, this gives an elaborate hierarchical segmentary series of descent groups of apparent rigidity.

The name of the descent group prefixed by the locative *ibu* is also used to refer to the territory occupied by the group. Gisu clans of between 1,000 and 5,000 adult men are always identified with a distinct territory and, indeed, at this level clanship and territorial identification are indivisible. Likewise the sub-clans of between 200 and 500 adult men also tend to have a residential base. The component lineages of the sub-clan, however, lack this co-residential basis and lineage members tend to live in small blocks scattered throughout the territory of the sub-clan. The lineage is only territorial in the sense that its members recognise certain collective rights over each other's individual plots of land. The identity of the lineages, in contrast to the descent groups of wider span, comes not through territorial exclusiveness coupled with putative agnatic descent but through demonstrable ties of kinship.

The transition between personal kinship and putative agnatic linkage is thus in Bugisu particularly well-defined and abrupt. It is only the members of the lineage, which tends to vary in size from between 50 and 150 adult men, who recognise each other as kin (*balebe*) by virtue of agnatic descent. The lineage is thus the widest unit within which classificatory kinship terms are extended. Since prohibitions on marriage are defined in terms of consanguinity, only the lineage is exogamous. Members of the sub-clan and clan are not regarded as kin and there are no prohibitions on marriage deriving from common membership.

The disjunction between consanguinity within the lineage and the idiom of kinship for describing the relationships between the higher orders of segmentation is reflected in genealogical reckoning. In tracing downwards from Masaba few Gisu have much difficulty in defining the major levels of segmentation down to the apical ancestor of their own sub-clan. Most men will here present a highly simplified version of territorial reality, with only those descent groups which are today eponyms for administrative units picked out for consideration. Men renowned for their genealogical knowledge may present a more complex picture, but even here genealogies tend to be remarkably telescoped, frequently giving as few as seven generations from Masaba himself to the most senior man alive.

However, if asked to trace upwards from themselves, few men will claim to know of any lineal ancestor above the founder of their lineage. As narrated by elderly men, such genealogies sometimes reach a depth of five to seven generations from themselves, but such a depth is rare. Other men often have great difficulty in remembering the name of even their great-grandfather. For this situation the Gisu interpret in terms of consanguinity and, in attempting such a genealogy, a man is trying to the best of his ability to make an accurate record of his agnatic kindred. Typically, above the level of a man's father only lineal ancestors are remembered and the collaterals are forgotten. Nevertheless it is felt that within the lineage there is a real possibility of tracing precise kinship ties.

People do not see this latitude in genealogical reckoning as in any way problematic and the same man might give both types of genealogy consecutively. Thus, unlike societies such as the Tiv (Bohannan, 1952), where the same genealogy defines both the major levels of politically relevant segmentation and also allows a man to trace his relationship to any other Tiv through this framework, Gisu genealogies, although seemingly all-embracing in this fashion, display a marked disjunction between that which co-ordinates intra-lineage kinship relationships and that which co-ordinates relationships with units outside the sphere of kinship. This disjunction is marked also by a hiatus between the two types of genealogy and most men will claim ignorance of the precise nature of the relationship between their lineage forbears and those of the sub-clan. When talking in a sub-clan context, the assumption of equality of status is deemed sufficient and, if pressed, elders will often say in a purely *ad hoc* way, 'Well, if there are so many lineages, then the sub-clan founder must have had so many wives or so many sons.' Beyond this, few see the relevance of genealogical co-ordination of units at this level.[1]

A distinction between kinship and descent relationships is, of course, common to most unilineal descent systems but in Bugisu it does not mark a transitional point from 'personal jural relationships' to collective obligations between groups of agnates (see Mayer, 1949). This latter feature, the external facet of lineage membership, is not stressed. The absence of any consensual genealogy which would relate lineage to lineage through their respective apical ancestors, or indeed pressure for any genealogical validation of lineage status, points to the fact that descent *per se* is not the most significant factor in determining the relationship of lineage to lineage within the sub-clan and clan. Nor does membership of the sub-clan or clan entail in itself any jural obligations.

GEOGRAPHICAL VARIATION

Before going on to describe the descent system of the central and southern areas of Bugisu it is important to indicate the main differences between these areas and the north as described La Fontaine on the basis of her fieldwork in Bumasifa in North Bugisu between 1953 and 1955 (especially La Fontaine, 1957, 1959, 1962). There are marked contrasts with regard to three features; the major levels of descent recognised and the degrees of territoriality and homogeneity. La Fontaine analysed the descent system in terms of four main levels of segmentation. Below the tribal section, she distinguished maximal lineages, internally segmented into major lineages, with these in turn segmented into minor lineages. These three lineage orders were all territorially based; the minor lineage of between 100 and 300 men being associated with a village, the major lineage with a cluster of villages and the maximal lineage with a district. Only the small exogamous minimal lineages, components of the minor lineage, did not form compact residential blocks as their members lived scattered throughout the village area. I have not adopted this terminology because descent in the southern areas fell more clearly into a tripartite model and a similar terminology would therefore be confusing. Moreover, I prefer, since it follows Gisu practice, to distinguish the lineage, where 'an accepted genealogical relationship is known between all members' (Middleton and Tait, 1958: 4), from the higher orders of descent, sub-clan and clan, where this factor does not hold.

The twin factors of homogeneity of lineage composition and territoriality may be dealt with together. One of the striking features emphasised by La Fontaine was the degree to which the patrilineal ideology was recognised in practice in North Bugisu. This was particularly evident at the level of the minor lineage (sub-clan) whose territory corresponded exactly to the then administrative unit of the village in the area she studied. In Bulwala village of Bumasifa sub-county, 87% of the men claimed to be members of the same minor lineage. The patterns realised in southern Bugisu are more variable. In the mountain areas sub-clans still tend to be identified with specific core areas but this tendency becomes less and less noticeable as one moves down towards the plains. A prominent pattern in some southern areas is for the sub-clans to be associated with a long strip of territory running from the mountains to the plains, interrupted in parts where areas have been colonised by other sub-clans. These patterns clearly bear the imprint of historical factors.

The clans north of Mbale have a tradition of migration in a northerly direction, pushing further and further around the mountain into the territory of the Sebei. La Fontaine estimates the eighteenth-century boundary between the Gisu and Sebei to have been in the vicinity of Mbale. When fighting occurred between sub-clans, La Fontaine maintains that the victors drove out the losers and presumably moved in as a unit, keeping their close-knit structure. To the far north, however, patterns are probably different for, with the setting up of the administration, Gisu expansion proceeded not by force of arms but by what was described in the administrative reports at the time as 'peaceful penetration' (Entebbe Secretariat Archives, series B 5, 1916). Between 1909 and 1916 the number of Gisu in Sebei increased from 100 to 2,200, and by 1959 they numbered 13,509, forming approximately one-quarter of the population of Sebei.[2]

The history of the southern clans presents a more turbulent picture, and the fortunes of war were not wholly in the Gisu favour. The southern clans, probably for some fifty years before the coming of the Ganda in 1900, were vying with the peoples of the plains for possession of the lower foothills and plains. Old men still recount stories of the intertribal wars with the Teso, Gwere and Nyole, dating mainly from the last two decades of the nineteenth century but with some outbreaks as late as 1918, well after the establishment of the administration.[3] These accounts tell of large-scale population movements as the Gisu occupied the plains and were then beaten back into their mountain valleys before partly reoccupying the plains lands again. Traditions relate their settlements as far south as Tororo in Bukedi and the southern tribal section is said to take its name from the rock overlooking that town, Buya. With the cessation of intertribal warfare, however, the Gisu migrated in increasing numbers to the plains as well as into Bukusu in Kenya, where many southern clans are represented.

Initially, however, the spread of the Gisu into the surrounding plains did not appear to ameliorate the effects of population pressure in the mountainous areas. In 1916, British officials reported that in what is now Manjiya the Gisu had cleared away the heavy forest as high as 10,000 feet. To alleviate this situation, the British decided to open up the Sirokho valley for settlement by people mainly from the southern half of Bugisu. This area now forms the North Bugisu sub-counties of Bunambutye, Muyembe and parts of Buwalasi. Thus the southern clans tend to be geographically dispersed, with segments found not only in the mountain zones of their origin but in the plains and as far north as Sirokho. Further, the southern areas also show considerable hetero-geneity of lineage composition, the need for allies making the hard-pressed clans fighting in the plains receptive to newcomers. As sub-clans and clans carved out more land for themselves in the plains, members from other clans moved also to these then relatively open areas.

The association of territory and clanship may now be considered. Clan membership is seen to derive primarily from rights to land handed down from the ancestors and the associated ancestral shrines; the clan is thus a homeland, established and validated by the fact of ancestorhood. Yet individual affiliation to a clan is a fairly rapid process, taking only the two or three generations needed to develop shrines to commemorate ancestors buried in the area. Until ancestors, both male and female, are buried in the new clan area, children and initiates must be sent back to participate in rituals in their area of origin. These ties are gradually severed as sacrifices to the ancestors become possible in the new clan areas.

THE LINEAGE

Of the series of descent groups, jural obligations among people are vested only in the smallest, that is, the lineage. The obligations associated with lineage membership are couched primarily in terms of land, marriage and the cult of the ancestors. The scattered plots of land owned by individual members of the lineage are thought of as 'lineage land', just as all women married to members of the lineage are considered 'lineage wives'. The lineage has a legitimate proprietal interest in both. As has been described in chapter 4, a man should approach his agnates if he wishes to sell land, giving them first option to purchase and, likewise, he should consult with them if the land is in dispute. In the same way, although bridewealth is paid by the individual, bridewealth negotiation is seen as a lineage responsibility and on a man's death, the widow may with her agreement be inherited by a member of his lineage.

The span of the lineage which effectively exercises these supervisory rights is, however, variable, depending in part on the degree to which named segments (*tsinda*) are recognised. Yet even where a lineage recognises no distinct segments within itself, the lineage is not an undifferentiated body, and obligations fall firstly on close agnates and diminish with genealogical distance. Three orders of genealogical segmentation may be distinguished within the lineage; the household, the family segment and the lineage segment.

The lineage is regarded as an association of equals, in other words of circumcised men, each responsible for his own household and with identical jural rights. The family goes through a cycle of development but in Bugisu it is not one of gradual augmentation into an extended family, which would occur if sons brought their wives to live under their father's authority. Rather, the conjugal family remains the basic domestic unit, and as sons reach adulthood they move away to set up their own households. Adult relatives, who may stay in the compound under the protection of the head, are regarded as 'attached' rather than as integral members of the household. Circumcised sons, awaiting the bequest of land and bridewealth from their fathers, are segregated from the household, sleeping apart and eating food prepared separately for them by their mothers. Divorced or widowed sisters and mothers, who may also take up residence, are given their own huts and plots of land to maintain themselves separately.

Yet while primary responsibility for the welfare of his dependants lies with the head of the household, the family segment, as I propose to call it, exercises some moral responsibility in this regard. The focus of a family segment is usually the dead father of a group of brothers. It commonly consists of between five and twenty agnates and tends to be co-residential. The primary responsibilities of agnates fall upon this grouping; their common interest in the patrimonial estate often being given symbolic rendering by their keeping a small plot of the dead father's or grandfather's land in common; land which is often designated for use by a divorced sister or sister's son.

Such a segment commonly recognises an elder, *umuxulu*, who is usually the most senior man. The eldership is not a post with defined rights and duties but solely a position of seniority; the elder is, in other words, respected as an adviser and may conduct negotiations for bridewealth and divorce. The family elder, together with the other senior men of the family segment, also consults with the other family elders of the lineage to sound out their opinion on a marriage or to seek their permission to a proposed sale of land. The number of elders it is considered necessary to confer with over such matters varies from lineage to lineage, according to the existence of recognised segments (*tsinda*) within them.

The existence of lineage segments is of course one aspect of lineage fission and, *pari passu*, the absence of such segments is an index of lineage strength which tends to be positively correlated with traditional forms of ritual collaboration. In the mountain areas of southern Bugisu, where lineages still participate with other lineages in the ritual cycles based on the sub-clan and clan, sentiments of common identity are stronger. Here the existence of segments within the lineage is often vehemently denied, and unity is given expression in the recognition of a single man as lineage elder, *umuxulu uwe cikuka*. Elsewhere, however, with ritual propitiation reduced to libations at the graves of grandparents, there is no ritual focus for greater spans of the lineage. Here little value is placed on lineage unity and effective co-operating groups are frequently reduced to that of the family segment. Moreover, in the lower foothills and plains such a pattern is further promoted by the geographical dispersion of the lineage throughout a far wider area than is common in the more densely-settled mountains.

In such lineages the constellation of close agnates can be seen to change with each generation. A span of the lineage is held together while members of the senior generation remain alive but on their death the juniors recognise a smaller span of kinsmen whom they feel obliged to consult. The wider lineage thus represents only a category of persons with whom they may not marry. They enjoy extended privileges, such as the option to buy land, only where individuals are bound by some supplementary tie forged on the basis of common residence or matrifiliation. Thus while agnation is not severed by the recognition of segments, it is often a weak principle in practical terms, carrying no mandatory obligations.

While differentiation within the lineage is seen as deriving from maternal kinship, the opposite process is as salient in Bugisu, with matrilateral affiliations acting to draw the lineage together. Most lineages show a generational depth far greater than that demanded by agnatic kinship alone, a fact which cannot be explained in terms of any value being placed on lineage exogamy as such. Rather, it derives from the interplay of maternal kinship ties within the lineage. Marriage in Bugisu tends to be parochial, with men choosing wives from among their neighbours and distant kin. Where agnates marry closely-related women their descendants are closer consanguineals than they would have been otherwise and exogamous restrictions are reinforced as a result. A preferred form of marriage is for real or lineage brothers to marry related women. Then they are drawn together by the tie of *bumasakwa* (see p. 148) and their children by their common maternal origins. Where such men are only distantly related patrilineally, their children will have the bonds of consanguinity renewed. Widow inheritance likewise has the same effect of creating a mesh of ties within the lineage, subsumed under agnatic kinship but not deriving from it.

The existence of matrilateral ties as principles of identification is significant also in considering sub-clan and clan organisation. Membership of the sub-clan and clan entails for the individual no jural obligations, but personal obligations are incurred through the matrilateral, patrilateral and affinal ties which ramify throughout such areas. Agnatic kinship thus is but one aspect of local identification, as La Fontaine emphasises when she says that 'although the lineage forms the framework of the political system, it does not of itself suffice to unify local groups' (La Fontaine, 1957: 92). Rather it is the tendency towards local endogamy and hence matrifiliation which promotes identification with local groups, strengthening the sentiment that they are all of 'one blood'.

THE SPREAD OF KINSHIP

A man recognises as kin (*balebe*) all people with whom he can trace a blood tie to a common antecedent four generations in depth from himself. Thus there are a total of eight stocks into which a person may not marry, up to and including all the descendants of his great-great-grandparents, with no distinctions being made between male and female links. However, the range of kinship is not absolute for classificatory terms are extended to people related through the fifth ascending generation, although the kinship term for people of that generation is *cirende*, a term in Central Bugisu which is also applied to strangers. Marriage is here talked about in preferential terms and marriage with more closely related kin is, in practice, often tolerated. The kinship pattern of the Gisu in fact is typified by the overlapping of ties over time; marriages unite men as affines, their descendants are kin and as this relationship becomes more distant, the tie is renewed by a further marriage.

Among men in any area, therefore, there is a continual realignment of relationships, as close kin are related to others by a variety of different ties and affinal ones become superimposed on the weak ones of consanguinity. Such marriages among neighbours create ties within local areas, economically important because of the rights of a wife to borrow land from her agnates and so by virtue of the privileges inherent in the brother-in-law, mother's brother/sister's son and cross-cousin relationships.

Apart from regulating exogamy, the tracing of a distant kinship tie does not presuppose any particular obligation, such as the giving of hospitality, but it does determine a man's demeanour while in the company of his kin. Fairly straightforward generalisations about kinship conduct can be made in Bugisu because of the overriding stress on generation as a categorising principle and the lack of distinctions made in terms of lineality. Relationships are thought of as on a scale from familiarity to distance and respect. Familiarity is the privilege of those defined as equal in generational terms, but between proximate generations the relationship is dominated by 'respect', *lukoosi*, and between members of the opposite sex by the added sexual inhibition of *tsisoni*

Throughout the kinship system the distinctive and antipathetic interests of the proximate generations are emphasised, with a corresponding identity among people of the same generation. In the sphere of kinship these lines of interest are drawn most tightly with regard to the prerogatives of marriage, with rights to the use of bridewealth and inheritance of widows determined along generational lines. The rules which determine the use of bridewealth bind together not only brothers and sisters but also cross-cousins.

Cross-cousins, both matrilateral and patrilateral, have rights to a portion of a girl's bridewealth and may also inherit each other's widows. Proximate generations are clearly opposed in these respects, for while in a single generation, marriage and consequent bridewealth redistribution forges close bonds of privilege among members, who may refer to each other's wives as 'my wife', this is translated into restriction and restraint between the generations.

Sexual distance is absolute with people of the proximate generation and opposite sex, whether kin or married to kin, who may be referred to collectively as *baxwe*.[4] With them incest or adultery is regarded as *imbixo*, 'polluting', and not just as 'bad' because it 'spoils marriage' as is the case between members of the same generation. Indeed the collective interest of men of the same generation in each other's wives precludes any compensation being levied for offences such as adultery since it is considered that the woman was paid for by the bridewealth of the generation as a whole. Further bridewealth received from the marriage of a woman may not be used for the marriages of the men of the proximate generation and nor may such men inherit each other's widows.[5] Thus, while the junior generation inherit land and other forms of property from the senior generation, the lines which serve to demarcate the divergent interests of the two generations are drawn with respect to sexual roles and privileges.

This has special relevance to affinal connections which present themselves as exaggerations of those found within the sphere of consanguinity. The twin constraints of *lukoosi* and *tsisoni* find their fullest expression in the absolute nature of the *bumasala* avoidance relationship between a man and his mother-in-law. *Bumasala* implies the ultimate in transgression, its breach nullifying all the social rules and discriminations upon which orderly human life is based. At the other end of the scale, the mutuality enjoined among members of the same generation, created through their common interest in women, is epitomised in the relationship between brothers-in-law. The term *muxwasi* (pl. *bamuxwasi*) is used to address both the wife's brother and the sister's husband. Such men are bound together initially by the successive use of the same cattle to marry a wife, and thereafter by the mutual interest they have in each other's affairs through their sisters.[6]

This interdependence of brothers-in-law is expressed in mandatory forms of gift exchange, particularly at the circumcision of sons and marriage of daughters, when these men are linked as mother's brother or father's sister's husband to the children of each other's unions. While such gifts are prescribed, the brother-in-law relationship is seen also as the basis for many other favours, particularly in the form of land loans or the option to buy land. Such grants of land are given most typically to the sister's husband, where they are seen as an extension of the obligations of a man to his sister. Yet while the obligations between brothers-in-law are related to the enduring bond between brother and sister, the importance of the relationship for the individual is not confined to the most closely-linked affines. The relationship is seen as the ideal basis upon which the individual can develop life-long friendships. Though amicability is built into the terms of the relationship, the onus is on the individual to cement such linkages over time. Between brothers-in-law this takes the form of reciprocal and competitive feasting, each individual selecting from among his range of *bamuxwasi* those with whom he wishes to develop this special relationship.

Of a similar nature is the *bamasakwa* relationship between men who have married sisters or between the parents of a married couple. While mild joking abuse is considered permissible and indeed desirable among brothers-in-law as evidence of their friendship, with *bamasakwa* more boisterous joking is considered possible. This is felt as particularly appropriate between those men who have married sisters and who are not directly involved in the exchange of property at marriage. Between the parents of a married couple who negotiate the bridewealth payments, such banter is said to be restrained for fear that real friction might develop between them if the marriage proves unsuccessful. For the Gisu a playful exchange of insults is only considered possible where the relationship is defined as one of equality and where, in addition, there is little possibility of real grievance. Thus grandparents and grandchildren, who are not directly involved in property transfers, may also tease each other in this way but it is not deemed suitable among siblings because of the likelihood of dissension over the distribution of property. Even among affines, it occurs only where the relationship between the two individuals concerned is one of true friendship and ceases if any quarrel comes between them; the insult would then cease to be a 'joke' and be taken instead as a serious affront. Since all relationships among kin and affines are bound up with the transmission of property, through inheritance, bridewealth exchange or gift, joking insults among kin are in fact always restricted in scope and run their full rein only with *bakulo*. These joking partners cannot marry and therefore cannot become kin.

The close companionship desired among brothers-in-law and *bamasakwa* may be compared at this juncture with the relationship between mother's brother and sister's son. Unlike many other African societies with a stress on agnatic descent, in Bugisu the mother's brother is not a benevolent figure nor a counterbalance to the authority of the father. Although he has a special relationship with his sister's son, he is at the same time closely identified with the father, as his brother-in-law, as a member of the senior generation and in terms of his obligations to his sister's son. The relationship is one of restraint. In general terms the mother's brother and his lineage are considered to have similar rights and duties with regard to a man as his own lineage, but of a supportive rather than primary nature. Thus while a man cannot usually expect to inherit land from his mother's brother, he may be called upon to ensure that his sister's son is treated fairly, and, in the last eventuality, is strongly obligated to provide the man with land himself. In the special circumstance where the sister's son is sent to be circumcised at the home of the mother's brother, as happens when there are three or more brothers, he is automatically allocated a little land by his mother's brother, though today this is rarely more than a token plot. Nevertheless, the circumcision of a sister's son at the home of the mother's brother emphasises the joint responsibility of matrikin and patrikin to assure the ritual and secular welfare of the individual. The shades of the mother's ancestors are thought as liable to attack a person as those of his paternal ancestors. Sisters and their children are thus summoned back for any ceremonies to placate the ancestors and the mother's brother is closely concerned in all the rites of passage of his sister's children.

The generational stress of the Gisu kinship system is echoed in the age-grading system which further stratifies the population into lateral sections. The names for age grades are primarily terms of reference but the more prestigious are also used in address to indicate respect, just as the kinship terms *papa* (father) and *kuka* (grandfather) are used to a large extent irrespective of actual relationship or relative age. In the past it is said that the young circumcised men (*basoleli*) were the warriors, and wars are often dated by reference to the names of the circumcision–periods of the men who fought in them. What remains of this principle is seen in the special ties which bind together contemporaries or *lubaka*.

The term *lubaka* may be used to refer exclusively to a man's age mates, his *bamakoki*, the men who were circumcised in the same year as himself. Such men are regarded as quasi-kin of the same generation and may not marry each other's daughters. Social equality is the keynote of the relationship, signified in the prohibition on them passing beneath each other's beer-straw while drinking. And, as all such ties, these are strongest in the immediate post-circumcision period after the boys have spent the months of healing in each other's company. In the past it is said that age mates acted as guardians of the male division of labour and would beat or fine one of their number who was caught doing 'women's work', such as cooking or carrying water. In the 1960s this was little heard of outside the healing period itself. Nevertheless, the bond remains and age mates have the power, as do kinsmen, to curse each other's sons, a power which is exercised if they are refused gifts at the circumcision of each other's sons. The term *lubaka* has additionally a wider sphere of application and can refer to the friends made by boys in the free and easy days of their childhood when they herded their fathers' cattle and courted girls of the neighbourhood. Boys, excluded from the social activities of the circumcised, particularly beer-drinking, must necessarily seek each other out for company. After circumcision, these friendships tend to decline in significance as each man, now able to marry and set up his own household, must turn his mind to the onerous task of supporting himself and his dependants. Moreover, as adults, they may now seek company with men of all ages and other relationships, particularly those with affines, become more vital for the individual to develop.

CONCLUSION

This chapter has outlined the implications of kinship for the structuring of territorial groups. The Gisu use the idiom of patrilineal descent as a way of describing the relationships between the higher-order territorial divisions of their country but, although in this way descent provides the framework for political loyalties, the distinctive character of Gisu kinship structure emerges from a strong pattern of intra-community marriages and the resulting mesh of affinal and matrilateral relationships.

These extra-descent ties also have great importance in considering what might be called the praxis of everyday life. For an individual man, the status relationships given by consanguinity can be contrasted with the exchange relationships he develops on the basis of age and affinal connection. Agnatic kinship involves competition over basic resources, competition whose outcomes can only be in zero/sum terms. In contrast, relationships deriving from marriage allow of a mutuality of interest and stress the exchange of favours. In terms of the particular Gisu structuring of sentiment in the kinship universe it is these latter which are 'marked' and empress the basic polarities of value of the kinship universe.

Put another way, Gisu lineages are deeply divided from within and this has importance in considering the lack of vengeance in Gisu life. Gisu lineages do not mobilise in support of their members. Rather the pattern is of individual self-help, a pattern which is predicated upon the individual responsibility of each man for his own actions (and enmities) and which in turn leaves him standing alone. In the next chapter, the distinctive nature of Gisu local relationships, with its lack of segmentary loyalties, emerges from a consideration of patterns of fighting and the payment of bloodwealth after homicide in the past.

NOTES

1   A similar point was noted by La Fontaine in North Bugisu, where genealogical reckoning would appear to be both more extensive and regarded as of greater significance (La Fontaine, 1957).

2   The territories of the tribes were consolidated according to the lines of occupation when the British administration was first established. Since 1959 the situation in Sebei District has been far from peaceful. (See 45–7.)

3   The naming of Gisu circumcision years after events that occurred at that time gives a chronology often lacking in oral history. These names indicate a succession of invasions of people from the west and north from the 1860s onwards with the main Teso invasion dated as 1877–78. According to the list held in the District Commissioner's office in Mbale, based on the testimony of Watexula of the Basoba, the decisive battle with the Teso was fought in 1881–82. This period became known as Bamaina, after the ancestral power associated with luck and riches. The note on the file said that those

circumcised in that year went on to become wealthy and successful and included a number of notable leaders, including Mumia of the Wanga, whose death in 1950 marked the passing of that generation.

4   In fact there are a number of cognate terms here. *Baxwe* emphasises the fact of marriage contracted through the payment of bridewealth, *buxwe*. *Basoni*, from the same root as *tsisoni*, can be used of the same relatives and gives notice rather to the element of sexual fear which reaches its strongest expression with those who are also *bamasala*.

5   In rare cases, it is possible for a man to inherit a wife from a member of the senior generation as long as she was married after he was circumcised and thus has never acted as a 'mother' to him.

6   There can be no direct exchange marriages. Marriages must all go in one direction with, in any one generation, related men taking wives from the same family and not vice versa.

7

LAND WITHOUT LOYALTY

This chapter provides a bridge between past and present by attempting to reconstruct the main principles which governed fighting in the pre-colonial era and relate these to the patterns which were found in 1960s. Unfortunately, the record does not allow a sequential tracing of changes in patterns of counteraction and fighting and this is beyond my present purpose. Drawing from the administrative records of the district and oral histories from Central Bugisu, the aim rather is to establish features of the pre-colonial political organisation which have a direct bearing on the present. The main argument here is not that the lineage system has broken down in any meaningful way but, on the contrary, that certain tendencies in Gisu life have a long history and that the individualism that is found is an accentuation of an old pattern. Gisu life never appears to have been marked by an all-embracing segmentary system and political loyalties were local, small in scale and highly schismatic.

COMMUNITY AND POLITICS

In terms of community relationships, lineages may be said to provide the warp and affinal and matrilateral ties the weft. Such a weft typically is woven most densely at the centre of a man's locality but it also acts to link him to those more geographically distant areas where his kin have migrated or his sisters have married. These distant patterns of affinal alliance also tend to be maintained from generation to generation as the younger generation meet each other at kinship gatherings. This has importance not only in considering the nature of relationships within the locality but, as La Fontaine (1962) has made clear, the nature of political leadership. The term used of traditional leaders was *bakasya*, 'men rich in cattle', and these men are best regarded as men of influence respected for the power they could exert by virtue of their wealth, a wealth in cattle which translated also to wives and thus affinal relationship. As Purvis writes, 'the strongest patriarch, or chief, is the man who has been able to procure the most cattle, and with them buy the largest number of wives' (1909: 274). As he makes clear their influence was largely moral and they had no authority to enforce their decisions. Indeed, such *bakasya* are best regarded with La Fontaine as 'first among equals' (1957, 1960a). Yet the favoured practice of choosing a successor from among the sons assured that the advantages of wide alliance were carried over from generation to generation and gave a hereditary stamp to such positions.

Not only were these leaders more polygamous than their fellows but they also tended to marry over a geographically greater area, thus establishing linkages with politically discrete areas. This is evident from La Fontaine's (1960a, 1962) analysis of Gisu chiefs and notables and was similarly apparent in the investigations I made in Central Bugisu. For example, of the nine wives of Mandali, a man who became one of the first sub-chiefs in Busoba, one came from Bukonde on the borders of Central and North Bugisu and another from as far south as Tororo in Samia Bugwe. Such far-flung alliances set them apart from their followers. As the first CMS missionary complained in talking of the difficulty in hiring porters, none but their chiefs would walk more than five miles from their homes.[1]

The pattern of affinal alliance also has significance in considering the level of political integration implied in the old *lukongo* (pl. *tsikongo*) divisions. While this word, which literally means 'ridge', is now archaic with this usage, such divisions are now identified in the southern areas with the administrative unit of the parish. In the north, when la Fontaine was working there in the early 1950s, the *lukongo* was identified with the administrative division of the village, then a sub-division of the parish. This rather wider degree of political integration in the south is consistent with the contrasting patterns of warfare and expansion noted earlier between the north and the south. However, it is perhaps as significant that in both cases the *lukongo* was equated with the lowest unit of the administrative system of the time, the old village unit of the administration having been abolished in 1961. Clearly, as its derivation suggests, its primary referent is locality.

It is somewhat difficult to reconstruct the social composition of such *tsikongo*. The walled and fortified Gisu villages of the plains and lower foothills were said to consist of between ten and thirty huts, though an exceptionally large one might have 100 huts. This size suggests they approximate to lineages of the size of present family segments based around a shallow lineage. The *lukongo* represented a coalition of such groups, but a coalition which was both tenuous and unstable. Deep and bitter factionalisation within local areas was evidently marked and receives much comment in missionary reports and letters, as it was seen to hinder the success of the missions because different families refused to work collectively on mission buildings or even attend church services together. It also receives early recognition by the administration. One indicative case in the archival record deals with the firing of a house at the Nyondo Catholic Mission in Busoba in 1913. Arson had by then become a recognised form of Gisu protest against the labour tribute demanded by their new chiefs and the missions who, following Ganda custom, regarded the land they were granted as *mailo* land and those living on it as 'tenants'. In this case, the men living on the mission *mailo* were required to repair a house which was then set on fire the following night. Following the administration's confiscation of their cattle, a District Officer held an enquiry and elicited a barrage of accusation and cross-accusation among the 107 Gisu families living on the land who, though all Basoba, were divided into four divisions, each with its own head. In rejecting the option of collective punishment in this case, the District Officer comments that he knew of no bond between such sub-tribes which should lead them to incur punishment on each other's behalf (Mbale District Archives, 1913).

Nevertheless, the nexus of cognatic and affinal ties within such areas, linking family segment with family segment through the individual ties of their members, provided a basis for an exceptional man to exercise influence and to assert a common interest over and above that of sectional difference. The spread of such influence undoubtedly varied from area to area and from time to time depending, presumably, in large part on the individual charisma of the leader as well as on the exigencies of the moment. Perryman (1937) reports the meteoric rise to fame of Manyu of the Balucheke in 1911, when his magical powers were seen to be effective against British and Ganda punitive expeditions. Through his sorcery he claimed defeat of at least three attempts to scale the mountain to his stronghold. Perryman's predecessor was struck down with a fever and Perryman himself was defeated on his first attempt by the sudden growth of an abscess and on his second by an urgent telegram summoning him back to headquarters. On the next occasion, Perryman judiciously gave no warning of his intentions and, making a forced march at night, surprised the Balucheke the following morning.

The *bakasya*, then, were the war leaders but they were also the formal spokesmen for peace. Indeed the Gisu, seeing in the *bakasya* the direct precursors to the modern chiefs, tend to talk about such men as essentially peacemakers, called in to 'cut' disputes among the people of the area. In talking about the equivalent leaders among the Babukusu, Wagner notes also that they were defined as 'men who talk gently and wisely and who can make people listen and return to reason when they want to quarrel or fight' (1970: 77). But peace and war went together, and the same affinal ties could be used to raise allies in war as well as to moderate tempers in disputes. Indeed, with no direct sanctions to support their decisions, it must be supposed that the effectiveness of Gisu leaders rested largely on the degree to which they could act as spokesmen for public opinion, a public opinion which was situated as much strategically as it was by general moral restraints.

The role of matrikin and affines as both champions or intermediaries in disputes is illustrated in the following brief quotation from an elder in Bungokho, who was describing the reactions of kin to fighting over land boundaries within the sub-clan:

> If the Babirabi fought the Babirabi and it continued so that they were beating each other badly then, one by one, they came. They came from up there in Ishikoli and from over there in Bumageni Bamweru and they all came and decided the boundary and replanted it. Mothers' brothers came and brothers-in-law and if they saw that the fight was continuing vigorously then they joined in and fought too. But if they saw that their side was losing then they went to the elders to make a settlement, and the elders said, 'Do not fight', and they went to fetch beer so that they could drink together.

With parochial marriage-patterns there were fewer checks on interclan fighting which, in contrast to that occurring within the *lukongo*, is described as frequently bitter and of long duration. Yet the *bakasya* could still be called upon as conciliators, the more renowned being summoned to go many miles from their homes to lend their weight to a peace settlement. Peace and war again went together as these marriage ties could also be used to mobilise allies in war, especially significant in the plains and foothills where clan contested with clan and with the encroaching peoples of the plains. And here land rights followed upon territorial occupation, giving rise in part to the pattern of affiliated lineages to the sub-clan and clan which was discussed earlier for the central areas. The following account was given by an elder in Busiu and dates back to 1900 when the southern Gisu were staking out rights to land in that area in competition with the Gwere, Nyole and Teso.

> The leader of the Bamasikye in Busiu at that time was Mwalie and he married a girl from Bungokho. Then her brother Mwambu quarrelled with his three brothers and went to Mwalie to ask him for a plot of land which was granted to him. At that time the Gisu had retreated from Tororo and had been driven back as far as Busiu but the Teso were still pressing in on them. Mwalie asked Mwambu to return to his people and ask for help. The Bamasikye then made a stand on Mumanye Hill and the Bangokho arrived and together they drove out the Teso and took their land and cattle from the river Manafwa up to Lwaboba. From that time, the Bamasikye and the Bangokho have been friends and Mwalie gave Mwambu more land for his descendants.

This story brings out clearly the fact that allies in war were not determined by the framework of descent. Sixty years after the imposition of colonial rule and the abatement of large-scale fighting it is obviously difficult to have complete surety in the stories recounted of past warfare, coloured as it is by being part of an almost legendary past when fighting, say the Gisu, was the main form of enjoyment of the young men. The old men – recounters of such stories – were but children when the first Gisu 'chiefs' were created. Nevertheless, collecting such stories one is struck by a contrast in the types of accounts offered. In some accounts lineage designations are used, giving the impression that forces were mobilised according to descent-group loyalties, while in others the emphasis is laid on the recruitment of matrikin and affines as allies. From an anthropological perspective concerned with the structural possibilities inherent in systems of descent, these accounts suggest completely distinct,

7   Gisu warrior, taken from Purvis, *Through Uganda to Mount Elgon*, 1909

even contradictory, models for warfare. In looking more closely at the contexts for these accounts it becomes clearer that they are not in fact different 'accounts', for the one in terms of descent in effect summarises the other. Just as descent implies locality, the particular fusion of consanguinity and descent in Bugisu allows the idiom of descent to be used as an abbreviated or shorthand framework for discussion, and one that is accurate enough when recounting the general features which affected the duration of fighting and the type of settlement likely. However, it does not imply that such groups ever mobilised *en bloc* on the principle of complementary opposition, and when accounts are offered of specific fights the emphasis is thrown on recruitment through extra-agnatic ties.

In coming across a somewhat similar discrepancy among the Bedouin, E. Peters (1967, 1975) offers an important commentary on the nature of lineage theory, arguing that ideological models used to explain and rationalise behaviour should not be confused with either normative models or sociological ones. Thus he argues that the lineage framework as used by the Bedouin is not a prescriptive one for action but is one by which they conceptualise and give coherence to it. This has been tied in to a debate on the nature of 'folk models', with the question being raised about whether the analytic priority accorded by anthropologists to the segmentary lineage model has not privileged that account over alternative models for action, models which might equally be given by informants (Holy, 1979, Salzman, 1978). One strand of argument here is that Peters's contrast between folk and sociological models is unfounded since the concept of the folk model has been unduly restricted to the lineage one. Salzman, for example, refers to systems where the lineage framework is supplemented by other principles such as residence and alliance as 'lineage plus' ideologies, and goes on to suggest a particular ecological niche for segmentary ideologies that are not realised in practice. He argues that it was 'suited to areas in which political conditions and productive activities result in an alternation through history of stable periods and periods of upheaval, periods of stable territoriality and periods of high spatial mobility and population mixing' (Salzman, 1978: 68). In such instances it may be seen as a 'social structure in reserve', a conceptual insurance called into operation only when needed, that is, when territorial stability is jeopardised or abandoned.

This is an interesting argument but one which, like other ecological arguments, is difficult to substantiate,[2] as the conditions may be said to be specified both too broadly and too narrowly. For example, the political actualities over much of East Africa in pre-colonial times could be described as unstable in Salzman's terms but segmentary lineage ideology, whether acted upon or not, is a far from universal feature. And the particular case of Bugisu would tempt us to reverse the formulation, as the segmentary ideology would appear to have been stronger in the north with its stabler and more tightly-knit territorial structure than in the central and southern regions. In Bukusu, just the other side of the border in Kenya, subject far more to the vicissitudes of warfare and migration, it fades away altogether. De Wolf (1977) is adamant that 'there is no evidence that traditionally there were strong corporate groups. There was no system of lineages in segmentary opposition' (1977:132). In these instances, territoriality and segmentary lineage ideology would thus seem to go together.

Indeed, the interesting thing about Bugisu is this very fusion of territory with descent – apparent equally in the north and south of the region – a fusion which has been reinforced by the administrative structure. This leads me back to Peters's argument that the segmentary model should be seen in such cases as a framework that people use primarily for interpreting their interactions. That is, it is not a prescriptive model for action, nor even a model which legitimises action, but it provides a simple – and simplified – framework for discussion. Yet my point with respect to the Gisu use of the lineage and affinal models is not quite the same, for I do not see the discrepancy in Gisu accounts as due to a contrast between ideal and real, ideology versus actuality. There is no question here of false consciousness or of an ideology being at odds with empirical political processes. Rather, as I see it, both accounts are equally *good* accounts and both are meant as descriptions of reality, but they are descriptions which belong to different contexts for discussion. The lineage model is the more general one and – when used – it is understood to imply the other. Common understandings – and, as indicated, the coincidence of territory and kinship – ensure that it does not conflict with the other account but summarises or glosses it.

Taking this view, there is no need to polarise action with ideology. Yet this difference in interpretation should not detract attention from the real differences between the elaboration of the lineage model as used by the Bedouin and the more skeletal version offered by the Gisu as a way of simplifying social reality, and its lack of prescriptive force in the latter case. This may be illustrated further with reference to the payment of blood compensation in the past.

BLOOD COMPENSATION

Discussions about the payment of blood wealth in the past stress the element of conciliation; they were made to 'cut the hatred'. Since the possibilities of vengeful hatred (*cixonde*) may be related in the first place to social distance, a simple schema of practice can readily be elicited. Thus it is said that no compensation was usually payable within the lineage for there there can be no *cixonde*. Within the clan, four head of cattle would have been offered and rather more, maybe up to ten head, outside the clan, for the hatred would be more bitter. But these are guidelines and are not prescriptions, as becomes clear in further discussion, for it is the feelings aroused by the killing which need to be assuaged. One is dealing not with legal principles nor with rules which state that a man's life is worth so much, as is the case with the Nuer, for example, where blood compensation is set at the level of bridewealth in order to marry a wife to the dead man and thus ensure his social perpetuity. For the Gisu, blood compensation is an aspect of reconciliation only and, as such, might be demanded also with intra-lineage killings to reconcile the murderer with the dead man's wife and the lineage of his mother's brothers. Perryman (1937) reports a case from the time when he was an administrator in the area in 1918 where, following a fratricide, the wife of the dead man demanded compensation and, when this was refused, her son tracked down his father's brother, the murderer, and killed him. Further, there is the question of pollution which adds further complication and demands higher rates of compensation to achieve reconciliation.

Killings within the lineage do not incur pollution (*imbixo*). They are regarded only as 'bad', as indeed is all killing. In all such cases a man is wise to purify himself on the grave of the deceased to guard against the vengeful spirit returning to harm him. In cases where murder is planned in advance, precautions too may be taken ahead of time. Intra-lineage killings in that respect do not differ from any other killing; they are not specially protected nor indeed regarded as especially reprehensible. However, killings of other categories of relation do incur pollution, particularly the killing of a mother's brother, sister's child, mother's sister's child, father's sister, brother-in-law, *masakwa* and age mate. These killings also incur a special risk of ghostly vengeance, with the enraged ghost of the dead man acting to send his murderer mad (*bukwat-sole*) so that he will lose his wits and become a vagrant. Elaborate ceremonies of reconciliation and purification (*xuxwiosa*) are then necessary as was higher blood compensation – often specified as of ten head of cattle – to cut the hatred such murders aroused. And, in fact, the only case I came across where compensation was offered at the present time was where a man killed an age mate who was also a close agnate. This case is worth recounting briefly:

Case 6: Pongo kills his age mate   Busoba, homicide survey, 13
In 1959, Pongo is said to have killed his father's brother's son, Nambafu, in a fit of jealousy, when he suspected that Nambafu was trying to seduce his wife. Pongo was arrested but then released by the police for lack of evidence as to his complicity. It appears that Pongo, together with some friends, had taken great pains to disguise the murder by hanging Nambafu's body on a tree to make it appear as if he had committed suicide. Suicide was, however, discounted on various grounds and blood compensation of four cows was paid by Pongo's father to his brother, Nambafu's father.

What made this murder particularly heinous was the fact that Pongo and Nambafu were still *bafulu*, initiands. They had been circumcised together the previous August and the aggregation ceremonies which finally admit the initiands to adult status had yet to be performed. The bonds between age mates are strongest at this time. Nor was Pongo believed to have escaped the awful consequences of his deed, for *imbixo* (pollution) is said to have caught him for killing his age mate and to have sent him 'mad'. Unable because of his kin's hostility to live on in Busoba, he was said to just 'roam around', incoherent in speech, always in trouble and dangerous. In fact, although compensation had been paid the rituals of purification had not been performed. Purification for such murders involves the sacrifice of a sheep, associated with the inauspicious and the removal of pollution. The intestines are then unravelled and one end is tied around the neck of the killer while the other is tied around that of the dead man's wife. The intestines are then cut 'to cut the hatred deep in people'. This procedure finds a counterpart in a number of other ritual situations where the intention is to cut the path of ghostly influence, to sunder a person from the harmful power of ancestors.

The payment of blood compensation in 1960s was the exception and indeed so rare that I cannot remember a single occasion when it was mentioned as a feasible strategy to reconcile families. The most obvious question to ask is why? In many areas of East Africa, it died out as a practice following the imposition of colonial rule, and the most obvious surmise is that legal procedures and punishment have replaced it. This conclusion might be justified and, apart from Gisu statements, is strongly suggested in the only other case of blood compensation I found. This was in the court records and concerned a case where the Probation Officer had taken it upon himself to arrange an extra-court settlement. Again the case involved young men who were contemporaries, though the record does not specify whether or not they were actual age mates.

Case 7 Blood compensation   Manjiya, 1961
In 1961 a young boy of eighteen killed his classificatory brother in a beer-party brawl. A note was attached to the case file to the effect that the boy had been placed on probation as a reconciliation between the kin of the two boys had been arranged. The killing had so obviously been without malice that the Probation Officer had been given leave to attempt such a reconciliation, which is allowed under Ugandan law at the discretion of the judge. The Probation Officer called a meeting of the boy's lineage and invited them to vote on the issue of blood compensation versus imprisonment. Of the fifty-one adult men present, twenty opted for blood compensation, thirty for imprisonment and none for both. Only one man, the dead boy's father, demanded the death penalty. Eventually he and the rest of the lineage was persuaded by the Probation Officer to accept blood compensation of two head of cattle.

Clearly, blood compensation and imprisonment are seen as a form of double jeopardy. Yet what is intriguing about this particular case is the relative lack of popularity of blood compensation even when the choice was offered. Here we need to return to the more general discussion of lineage organisation. It is apparent, with respect both to fighting and warfare in the past and to the lack of vengeance and payment of blood compensation in the 1960s, that the 'lineage model' offers a model which, if taken too literally, would seriously distort an understanding of Gisu social process.

THE LINEAGE AND LINEAGE THEORY

It is widely recognised that the segmentary lineage system as originally formulated by Evans-Pritchard delimits a set of structural possibilities whose realisation varies from society to society and from context to context within any
society manifesting that structural form. Descent is a way of conceptualising
social processes but, as the debates over the relevance of African models for the
New Guinea Highlands have made clear, it does not automatically provide the
means by which men are mobilised for political action (Scheffler, 1966; La
Fontaine, 1973; Strathern, 1973; Karp, 1978). As Karp writes, 'the ideology of
descent does not necessarily specify a set of rules in terms of which behaviour
may be articulated nor does a descent ideology necessarily determine or
constrain patterns of choice' (Karp, 1978:3). Descent is an idiom which can be
put to use in numerous different ways according to the way it articulates social
processes. The Gisu descent framework identifies kinship with territory at all
levels of segmentation but it provides in itself no basis for collective action.

In segmentary lineage societies such as the Nuer, groups perceive their
common interest, their unity, only in times of war and in opposition to like
groups. Mobilisation defines the system. In order for this to occur groups must
be clear-cut, defined by reference to agnatic descent, for example, and this
identification must override all others. The evidence from the past does not
suggest that the Gisu descent system had this degree of definition. Further, it
could be argued in the case of Bugisu that the establishment of an administrative system has not subverted the lineage system but rather strengthened its
ideological aspects. The territorial aspect of Gisu descent initially allowed for a
merging of the framework of descent with the colonial administrative structure
and this in turn gave the descent system a far greater coherence, producing a
pyramidal organisation of groups with political functions. At higher levels
these groups represent degrees of integration which had no counterpart in the
pre-colonial political formation. At lower levels, lineages certainly fought
lineages, but genealogical reckoning above the level of the lineage would
appear too uncertain to have allowed for any automatic mobilisation of larger
groups. Rather, as has been indicated, allies were recruited on the basis of
extra-agnatic relationship, and it was the nexus of these ties which allowed for
collaboration, however temporary, within the sub-clan and clan.

Further, when compensation was paid it seems it was less a matter of
redressing relationships among blocks of agnates as of achieving reconciliation
between specific categories of non-agnatic relative. This point must be
stressed, for the closer one looks at the system the clearer it becomes that
compensation was offered among kin and usually *only* among kin. Its purpose
was thus not of redressing a balance between lineages as part of a *quid pro quo*
between feuding groups but of allowing for the resumption of kinship relationships. In contrast to compensation, it appears that the Gisu used another –

and unique – way of achieving peace and re-establishing relationship when the killer and victim were unrelated. This was the institution of *bukulo*, joking relationship.

In the 1960s, *bukulo* was a hereditary joking relationship which held between members of different lineages and linked members as joking partners (*bakulo*) to each other. In outline, the pattern conforms to that widely reported in Africa in that the partners have licence to revile, abuse, and insult one another and this licence extends to the snatching of property.[3] It differs from those reported elsewhere in that joking partners are neither kin nor affines and nor are they linked by the performance of any mutual service, such as funeral or purificatory rites. Nor do they possess any other role in community or kinship affairs such as mediation in disputes. The relationship is thus defined and has meaning solely in terms of the licence given by 'joking', and this licence is explained in terms of prior hostility between the linked lineages. *Bukulo* is thus presented as a peace pact and all its symbolic forms build upon this notion and its dual correlates of amity and enmity.

Though no longer contracted *bukulo* remains important in central and southern Bugisu. Typically these linkages are found between small lineage segments of approximately three generations in depth of the same clan or sub-clan area. Such lineage segments tend to maintain only one such alliance, though some claim more, but there is no regular pattern. In the present context the broadest generalisation that can safely be made is that the relationship tends to hold between neighbouring but not immediately contiguous lineages. *Bukulo* is incompatible with the etiquette and courtesy which are demanded by kinship and, further, where through migrations and shifts of house-site, *bakulo* find themselves living in immediate proximity to each other, the relationship tends to become subdued in the interests of neighbourly cordiality. *Bukulo* behaviour is at odds with that expected in ordinary social interaction.

The chief characteristic of *bukulo* behaviour is abuse and this is distinguished from light-hearted jesting and chaffing. It is stressed that *bukulo* exchanges are 'not play' (*xung'aa*) but 'abuse' (*xuxomana*); abuse which may take no note of normal etiquette and of the restrictions of relative sex, age or generation. In practice, the most extreme forms of verbal abuse tend to occur only between those men who are contemporaries and, in my experience, interactions were more restrained between those of the opposite sex. However, in principle, such restraints may be set aside and any type of abuse is licensed. It thus may run the gamut from relatively innocuous remarks over personal appearance ('big head', 'shrivelled body', 'unkempt hair' and the like) to more direct accusations of witchcraft and the type of animal and sexual obscenities which, in other circumstances, would undoubtedly precipitate fighting. All rude personal remarks indeed tend to carry the implication of witchcraft since they play upon the kind of objectionable characteristics which can be taken as the mark of a witch. If witchcraft is imputed to the recipient, however, it is equally incurred by the perpetrator since open abuse and the use of obscenities are seen as a form of cursing (*citsubo*). This is not to say that witchcraft and *bukulo* are in any other ways identified but to emphasise the abnormality of the behaviour; it is beyond the pale.

While the *bukulo* relationship holds between lineage segments, individuals contract special relationships on the basis of the tie. While it is said that such relationships may be formed between women they are generally contracted between men, either following the final mortuary ceremonies for one of their fathers or after their own circumcision. This relationship is developed by the reciprocal 'snatching' – known by the special term, *xutubuta* – of each other's property. These thefts begin with small items, such as pots or chickens, and progress to goods of higher value, with the aim being finally to snatch cows from each other. Such snatching is done strictly by turn, with one man initiating the exchange and then waiting until his partner retaliates by taking an item of equivalent value. The way is then open to snatching items of greater value and so on, with the taking of cows effectively ending the cycle of escalation. Any further snatching between the two is then said to begin again with the taking of chickens. The 'negative reciprocity of abuse', as Richards (1937) called it, is here carried over to the expropriation of property.

Snatching of this kind takes place at yearly or even longer intervals and Christmas has become a favoured time for it. The Gisu see this progressive snatching as a way for the two men to 'test' their friendship and thus the strength of the *bukulo* relationship. The toleration of such thefts is seen to strengthen the bond between the two. Yet this bond is of *bukulo*, not of friendship (*busaale*) from which it is held to be qualitatively different both in terms of its enduring nature and in the element of hostility. Unlike friendship, *bukulo*, it is said, cannot die since it depends not on personal whim nor the vagaries of individual affection but is a relationship which is renewed with the same force in each succeeding generation. In the second place, the symbolic theme of violence and hostility sharply distinguishes *bukulo* from normal friendship.

The *umukulo* is both enemy and friend; his attitude and behaviour are seen as a direct expression of the peace pact once concluded between the families. Hatred, *cixonde*, is re-enacted in the omission of greetings on meeting each other, in the seriousness of the abuse and in the mock thefts. This symbolic theme is further developed in the rules associated with the snatching. The *umukulo* cannot snatch from his partner until he has provoked him into responding in like terms. Apprehensive as to what he may take, those in the homestead usually attempt restraint, for once he has successfully 'picked a quarrel', then he may strike the object he wants and make off with it.

Moreover, when livestock is taken then the animal must be slaughtered on the path on the way home: it cannot be taken into the partner's home alive and then used for breeding. *Bukulo* is equated with destruction: with the taking of life and consequent enmity, *cixonde*.

Yet while hatred is said to underlie the particular forms taken by the relationship, the pact equally implies peace and friendship. *Bakulo*, under pain of the destruction of their lines, may not take offence or respond with real antagonism. Nevertheless, hatred is an ever-present facet of the relationship and is said to rise once more to the surface – to be an emotive factor in the situation – at times of illness and death when *bakulo* are identified once more as 'killers'. *Bakulo* do not visit each other during illness for it is said that if they do then the sick person will die and, following a death, they practise total avoidance, again like enemies, neither meeting nor greeting. All deaths thus bring to mind the original situation of enmity and this is given further elaboration in southern areas of Bugisu in beliefs that the ghosts of the *bakulo* 'snatch' the shadow soul, *cisimu*, of the dead person, keeping it until the final mortuary ceremonies are performed.

JOKING AND FIGHTING: COMPARATIVE CONSIDERATIONS

The association of joking with fighting and rivalry has been widely reported in East and Central Africa and there has been some comment and speculation on the origins of joking relationships in these terms.[4] Moreau (1944) was the first to raise the issue on the basis of information collected in Swahili from thirty-two Tanzanian men belonging to seventeen tribes. He classified *utani* into two main types, internal (between members of the same tribe) and external (between different tribes, typically associating all members of such tribes as *utani* to each other). The origin of these external *utani* links, found for as many as fifteen of the seventeen tribes, was the subject of considerable unanimity of opinion. Asking each informant how he thought external *utani* had originated, Moreau reports that 'without exception he said that his ancestors had fought (*pigana*) with the tribe with whom he now has *utani*' (1944:388). More precise or circumstantial information was not, however, forthcoming and Moreau comments on the difficulty this explanation poses where *utani* links tribes widely separate geographically. Though not conclusive, the existence of long-distance caravan routes and porterage goes some way towards explaining the pattern of linkages found. This, however, points to a relatively recent historical origin for such ties.

An even more recent origin has been suggested by Wilson (1957) and Gulliver (1957) on the basis of studies of the Nyakyusa and Ngoni. They argue that the *utani* relationship has been used to facilitate easy relationships between tribal groups with a tradition of rivalry and hostility in the colonial conditions of labour migration. As such they see it as modelled on the undoubtedly traditional forms of joking found within the tribe. For example, Wilson, stressing the fact that the tradition of rivalry is linked to mutual respect and carries the implication and obligation of mutual aid, sees it as a metaphoric extension of cross-cousinship for the Nyakyusa. She writes: 'In quality the *ubutani* between peoples resembles the traditional rivalry between cross-cousins because the quarrels are "family quarrels" which should not lead to action in court, and the rival with whom you spar will come to your rescue in a real fight against strangers' (Wilson, 1957: 111).

Yet if external *utani* shares some of the associations of internal *utani*, the question of origins remains obscure in the Tanzanian cases since the pattern of external alliance had been crystallised before fieldwork was done and *utani* was not apparently being used to create new alliances in the changing conditions of labour migration, as one might perhaps expect. What appears clear from the reported instances is that the idea of hostility, of mutual respect bred from prior fighting, is strongly associated with intertribal *utani* but forms a less prominent part of the repertoire of ideas associated with intratribal *utani* whose essential definition is seen in other terms, e.g. as dependent on kinship, intermarriage, purificatory services, etc. Nevertheless it is an aspect of the *utani* relationship. Thus Moreau reports that 'None of my informants can say with any confidence how his hereditary internal *utani* originated, but three different men suggest vaguely that the ancestors of the families concerned may have fought (*pigana*) or disputed (*gombana*)' (1944: 390). For the Kaguru, Christensen (1963) reports that interclan *utani* is seen as having developed as a result of warfare during the initial occupancy of the area, with victors and vanquished forming such an alliance and jointly settling a territory. Similarly among the Gogo, where Rigby (1968) reports that some clans relate their *utani* relationship to previous warfare or the usurpation of land by an immigrant group. More examples can be adduced (see Tew, 1951). Thus what seems to be the case is that the idea of prior hostility is widespread in East and Central Africa, forming one strand in the often complex cluster of ideas associated with joking, and subject to variable elaboration in local myth and traditions.

In this context, the Gisu elaboration of this theme forces the question as to whether the relationship was used as a pragmatic strategy to compact peace. Speculation as to such an origin is always difficult, especially when fieldwork was done some sixty years after the setting up of British administration and when other traditional measures for dealing with murders had long fallen into disuse. Nevertheless, the emphatic statements of the Gisu on the issue and the circumstantial nature of some accounts of the origin of specific linkages do strongly suggest that this was one way of resolving disputes between neighbouring families, providing a means of turning a situation of enmity into one of alliance.

Firstly, some of the main contrasts between the Tanzanian and Central African *utani* relationships mentioned above and the Gisu *bukulo* may be briefly outlined. The main point here is that *bukulo* is essentially a local, neighbourhood phenomenon and is said only to have been contracted between fellow Gisu and never used to create alliances between Gisu and neighbouring peoples. Thus the lines of speculation concerning external *utani* in Tanzania are irrelevant in the Gisu case as it cannot be associated with the exigencies of either long-distance trade or labour migration. Further, with the unstable and unresolved competition between the Gisu and the other peoples of the plains that existed in the nineteenth century, there perhaps would have been little call for the kind of permanent peace pact enshrined in *bukulo*. Rather, relationships between individuals of different tribes were established through blood brotherhood, which carried no hereditary implications.

Blood brotherhood, *busaale bwe sale*, literally 'friendship of cuts', referring to the incisions made on the forearm to draw the blood to be shared between the two parties to the relationship, carries similar connotations to the practice found widely elsewhere, namely the unconditional guarantee of mutual protection and aid in times of need. It is further associated by the Gisu with intertribal linkages, and specifically seen as a strategy which enabled the negotiation of peace treaties in the past. There are well-attested accounts of such relationships being formed between Gisu leaders and those of the invading plains tribes before the turn of the century. Breach of the terms of the relationship was here believed to result in destruction of the tribe of the defaulter. Blood brotherhood thus is seen as having a relatively definite purpose and tends not to be thought of as a strategy which may be used to create binding friendships between individual Gisu – at least between men. I did come across one case where it was used by a boy and a girl as a pledge to future marriage.

Accounts of origin of *bukulo* were rarely elaborated beyond the statement that there had been prior fighting between the two lineages. Alternatively, accounts of fighting between lineages might conclude with the statement that 'then they made *bukulo*'. Names of those killed and dating which would have given more historical substance to such accounts were thus in general lacking. This is not altogether surprising given their distant origin and the emphasis on hereditary transmission. However, I did come across one case where the details were still remembered, partly one suspects because the relationship had proved stillborn. In this case an elopement occurring almost immediately after *bukulo* had been contracted had effectively replaced *bukulo* by affinal ties. This had evidently not been popular among the families concerned since the *bukulo* relationship is incompatible with close affineship.

THE SYMBOLISM OF PEACE

Accounts of peacemaking ceremonies are subject to greater elaboration. There appear to have been two main forms of peacemaking ceremony and opinion varies (largely according to clan area) as to which was used to initiate *bukulo*. The first, in essentials, appears to have been the general form for all peacemaking, whether the parties were kin, other Gisu or members of other tribes, though the actual ceremonies undoubtedly varied considerably in scale. Here, a cow or goat was sacrificed on the boundary between the two opposing sides, either a path or more commonly a stream, and cut in half 'like a rat', that is across the middle, thus separating the forequarters from the hindquarters. The stomach was then extracted and the chyme mixed with blood into which leafy branches were dipped by the warriors of each side to spray the other. Sometimes, in the course of this mock fight, beer is said also to have been mixed with the chyme and sprayed in this way or, alternatively, beer was blown explosively from drinking-gourds. Each side then roasted its meat separately but shared the flesh, one man taking a piece of meat, cutting it in half with his spear and offering it to a member of the opposing side, and so on.

Peacemaking of this kind involved the killing of the *ingafu iye ifugi*, 'the cow of blood'. As a signifier and pledge of peace killing an animal in this way was potent for the Gisu as it is said that it was one of the few occasions when blood was spilt during animal sacrifice. Blood was preserved for the purposes of most sacrifices; chickens had their necks wrung, goats were strangulated and cattle stunned by a blow on the head. Such sacrificial forms are regarded as specifically Gisu, being indeed the only ritual observance in addition to circumcision which was said to have been common to all the clans. However, in the context of *bukulo*, one man explained as follows: 'They threw the blood to show that *bukulo* is strong. Even if those making peace die and their children after them, *bukulo* itself cannot die because they have killed the cow of blood.'

In other areas, including Busoba, it is said that for *bukulo* a special form of peace was made and that a dog was slaughtered in place of the cow. Interesting corroboration of such a practice is provided by an account given by Rev. J. B. Purvis, who gives an account of such a ceremony in terms which suggest that he witnessed it:

When two clans have been engaged in war, and each has tried in vain for the mastery, they decide to make a compact which no man or woman would dream of breaking.

A dog is brought to the boundary and there cut in two, where so many fights have taken place. One half is placed on the land of one clan and the other half on the land of the other clan, and the warriors of each clan march in procession between the two halves, which are then spurned by both parties.

There is much hand-shaking and merriment, and from that time the clans are friendly. (Purvis, 1909:292)

Purvis comments that the people gave no clear reason for such a practice but he considers that the underlying idea is the wish that whoever broke the compact would 'end like the dog – disowned, cut in two, and spurned' (Purvis, 1909:293). It is possible to extrapolate further, however, by examining the matrix of ideas and attitudes which are associated with the dog and which make the killing of a dog a particularly apt symbol for peacemaking, providing not only a graphic representation of the ending of hostilities but an act which can be seen as striking at the very motives which provoke them.

For the Gisu the dog epitomises anti-social troublemaking, *kamaya*. It has 'bad blood' and is described as indiscriminate in all its habits and proclivities, whether sexual, aggressive or in eating. As such, dogs are universally despised, making the Muslim abhorrence of the dog readily comprehensible. Emphatically, the Gisu do not see the dog as a friend to man but more the enemy within the camp; the unsocialisable domestic animal inherently opposed to the discipline and conventions of human social order. The dog is also the only domesticated animal which is not eaten, a prohibition which extends to all animals which fall into the dog class, a class which includes most of the wild carnivores, leopards and lions. All associations reinforce the idea that the dog is a hostile predator which is tolerated within human society for one purpose alone – its use as a guard animal, where its natural aggressiveness can be used to warn and fend off the danger from human enemies. To this end dogs are frequently both beaten and starved and fed 'medicines' in order to make them more fierce. The killing of a dog to cement a peace pact thus forcefully carries the idea of destroying 'disorder' and all its associated evils. The dog represents both *kamaya*, the disregard for normal conventions and rules which leads to trouble and ill-will within the community, and its outcome, hatred, *cixonde*. Once the dog has been killed, the two parties may freely enter each other's houses, hatred removed but not forgotten.

At the most evident level *bukulo* represents the renunciation of the feud and feuding relationships within the locality. Unlike the payment of blood compensation, which may only partially atone for a death and which may thus form part of a feuding relationship, the terms of the *bukulo* relationship in this respect are unequivocal. The structural context for such a unique form of peace pact would seem to be that of small and relatively weak kinship groups living in close proximity and linked by marriage and matrifiliation.[5] Where no prior ties exist, *bukulo* may be said to capitalise on a situation of hostility by converting it into friendship and, in so doing, provide yet another extra-agnatic tie which extends the individual's social network and the density of extra-agnatic affiliations. Yet the tie remains distinctive, combining as it does the polarities of affect, of friendship and hatred. This aspect demands a broader, even existential, treatment and forms the topic of a later discussion.

If *bukulo* may be taken to represent the rejection of the feud in the context of interlineage relationships, there are also negating factors internal to the lineage itself and it is to these that we now turn.

LINEAGE AND THE LACK OF LOYALTY

Moving from *bukulo* to the current reaction to murders in the community we may pick up the earlier discussion of homicide and the lack of lineage identification. Gisu lineage groups provide an axis for loyalty and support of the individual but it is one that he can by no means count on. While a man may approach his lineage elders when he is in trouble, he is never bound to consult them with respect to most of his affairs, nor are they bound to support him in quarrels. Indeed, it is only at the lowest level of lineage identification that the principle of *lex talionis* is operative at all, with members of the elementary family (brothers, fathers and sons) sometimes taking vengeance or being held culpable so that vengeance is exacted upon them. Even here – and crucially – the principle is not invoked in an automatic way and where such vengeance was taken I never heard it justified in terms of a principle of substitution. Rather, it was accompanied by the accusation that the kinsman was an actual accomplice in the crime and thus directly shared in the culpability. This can be illustrated by the following case.

Case 8 Vengeance witchcraft   Busoba, 1968
Xauxa, an extremely old man, returned home one day to find his house broken into and his money, carefully buried in the floor, gone. The amount was said to be the small fortune of 1200s. He immediately suspected Wangolo, a man in his twenties whom he had employed a month or so before in the building of the house, on the reasonable grounds that Wangolo knew of the existence of this money and its probable hiding place. Since Wangolo was in any case a well-known thief the accusation had wide currency and immediate moves were made by neighbours to find and arrest him. However, he had already absconded to Mbale and could not be found.

Three days later, Muslim diviners said to come from twenty miles away in Bukedi were seen at Xauxa's house. Muslim diviners are regarded by the Gisu as knowing the most potent forms of retaliatory magic and distance further adds to the reputation for power. The very next day Nacimolo, the father of Wangolo, fell seriously ill and died four days later. The body immediately began to swell, indicating witchcraft. At the funeral, which was very well attended, most people were careful to stay a good way off and few had the courage to enter the house where the body was laid out for fear that the witchcraft substance might still be active there. Xauxa himself did not attend and could just be made out from the site of the funeral sitting in his own courtyard. Nor was Wangolo there, though whether his absence was due solely to his fear of arrest or whether from the possibility that he too was bewitched remained a moot point. One of his sisters brought news from Mbale that he was indeed ill, 'running as if he were mad' and unable to speak coherently.

For many months these dramatic events served as a cautionary tale of just vengeance against two thieves. For the action of the witchcraft against the father was thought to be possible only because he too was implicated in the theft and had shared the proceeds with his son. This possibility of joint culpability carries with it a sting in the tail. For far from supporting the individual, it is often members of the family who are most concerned to repudiate him and act thus to protect themselves from each other's felonies. To a lesser extent, the wider lineage is under the same constraint since the misdeeds of its members tend to get it a bad reputation as bad habits are believed to run in families. Thus the wider kindred too often feel bound not only to warn an impenitent individual but also to indicate publicly that they too deplore his actions.

An absence of retaliatory killings thus can be associated with the reluctance of kin to bear responsibility for the actions of their members. Support is always qualified. Indeed, they may feel under particular pressure to disown troublesome elements in their midst. The moral lesson seen to lie in the above events can be contrasted here with the exemplary tale told of a famed leader, Lutiko of the Bangokho, who was credited with making the peace with the Teso at the turn of the century. In discussing the actions to be taken against thieves, an elder from the Bangokho brought up the following story:

Lutiko himself killed his son because he was a thief. His wife was the first one to kill one of their own children. She killed him because he stole pieces of meat from the cooking pot. She said to her husband, 'Husband, you complain that I have eaten all the sauce and there is none left for you. But now you see what that child has done.' Lutiko told her to kill that child for he was just a troublemaker and had let her be called a thief. Nambozo killed her child, over that meat itself, she hit him and he died. That son was still young and when the one that followed him grew up he stole a goat from Lutiko. He stole it with the help of two friends. Lutiko followed them and while it was still day he killed his son and one of the others. The one that escaped hid for a long time. When he returned he paid two cows to Lutiko.

This story has an apocryphal ring but its message is clear. Lutiko's action, running against parental sentiments, attests to the greater fears of breeding wastrel sons. More, it shows him as an honourable man and implicitly contrasts him with fathers who are themselves thieves and thus in league with their sons in their misdoings. While in the discourse on morality the veracity of the account is irrelevant, it is not *prima facie* unlikely. Killings within the elementary family, as has been discussed, do indeed occur and are given moral justification.

Killings within the family of this kind are not foreign to segmentary systems where the principle of *lex talionis* operates at all higher levels of segmentation. For example, Schapera (1955) has argued that the operative principle here is the right of self-determination by the kinship group, and the smaller the group, the more likely it is that the individual himself will be deemed wholly responsible for his acts. The issues here are seen as interpersonal and not matters which invoke the principle of collective indemnity. Thus in talking about fratricide among the Biblical Hebrews, Schapera writes that the attitude taken towards it depended 'not so much on fixed legal rules, as upon the size and monetary composition of the family, the domestic balance of power, the circumstances of the killing, the personal feelings of the people involved, and other factors of the same general kind' (1955:42). Such an attitude has been put in a structural context by Sally Moore (1972). She argues that any group recognising collective liability will have the corresponding right to exercise discretion as to whether or not to support a member: 'if an individual can commit a corporate group to act, there is the possibility of being expelled by it' (Moore, 1972:90). 'Public' and 'private' law may then be seen as complementary aspects of the same structure. While the 'private' aspect may be seen in the self-help taken by the group to avenge its members, 'what is equivalent to a criminal penalty is the kind of individual assessment of character inside corporate groups which can lead ultimately to expulsion or exclusion' (Moore, 1972: 95). Thus the group may take action itself against the individual it has condemned or may simply withdraw support, leaving the individual open to retribution from others.

However, there are nuances in the Gisu system which point to a difference again from such segmentary forms. In the first place what seems to be at issue in the Gisu case is not a fear of collective identification that must lead them to unite in a solidary fashion but a fear of moral identification of character. The Gisu are afraid that the moral opprobrium of the 'bad lot' will attach to them also as a group but, more particularly, as individuals. The battle in so far that it is a battle of reputations is played out within the group as much as between groups. And this is true of all judgement; the lineage is neither the only nor a discrete arena for the assessment of character and motive. Lineage judgements are in line with community ones. There is thus, in Bugisu, no 'continually changing moral perspective' (Read, 1955) in line with segmentary loyalties. Lacking such loyalties, the Gisu moral system lacks the relativity of morality and judgement which has been seen as one of the distinctive characteristics of such acephalous communities.

Nor is the individual protected by the group. The lack of a principle of absolute collective liability of kin in Bugisu has decisive implications both for the support an individual may expect from his kin as well as for the nature of moral judgement. Where this principle is important we may hypothesise that there are pressures which militate against common recourse to the loopholes in communal obligation. Such would tend to undermine the balancing of force with equal force which serves to define and redefine group relationships, just as it would weaken the basis for trust essential for the cohesion of the group. It is of interest that such measures are not reported for the 'classic' segmentary societies known to us from the literature; not, for example, among the Nuer (Evans-Pritchard, 1940: Howell, 1954), nor for the Bedouin (Peters, 1967). In an important discussion of segmentary lineage organisation, Gellner (1969), for the Moroccan Berbers, mentions two institutional ways in which a group may escape the consequences of a member's action: partial exemption obtained by letting him down in the communal oath and the ultimate sanction of the 'good fratricide' against a recidivist member. But set against these measures being resorted to with any frequency are the countervailing pressures arising from the nature of segmentary lineage organisation which puts some premium on in-group loyalty, albeit situationally determined.

However, the sentiment that fires the feud, summed up in a Kabyle saying, 'Help your kinsmen whether they are right or wrong' (Bourdieu, 1965: 229) finds no recognition in Bugisu. The Gisu man stands firmly alone, unable to commit his descent group either morally or in action on his behalf. The group not only provides little in the way of support for its members but may indeed be the first to withdraw its support. I can think of no Gisu word that one could translate as loyalty. The word that would be used to indicate such support would be the verb *xufukilira*, which translates best as 'to agree', or 'to be in agreement with', thus carrying much more contingent implications. It is used for the agreement of terms in contracts, to indicate support for the arguments or statements of others and to aver concord. It is interesting to note that the first missionary in the area was given this word when he sought a translation equivalent for the Christian 'love', reporting with some disappointment that it was also the verb used with the sense of 'to agree'.[6]

Nor are killings within the family, of brother by brother or son by father or father by son, regarded as especially bad. In the segmentary situation, the 'good fratricide' rids a group of an undesirable member, thus averting feuds and disputes with other groups. It is a necessary evil and with other kinds of fratricide vengeance is seen largely as self-defeating, the group taking double punishment in a situation where the strength of the group depends on the physical force it can muster. However, such killings may incur special dangers of pollution, and may result in the expulsion of the culprit, either temporarily or permanently, from the group. In Bugisu such murders incur no special pollution (*imbixo*). In asking this question, a typical response ran as follows: 'But why should there be *imbixo*? they say, "They have killed each other: when a son kills a father or a brother kills a brother it is finished." They just bury the dead man and it is all over. There cannot be any hatred.'

In actual cases there may well indeed be hatred, as much here as with any other killing. A local man was well-known for his saying, 'there is not much in kinship', a saying which related to the death of his father at the hands of his brother some thirty years earlier, but one which was taken as a more general comment on the nature of family relationship, inspiring wry humour. And the fact is that reactions to killing within the family do not differ greatly from reactions found to any other kind of killing. We are dealing here with a system of self-help that is so individualised that it differentiates little between kin and non-kin.

All that remains of a segmentary principle is the sentiment that killings within the family do not, by and large, involve outsiders. Even so, the rarity of blood vengeance appears as an anomaly, given the high rate of interpersonal violence and the expectation of violent retaliation in situations which inspire hatred and where men are aggrieved. In order to understand better the pressures that are operative in counteracting blood vengeance we now turn to the nature of neighbourhood relationships and the valuation of conduct in disputes at the present time.

NOTES

1　Crabtree, letter 1901: Church Missionary Society Archives.

2　For example, as with the extensive debate over Sahlins's (1961) thesis that segmentary lineage organisation is an adaptation for predatory expansion. On Salzman's thesis, see Holy (1979).

3　Radcliffe-Brown (1940a, 1949) defined these joking forms in terms of their essential ambivalence as a 'peculiar combination of friendship and antagonism' (1952:91) which gave expression as he saw it to both the common and the divergent interests of parties to an alliance. See further, p. 217.

4　It is not being argued that this is the only theme apparent in African joking forms. Another contrasting and widespread theme in the joking patterns of Central and Southern Africa has been analysed by Kuper (1982) where the joking is based on the ambiguities involved in cross-cousinship, sexuality and marriage. See also Beidelman, 1966; Rigby, 1968; Freedman, 1977.

5　A similar line of reasoning is given by Tew (1951) in discussing the structural context of funeral friendship patterns in Central Africa.

6　First letter from the Rev. W. Crabtree from Bugisu to the CMS in 1901.

8

COMMUNITY AND CONFLICT

The infrequency of vengeance and the demise of traditional institutions of conciliation point to the general weakness of kinship groupings, their lack of collective responsibility and their corresponding lack of coercive power over the actions of their members. Indeed, what one finds instead is an almost universal stress on individual autonomy, with homicide and indeed any resort to violence being seen as an individual prerogative. Hostilities are interpreted in interpersonal and not in intergroup terms. Group membership thus does not structure patterns of violence; it does not regulate killing nor does it provide any security for the individual.

Further, killing is largely a matter of kinship. In an overwhelming proportion of the cases in the court records both the accused and victim came from the same parish and were often also close neighbours. In two-thirds of the thirty-seven cases I investigated in some detail in central Bugisu both accused and victim lived within 200 to 300 yards from each other and in the remaining cases not more than one mile away. In some 40% of the court cases it was possible to ascertain that at least one of the accused was related to the victim and this proportion is undoubtedly underestimated because of the difficulty of establishing kinship relationship from the court records. Nevertheless, the proportions are indicative; in twenty-eight cases a spouse was killed, in twelve an affine, but in the vast majority, 110, the victim was a consanguine.

This chapter will not be directly concerned with the escalation of grievances into murder but will deal with what, in many respects, is the other side of the coin – the ways in which he repercussions of disputes between individuals are limited and prevented from spreading to involve others. The main body of the chapter is an extended case study which follows the reactions of people after a murder in the community in order to see how the strong emotions aroused by the event were eventually dissipated in a way which allowed kin to renegotiate their relationships with others. The strategies used to minimise the disruptive implications of such deaths provide the focus for this study, as they illustrate both the way individuals are unprotected by kinship loyalties and the nature of moral discourse. This opens the way for a more general discussion of Gisu morality in chapter 9. The context for the present discussion is the neighbourhood and relationships within the neighbourhood as they were in the mid-1960s.

NEIGHBOURHOOD

At higher levels of the descent system descent groups are associated with specific territories which, in the main, have been consolidated as administrative units. The lowest administrative unit in the 1960s was the parish, varying in size from one to ten square miles and with a population of between 2,000 and 5,000. Within this area, the names of the former village divisions are still used for locational reference, as are what might be called the 'unofficial' divisions of the parish created by the parish chief for convenience in tax collection.[1] These areas denote the sphere of influence of a *mutala* chief or headman who acts as a personal and unpaid assistant to the parish chief. All these areas are clearly defined, their boundaries following the course of streams or established paths and roads. They are also named, either after a lineage or sub-clan or a feature of the natural environment, these latter also being used for the finer distinctions used to refer to the exact site of a man's house.

The division into parishes – the lowest unit of the administration – is fundamental. In everyday life a man's dealings with the administration are most affected by his parish of residence which determines the chief to whom he must pay his taxes, the councillor for whom he can vote and the court in which he can sue his fellows. No territorial subdivisions which exist within the parish provide a similar focus for commitment and, at the level of the *mutala* divisions, descent-group affiliation provides no framework for community values. The *mutala* commonly consist of between fifty and 100 taxpayers (adult men), drawn from various lineages and even sub-clans. Members of a *mutala* never see themselves as an exclusive community with special obligations to each other by virtue of inclusion in a *mutala*.

Indeed what strikes an observer is the straggling, diffuse nature of social life and the lack of bounded communities. There is nothing in the spacing and distribution of homesteads which marks out one area from another at any territorial level, men happily building their houses straddled over administrative and other divisions of the countryside. Nor in everyday life do such boundaries have any significance in defining communities or neighbourhoods. Indeed, there are no defined neighbourhood areas with a focus where men might meet to discuss the day's events, although shops, crossroads and beer clubs scattered irregularly over the countryside do serve this purpose to some extent. The exigencies of defence which led to the clustering of homesteads in the past have long since disappeared and today there is no incentive, either indigenous or governmental, which would favour such concentrations. Men feel free to build their homes on any portion of their own land, whether this be thirty or 300 yards from their nearest neighbour.

Yet despite this lack of clearly delineated communities, locality is an extremely important principle in social life and marks out for the individual a highly significant arena of social relationships. A man's neighbourhood is not a discrete area, for the obligations incumbent on neighbours (*bawesana*) weaken with distance. Nor is it of any particular size, as each individual will have greater or lesser interest in extending such obligations to include more people. For most men, however, a radius of about a quarter of a mile from their own house marks the area in which they will spend most of their time with regard to both work and leisure. Again, for the majority of men, most, if not all, people living in such an area will be kin; a few, perhaps from one to ten adults, will be his agnates, and to the others he will be related by diverse ties of affinity and consanguinity. The neighbourhood is obviously not an exclusive area and it is unique to every man; those living near to one another having an overlapping but distinct constellation of neighbours just as they also have distinct networks of kinship and friendship which stretch outside such an area.

Neighbours extend to each other certain rights over their land. Thus streams, springs and waterholes are considered to belong to the area, rather than to the individual who owns the surrounding land, and all may use them freely. Similarly rights to fishing, although of little economic importance in most areas, are held by neighbours, not the individual. In addition, neighbours usually graze their cattle over fallow fields and along the verges of paths and may collect thatching grass and firewood from the same areas. As these economic privileges indicate, the emphasis in neighbourly relationships is on friendship and mutual assistance. In the past working bees of women and men were based on the neighbourhood, neighbours helping each other in major agricultural tasks. While the formal work associations had disappeared by the 1960s, work parties remained a neighbourhood concern, with those participating rewarded by a beer party after the morning's work. It is within the vicinage too, that the more informal norms of hospitality are stressed; a passer-by shares the food of the household as he steps in to chat for a few minutes or is invited to comment on the strength of the day's brew of beer. Indeed failure to eat with others, to accept food as well as to offer it, is such an arrant breach of neighbourly norms that it indicates serious discord among the people concerned.

It is neighbours as well as kinsmen who recognise the important rites of passage of the individual, bringing small gifts at the time of births, circumcision, marriage and death. Most such gift-giving is personalised, accompanying for example the first visit to a mother after her confinement. At marriages and deaths, however, neighbours are expected to help collectively by bringing baskets of cooked food to feast the bride and to contribute towards the cost of the mourning rites. The importance of the locality is also stressed by religious observances on all such occasions, and it is considered dangerous for either a woman to give birth or for a person to die away from home. Indeed there are specific taboos (*kimisiro*) which confine the participants and their immediate kin to the locality during all major life-cycle rituals. During these times, they may not walk far from the house, nor cross major paths and streams.

Yet residence is not static and the population in any area tends to fluctuate considerably. The Gisu are a mobile people, always open to the lure of fresh land. Since the turn of the century such pioneering has taken them far from their tightly-packed mountain valleys down to the plains and, as such open spaces have been populated, further afield, to take up settlement in Kenya or Buganda. Added to this migration, the Gisu also quickly accustomed themselves to temporary migration in search of work, leaving the area for a few months or years but occasionally, in the case of skilled artisans or professional people, for the course of their working lives. Even within the parish men are continually shifting their place of residence. In the normal course of events, the clay and thatch houses require rebuilding every five to ten years and men then often choose to build on another piece of their own land or buy land elsewhere on which to re-settle. Such movement is little hindered by ties of sentiment to particular tracts of land. Lineage land consists merely of those plots at present held by members of the lineage. The composition of any area is thus not only heterogeneous, with members of different lineages living in close proximity, but also fluid as men shift their residence and the land itself changes hands from one lineage group to another.

With residence primarily a factor of personal choice, even small shifts in a man's house-site, 100 yards away or across a small valley, mark significant changes in the patterning of his social relationships and redefine the individual's vicinage. Indeed removal of a house-site is indicative of a desired change in personal relationships and is invariably precipitated by quarrels or bad feeling. This holds true for such cases as the son who on achieving a tardy independence from his father settles himself on the furthest-flung plot of his father's land. Similarly a man who moves to avoid incessant quarrels with his neighbour or, in the extreme case, finds it expedient to move out of the area altogether, perhaps for a spell of work in the township or in order to settle on the plains, is escaping from a difficult, perhaps even dangerous, situation.

The neighbourhood is seen ideally as the place of relative safety. In talking about the obligations incumbent upon neighbours, the Gisu emphasise this characteristic together with the obligation to answer any alarm raised at night, a rule codified in by-law. It is also here that men usually say that they feel safe to walk home after dark. This relates to the preference to drink nearby, for if a man drinks elsewhere he must choose either to leave early or be prepared to stay the night to avoid the dangers of walking alone at night. The fear of inadvertently drinking with enemies also tends to support parochial drinking patterns. Within the neighbourhood an individual feels able to pinpoint his enemies and take what evasive action he can. The intimate nature of social interaction within such vicinages makes any breakdown in normal social relationships immediately apparent, and slight changes in a neighbour's demeanour are noticed as well as those dramatised by avoidance, lack of greeting and open quarrels. Outside this area, grievances may not only simmer undetected but a man faces in addition the threat from 'strangers'. Men thus tend not to venture far from home to drink beer, unless they go under the protection of a friend or in the company of fellows to the relatively neutral ground provided by a licensed beer club.

Yet the very intensity of social relationships within the vicinage both adds to hatred engendered by dispute when this occurs, just as it gives more opportunity for grievance. It is in a vicinage setting that the critical and endemic disputes among close agnates over the distribution of land and cattle occur as well as quarrels over the exact boundaries of adjacent plots. Likewise, when cattle break loose from their ropes, it is a neighbour's field they ravage. Whatever the cause, such disputes among men who see each other daily are not easily forgotten, and associated with all disputes are fears of violence. Neighbours who can watch each other's comings and goings are the clearest suspects when it comes to ambush, theft and witchcraft. Indeed an undercurrent of witchcraft fears is rarely absent from the vicinage. When people sicken it is usually neighbours who are the first suspects since they have easy access to the bodily waste matter necessary for some kinds of witchcraft. On account of this, witchcraft fears attach to all communal gatherings, whether beer parties or the periodic ritual feasts which ostensibly express amity and mutual concern. Such fears, superimposed upon other grievances, often taken disputes outside the realm of settlement, and instead of the easy companionship and trust which the Gisu desire among neighbours, relationships deteriorate and erupt in violence.

THE BEER PARTY AS A SITUATION OF DEATH

The beer party is in fact the place where murder is most feared. To understand this attitude, it is necessary to outline the general significance of beer-drinking for the Gisu and the part it plays in social life. In the first place it is a daily occurrence, not only essential for the celebration of any special or ritual occasion but operating more generally to facilitate neighbourly co-operation and sociability. Thus beer is offered freely at feasts, in return for work and also for sale. The beer party or the beer club provide the main venues for drinking. The former are essentially private parties where an individual obtains a beer-brewing licence and then offers this beer to his or her kin and neighbours, often in return for work but also for sale. Millet or maize beer is the most popular and this is usually drunk around a communal pot, with the thick porridge of fermented grain being diluted with successive buckets of almost boiling water. The beer is sucked up through long reed tubes which vary in length from four to eight feet to allow staggered seating around a central pot. Permanently licensed beer clubs or bars provide a more neutral setting and attract a wider clientele. Here beer is sometimes sold by the pot but more usually by the gourd or bottle, and there is usually a choice of alcohol available.

Alcohol, then, is very freely available and, with beer parties starting about lunchtime and continuing until well after dark, so is drunkenness. Sometimes this leads to violence, sometimes after an apparently trivial quarrel. A case from the court records can be taken to illustrate this.

Case 9 Mwenyi gets a beating   (Muyembe, North Bugisu)
Wafula had called his brothers-in-law together to help him pick his cotton crop and afterwards offered them beer. The two sets of relatives, the party of his wife and the party of his sister's husband, were offered beer in separate houses, as is customary because they came from different areas. They all began drinking about 2.00 p.m. and between 5.00 and 6.00 p.m., a woman, Janeti, decided to leave. Mwenyi, who was distantly related to her and who had brought her to the party, was intent on leaving with her but was prevented by two other men in the same group on the grounds that she was married. Mwenyi responded angrily with the taunt, 'Are you yourselves offering to sleep with me as you have stopped me following my girl?' They then began to beat him, knocking his head against the wall. Wafula was called from the other group with whom he had been drinking and managed to put a stop to the fight, but not before Mwenyi had been injured severely enough to die a day or so after. In court the accused admitted the offence and claimed that the real issue was not Janeti but the fact that Mwenyi had been making too much noise and preventing them listening to their radio.

The Gisu are well aware of these kinds of effects of alcohol and many men fear their own aggressive reactions when drunk, sometimes to the extent that they avoid drinking altogether. This is a high price to pay for, as Ivan Karp has written of the neighbouring Teso, in the absence of specific contractual obligations attendance at beer parties indicates 'intentions to interact in a cooperative manner' (Karp: 1980b:89). It thus facilitates both long and short-term exchanges. But more, it is a measure of sociability, both that of the individual and that of an ideal form of commensality. And herein lies the problem. The Gisu have a proverb, 'Witchcraft thrives on friendship': not only can the ideal not be achieved but it carries the seeds of its own destruction. The collective occasion, the company of friends, can never be altogether trusted. And this cannot simply be laid to the disinhibiting effects of alcohol. As Jean la Fontaine has emphasised, the Gisu do not kill 'blindly in their cups' (1960b: 95); drunken killing tends to be motivated by older scores. Knowing this only too well, most Gisu are extremely careful about their choice of drinking companions, but no man can be totally on guard against those who choose to dissemble their intentions. Under a show of friendship a murderer may buy his intended victim beer and, thus disarmed, attack him later.

Case 10 Get the victim drunk   (Busiu)
                                                                    homicide survey 3
After selling his cotton at the local co-operative society, Walubongo called in at the beer club for a drink. There he met both his brother's son and grandson, Mbesho and Kisamba. They began to drink with him, and when the pot was finished

Kisamba bought Walubongo a separate bottle of banana beer mixed with *waragi*, a favourite mixture. The drinking continued until well after nightfall, with Walubongo leaving about 8.00 p.m. The owner of the beer club, another relative and son-in-law to Walubongo, then gave evidence that Mbesho and Kisamba conferred together for some fifteen minutes before following Walubongo out. Other people gave evidence that the two men returned home for their spears. Walubongo was attacked while still on his way home a little later but nobody answered his alarm. He was found dead on the path the next morning. The two younger men both suspected Walubongo of bewitching them, a fact which was not reported in the case records, and the two were later discharged owing to lack of evidence.

The beer party then is seen as the scene for planning murder. The noisy confusion of a typical beer party, where between ten and fifty men and women might be crowded together in the main room of a house, is seen to give ample opportunity for conspirators. And it is here that the fear of poisoning enters and enters in a way which epitomises such fears. This poison is believed to be placed in the mouth of a drinking-straw, thus contaminating not the whole brew but just the specific straw. Yet it is customary, an act of friendship, for a person to offer his straw to another to drink from so that those who come without their own straws may also drink. Again, when he leaves the room temporarily, a man also leaves his straw with a friend to use. These practices and associated fears would thus seem to underscore the fragility in friendship, the necessity for trust and the inevitability that it will be abused. Further, they are all pervasive, so that all social gatherings and celebrations carry fears of witchcraft and poisoning. All rituals, whether at marriages, circumcisions or death, involve feasting and beer-drinking and they are all seen to hold the risk of poison, so that people are obliged to share and eat food that in fact they deeply distrust.

STRATEGIES FOR LIVING

As has been said, in ordinary life the individual stands out as the autonomous unit. Once a man has been circumcised, marries and builds his own house he is regarded as a fully mature man. He is expected to be self-sufficient and self-reliant, a master of his own affairs and not subject to group discipline or group control. His own 'toughness' and strength is all: he must make his own decisions and personally redress the wrongs done to him. Self-help thus lies on the individual level and largely remains here. In his dealings with others a man aims to build up a network of support in his neighbourhood and he relies on such friends to listen out for him at the beer parties they attend, bring him back news and warn him of the dangers that may lie in wait for him. But such friends do not necessarily become involved directly in his disputes, most frequently, indeed, disclaiming any such intention with the words, 'I just turn your millet over but am not eating it'. Partisanship implies danger. Just as a man who intervenes to stop a fight may well find himself more soundly beaten than the original combatants, active intervention in the affairs of others is avoided as far as possible.

The rules and values which inform everyday life stress the importance of judicious conduct, to keeping to the tried and tested maxims of living. Proverbial wisdom exists in plenty with its message of the general untrustworthiness of others, of avoiding open strife and guarding against the hidden enmity. In any situation open support for another must be balanced both against the dangers it might bring to the individual offering it and the potential disruption it might have on his other social relationships. The tactical rules of everyday life then tend to place a premium on what one might call ways of disclaiming responsibility. People assiduously avoid taking sides and a public fiction of ignorance is maintained in many situations of conflict. The scandalmonger is doubly abhorred; he not only spreads knowledge of offences but in so doing he evokes enmities and thus may precipitate violence.

This is not to say, of course, that quarrels are not talked about, but that they are talked about covertly and with circumspection. Through the face-to-face exchange of news gossip travels fast and, between those who trust each other, may be freely commented upon. However in public gatherings, such as beer parties, scandal of any kind is phased warily, by allusion and with an obliqueness only to be picked up by those already cognisant of the facts. Indeed, people develop effective secret languages for use in such situations. Some are developed between friends by selecting key words from the stock of proverbs and riddles to convey their meaning, and among old men these languages may become so elaborate that they are truly impenetrable by outsiders. Dissimulation becomes, if not exactly a virtue, a necessary skill for daily living.

The repercussions of disputes are to this extent controlled, for the ordinary congress of daily life may proceed with politeness while grievances are left to simmer below the surface. There is a general and important contrast between morning and afternoon here. The morning is regarded as a propitious time, the time for work and quiet sociability around the home, but also the time for sacrifices, starting ventures and long journeys. The afternoon is less propitious, even unlucky and dangerous. It is the time for doing 'tough' things, for circumcisions, burials and collecting debts. With beer-drinking starting usually in the late morning, this division also takes on the overtones of sobriety versus drunkenness. Life does indeed get noticeably more raucous and dangerous as the afternoon progresses into night and brawls and fighting break out. Each night brings its accounts of trouble and sadness, of illnesses, thefts, woundings and arson.

At this point we might look at the structure of the local government administration and particularly at the courts, which ostensibly existed to keep the peace. At the time in question these were manifestly under pressure and complaints of their inadequacy were widespread. Indeed, as will be detailed later, it was this perception which led to Gisu moves to establish their own parallel system of control through the establishment of drinking companies and vigilante groups. To a large extent the failures of the local administration at this time can be related to the fundamental changes in structure which were instituted as part of the transfer from colonial to post-colonial state. The following section concentrates only upon the powers of the local chiefs and the workings of the courts and moots in the local areas in the mid-1960s, at about the time the new associations began to gain momentum.

THE COURT SYSTEM IN THE 1960s

During the 1960s there were several changes in the judicial system which affected dispute settlement in the rural areas. The Magistrates' Courts Act of 1964 marked the unification of Ugandan law and, with this, the separation of the judiciary from the administration. Up until then, the chiefs and District Commissioner had acted as judges and a bipartite system of law had been in force. The District Commissioner had tried cases under the Ugandan penal code, while the chiefs had tried cases under the jurisdiction of the Native Courts Act. While serious offences could only be tried under the penal code, the chiefs' courts had jurisdiction over all other matters of customary law and local by-laws. With the implementation of the 1964 Act, all the courts of the native judiciary were disbanded and replaced by a series of Magistrates' Courts at the sub-county and district levels. These courts had jurisdiction over all Ugandan law and, while offences under customary law could still be tried in these new courts, the set penalty often differed from that which had held previously. In addition, some criminal offences under customary law could now only be tried under civil law and thus the plaintiff now had to pay a registration fee. Together with these changes in the law the chiefs, who had sat with two local men as assessors, were replaced as judges by new magistrates. At the sub-county level, these magistrates were in the main young men who had been given six months' training and, in accordance with the government's nationalist policy, were rarely Lugisu-speaking.

Suspicion of the new magistrates, uncertainty over the new form of the law as well as the distance to the sub-county headquarters and the expense, all deterred people from making full use of these courts. In the local areas then, the parish chief and his deputy together with the headmen continued to fulfil their old role as judges in disputes. As before, they sifted cases, reported the more serious to the police in Mbale or to a higher magistrate and attempted to settle those which had been within their jurisdiction since the establishment of the Native Courts in 1919. However, the legitimacy of the chief still acting as a judge in this way was challenged in 1967 when a notice was promulgated to the effect that from now on all disputes, whatever their nature, were to be tried in the Magistrates' Courts. In most areas the chiefs stopped holding public moots at this time and unofficial arbitration was further challenged in the following year when the District Council outlawed the 'employment' of headmen by the parish chiefs.

With the chiefs and their assistants under threat, the arrangements for local dispute settlement during this period varied over time and from parish to parish (see Heald, 1982b). These arrangements may be divided into those which directly involved the chiefs and his assistants and those which were the primary concern of lineage elders. While lineage elders were also in some cases headmen, the part they played was more generally that of counselling. Apart from their persuasive powers, they had no other sanctions to achieve settlement and the Gisu had long been used to look to the official courts for judgement.

Formal dispute settlement in the rural areas usually took place under the aegis of an official, either a headman or a chief. For example, in one area of Busoba a weekly moot was held on the boundaries of three *mutala* areas and consisted of the three headmen together, sometimes with the parish chief. People from all three *mutala* brought their disputes to this moot, though the chief and headmen would also be called to an individual's house to attempt to settle the more urgent matters. The parish chief (and the headmen by virtue of their relationship to him) had definite powers to enforce his decisions. Despite the fact that at this time the chief's judicial authority had been considerably reduced (and legally did not exist at all), the parish chief and his deputy still retained wide powers through their overall responsibility for the maintenance of law and order in their area. For example, the threat of arrest was often a powerful incentive to acquiescence in the cases tried by the chief. This practice depended upon the discretion of the chief, his assessment of the participants and the consequences which might arise out of the dispute. Where, for example, a man was persistently troublesome, the chief might arrest him for the infringement of a by-law (brewing the spirit, *waragi*, illegally, lack of a latrine and so on), offences which in the normal course of events he would overlook. Most chiefs resorted to such measures sparingly, for no chief likes to get a reputation for putting a man in prison for minor offences. However, threats of such action occasionally put a recalcitrant member of the community effectively 'on probation'.

Yet the fact remains that the registration of a case with either a headman or chief was hardly a guarantee of eventual settlement. To a certain extent the nature of the grievance will determine the ease with which it can be settled by the chief. Land disputes, for example, are of a notoriously intractable nature since the evidence produced frequently goes back for generations. Cases of debt, on the other hand, where small amounts are involved and the loan well authenticated, are fairly readily settled; the chief can always fall back upon his powers of confiscation. Nevertheless, the triviality of a grievance is no sure index of judicial settlement. It may simply represent the tip of the iceberg, so that further enmity is produced by the process intended to resolve it. Courts are used as much as a mechanism for gaining retribution, for enforcing rights and for the expression of anger as they are for 'settlement' of grievances. To take a complaint to a court is the act of an enemy, and the Gisu at all times maintain a burning sense of personal justice and do not concede defeat readily. Where a decision of a court goes against him, the individual perceiving himself wronged will often threaten further violence. The machinery of the court may indeed be knowingly exploited as a means to escalate a quarrel. To avoid this, elders frequently attempt to dissuade an individual from taking a dispute to any kind of court in the first place. In fact the registration of a case in the first flush of anger is common, a man sometimes going to register a case directly with the police in Mbale. After consideration and when the case comes up before the courts (usually several months after the event), he may then withdraw, preferring to let the case rest there and not produce a confrontation. Similarly many cases reported to the chief or headman are later withdrawn.

THE CONTROL OF DISPUTES

For those in dispute who wish to avoid open violence, physical avoidance is recognised as the key strategy. Enemies do not greet each other, avoid walking past each others' houses or attending the same beer parties and ultimately, in situations of intractable hostility, rebuild their houses further away. Over time they may once again observe the small courtesies of everyday life and ostensibly forget their quarrel. Drinking together once more is a tacit statement that men no longer fear each other. Yet in the words of one of many Gisu proverbs in the same vein, 'He who shits forgets but he who steps into it remembers forever.' And, at any time, other events in the vicinity may rekindle such hatreds.

Murder in particular is likely to reawaken many old enmities as well as create new ones. It incites anger and is thus, perhaps, the most dangerous social event for this reason. The complex processes involved here are best explored through a case study. In the following case, the course of events following a murder is described since it exemplifies certain reactions to murder which were apparent in almost all the cases that I was able to investigate while I was in the field. I lived a little under a mile from the house of the victim in this case, and I take as my base here the various interpretations given for the murder over a period of approximately one month after the killing. I have divided these into three phases, according to the different turns the gossip took as to the identity of the killers and the motivation for the murder. These different directions are important in understanding how the strong feelings of both fear and anger which were aroused by the murder were eventually dissipated, or apparently so.

Case 11 The death of Wafaxale   Busoba, 1966
                                                                    homicide survey 7
Phase one: spreading the scandal
On the last Friday in May, Wafaxale collected his wages from the local school where

he worked as a painter and after going home set off to drink locally distilled spirit at a neighbour's house. He left a couple of hours after nightfall, at around 9.00 p.m. and a few minutes later, according to some accounts, was heard screaming, 'They are killing me!' No one ventured on the scene until about half an hour later when they found that he was dead with his neck severed.

The killing was the main topic of conversation the next morning. I lived about three-quarters of a mile from Wafaxale and my neighbours were avidly discussing the case. Since I did not know the dead man they told me that he was a good man when sober, married and with three young children. However, when he was drunk he was a troublemaker (*uwe kamaya*) and was unpopular on this account. He was a scandal monger, not only indulging in private gossip but bawling it out when he was drunk, making it known to all and sundry. And his language was abusive, using obscene words and phrases. This use of language, crossing the barrier between acceptable and forbidden, is believed to take on a power of its own to harm those at whom it is aimed, and is regarded as a form of cursing, *citsubo*. It was felt that this provided ample reason to kill him and a reason that was not only understandable but justifiable.

On the question of who killed him there were from the beginning a number of theories. It could have been thieves after his salary but this was discounted, as it was said that about 5*s*. had been found on the body. Or it could have been one of his brothers. There had been numerous quarrels among the brothers over land and they lived apart because of them. However, there were also other people in his kindred that Wafaxale was known to have offended. The net of possible suspects seemed very wide indeed, and so it was to prove.

Wafaxale's immediate family was quite large as his father, Malitsi, had six adult sons by his first wife and a number of smaller children by his second. Of the adult sons only four were still living in the area; in birth order these were Jemus, Yovana, Letero and Wafaxale (see figure 9). The two younger sons had both migrated away to obtain work, one to Mombasa and the other to Buganda where he had bought land. There was very little land for the sons that did remain, however, as Malitsi had migrated to this area as a young man and had been given land by his maternal relatives. This land fell into two pieces, with Malitsi and Letero having houses on one piece and Wafaxale on the other, about three-quarters of a mile away. Jemus, the only adult brother to remain a bachelor, had bought his own land from money saved from working in Kenya for six years and lived together with another bachelor quite near to Wafaxale. Also in the immediate vicinity of Wafaxale lived the large families of his mother's brothers and of his father's mother's brothers (see figures 8 and 9).

Wafaxale's body was returned by the police on 3 June, following the *post-mortem* examination, and was buried the same day late in the afternoon. The funeral provoked an intense display of collective grief. Unaccompanied by the usual drumming, the women came back from beating the bounds wailing and crying as they brandished their sticks in the funeral dance. Malitsi, distraught, wandered around the courtyard and among the dancers making thrusts with his panga. The women continued to dance around the coffin as it was brought from the house for burial and the crowd gathered tightly around the grave.

At the graveside, a man noted for his ritual knowledge performed the magic to make the spirit (*cisimu*) of the dead man speak. I was told that Mutsonga (see case 3), who was Wafaxale's mother's mother's brother's son, had already cut small pieces from the skin of the corpse while it was laid out in the house. These fragments, which included a lock of hair and nail-parings, were wrapped into a bundle of dried banana fibres, just as would be done in the witchcraft technique of *kamarolo*. Mutsonga now placed this bundle under the dead man's head, incanting as he did so:

'I, your mother's brother who has cut your nails, say this to you. If you were caught with someone's property, just die. But if he caught you without such things then tell us quickly so that we can act. If you call one of them, he will follow you (to the grave). Do this within one year. We want this. But if you tell us then we who are still above will take vengeance.'

At this point, as this ceremony shows, the desire for retaliation was strong although there was little consensus as to the identity of the killers. I never again witnessed a ceremony to make the *cisimu* speak, nor did I hear of one being performed.[2] Yet the police enquiry appears to have been cursory and no one was arrested even for questioning. Whether this was because no one was ready to volunteer information or because of the obstructive attitude of the parish chief – who had been heard to say that the area was well rid of a troublemaker – remained unclear. The attitude of the parish chief was certainly shared by others and indeed, for those not immediately related to Wafaxale, his death was incorporated into this general category of murders. This allowed of a consensus of indignation not against the possible murderers but against the dead man himself. Throughout all the events which were to follow this tended to detract from full odium falling on the suspects.

Phase two: the spread of suspicion
On 11 June, Jemus, Wafaxale's eldest brother, gave news that he had heard the *cisimu* speak. As he had been passing Wafaxale's house, the *cisimu* had cried out that he had been killed by the four men with whom he had been drinking. They had killed him and then carried his body out of the house to the path. Wafaxale had been unable to use his own knife but had managed to bite one of the assailants. The murderers had in addition robbed him of 120s, an amount that roughly equalled his salary.

This account was circumstantial enough to satisfy a number of people and Malitsi and Jemus evidently felt that it gave them enough evidence to put greater pressure on the parish chief. Two days later the chief arrested six men for questioning on the grounds that four of them had failed to answer the alarm and that the other two were the first on the scene of the crime. Not answering an alarm is an indictable offence but, as in this case, answering it frequently carries its own judicial penalties. However, these circumstances provided only the overt justifications for the arrests. Other people also had failed to answer

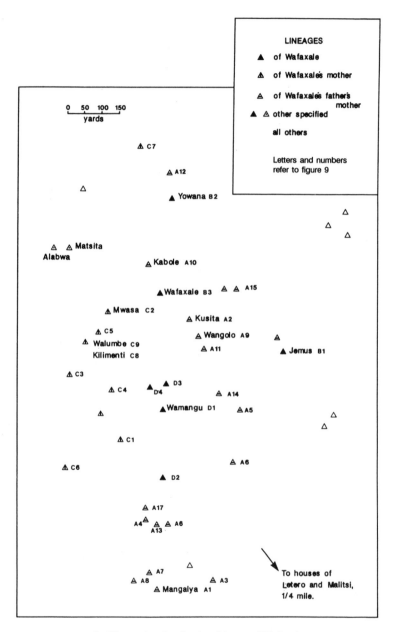

8   House-site plan for the vicinage of Wafaxale

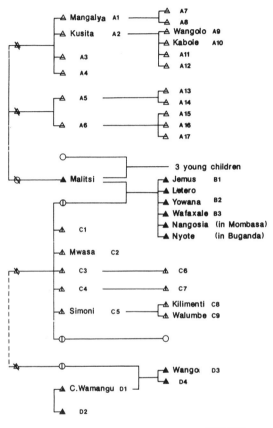

LINEAGES

Sibling Tie

△ Man   ▲ of Wafaxale

○ Woman   ▲ of Wafaxale's mother

Assumed Sibling Tie

⚠ Lineage   ▲ of Wafaxale's father's mother

Marriage

⚠ Dead   ▲ other specified

Letters and numbers refer to figure 8

9   Skeleton genealogy for the kindred of Wafaxale

the alarm and those arrested were all those who had earned suspicion on other counts as well.

Three were the men with whom Wafaxale had been drinking. **Matsita**, the owner of the house, had not answered the alarm, nor had his brother Alabwa who lived with him, though he was not arrested. These two brothers were not related to Wafaxale but his other drinking companions, **Walumbe** and **Kilmenti**, were the sons of Simone, Wafaxale's mother's brother. They were arrested for being first on the scene of the crime but claimed that they had left the party some time before Wafaxale and heard him leaving in his usual drunken fashion, shouting out curses as he went. These three men were all arrested on situational criteria which suggested an association with the crime, but none were known to hold any personal grudge against him. The possibility of theft provided the only motive here, but the parish chief explained that he had arrested them because he believed that they knew more than they would tell. This applied also to a fourth man arrested, **Mangalya**. Many people claimed afterwards that they had heard rumours of the impending murder and these appeared to have stemmed from Mangalya, Malitsi's mother's brother's son. When I visited the accused where they were held in the sub-county gaol, he freely admitted that he had spoken at a beer party two days before the murder of the likelihood of Wafaxale being killed for his behaviour, but claimed that he had implicated no one.

The other two men arrested, both senior relatives of Wafaxale, had specific grudges against him. *Wamangu* was a classificatory father to Wafaxale as he had married a woman from the same lineage as Wafaxale's mother. He held Wafaxale largely responsible for defaming him as a witch (*umulosi*) and spreading scandal about incest. The two accusations were related. The incest in question went back four years to 1962 when Wafaxale discovered that Wamangu's son, Wango, had been sleeping with Mary, who was related to him as his mother's sister's daughter. People related matrilaterally in this way are known by the term *umusoni*, which distinguishes them terminologically from all other relatives of the same generation, who are all called 'brothers' or 'sisters'. Incest with a sister is a small offence but incest with an *umusoni* is one of the most serious sexual misdemeanours and incurs pollution. This risk of supernatural retribution becomes more likely when, as in this case, the affair is found out. In any event, the incest had caused a furore among the elders of the family but, although speedily ended, no ritual was performed to cleanse the couple.

Wafaxale was blamed not only for spreading the scandal but also for keeping it alive. He would abuse Wamangu when he was drunk and accuse him of teaching his son witchcraft, *liloko*. This charge also relates to the incest which can also be termed *liloko*. As previously discussed, this does not mean that committing incest is a necessary prerequisite for becoming a witch, only that abhorrent acts of this kind give notice of witchcraft potential. Wamangu was, moreover, associated with the taint of night dancing (*bubini*), one of the forms of witchcraft believed to be passed on from father to son. Nevertheless, until a few months before, the incest had largely been forgotten. Then it was discovered that Mary was pregnant. She was forced to leave the teachers' training college where she was a student and then the child died shortly after birth. While it was commonly believed that the child was fathered by a teacher at the college and that Wango was not involved, these events aroused all the old hostilities, and the death of the child was taken as an indication that all future children born to Mary would meet the same end. Such retribution could follow upon incest. Wafaxale again had been loud in his abuse of the father and son and Wamangu became so enraged that he had not only muttered to his neighbours about the need to 'do something' about Wafaxale but on one occasion in April had openly threatened him.

Wafaxale had also accused **Mwasa**, the sixth man arrested, of being a witch. Not only Wafaxale but the whole set of brothers believed that Mwasa, their mother's brother, had cursed them by invoking the ancestral ghosts. This suspicion went back even further in time and again involved a sexual offence. In 1946, Jemus returned from fighting with the King's African Rifles in the Second World War. Soon after Mwasa suspected him of committing adultery with his wife and threatened to kill him. Jemus escaped to Kenya and did not return to the area for six years. However, the brothers believed that Mwasa had cursed them in retaliation and, as a result, only two of the six (Wafaxale and Letero) had children.

Such a set of grievances is not in itself unusual. Indeed, if anything, it is essentially incomplete as it concentrates solely on the family ill-will that could be related in a direct way to Wafaxale, ignoring other and older disputes between, for example, Malitsi and his brothers-in-law. Nor was there any supporting evidence to link these senior relatives to the murder. Indeed, they were all so old that it seemed highly unlikely that they could have been physically capable of it. The parish chief seemed to be acting more to avert criticism from Wafaxale's brothers and perhaps to issue a salutary lesson to the accused, especially Mwasa and Wamangu who were both reputed to be witches. In any event, the six accused were only held in the sub-county gaol for a little under a week. When I spoke to them in prison they all spoke of the reasons why they had been arrested in identical terms to those being circulated in the community. All denied any involvement, though Matsita admitted that he had taken the precaution of sending his wife back to her parents for protection.

The net of suspicion was in any case wider than this. Many other people now admitted that they were afraid for their lives, especially those who had had any previous quarrels with the family of Wafaxale. Crises such as murder expose the tenuous basis of relationship; anger rises to the surface and conflicts which are masked in the civility demanded of day-to-day living become open issues.

Alabwa, the brother of Matsita, certainly had some reason to fear for his life at this time, as did the local headman, Calo. He was not only a matrilateral relative of the brothers Kilimenti and Walumbe but had also had a hand in exposing a tax fraud perpetrated by Letero. Both Alabwa and Calo were avoiding all beer parties and it was noticeable that the average attendance at these had dropped sharply in the neighbourhood. The atmosphere was as tense as it was uncertain. Mangalya had voiced the opinion of all when he told me in prison that 'No one knows who to be angry with as we don't know who is being bad.'

With the release of those held in prison and nothing conclusive proved against any of them, the pattern of suspicions seemed suddenly to change. The accusations against the senior kin had exposed the basic grievances among members of the kindred to the public eye and, in so doing, had given public credence to the bad characters of some. The question of who was being bad was indeed a moot one. Guilt and character rather than simply guilt and motive were linked together and the accusations suggested that not only had Wafaxale been 'bad' but so too had others. Those who had been singled out in this way undoubtedly felt the pressure and it is not surprising that on their release from prison both Mwasa and Mangalya became more vocal in the supposition that the culprit would be found among the brothers of Wafaxale himself. This possibility, directing attention and censure away from the wider kindred, now became the talking point.

Phase three: the focus on the family

It had been Malitsi and the eldest brother, Jemus, whose adultery it was believed had led to the brothers being cursed, who had taken most action to identify the killers. Jemus had not only reported on the crying of the *cisimu* but had also visited Muslim diviners on several occasions in the weeks following the murder. Of the other brothers, Yovana appears to have remained relatively uninvolved, taking little part in the discussions. Letero now became the main suspect. Although since the beginning people had known about the quarrels between Wafaxale and Letero, opinion had largely discounted them. They were now evaluated differently. The quarrels again went back in time as Wafaxale coveted some of the land which Malitsi had allocated to Letero in 1959. Letero had, however, refused to share it and had, since 1962, lived on this land together with his father. Wafaxale was also said to claim the debt of a cow which he had lent to Letero for his bridewealth. These quarrels were old but, just prior to the murder, there had been a violent confrontation between the two.

On 22 May, the fourteen-year-old son of Malitsi by his second wife fought with the ten-year-old son of Letero and cut his head open. Letero demanded that his father take the child to the dispensary for treatment but Malitsi had refused, saying that the wound was not that serious. Letero's wife then joined in the affray and abused Malitsi, crying that her child would die because of his negligence. Wafaxale, overhearing this altercation, became incensed at his sister-in-law flouting the respect rules of *bumasala* in this way and rushed off to fetch his spear. While the two brothers were prevented from fighting both threatened the other, Wafaxale saying that he had money and his brother 'would see' and Letero retaliating in like form.

The next day Malitsi called together the elders from his mother's lineage and his brothers-in-law, including both Mwasa and Mangalya. They decided that it was Wafaxale who had been in the wrong and Letero should if he wished take out a case of threatening violence at the sub-county court. Letero in fact registered this case.

By the end of June the suspicion that Letero was involved in the murder was apparently confirmed by two other rumours. A young daughter of Malitsi was said to have told her father that she had overheard a conversation between Letero and some visitors from his wife's lineage area. They had demanded money from Letero, claiming that Letero had only paid them 300s out of the 1,200s originally agreed. The other rumour originated from Jemus. He claimed that one of the diviners he had visited had told him the day on which the murderers would come to purify themselves on the grave. He had waited all that night and no one appeared but on the next he surprised two men throwing chyme on the grave. He only caught a glimpse of one but claimed that he recognised the other as Mwasa, their mother's brother. Since it is better if senior relatives perform this ritual action to prevent the ghost of a dead man visiting evil on his murderer, it was generally believed that Mwasa had been purifying Letero. The fact that Malitsi at this time moved his house back to the place where Wafaxale had lived seemed only to confirm this interpretation.

As far as most people in the vicinage were concerned the affair ceased to hold any further interest at this point. It was noted that neither Jemus nor Malitsi were drinking with Letero. It was supposed that Letero had hired murderers. The amounts mentioned seemed high, given that it was commonly believed that men would kill for as little as 5s, a comment perhaps on the evil nature of such men rather than on the realities of the situation. In any event there was little comment on the discrepancy. Thus suspicion, though hardly proof, centred upon a member of the dead man's family. As far as everyone else was concerned that was the end of the matter. When I asked what might happen next it was suggested that if Jemus was still angry he might well resort to retaliatory sorcery against Letero.

THE DEVELOPMENT OF RUMOUR

I have not been concerned in this case study to unravel fact from fiction, and indeed such a task would be impossible for the factual core of all the rumours was embroidered upon to a greater or lesser extent in gossip. Rather, my purpose has been to document the growth and development of the rumours themselves; with the information that was disseminated in the vicinage and the credence given to different versions over time. If one looks at these clear patterns emerge; patterns which can be seen as generated by common familial conflicts and the way the Gisu attempt to rationalise and thus normalise a situation of danger and uncertainty. In attempting to impose an order on events the need was not only to assimilate this case to known patterns but to known patterns that reduced risk and circumscribed danger. Two main strategies emerge in this context which, although they operate in contrary directions, both operate to limit involvement. The first seeks to justify the murder in terms of the bad character of the victim and thus to exonerate the killers and remove grounds for vengeance. The second strategy seeks to limit the involvement of people by locating the murderer in the immediate family of the deceased. The affair then becomes a purely 'private' affair and need concern no one else.

In the case of Wafaxale, and indeed in practically all the homicide cases that I was able to investigate *in situ*, as it were, the rationale for the man's murder was sought initially almost entirely in his character and behaviour traits. Appeal is here made to community values; the victim is a troublemaker and the murder thus a 'good' murder. There is undoubtedly an element here of *ex post facto* dossier-building for the vilification of the dead man in this way has several important implications. In the first place it acts to justify the killing and in so far that it is felt that he got what was coming to him it tends to a greater or lesser degree to detract from the culpability of the act of murder. The sentiment that a bad man should not be avenged is strong and is held equally among kin and non-kin as the rite at the graveside showed: the elder reiterating that no vengeance was appropriate if Wafaxale had been killed as a thief. The possibility that the killing was justified on such grounds also acts to restrict the dangers of being murdered to certain categories of people. Not all need fear such a death.

If what I have called phase one following Wafaxale's murder was marked almost exclusively by giving this kind of reasoning, at least by those in Wafaxale's more distant vicinage, phase two took a different turn as the task of identifying the killers got under way. The battle at this stage clearly was a battle of reputations. The question, as Mangalya put it, of 'who was being bad' was clearly crucial just as it was clear that many had a motive or potential motive for the murder. A clear split developed at this point between the immediate family of Wafaxale and the wider kindred: the murder had destroyed the uneasy truce of everyday praxis and, with fear running at a high level, open accusations were made, particularly by Jemus who, because of his past history, undoubtedly perceived himself as not only already suffering as a consequence of the past anger of his matrikin but now also as in danger of the same fate as Wafaxale.

Jemus's story indeed bespoke cursing: he had no wife and no children. And, given the small size of the family and their position as 'sister's sons' in the area, it was perhaps only too easy to project a more general malevolence. The ability of Jemus and his brothers to survive in the area certainly depended to a large extent on their matrikin. Short of land as they were they needed to buy some and, as close kinsmen, would expect the same preferential treatment as agnates in this respect. Three of the brothers had indeed bought land in this way: Jemus with the money he had saved from working in Kenya, Letero from his teacher's salary and Wafaxale again from savings from the income he earned as a carpenter. The scarcity of land and the corresponding high price by and large precluded purchase by those without off-farm incomes. A good indication of the difficulty both for this particular family and in general is given by the fact that two of the brothers had evidently given up the struggle to keep a foothold in the area and migrated elsewhere on a presumed permanent basis. For the brothers that remained, however, there was little to be gained and much to be lost from perpetuating a general schism between themselves and their wider kindred. It was one thing if consensus could be reached on one murderer, one 'bad man' on whom to blame the murder, quite another to promote a general hostility in which their own positions and reputations could only become more marginalised.

Jemus, again, was most at risk here. As a bachelor, with no job and thus no evident prospect of earning the money necessary for bridewealth, Jemus's reputation was undoubtedly on the line. The role played by Jemus – alone of the brothers – in championing the cause of Wafaxale now becomes somewhat clearer. From a number of contrary directions he had most to fear: as a target for the continuing anger of others he felt himself already a victim but potentially he was himself also a suspect. The very success of Wafaxale in marrying and having children could be supposed to elicit envy in Jemus, a man who had so little regard for kinship norms that he had committed adultery with the wife of his mother's brother. In fact, I never heard such a construction put on events but Jemus's particular history implied it just as did the ill-will that existed among the brothers. Jemus thus had much to gain from acting as 'public prosecutor' in the case, making appeals to public opinion which threw the weight of suspicion elsewhere.

However, it is clear that fear was not restricted to Jemus for at this time all the victim's social relationships came under scrutiny, as did the characters of other men in the neighbourhood. This process, uncovering hostilities, spread outwards and in ever-widening circles as, with inflamed emotions, any dispute or grudge with a member of the dead man's close kin now became a potential cause for suspicion. For a while, approximately a month in this case, the affair was the main subject of public gossip and concern, engendering insecurity. Men went warily about their daily lives. What I have called phase three can be seen to have brought some resolution to this situation at least as far as the wider kindred and community were concerned. With nothing conclusive proved against any of the original suspects, locating the murderer within the elementary family limited both involvement and concern. The affair was seen to rest between Letero and Wafaxale, with the option of continuing any hostility resting with Jemus. The matter could be regarded as a dispute which concerned a single family alone and which had little implication for the wider social networks with which they were associated. And again, through his own actions, Wafaxale could be held at fault.

One can now comment further on the problems encountered at the beginning of this section on the apparent reluctance of the Gisu to see murder as a group or lineage matter. The general tendency, as this case study shows, is to regard all murders in essentially interpersonal terms, the product of a specific situation of conflict. Thus each murder is seen as a unique event to be judged solely in terms of its own specific rights and wrongs. The reasons for a man's death are sought in his character and the culprits are found among those with whom he is known to be on bad terms. Moreover, the overriding tendency is to try to find exonerating rationales for the killing. This is not to say that the murderers necessarily go unpunished or that the reputations of those accused remain unscathed. Indeed, in the above case, all those implicated were afterwards thought of as *batemu*, dangerous men, though it is fair to note that most had already earned such a reputation. But this focusing on the characters of the principals operates to detract from the possibility of seeing offences in group terms, as part of a continuing feud, for example, between two groups.

To some extent, then, the lack of blood vengeance among the Gisu may be more apparent than real, for anger over a murder is as potent as any other cause for hatred and may well have repercussions for the future. It is the definition of the situation, the unwillingness of the Gisu to contemplate this as a necessary consequence, which is at issue. To take the case of Wafaxale further in time, Matsita, the only non-relative involved, certainly had reason to fear for his life in the months ahead. A few months later, in October, he reported that after tying up his cattle he returned home to find chicken and food laid out on his table. He said that he then knew that somebody wanted to kill him as undoubtedly the food was poisoned. Again he took the precaution of sending his wife and children back to her father's home, was very cautious for the next few weeks and did not walk at all at night. Yet nothing further happened. However, some two years later his brother, Alabwa, was attacked and very seriously injured as he returned from a beer party (homicide survey case 18). He was saved by the timely intervention of another neighbour walking home in the dark and spent ten days in hospital recovering from the effects of strangulation. He said his assailants were Wangolo and Kusita (the sons of Wafaxale's mother's brother), with whom he had been drinking but refused to give their names to the police. It was said that the subject of Wafaxale's death had come up at the beer party and tempers had become inflamed but no one, with the exception of Matsita, was willing to consider this as the real motive for the attack. Opinion held, equally plausibly. that the attack was due to the ill-will that had lingered between Alabwa and the brothers from the time when they had all been employed together at a local school.

CONCLUSION

The lack of serial identification of cases detracts from there being the possibility that group will oppose group. No tally of deaths is kept. In this respect murders operate like witchcraft deaths. In the normal run of events, deaths from witchcraft – which effectively are all other deaths – do not call up in peoples' minds any previous death or deaths among the kin of the individuals involved. When a person is seriously ill his kin usually attempt through divination to identify his enemies, in the hope of either placating or counteracting the evil forces pitted against his life. Death, however, is usually held to be the end of the matter and, although rumours as to the culprit are aired, action is rarely believed to be taken against the supposed witch or witches. Significantly, the death of children is most likely to precipitate direct vengeance sorcery, as the act of witchcraft in this case is thought of as aimed directly at the parents rather than at the child. Where witchcraft causes the death of an adult, however, it is seen to emanate from the specific hatreds which he has aroused and thus not considered necessarily to pose any further threat to his kin. The lack of conclusive proof is usually considered sufficient justification for not pursuing the matter.

Further, divination rarely produces a certain culprit. Gisu diviners are specialists who have been caught by the ancestral power of *bufumu* (divination) and whose main mode of divination is through gourds, which they shake to make contact with their tutelary spirits who speak through the mouth of the diviner, or sometimes from the gourds, depending on the style and the ventriloquist skills of the practitioner. Once the causal agent of the illness or misfortune has been determined then the diviner usually takes it upon himself to undertake a cure or counteraction, and most such diviners are also witchcraft-finders able to smell out hidden sorcery substances around the home and environment of the victim. They may also undertake vengeance as was so in case 8, though most local diviners are wary of gaining such a reputation.

Nevertheless, we can see the system of divination exists as a complete parallel system of action and counteraction. The diviner whom I knew best clearly modelled his procedures on those of the old chieftainships. He sent his spirits out as *banalukoosi*, the word used of agents of the chief in colonial times who were used to bring in the accused or, in this case, their spirit/shadows (*cisimu*). These he interrogated, with the *banalukoosi* delivering beatings at his request in order to elicit a confession. If the accused witch in this instance refused to withdraw his powers then the diviner would draw out his *cisimu*, something which was said not to kill the witch but simply to weaken his motivation and powers. Divination thus tends to exist at a *sub-rosa* level; its procedures and powers all shrouded with secrecy. Indeed, in order to take action or make a public accusation of witchcraft it is said to be essential to gain the same verdict from three diviners operating independently, and thus preferably at some distance. Even for those prepared to bear the cost of such extensive divination, a unanimous verdict of this kind is not easy to obtain. It was a rare divinatory seance – and I attended many – where only one causal agent was identified. A sick person was more often seen as under attack from a multitude of different sources, from the ancestral ghosts and powers and from several witches, acting sometimes in consort and sometimes independently.

The ambiguity of divination and the reluctance of the Gisu to serially link murder or indeed any deaths gives an immediate, atemporal dimension to all such events. They are not seen as part of an ongoing history, as a series or regularised flow of events as is produced by the action and counteraction of feuding situations. The Gisu recognise only too well that as in the words of one of their proverbs, 'The thing which kills you comes from your past', but such an event can only be known *ex post facto*, generally through divination. There is a timeless quality too in the way that current events pass almost immediately into proverbial usage. Collecting proverbs, I was struck by the way that local *causes célèbres* were used as part of the currency of stereotyped comment and warning. Thus a variant of the proverb, 'Greediness killed the sunbird', was given as 'Greediness killed Sakulule', referring to the murder of a local thief (homicide survey case 23). Again 'Namanda called Wapuwa' referred to another recent murder (homicide survey case 8); in this case a fratricide, and carried the warning that friendly acts do not necessarily bring friendly consequences. Presumably, these sayings pass out of usage as speedily as they pass in, leaving no trace, just as events within the community are always moving on, with the troubles of yesterday overlaid by the troubles of today.

This is not to say that the Gisu do not have a sense of the past. The circumcision periods are named and thus major events can be dated fairly accurately with reference to these two-year intervals. But past events have little significance in themselves. They may have been times of hardship or joy but they are things that one has lived through. The things which have present meaning are the things which live in the memories of others, in their feelings, and particularly, in their anger. And this is essentially unknowable. As the Gisu say, 'When it kills you then you will know it.' This is the vision to which divination attests. It brings together events which have occurred at different times into a single constellation and posits that the emotions they aroused are operative in the here and now.

This brings us back to the importance of character and character assessment. In the account of events following the death of Wafaxale, it was emphasised how blaming the victim acted as a justification for murder and how this in turn may be interpreted as a strategy for limiting the repercussions of such events. In this context it might be said to be a strategy of impotence in a context where groups are unwilling to bear any responsibility for their members. The individual alone bears the consequences of his actions. But the pinning of moral blame on the victim is successful as a strategy only because it does mobilise public opinion and allows for something approaching unanimity. Killing in such instances is justified self-help, ridding the community of troublemakers.

Mobilisation against deviants, in the Durkheimian tradition, has been seen as one of the main ways in which the values of a community are symbolically affirmed. In a situation approaching anarchy – as Bugisu in the mid-1960s may fairly be described – it was also to become a forceful statement about the need for control and the assertion of it. The 1960s were to see the rise of two new forms of neighbourhood association, vigilante groups and drinking companies, which both sought to reconstitute effective controls over behaviour by introducing new forms of 'discipline' backed by force. This, what we might see as a political solution to the Hobbesian dilemma, forms the topic of part four of this book. The next chapter tackles the problem from a very different point of view in examining a Gisu concept of 'order' – or rather, of rightful living – itself and the way it is realised in Gisu social forms.

NOTES

1   The village unit of the administration was abolished in 1961, some years prior to the date to which this description refers.

2   Fear of the *cisimu* speaking out in this way is said to lead murderers to cut out the tongue of their victim in some instances.

9

EXCESS AND RESTRAINT IN
THE MORALITY OF KINSHIP

This chapter is divided into two sections which tackle a number of linked
themes concerned with the nature of Gisu morality and the way this is depicted
in their kinship system and beliefs about ancestors. The overall problem may
be stated thus: harmonious social life is seen in terms of the necessity for
restraint, enjoined both by kinship etiquette and a wealth of proverbial sayings
which counsel caution and judiciousness in dealing with others. Yet with no
coercive authorities and no segmentary loyalties, such acts of restraint depend
on individual submission, a submission which runs against the forceful individualism enjoined in other aspects of Gisu culture. Not only, as has been seen,
do people attempt to break or bend the rules but breaking the rules is
associated with violence, a violence which is seen as a male prerogative.
Indeed, more than this, the very capability of it acts to define manhood and is
valorised in the most important ritual the Gisu possess, that of circumcision. If
we see this contradiction, of violence versus restraint, as a basic personal
dynamic for Gisu men then, perhaps, we may see the formalised structures in
which that life is lived as offering an important commentary upon it.

This topic entails a change of approach away from what might be called the
more pragmatic aspects of social living and relationships with which I have
been concerned in the last few chapters towards a consideration of the more
implicit coding represented in kinship custom. In an earlier chapter I examined Gisu concepts of the male person and how this was constructed in and
through the ritual of circumcision. The argument was that the ritual did not
just display or dramatise norms and values but that the experience provided
the direct means which enabled individuals to identify with them, realising
them in terms of their own capabilities. Thus the ritual could be seen to have
direct efficacy in shaping self-understandings and attitudes. I now want to
place this in a wider context by looking at the largely implicit metaphysics
embodied in Gisu ancestral beliefs and their implications for morality. My
approach here is that of an observer's hermeneutic, a seeking-out of a structure
of meaning which I argue is apprehended by the Gisu and informs their

understanding of their social world but which is not articulated by them in systematic terms. This is so particularly in the second section of the chapter, where I seek to interpret the significance of Gisu kinship etiquette in terms of the necessity of restraint and self-control.

Nevertheless, the task can proceed only through an examination of Gisu concepts and constructions. Fundamental to an understanding of how the Gisu conceive of the good or righteous life and how it might be achieved is that of *lukoosi*. As with all such notions, it has a large range of reference which derives from the very generality of the 'good' it describes for *lukoosi* may be translated as 'order', 'peace' or 'respect'. Indeed, *lukoosi* is 'respect', a respect which implies not only the proper esteem rendered to persons but embraces a sense of the proper ordering of things, of custom and tradition. *Lukoosi*, in this general sense, is the fundamental principle upon which all orderly social relationships and conduct are based, and it equates order with peace. A person with *lukoosi* is thus not only a courteous individual but also respectable, honest and law-abiding. At the most obvious level, *lukoosi* finds expression in the detailed, concrete rules of everyday etiquette. In a slightly more specific sense, *lukoosi* is mandatory between all kin who must show a proper respect for each other, that is, observe due decorum. More specifically still, it is the guiding norm for relationships among people of adjacent generations where it carries more forcefully the connotations of distance and formality.

Lukoosi, then, can be seen to exist in the extraordinary politeness of the everyday forms of social interaction. All people must be treated with respect and greetings should never be omitted and take a deferential form, with it being usual to address everyone as 'father' or 'mother'. To show particular respect, the terms *umusaxulu* and *umuloosi*, for a man and woman respectively, are used and carry the implications of worthy and respectful old age. These terms all tend to be used reciprocally, honour given on both sides irrespective of relative age or kinship position, thereby expressing the egality of Gisu life and not the subservience of hierarchical structures. Politeness exists too in the forms of discourse: the imperative is rarely used and there are special verbal forms for phrasing requests.

Yet *lukoosi* in normal usage is not an abstract principle of 'order'; it exists, as has been said, in concrete forms of behaviour. Further, it is more an attitude than it is a 'thing'; it applies to behaviour and the motivations that are associated with it. It is people who 'have it', 'do it', 'are of it' or 'with it'. And here, it does not just apply to keeping the rules but is best summed up as 'goodwill'; it exists in a generous, altruistic, caring and responsible attitude towards others, and in the reciprocating attitudes of gratitude, admiration and respect. The verbal form *xukoosa* is generally used of treating people well. Thus we may say here that it represents the positive reciprocity of life and relationship, the mutuality of obligation and return. When someone does you a favour, that is *lukoosi*; when a man gives his son land and the son is grateful, that is *lukoosi*; when a chief rules well and there is peace in the country, that is *lukoosi*.

Lukoosi thus would appear to apply to all attitudes and actions which breed accord among men; respect and deference, goodwill and gratitude, obeying the rules and being a good citizen. As such it is opposed in all respects to *lirima*, as goodwill to hatred, as co-operation to anger, as peace to violence and disruption. Yet both are recognisably present; a dialectic of good and evil in the community and in the attitudes and heart of man. The problem for this chapter is not to document the manifestations of *lirima*. That has already been done and at length, but to begin on the questions of how *lukoosi* is manifest in the forms of Gisu life, of how the Gisu apprehend it and how it might be achieved, a topic that now carries us through to the end of the book.

The first section of this chapter engages in a debate with Fortes's work on the concepts of self, morality and ancestors among the West African Tallensi, partly because of the importance of this work in itself for an understanding of the nature of ancestral belief and partly because it allows me to highlight the distinctive nature of the Gisu moral universe. Fortes writes of the West African Tallensi that their ancestor cult 'is the religious counterpart of their social order, hallowing it, investing it with a value that transcends mundane interests and providing for them the categories of thought and belief by means of which they direct and interpret their lives and actions' (1959: 13). Indeed, the distinctive mark of Fortes's work was to enquire into the nature of self-understandings, not only in terms of the moral person as it was depicted in customary beliefs, i.e. those qualities and capacities with which a culture endows a person which 'enable the person to be known to be, and also to show himself to be the person he is supposed to be' (1987:251), but to enquire into the subjective side of what Mauss (1985) called the 'moi'. Informed by his continuing interest in psychoanalysis, the complex line of Fortes's arguments was developed in his analysis of Tallensi personhood, fate and the life course in *Oedipus and Job in West African Religion* (1959), in his analysis of taboo (1966) and through numerous articles, especially, 1972, 1976 and 1977. Among the Tallensi, through the overarching cult of the ancestors and the belief in their omnipotent power, he argued that the person may be reconciled to a harsh destiny. This forms the framework for discussion because it touches so closely upon the themes of this book. It also allows me to engage in a dialogue between the forms of Gisu and Tallensi life, an extension to one also embarked on by Fortes (1977).[1]

One of the key differences that must be indicated here is the fragility of authority in Bugisu. Indeed, it is really hard to see that there are any 'authorities' in the Gisu system. This statement must be qualified with respect to the system of chieftainships which have considerable legitimacy, albeit diminished at the time in question. However, these derive their legitimacy from the government – in effect, 'outside' Gisu society. 'Inside' there is a greater ambivalence to the manifestations of potential authority. For example, there are principles of seniority implied in both age and kinship. Elders (*baxulu*) should be given respect, but respect here is different from authority. They may be given precedence on account of their age, it being recognised that they should be 'first to eat', or they might be respected for their knowledge but they, no more than any other, have any right to interfere in the affairs of someone else, nor do they have any sanctions to enforce their mediations when requested to 'cut cases'. But it is not just that their genealogical authority is weak in these respects, for it is also regarded as dangerous. Indeed, an attribute of old age, *kamaxura*, wisdom, is not an unmitigated good for it carries the overtones of illegitimate knowledge, of witchcraft. It is tainted knowledge, as indeed is the ability, *bunyali*, which also is seen as growing with age and carries the imputation of witchcraft. Indeed it is on this question of witchcraft that the Gisu ambivalence to the powers of age and genealogical seniority is most clearly articulated. Genealogical seniority bestows the power (in this case given by the word, *bunyala*, which, like *bunyali*, derives from the verb *xunyala*, to be able, but carries the implication of categorical right) to invoke the ancestral ghosts in the curse. But again, it must be stressed that this is never considered legitimate, and that far from buttressing the authority of the old it emphasises their illegitimate malevolence, giving graphic expression to intergenerational tensions.

Nor do ancestral beliefs in other respects give any support to authority, and I conclude by arguing that because of this, and in contrast to the Tallensi, Gisu ancestral beliefs enshrine neither piety nor amity. This leaves the idea of perpetuity as the main – indeed even only – strand in Gisu kinship. Nevertheless, the rules of kinship and ancestry do provide the basic template for moral living. This leads on in the second section of this chapter to an examination of the formal etiquette of kinship itself. But we begin with a description of the main ideas embodied in Gisu beliefs about ancestral power and powers. With Fortes, it is taken that such beliefs provide an implicit philosophy of being, the constituent ideas with which and against which the Gisu live their lives. Descriptions of these form the necessary background against which to explore the nature of the Gisu moral universe, of kinship and the concept of social rule.

1 ANCESTORS, MORALITY AND KINSHIP

ANCESTRAL POWERS: THE INTERDEPENDENCE OF DEAD AND LIVING

The complex relation between persons and their ancestors takes a number of different forms in Africa. In Bugisu the interdependence of flesh and spirit is perhaps the strongest theme, with its corollary of the regeneration of life and powers. Death and birth set up a complex cycle whereby spiritual force is released into both the worlds of the dead and of the living, replenishing the powers of both. It is this continuity rather than the authority of ancestors and the principle of seniority which is emphasised. The Gisu ancestor cult is thus no morality cult. Thus, it cannot be said of Gisu ancestors, as it can for example of those of the Lugbara, that ' "Our ancestors" are seen as good people who set an example that men should follow and who maintained the idea of the social order and social behaviour merely by their having lived as they are said to have lived' (Middleton, 1960: 23). Gisu ancestors are not presented as examples of rectitude nor are they concerned with this aspect, either in the establishment of moral standards among kinsfolk nor the protection of such specific kinship morality. Rather, the ancestral world is seen as ensuring the continuity of the people as such, in both their physical and spiritual aspects and for the perpetuation of the critical traditions which define them.

The Gisu postulate a continuity of spirit, seen as the source of vital life, *bulamu*, and identified with the shadow, *cisimu*. This exists on a parallel plane to physical procreation. The body of the child is believed to be created equally from the mixing of the 'red blood' of the woman and 'white blood' of the man but to be animated at birth by the life force, *cisimu*, of a person in the kindred who has recently died. This spirit must be identified correctly and the baby then takes this name, though no further cult is paid to the named ancestor, who is not believed to act as a spirit guardian or especially influence the course of life of his namesake. It is the life itself which goes on. Names thus tend to be inherited from the generations of grandparent to grandchild; the biological succession from parents to children complemented by the transmission of 'life' from grandparents to grandchildren.

The *cisimu* itself is identified with the penumbra around the shadow and on death the *cisimu* is said to escape from the body and to take a purely ethereal form, described as white and bright like the sky in the dry season. For some time after death the *cisimu* retains its links with the corpse: it is said to linger near the grave and appear in the form of the person. Precautions are taken to avoid inadvertently seeing such manifestations before burial. After burial such apparitions are regarded as of ill-omen, attesting to an unquiet spirit. With the completion of the mortuary rituals the *cisimu* dissolves into two more or less distinct aspects. On the one hand, it is said to become the ghost (*umumakombe*) of the dead person, and drawn into an association with the powers of the ancestral spirits, *basambwa*, the collective spirits of those who are no longer remembered as distinct personalities by the living. On the other hand, it returns to become the *cisimu* and thus the *bulamu* (life) of a new-born child in the kindred. Death and birth thus set up a complex cycle whereby spiritual force is released into the worlds of both the dead and the living, replenishing the powers of both.

The personalised aspects of the dead are subsumed by the *umumakombe* which can be translated as ghost or shade. This is also sometimes referred to by the term *kusimu* (large shadow) in contrast to *cisimu*, with the prefix *ku* indicating both larger size and having strong derogatory implications. *Ku* is used to describe bad things. In talking about the fate of the dead, the *kusimu* may also be identified as the shadow proper (*cicinini*); in this context as the large black shadow, the adjective 'black' again carrying negative feelings, for the Gisu perceive the *bamakombe* as almost entirely malevolent. They are thought to be resentful of the fact of death and motivated by selfishness. They visit enervating illness, barrenness and even death upon their descendants as punishment for small slights to their memory. The *bamakombe* appear in dreams to demand sacrifices or other marks of respect to their personal memory. A frequent request these days is for the erection of a permanent concrete grave. A point to be returned to is that moral fault as such is not at issue in dealing with the *bamakombe*; they are not thought of as impartial judges punishing breaches in kinship rules but to be motivated by individual selfishness and greed.

The power of the *bamakombe* diminishes over time, fading as the shadow itself is said to fade. The Gisu hold that the power of the dead is always less than the power of the living; only the living have real vitality. Once the *bamakombe* are no longer remembered by the living then their individuality is merged with that of the collectivity of Gisu dead, the *basambwa*, ancestral spirits, who have no corporeal or visible existence but are described as 'like the wind'. The *basambwa* are associated with the powers of the *kimisambwa* (sing. *kumusambwa*) and, as such, are seen as the repositories of Gisu tradition. The *kimisambwa* embrace the important Gisu traditions which are transmitted from generation to generation by 'catching' people, usually with a characteristic affliction. Through ritual the person is then both cured and further identified with the powers of that *kumusambwa*. These they exercise during life and transmit in the same way to their descendants on death. The powers transmitted by the *kimisambwa* are various; most of them being associated with sickness and its control and having also a totemic aspect. Thus, for example, the *kumusambwa kw'ingwe* (the ancestral power of the leopard) is manifested in a particular skin disease, and all people who have this power in their kindred respect the leopard and keep the speckled hen known as *nangwe* in their homesteads. Other *kimisambwa* give their possessors powers to both inflict and cure the illness in question, for example, *murabula*, identified with polio and associated with the centre pole of the house, is believed to strike anyone down who attempts theft from such a homestead. Others bequeath more general powers such as that of twinning, divination, rainmaking and circumcising, leading thus to occupational specialisations.

In addition to the *kimisambwa* and seen as forces of much the same character are those of the *were*. In contrast to the *kimisambwa*, as spirits incorporated and perpetuated through kinship, the *were* may be regarded as unincorporated spirits. They may be divided into three broad classes. The first are simply the *kimisambwa* in their unincorporated form, the usage of *were* as opposed to *kumusambwa* indicating no prior ancestral association with that power. Thus if someone is diagnosed by a diviner as suffering from the power

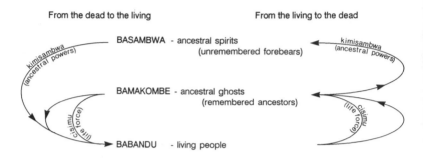

10   The transmission of powers

of the circumcisors and no kinship linkage can be established then the power would be referred to as *were w'inyembe* and not *kumusambwa kw'inyembe*. Once accepted and thus incorporated as a power of the person it would be transmitted by descent in the way of other *kimisambwa*.

The second category of *were* are the spirits of the unpropitious dead whose names are not inherited. Those who die childless or of certain deformities such as lameness or a hunchback are not renamed. Some attempt is usually made in these cases to prevent the *cisimu* escaping at death by tightly wrapping the corpse and not leaving the usual gap to allow free movement and thus the escape of the *cisimu*. For such *bisimu* are doomed to become the hostile spirits of the bush, rivers and paths, which prey upon and haunt human life. Seeing such a spirit is usually taken to mean death. The spirit may take the form of a ghost but is also said to be manifest in trees which blaze at night when there is no fire and to be heard in the guise of a child crying in the centre of the blaze. Not quite all the *were* take this hostile predatory form; Nabende, for example, comes from the spirits of those who cared for their bananas well and will protect one's banana grove, while Maina, who may be seen around the homestead, protects both people and cattle. Both these two classes of *were* derive from the dead in essentially the same way as the *kimisambwa*. There is one main exception to this in Central Bugisu and that is of *were we lufutu*, the *were* of the rainbow – which is seen as existing and having been created outside human life. The rainbow is associated also with waterfalls and is regarded as extremely unpropitious. To be caught by a rainbow in the water is the most unlucky act of all; it will dry you up, causing your death and the death of all your children. The rainbow is associated with barrenness.

The refractions of the dead, the *cisimu*, *bamakombe*, *basambwa* and *were*, may be said to represent different degrees of separation of power from remembered personality and materiality. In part their attributes suggest a basic conflict between the dead and the living, an ambivalence of sentiment. Certainly, interventions of the ancestral ghosts never bode well in human affairs and the misfortunes they send, the death of children and barrenness, strike at the very meaning of kinship. The ghosts have power only as long as the living recall their memory and their actions are thought of as prompted by essentially personal grievance. Mbiti (1969) refers to this order of ancestor as the 'living-dead', those dead who still retain a foothold in the land of the living. Thus these individualised shades are still mindful of what is due to them and sensitive to the signs of respect which acknowledge their power. The powers of the *basambwa*, the collective and 'forgotten' dead, on the other hand, are essentially impersonal; they have no feelings and no specific motivation for their interventions. While such interventions are generally unwelcome since their sign is sickness, yet misfortune here is a sign of empowerment and offers the possibility of turning the negative symptom into a positive attribute.

The attributes of the ghosts suggest the malleability of substance and the transience of the individual personality as against the continuity of the spirit line represented by the *basambwa*, whose powers are said to be transmitted from generation to generation with the same force. Indeed, the strongest theme in Gisu beliefs about the dead is that of continuity and mutual dependence. The interventions of the powers of the dead, although they harbinger ill in the here and now, are an aspect of the mutual dependence of dead and living, part of the way in which the powers upon which both depend are released and perpetuated. This suggests that one should think firstly of the relationship between living and dead in terms of process rather than in terms of a static opposition.

Regeneration and recycling are the dominant themes, imaged in the compound rubbish heaps and mounds of dung (*isina*) which are said to be the favoured haunts of both the *bamakombe* and the *basambwa*. They choose to associate themselves with the waste products of the moment which replenish the fertility of the earth. Boundary images reverberate throughout Gisu practices towards their dead; the dead and the ancestors are of the house but not in it. Only diviners and circumcisors and a few other ritual specialists have permanent shrines to the ancestors in their courtyards or in the house itself. Otherwise, the place of the family ghosts remains their graves at the compound edge and the associated groves of trees which are allowed to seed around them. These trees are left to regenerate naturally and must be neither seeded nor felled. Even when sacrifices are made to elicit their goodwill, at times of circumcision for example, shrines are erected in the public courtyard and not inside the house. Small spirit huts are erected together with a forked stick of *lusola* to carry the sacrifice. The heart and lungs of the animal, signifying its life and intentions, is placed there while the windpipe, the link between inside and out, of the inner thought and the spoken word, is placed above the door of the house. At circumcision other portions of the sacrifice are also often placed inside the curing house at the interstices where the roof joins the walls; there to placate any invading spirit.

This brief summary has described the main elements of Gisu belief about their ancestors and the relationship they have with them. We may now extend the discussion into the area of morality, considering firstly the implications of ancestrally-validated rules.

RULES, RELATIONSHIPS AND MORALITY

It is the nature of the power they give and the special mode of transmission which distinguish the *kimisambwa* both from ordinary custom (*isambo*) perpetuated by tradition and social expectation and also from ritual prohibition (*kimisiro*) where breach results in pollution. Such a classification cuts across our usual way of talking about rules with its mixture of content and sanction since it introduces an additional mechanism operating to make some social rules binding; that of ancestry.

To take these Gisu categories one by one, *isambo* (custom) applies to all customs and habits, whether of an individual or a group, which are not marked by pollution fears or associated with ancestry. Since custom in this usage applies to many – even most – of the basic ethical norms in Gisu society this is evidently not to say that customs are seen as a matter of choice or that they are necessarily unbacked by sanction. This indeed is the arena of interpersonal sanctions and of a 'do-as-you-would-be-done-by' ethic. Good may not always bring an appropriate reward, as the Gisu recognise too well, but bad deeds are expected to return as those harmed seek to retaliate. Nevertheless, we might say here that such norms are 'unmarked'; in themselves they carry no coercive power. Thus good sense and morality conspire to keep such custom current or indeed to modify it, as is the case today with customary by-laws which are enacted by the local government. We may also add here the rules and regulations known as *kamakambila*, the word deriving from the verbal root, to warn/advise.

In contrast, the *kimisambwa* and *kimisiro* cannot be changed in the same way; they are essentially a part of a person's identity and social potentiality. With the *kimisiro*, ritual prohibition, breach results in pollution (*imbixo*) and the risk of incurring punishment, usually in the form of a skin disease. Although associated with the ancestors in a general way, breaches of the rules are not directly punished by them. The punishments are seen as self-operative, self-triggering, rather than, for example, consequent on the enraged authority of the ancestors. The restrictions themselves are associated particularly with sexual status and roles including the division of labour between the sexes and more generally with the *kimisambwa* and all ritual. It would be difficult to catalogue the range of *kimisiro*. The more obvious are those associated with the division of labour between the sexes, and all are couched in the form of negative precepts. It is said to be *kumusiro* for a woman to thatch a roof, climb a tree, skin a cow, bury a person, or speak in the same way as a boy going to be circumcised. Women here are clearly being forbidden male prerogatives, for there is no comparable list of prohibitions for men, and associated with these rules are a wide range of food restrictions which only affect women. Thus women (and children) are forbidden chicken, eggs, fish, the windpipe and genitals of a goat or cow. While some of these *kimisiro* – particularly those associated with the division of labour between the sexes – are probably general throughout Bugisu, many of the others are highly particularistic as they are associated also with the *kimisambwa* and thus specific ancestry. Thus one may to talk of people having the same kinship, the same *kimisambwa* or the same *kimisiro*.

Kimisiro, like the *kimisambwa*, are thus essentially an aspect of a person's identity. Following Fortes (1959; 1966) these rules are probably best thought of as rules of relationship and the identity which comes with it. A person is born into a given constellation of *kimisambwa*, subject to the power of both those of his mother and those of his father. Thus the effective range of the *kimisambwa* of close kin overlaps but is not coincident except in the case of full siblings. Some of the restrictions associated with these *kimisambwa* a person will observe all his or her life; others become manifest in the course of life. These will be observed when circumstances and divination indicate that the person has been 'caught' by them.

The interventions in human life made by the anonymous powers of the *kimisambwa* are essentially individual in the sense that they affect only the person directly afflicted who must then go through the procedures of divination, cure and initiation into the cult. No moral lapse or fault is implied. The situation with respect to the ghosts is different and more ambivalent. In the first place the ghosts inflict individuals as representatives of their group. Thus, when children are dying or women are barren, this is seen not just as attacking the individual but to pose a threat to the whole kinship group who must as a group undertake the rituals to remedy this situation. Further, it could be argued that some moral fault is involved since the ghosts are seen as acting as a response to their neglect. This aspect is difficult and needs to be considered at some length.

Fortes's writings on Tallensi morality and concepts of ancestorhood provide possibly the most deeply considered work in this area. He regards ancestral observances of the kind described as an aspect of kinship morality, signifying submission to the ancestors and thus of one's own place in the kinship structure. For the Tallensi, it is the fact of rule and observance which he sees as the basic moral act rather than the content of the rules as such: 'morality in the sense of righteous conduct does not count. All that matters is service and obedience' (1959: 24). Tallensi ancestors are thus not moral guardians in any easy sense: they do not distinguish between righteous or unrighteous conduct among their descendants and their interventions have a hostile and punitive character. Yet still he regards the ancestor cult as the moral foundation of

Tallensi society, for

> What the ancestors demand and enforce on pain of death is conformity with the basic moral axioms in fulfilling the requirements of all social relationships; and these are the counterpart, in the domain of kinship, of the obligations posited between persons and their ancestors in the religious domain. This is understandable since the latter are derived from the former by extension and transposition to the religious domain. (1959: 25)

For Fortes, kinship is binding and the ancestors demand conformity. Further, kinship implies amity and this value too receives recognition in the ancestor cult, a cult which takes its meaning and is built on the fundamental experiences of kinship, itself predicated upon parenthood. It is these experiences also which he takes to account for the affective ambivalence displayed in ancestral belief, for they answer to the 'tragic dilemma presented by the inevitability of the succession of the generations' (1976:7), to the desire of parents for children to ensure their own immortality and the continuity of their line and the fact that children will ultimately displace their parents. Fortes argues that ancestral beliefs, by simultaneously submitting to the reality of death while keeping the parents alive symbolically, provide a resolution to this dilemma. The aspect kept alive is that of 'the parent as the inescapable source of discipline and frustration in the tasks of socializing the offspring to conform to custom and to take their proper place in society' (1976:14).

Thus the ancestors represent a particular transposition of the relationship between parents and children, a transposition which is partial and distorted for, as he makes clear, it is only the *authority* of the father, magnified and made absolute, which is represented in the cult. And, while some of his argument is phrased in universalistic terms – for example, the inevitability of the succession of the generations – it is clear that his transpositional theory ties his argument to the particular forms of Tallensi society where parental authority is strong and a person's place in society is determined by parentage.

In many respects the Gisu ancestor cult is very similar to that of the Tallensi. Yet while one could say that the ontology is the same it differs at the level of praxis. Piety, obedience and the willing submission of the self to the ancestors is basic to Tallensi morality as Fortes explicates it, but it is clear that this piety belongs to practice and to the actual obligations that a man owes his father, and which are ultimately demonstrated by the first-born son erecting a personal shrine to his father and thereby ensuring his rightful place as an ancestor. It is this piety which transforms the aggressive power of the ancestors into moral value. The Tallensi align with Job, when 'He perceives that submission to his god must be absolute, whether or not it corresponds to norms of righteous conduct among men' (1959:37).

As has been seen, parental authority is not strong in Bugisu. Further, fathers and sons are seen as in direct conflict over the land on which they jointly depend, and the conflicts which occur are little tempered by any attitude of filial piety. Indeed, to repeat once more, once a man has been circumcised, he is seen as jurally the equal of his father: ideally, an independent homesteader responsible for his own affairs, which includes the ritual protection of his household. Once circumcised then, a man may erect shrines on his own behalf to the ancestral powers which inflict him and his family; he needs no outside mediation. Nor is his relationship to the ancestors essentially changed upon his father's eventual death for, unlike the Tallensi, no specific cult is paid to the parents and the first-born assumes no particular role in ensuring the ancestral status of his father.

Since there is no piety in the relationship of son to father in Bugisu it is not surprising that this aspect is hard to find in their ancestor cult. Especially with regard to the *bamakombe*, hostility may be said to be little tempered by piety. People submit to ancestral will because they must. Using Weberian terms, we could say that it is 'power' and not 'authority' which the ghosts possess. When the ghosts attack, the kinship group ideally should rally round, take their dreams to the diviner for interpretation, ascertain which ghost has been affronted and perform the necessary rituals to placate the angry shade, for example, by disinterring the bones to establish new contact and then remaking the grave, very often with concrete. Yet placation is only one route, and where the Gisu can combat the ancestral ghosts they do, attempting to frighten away unwanted ghosts or, as a last resort, to capture and destroy them in ordeals of fire and water. Indeed the ghosts do not differ on a moral level from the other forces for mystical destruction in the Gisu cosmos, that is the witches, and particularly the cursers, whose motivations they are deemed to share.

What then, we may ask, are the values inherent in Gisu kinship and ancestry? We are still left with the idea of rule and observance, a template for living which is seen as obligatory. This may be, indeed must be, regarded as moral in the Durkheimian sense which Fortes clearly follows. But it could be said that this is 'moral' only in a weak sense, for it applies to all social rules and thus does not give any special status to those which are associated with ancestry. Further, without piety, without the submission of the individual to a personalised and positively valued authority, their ethical dimension remains in doubt. Expediency, opposed to the sense of obligation which Durkheim identified with the moral, remains as a possible attitude. Perhaps, given the indeterminacies of what we might here wish to regard as moral or ethical, the key point is that the question in itself tends to divert our attention away from the truly distinctive nature of these beliefs which hinge on the particular view they posit as to the nature of social transmission and reproduction.

Here we are left with the fact of continuity. Kinship continues; it 'cannot die', as the Gisu say when contrasting kinship with other forms of relationship. Kinship and the *kimisambwa* continue down the generations with the same strength and with the same implications. This, we could say, is kinship stripped to one form of essential – not amity, as Fortes maintains, nor long-term generalised reciprocity as Bloch (1971, 1973) has it – but simply continuity. Its rules carry an inevitability not associated with other kinds of social rule and which are carried with the very fact of birth. But they do not necessarily carry other ethical or moral values. Indeed, among the Gisu, it would not be too strong to say that kinship and ancestry enshrine neither piety nor amity, and this leaves perpetuity as their cardinal and only value. Service and obedience are not at issue. In this way, then, it could be maintained that the ancestral spirits enshrine a cult of identity, as Fortes argued, but not one of morality.

This is not to say that kinship does not carry as elsewhere the implications of generalised reciprocity and mutuality. The point is that these values are not protected by the ancestor cult and, to the extent that they are not, are contingent rather than categorical. One may bemoan the treachery of kin but this is not an unexpected evil, nor is there any to take redress apart from oneself. *Lukoosi*, in so far as it is made into an enforceable value in Gisu kinship, is the *lukoosi* of respect and deference, of distance and formality. This attracts sanction. The *lukoosi* of altruistic generosity, while it is hoped for as an ideal, has no such privileged ultimate status. One gains no support from others in complaining of a father's meanness: that is his affair. Moral indignation cannot be guaranteed on such issues. But to accuse him of a breach of *lukoosi*, of breaking the rules of kinship etiquette, is to accuse him of sinning, an offence deemed threatening to the very basis of the community. Of course, in the praxis of life, the two issues are linked since breach of the rules is often the outcome of dissension and bad feeling. However, it is important to make this distinction for the issues which mobilise indignation are those which we may call the rule, in the sense of the basic template laid down for social living.

Before taking up this theme we might consider more fully the nature of the tradition which is here implied for it is important to point out that there is a certain pragmatism in Gisu attitudes towards ancestral rules. Thus, while one might say, with Fortes, that the implications of such rules are immutable, which rules apply is a rather more open question.

ANCESTRAL RULES AND TRANSGRESSION

Custom, no less in Bugisu than elsewhere, is not unthinkingly followed. Indeed, the concept of tradition here does not imply a set point of historical origin which has laid down a fixed template of behaviour. On the contrary, when tied to ancestral power, it implies an inevitable malleability. Ancestral powers wax and wane as they are brought into different constellations with each other over time. And the applicability of such rules can often be known only contingently; a fact which, if only in a superficial sense, renders Gisu attitudes experimental in nature for many can be tested out only in practice.

Thus while some are unquestioned imperatives – such as the mother-in-law avoidance rules which hold for all Gisu – others are rather less absolute, and because of this it is often difficult to state exactly what the rule is. Incest rules, for example, tend to vary from family to family and indeed even members of the same family may give different degrees of consanguinity as marking the effective boundaries for marriage or sexual intercourse. Attitudes here follow the perceived consequences of such unions. Thus, in talking about prohibited unions, one neighbour was unwilling to state a rule because, as he said, he knew what it had been when he was young but he did not know what people could do today. He then went into some detail as to how his father's sister had married a distant cousin, within formerly prohibited degrees, and she had not only lived but flourished and had eight children. Another person told me that he also had a classificatory relative who had married within prohibited degrees and their children had all died. The lesson was clear in both cases, but in neither case was it a lesson which could be generalised to others. The distinctive nature of everyone's kinship make its rules particularistic. And this goes for all ancestral practices. Thus one of my neighbours no longer mixed her millet seed with an egg and various other medicines prior to sowing. No one else followed her example – the fact that her crops appeared not to suffer was no indication that other people's *kimisambwa* would be equally unresponsive. Ancestors create diversity as well as unity, and some people clearly are willing to take more risks than others.

The idea of ancestrally-derived order and rules allows – and possibly even invites – a degree of pushing at the boundaries of custom, a testing-out of what is and what is not in force. Misfortune and calamity mark the boundaries of the permissible. Yet even here transgression is not automatically punished by ancestral agency: this is seen as a risk and not as an inevitability. And it is a risk that the Gisu say is most acute where the offence becomes known. To some extent this depends on the seriousness of the offence. Breaking of the avoidance rules between in-laws of the opposite sex and generation automatically evokes *imbixo*, pollution. Most forms of incest do not. Here *imbixo* is contingent on the affair becoming known, on it actually affecting relationships and thus public morality.

Nor is this kind of pragmatic morality specific to the Gisu. As Mbiti (1969) implies, it is widespread in East Africa. He writes that

what lies behind the conception of moral 'good' or 'evil', is ultimately the nature of the relationships between individuals in a given community . . . It is not the act in itself which would be 'wrong' as such, but the relationships involved in the act: if relationships are not hurt or damaged, and if there is no discovery of breach of custom or regulation, then the act is not 'evil' or 'wicked' or 'bad'. (1969:213)

Nevertheless, where offences are found out then the punishment falls automatically, irrespective of questions of intent, degrees of moral culpability and so on. In Bugisu, the punishing force of *imbixo*, bringing skin disease, wasting, madness or even death is only loosely linked to the idea of ancestral power. It is seen to operate, where it does operate, of itself and without the direction of specific ancestors or their influence. The individual thus operates in an uncertain and unpredictable situation. Where there are secular authorities, there may be remorse, punishment and forgiveness; offences can be negotiated, assessed and open to mitigation. Where this does not hold, offences are seen to rebound in some absolute way on moral order and on the moral standing of the individual.

At this point it might be enlightening to discuss the issue of culpability with respect to the two paradigms of Oedipus and Job that Fortes used in his elucidation of Tallensi beliefs, and consider what the contrasting themes are in Gisu culture. In 1959, Fortes used the Oedipal paradigm to include both the idea of inevitable rivalry between fathers and sons and the idea of predestined fate. Among the Tallensi an individual is deemed to chose his own fate before birth and this pre-natal destiny may be for either good or bad. A bad destiny becomes manifest in the course of life, in the failure to achieve a satisfactory life course and thus the resulting dislocation of kinship and ancestry. At one level, then, responsibility lies thus with the individual. Yet Fortes writes that the belief in the supremacy of ancestors and their control over the life course, to an extent, frees the individual from ultimate blame. Job stands for this submission of the individual to this rightful and all-powerful authority.

Indeed, there is more to it than this. Fortes (1977) went on to speculate on how such submission might operate on a cathartic level to reduce the burden of guilt, grief and anger inevitably encountered in the course of life. In so doing he provides yet another insight into one of the problems that had puzzled him throughout, that is, why the all-powerful ancestors, the ultimate source of morality, at the same time were depicted as hostile and predatory? He now suggests that this effectively removes conflict from the domestic arena; the transposition of the potentially destructive part of parental authority on to the ancestors leaves the caring aspect 'intact for living relationships' (1977: 147). The ancestor cult thus siphons off tensions within the family and in so doing resolves them. And, as for family so with individual, for 'Tallensi can consistently off-load ultimate responsibility on to their parent surrogates who serve as external foci for conscience' (1977: 150).

If we consider what the corresponding paradigms inherent in Gisu beliefs might be, we would posit those of luck and the destructive power of witchcraft. The first places emphasis on chance in an essentially amoral world; the second that of bitter and ruthless competition which stops at nothing. And again the two are related, for while one is helpless in the face of chance, all misfortune is deemed as ultimately coming from the malevolent power of others, including in this case the ancestral ghosts. For the Gisu, therefore, the human world is ultimately turned in upon itself with no escape, unlike the Tallensi where responsibility for failure is projected elsewhere outside the body politic. The Gisu have no external agency on whom to blame misfortune; their enemies are other people whose constitution is essentially similar to their own. In this battle, success, both in pursuing one's own goals and warding off the attacks of others, depends solely on one's own strength, power and knowledge.

Again to follow Fortes and to enquire into the way these beliefs are grounded in social experience (just as they reflect back upon it), we might say that both the concept of luck and the belief in witchcraft, open to any with sufficient power, may be seen as the conceptual correlates of the unrestrained individualism that is found in Gisu social relations. Unlike the Tallensi case, the conflict bred in kinship, in the unit of the family and especially in the competing interests of father and son, cannot be seen to achieve a reconciliation in ancestral beliefs. The conflict in itself is given straightforward representation in the beliefs of the mystical powers of age and seniority, in the ability to use witchcraft and the power to curse. Indeed the curse may be seen as the ultimate act of treachery, involving the combined malevolence of ancestors and elders in destroying their own kinship and ancestry. Far from restraining conflict among kin, such beliefs fuel it. As Mary Douglas wrote, against the prevailing interpretations of witchcraft at the time which tended to stress their positive 'functional' role in community processes, witchcraft may also be 'an aggravator of all hostilities and fears, an obstacle to peaceful cooperation' (1963:141). This too must form part of the analysis.

In a social world predicated on fear and competition with others a consequence might well be an exaggerated respect for the idea of 'rules'. They are seen as the main way in which social living might be rendered predictable and the actions of others accountable. In following rules one acknowledges oneself and others as morally responsible. Responsible action thus implies a discriminating mind; of knowing the conduct appropriate to different circumstances and to different categories of people to whom one is related. In the most general terms it is this ability to discriminate which opposes men and animals: confusion is despicable and animal-like. It follows that the most heinous faults are seen to be those of non-discrimination, disregard and disobedience. It is the way of children, of the mad and of the foolish. It is also the way of witches and thieves; those who are seen as having opted out of responsive human society. Rule-following thus also provides the way in which the essential constitution of the person can be judged.

Yet here again we meet the lack of authority in the Gisu system and the fact that the ideals of *lukoosi* do not receive any positive reinforcement in ancestral beliefs. Further, in both this chapter and chapter 3 I have argued that the locus of responsibility for moral action lies with the individual and his dispositions. The lack of external sources of social control throws the emphasis on self-control. At this point we may try to develop this argument further by looking again at the nature of kinship etiquette itself, since this clearly embodies the idea of restraint. However, it also embodies other themes, including that of violence, and this invites a more speculative line of interpretation, seeking to show how it codes the dilemmas of Gisu society, for what it says about the nature of social living, of the bases of responsibility and particularly about the control of the self. I say 'codes' rather than 'describes' or 'depicts' here because I assume that the meaning involved is not to be read from the surface of things but inevitably involves a hermeneutic approach, a 'reading'.

At this point therefore I move away from Fortesian concern with the social construction of the self, and what particular constellations of ancestral beliefs imply for human existence, to an examination of the formalised etiquette of kinship itself. Kinship norms, in so far as they relate to demeanour, are concrete but I argue that their implications for action are wider than this since they may also be seen to carry more general messages. Here I envisage a reflective self using the materials of collective life, in this case of kinship etiquette, not just to specify appropriate types of contextualised behaviour but as more generally orientating, providing a way by which the individual may apprehend the nature of his social existence and its problems. Again my concern is not so much with the pragmatics of daily life but with what might be called the philosophy of Gisu social forms.

2   JOKING AND AVOIDANCE: ANOTHER READING OF KINSHIP

In this section it is proposed to look again at Gisu kinship structure and at the contrasting formulations of the avoidance relationship, *bumasala*, and the joking relationship, *bukulo*. In an earlier chapter *bukulo* was placed in its historical and structural context as a unique mode of peacemaking, a strategy of the past. But it also has present significance; as an aspect of daily life its surprising and usually unexpected encounters serve to break the complacency of everyday interaction. Such encounters take many forms: from tentative abuse, as perhaps exchanged between a young man and woman little versed in the forms and still circumspect in their dealings with each other, to the ribald jest or uninhibited hostile pretence of established partners. And it is important to note that while many such exchanges are taken in apparent good heart and are often accompanied by considerable jocularity, they can also be 'played for real'. In such cases, for an unsuspecting observer, they may be indistinguishable from a real conflict. On one occasion, when travelling in an area which we did not know well, my assistant and I were caught in this way and I still remember vividly the panic of our reaction when our guide was suddenly embroiled in what appeared to be an extremely ugly situation with a man whose house we were passing. Our evident fear eventually prompted explanation, as well as some amusement, as the apparent venom and extreme abuse gradually gave way to more ribald and standard forms of insult as the two men disengaged from the encounter.

Yet even when less extreme than this, in a very real sense all such encounters are startling and provoke extended commentaries on the forms of the relationship and its possibilities, some of which were given in chapter 7. Further, we might go on to say that as a formalised relationship it offers a fixed point in the constellation of Gisu relationships and gives direct recognition to the problem of hatred and aggression.

My aim in this section is thus again hermeneutic. More than that, it seeks to provide a new way of looking at joking and avoidance relationships. Levine (1984) has argued recently that these behaviours are best seen as setting the parameters for moral discourse and behaviour – that is, he argues that they should not be interpreted just as odd quirks of a system of classificatory kinship, but seen as essential for establishing the moral verities it posits. I want to extend upon this view to argue that these patterns provide not just a template for moral action but an implicit philosophy, a metacommentary on the nature of social life and its possibilities.

The very 'oddness' of African joking forms has ensured that an interpretive literature has been developed around them and the critical parameters of kinship structure with which they are often associated. Radcliffe-Brown defined joking relationships in terms of their essential ambivalence. They are a 'peculiar combination of friendliness and antagonism' (1952: 91), a play upon enmity, which gives simultaneous expression to the common and divergent interests of parties to an alliance.[2] Avoidance relationships he saw as another means of achieving the same end, namely the giving of a stable and institutionalised form to a relationship of alliance. The Gisu have both these forms; indeed, they might be said to have extreme versions of them with avoidance between mother-in-law and son-in-law being pretty well total and an extra-kin joking relationship which brings the element of hostility to the fore.

Yet it is not just that these relationships are odd – though they are – but that from this point of view so is the whole system of classificatory kinship. Why, we might ask, all this specification of conduct? Why is appropriate human conduct chopped up, so to speak, into chunks and then distributed among different categories of relative in the way that it is? We might accept, of course, that it acts to regulate action, but we might go further by enquiring into what it is saying about the basic parameters of moral action, of the essential categories of social life and of human possibility.

To begin with a summary of the major themes in Gisu kin classification and etiquette, firstly, as has been described, all kinship relationships involve restraint, *lukoosi*. Secondly, this restraint is more stringent among those of adjacent generations and opposite sex and these two forms of restraint combine to magnify each other. Thirdly, this goes along with the separation of the sexuality of the generations, and a rigid distinction between procreative and conjugal roles. Fourthly, affinal relationships are exaggerated versions of consanguineal ones: intimacy is both more intimate and respect is more compelling. Thus, in relationship to a man a wife thus stands at the opposite extreme to her mother, and brothers-in-law are more 'familiar' than brothers. Thus brothers-in-law, parents-in-law and men who have married sisters may indulge in light jesting with each other, but brothers never. In the opposite direction, the twin constraints of respect and sexual inhibition find their fullest expression in the absolute nature of the *bumasala* avoidance relationship between a man and his mother-in-law.

The term *bumasala* applies both to the relationship between mother-in-law and son-in-law and to the behaviour that is prohibited and it is this relationship which stands as the prototype for all relationships in the category. The avoidance combines both fear and respect. Men say both that they respect/honour their mother-in-law because women are more fertile than men and equally that they are afraid to see them in case they find them beautiful. Indeed, the prohibitions hinge on the fear of sexual contact and focus on the issue of touching or seeing one another naked. However, the concept extends beyond this to include all that is obscene. Abusive language is referred to as words of *bumasala* and is regarded as a form of cursing with the words taking on a power to harm irrespective of the relationship between people. Yet the essence of *bumasala* is the sexually forbidden and these restrictions constitute such cardinal value that breach is felt to be an abomination. One cannot overstress this aspect.

The set of attitudes associated with *bumasala* can be examined further by looking at the connotations of *lukoosi*, *tsisoni* and *kamanyanyu*, with their overlapping sets of connotation and reference. *Lukoosi*, described earlier, can be glossed in the present context as 'respect'. *Tsisoni*, while it too inspires respect, is a respect which is best rendered as sexual reticence or inhibition. *Tsisoni* 'catches' you when sexual distance is breached. The affect experienced here is likened to that of *kamanyanyu*, the word more generally used for shame. Yet shame provides only a partial gloss as it is not adequate to either the strength nor the range of this affect which again also implies fear. Thus *kamanyanyu* may catch a child when he is scolded but equally it might catch an adult in a variety of different but dangerous situations. One man gave the following list of things which might inspire *kamanyanyu*. Firstly, all situations where *tsisoni* is present, but also walking alone at night or sleeping alone in a house, seeing a snake or a wild animal, walking in a town or seeing a murdered and mutilated body. *Kamanyanyu* then seems to apply to raw fear, a sense of the ominous; it is the type of fear which makes your skin crawl.[3] And *tsisoni* is the strongest fear/shame of all. Felt on the skin; if you look directly at your mother-in-law *tsisoni* can catch your body all over. Fittingly perhaps, the punishment, as with all pollution, takes the form of a skin disease.

The *bumasala* relationship is clearly at one extreme pole of Gisu sociality. Keeping to the context of kin classification, we can note that mother-in-law and son-in-law are asymmetric with respect to the basic polarities around which the Gisu have constructed their kinship universe, that is, of sex and generation. Added to these principles, there are those of conjugal/sexual as opposed to generative/consanguineal linkage. Here the patterned discriminations extend into the most private and intimate sphere of social life. A woman's maternal or procreative role is clearly separated from her conjugal, sexual one, with the intimate physical relationship a woman has with her husband, on the one hand, and her children, on the other, being demarcated by ritual restrictions (*kimisiro*). Thus if a man becomes seriously ill or incontinent a wife cannot nurse him for only a woman related as 'mother' can wash and clean his anus and genitals. In a like manner, a man may never touch or suck his wife's breasts for these 'belong to the children' and any injury here is an offence which pollutes the couple and requires ritual annulment and compensation. If, in relationship to a man (and there are strong grounds for considering the kinship system to be constructed around the male person because the system is more elaborated with respect to men than it is with respect to women), a 'wife' and a 'mother' are very different kinds of relative, the 'mother of a wife' becomes doubly charged.

Further, a women's fertility is largely credited to her mother who is said to have 'grown her' and to have protected her from the dangers of sorcery and other misfortune during her childhood. A girl is most vulnerable to malignant supernatural force during her first menstruation and this tends to be specified as the particular charge of the mother, the essential part of any safe rearing. When a girl marries the debt to her mother is recognised in the gifts of clothes, hoes and other household utensils which she receives, items which fall outside the bridewealth proper and are not repayable on divorce. Yet, in a very real way the debt to the mother-in-law can never be repaid. She has no stake in the exchange of livestock which procure wives for the male members of the family and, Gisu marriage rules ensure, that women are not directly reciprocated between families.

These lines of exposition set forth the major contrasts which place the relationship with the mother-in-law at one end of the spectrum of possible social behaviours. As has been described, the mother-in-law/son-in-law relationship is associated with fear, a fear which hinges on a sexual reticence so strong that it amounts to dread and imposes avoidance. In the normal course of events violations are unthinkable and witting breach unforgivable. Breaches, where they occur, are thus diagnostic of relationships which have broken down and arouse anger in a way little else does. This is much less likely between mother-in-law and son-in-law because of the absolute nature of the distance imposed, at least between those most closely related. However, disputes between brothers or between father and son in the domestic setting frequently have such outcome as daughters-in-law also get embroiled in the issues, as was the circumstance in case 11, that of Wafaxale. And such violations take the form of insult, physical violence or, in extreme cases, the exposure of the genitals. All, in this situation, carry the threat of witchcraft and prelude further violence within the kindred. Breaches of *bumasala*, given as the cause of grievance and anger, thus tend to overlay quarrels which we are inclined to see as more basic. Land issues, quarrels over its allocation or the boundaries between plots, between father and son, thus tend to reach public attention as pollution issues.

What then do we make of the joking relationship, *bukulo*, who freely make play with the things of *bumasala*, with the sexually obscene, with violence and hostile abuse? The terms of the relationship are clearly reversed.[4] To this extent we might follow Radcliffe-Brown and see the avoidance and joking forms as mutually illuminating each other.[5] However, it is important to see the two relationships as embedded in a system of meanings which extends beyond the simple regulation of behaviour to embrace a wider social vision, a social vision which I will argue emphasises throughout the necessity for emotional and behavioural restraint. While this message seems clear enough, even self-evident, with respect to mother-in-law avoidance, it appears less obviously applicable to joking relationships. The argument thus needs to be developed.

Firstly, we might summarise the contrasts between the two relationships. Thus, the mother-in-law is the focus for the most stringent restraint, and the relationship effectively epitomises the nature of kinship rules, while the joking relationship rides roughshod over all the distinctions of kinship. Clearly it is incompatible with either kinship or marriage. Further, it can be opposed to mother-in-law avoidance in that cosmologically the mother-in-law is associated with the gift of a daughter and life and the joking relationship with death. So the oppositions, kinship/non-kinship, restraint/licence, life/death, are apparent and may be elaborated still further. Indeed, one of the problems – or perhaps I should say challenges – in interpretation here is precisely the range of themes, contrasts and polarities that it is possible to identify. Added to which, both relationships in themselves involve a reversal. In the case of *bumasala* a marriage in effect transfers a whole set of people of the opposite sex from permitted sexual partners to a category which is absolutely forbidden. In the case of *bukulo*, a fight or war enables a positive transformation of enemies into allies, conceived in terms of enduring and absolute friendship. To the fact of such contrasts we can relate the numerous different emphases that are present in the anthropological literature on joking and avoidance.

To pick a way warily (and partially) through this literature. I think it is fair to say that of recent analyses of joking many of the more interesting have taken their lead from Radcliffe-Brown. Thus, while decrying his functionalism, they too have put the emphasis on ambivalence and the theme of reversal. In so doing they have extended the interpretive framework by taking analysis away from the simple regulation of behaviour to explore the cosmological dimensions of the pattern. Beidelman (1966), for example, considered the problem in terms of transformations, with jokers being seen as ambiguous/liminal figures. Jokers then are mediators, but if they are to be seen as mediators the question as to what they might be said to mediate between is posed. What are the relevant boundaries of the social universe? How indeed should the social universe be conceived?

In fairly orthodox terms one can see the social universe in terms of sectors of sociability, the gradual phasing-out of moral responsibility in line with social distance, as Evans-Pritchard (1940) has explained for the Nuer and Sahlins (1972) for the gift. Kinship at the core then may be taken to contrast with enmity on the periphery. Thus we might see both mothers-in-law and joking partners are intercalary figures, the point of transformation between solidary kin and hostile outsiders. But neither of these polarities is particularly well-developed in Bugisu: kin are neither solidary nor are outsiders necessarily hostile. In part this arises from the fact that the kinship universe is pretty well all-embracive. At the interactive level all are kin, either by consanguinity or by intermarriage. Parochial marriage patterns and the wide extension of kinship terms ensure that effectively everyone is related. In any event, everyone is addressed by kinship terms. And, working outwards from the self, relations with distant kin or neighbours with whom only a remote connection can be traced take the form of a dilution of kinship conduct. Taboos fade out, incest ceases to become meaningful, obligations dissolve rather than abruptly cease. And, at some point along this line, kin become marriageable once more. And, in fact this is what happens, with Gisu marrying distant kin, and marriage thus being not so much the way kinship is created as the way it is renewed.

Joking partners alone stand outside this normal schema of sociability. Effectively they are the only 'non-kin' in the Gisu social world, the only people not linked by the bonds of sexuality. But, while one could see these relationships as existing at the point of divide, mediating between a world of kin and a world of non-kin, this is not altogether convincing. Besides, there is, in any event, a more interesting line of interpretation. That is, we can also see the social universe in more existential terms, and see the relationships of joking and avoidance thus as representing the contrasting tendencies present in everyday life. The emphasis is then thrown not so much on ambiguity and mediation but on the role of reversals in social life.

Analysing the reversals found in carnivals, Abrahams and Bauman (1978) have written that we should not understand these as literally involving 'the antithesis of behaviour at other times' but as giving expression to the disorder present, if disapproved of, in normal daily life. This is clearly relevant for the Gisu. The neighbourhood is the sphere of the most embittered enmities where conflicts over land, women and breaches of norms are most evident and serious. Avoidance of overt and public strife is an ideal, just as physical avoidance is seen as the main strategy for peaceably dealing with an enemy, allowing time for tempers to cool. Such an ideal is frequently broken. Thus one could argue that joking gives expression not only to the hostility present at the edge of the kinship universe, but simultaneously gives expression to the hostile sentiments present within the community itself. One could make a similar point about incest, but to continue with joking . . .

Like kinship, *bukulo* is a perpetual alliance; unlike kinship it is based on the recognition of violence, on the toleration of the intolerable. To return to the symbolism of dog-killing, the dog represents *kamaya*, the disregard for normal conventions and rules which leads to trouble and ill-will in the community and its natural outcome, *cixonde*, hatred. One could say that *bukulo*, like the dog, represents the confrontation and confounding of the two systems; with disorder and anarchy invading – and then contained within – the sphere of order and etiquette. This is reminiscent of Mary Douglas's commentary (1968) on the subversive nature of the joke with its juxtaposition of control with non-control. At one level, joking partners represent the reversal of the normal moral order and freely indulge in the forbidden words of *bumasala*, obscenity and insult. Yet it could be said that the very possibility of such a reversal underlines the essential relativity in human social conventions and the creativity of social experience. Pollution can be contained and enmity transformed into friendship; men can not only come to terms with their bitterest experiences but do so in a way that creates positive social value. In the pool of human experience, the joker, like the trickster, can transform all things, making mockery of the most deeply held canons of propriety and generating value from the apparently valueless.

This broadly is Mary Douglas's view. In her important article on joking, she argues that 'by the path of ritual joking these African cultures too have reached a philosophy of the absurd' and they do so 'by revealing the arbitrary, provisional nature of the very categories of thought, by lifting their pressure for a moment and suggesting other ways of structuring reality' (1968: 374). In a similar vein, Handelman (1982) argues for the reflexive potentialities of 'play', with its power to take apart the 'clockworks of reality'.

However, despite the appeal of these formulations, I do not see the significance of Gisu joking patterns to lie here. I am not at all sure that I see these formalised encounters as creative and freeing. Rather, I think the message may well be more straightforward. For, if it is possible to phrase *bukulo* behaviour in terms of a reversal of normal ideal sociability, it is equally possible to see it as an extreme type of it. We might then see the relationship as representing not mediating ground nor reversal, not liminal nor ludic, but as giving yet another twist to the theme of restraint.

This view raises different interpretive possibilities. For example, if one emphasises reversal then the joking relationship may be said to give notice of the 'hidden' dimension, the underside of social experience; human nature perhaps set against the repressive forces of the social order. This tends to imply a cathartic model of process; with emotion being channelled and possibly transmuted, as was the case with Radcliffe-Brown's theory, just as it also invites a Freudian perspective. Alternatively, if one sees it as an extreme type of permissible relationship, one end of the spectrum of possibility, then we might say that though it appears like licence, in fact like other relationships, it embodies, as I have indicated, its own given mode of restraint. *Bukulo*, as the Gisu say, is a bitter thing.

To expand on this, *bukulo* involves the systematic turning of the other cheek. Violence on one side is met with restraint and even generosity on the other and natural retaliatory impulses are suppressed. A text illustrates this point:

When they first started *bukulo*, my grandfather went to snatch a bunch of bananas in the plantation of his partner. He struck that bunch so that it shattered completely and each banana fell to the ground. Then he went and struck down another bunch. After that he slashed the stem of the trees, felled them and went away. When the owner discovered this damage he asked angrily who had come to spoil his plantation. Neighbours told him that it was his joking partner who had scattered his bananas on the ground. So he went to his joking partner and said, 'You have spoilt my bananas but as it is you who have struck them down then you may eat them.' This act strengthened *bukulo*. Then, on another occasion, he ran to his joking partner's and caught hold of a cow; he hit it, snatched it and killed it. He even ate it but his partner did not pursue him as a thief. And so *bukulo* continued from strength to strength, and it does so in the same way today.

To move to a conclusion. I have wanted to argue that the structuring of kinship contains an implicit philosophy of being in so far as it patterns experience in terms of the possibilities inherent in social relationships. The basis of the Gisu social order is seen to rest with *lukoosi*, a restraint which is sanctified in the person of the mother-in-law who is revered by avoidance. With her there can be no social contact; *bakulo*, on the other hand, may revile each other with impunity. With them all and any contact seems possible. However, rather than either ambiguity or reversal being the main theme, I argue that the keynote is again restraint. The joking relationship may then be seen as a fixed point in the 'normal' constellation of social relationships; not a fake form but a real form of social interaction. And, like others, it may also be seen to encode its own drama of renunciation, a ritualised form of self-abnegation. Licence is possible *only* because one has forsworn vengeance. Mother-in-law avoidance and *bukulo* then may be said to encode contrasting dramas of renunciation; of love and sexuality in the one instance and of hatred and warfare in the other; Eros and Thanatos.

If, as I have argued, it is restraint and denial which are being dramatised in both these relationships we might return to the question of how far their forms answer to the particular dilemmas of Gisu society. As I see it, they objectify the 'problem', perhaps more in parable form than as a direct moral lesson, but nevertheless they stress the importance of restraint, a restraint which is centred upon the self, and which, in the absence of both segmentary loyalties and strong patterns of authority, exists as the main force for consensual social living. The extreme forms that both joking and avoidance take among the Gisu may be set in this way against their equally dominant egalitarian ethos. The importance of control gains further power when considering the constituent powers of the personality. In particular the defining power of the male person is seen in terms of a capacity for anger, an anger which leads to hatred and thus is inevitably a force for disruption in social life. This capacity for anger gives added poignancy to the dilemmas of control, a control which is centred as much upon the self as upon others.

CONCLUSION

In the first section of this chapter it was argued that Gisu metaphysical beliefs were in accordance with everyday realities where authority is but poorly recognised. Unlike the Tallensi, Gisu ancestral beliefs provide no resolution to the inherent conflicts in the familial setting, whether one sees these in the universalistic terms proposed by Fortes or as related to specific cultural features such as the Gisu inheritance system. And the hostility which this breeds knows of no natural limits, permeating all social relationship as the rationale for misfortunes is sought predominantly in witchcraft and those punitive powers of the ancestors which are linked to witchcraft. Luck and witchcraft, uncontrollable chance and the evil in others, equally uncontrollable, form the dominant explanatory schemas. This exposes a tenuous basis to community life and, indeed, social life is a matter of constant wariness as the intentions and dispositions of others are scrutinised for clues as to their feelings. At a very real level, safety, indeed very life itself, depends upon such vigilance.

It is in this context that I have sought to interpret the significance of kinship and its etiquette, a product of an egalitarian society where fear of the hostility of both oneself and others is a dominant feature in social interaction. The insistence on rules provides the basis for predictability in social affairs, yet it is a predictability which is seen to depend on the control by each individual of his own hostile feelings. The message of kinship, which is in effect the message for the management of all social relationships, can in this way be rendered in terms of the need for self-control. It is this alone which may curb the socially disruptive nature of agonistic competition among men. And the forceful reiteration of this message may again be referred to the lack of external authorities; of repressive mechanisms which could provide institutional support for an otherwise 'voluntary' submission of the individual to the demands of social living.

Yet clearly this is only one strand. In so far as the etiquette of kinship is enforced in the fear of other peoples' anger, force is also part of the story. And further, I have been dealing with the topic as though the apparatus of the Ugandan state was irrelevant or non-existent. To an extent this is justified, partly because I have been concerned to identify tendencies which may be regarded as deeply embedded in Gisu social forms, and partly because of the very inadequacies of the state as a source of authority and order at the time in question. Yet the Gisu experience of fifty or more years of authoritarian rule is not irrelevant to the argument, nor indeed to the way the Gisu conceived of the problems that were besetting their society and the remedies available to them. For it was through discipline and control, more rules and regulations and the more systematic use of force that the new associations developing in Bugisu in the mid-sixties sought answers to the problems of increasing insecurity. In the process they were to give a new twist to the theme of *lukoosi*.

It was in the name of *lukoosi* that both the vigilante groups and drinking societies developing in Bugisu in the mid-sixties demanded support. It was a self-evident good. *Lukoosi*, as has been seen, is enshrined in the rules of kinship, the detailed specification of kinship conduct. This conduct is not about rights and obligations, it is about rendering through one's manner and behaviour what is due to others, demonstrating proper respect. Nevertheless, as outlined at the beginning of this chapter, its sphere of reference is far greater than this, including all action which may be seen to foster peaceful co-operation among people. Thus, *lukoosi* also can be applied to authorities, to those who make rules, those who obey them and those who put them into effect. Obote, then the president of Uganda, was often described as an *umu-koosi*, or as having *lukoosi*: many Gisu supported his government and identified with its aims. So were the chiefs when their actions were approved of. I was more mystified when some neighbours told me that, in the past, when the colonial police came to the rural areas in search of suspects they would round up the people of a neighbourhood and threaten or beat them until some gave evidence. This too was described as *lukoosi*, for it was seen to carry positive consequences. Without such coercion people, I was told, would have been too afraid to speak out: with it, they were felt to be absolved from blame. Peace, then, can also be achieved through coercion and the imposition of controls. This was the message that the vigilante groups and drinking companies promulgated and it was a message that drew widespread support.

NOTES

1 A theme also taken up by La Fontaine (1967). However, my interests in this section remain the elucidation of Gisu forms rather than to provide a critical commentary on the work of Fortes.

2 There have been extensive critiques of Radcliffe-Brown's theory and the explanatory role he gives to catharsis, with the argument that the expression of hostility in itself promotes or facilitates the formation of stable institutional relationship, particularly Beidelman, 1966; Apthorpe; 1967, Douglas, 1968; Rigby, 1968; Sharman, 1969; Kennedy, 1970; Howell, 1973; Freedman, 1977; Stevens, 1978.

3 Parkin (1986) has contrasted 'raw fear' of this kind with 'respectful fear', with the latter being seen as an instrument of hierarchy and being calculable in its consequences in a way that the former is not.

4 *Bukulo* may also be contrasted with the pattern of brother-in-law feasting friendships. Both relationships are cemented over time between two men by increasing the scale of their reciprocities, but while brothers-in-law feast one another, *bakulo* engage in negative reciprocity, a sanctioned appropriation of goods which are destroyed or 'eaten' by one side alone. Moreover, the verbal component is again

sharply contrasted, with the gentle chaffing of brothers-in-law – who must always be concerned lest their remarks are taken ill – having little in common with the kind of insult permissible among *bakulo*.

5   In contrast to the extensive commentaries on Radcliffe-Brown's theory of joking relationships (see note 1), his account of avoidance relationships has been little questioned and thus one may suppose is the subject of at least tacit acceptance. But the functionalist thesis he proposes is much less convincing here. If it were solely a question of separating those with divergent interests in order to promote social harmony, as he suggests, then the restrictions should apply equally to other affines. In the Gisu case, with a pattern of easy divorce requiring the return of bridewealth, one could argue that the affinal relationship most under stress from potential conflict over property is that between father-in-law and son-in-law, and this is not marked by either joking or avoidance. They are bound only by the *lukoosi* respect rules which hold between adjacent generations. Or, again, one could argue that the functionalist hypothesis runs into trouble in accounting for observed patterns of behaviour, for restrictions such as that of *bumasala*, far from preventing trouble, can be seen to create it. While it is possible that in many societies the avoidance rules only affect those with whom there is little contact in any case, in Bugisu the wide extension of *bumasala* coupled with parochial marriage patterns means that fear of inadvertent breach of distance is ubiquitous. People must be constantly wary of activities which might bring them into contact with *bamasala* but, even with such vigilance, breach in many cases is inevitable.

PART 4
Community in the making

10

'WE ARE THE GISU GOVERNMENT':
THE NEW MOVEMENTS

In the 1960s the Gisu perceived themselves to be facing a crime wave of unprecedented dimensions, a crime wave of witches and thieves. Nor was Bugisu the only area to experience this problem, for it appears that it was general to East Africa, with popular fears focused on the figure of the *kondo* or armed robber. The national newspapers of both Kenya and Uganda carried regular bulletins of *kondo* attacks and the degree of public concern was clearly articulated in 1966 when Uganda made robbery a capital offence. Yet crime continued to rise.[1] The Uganda Government Annual Report for 1968 shows a general increase in the number of offences reported over the previous year, with a 22% rise in offences against the person and an 8.6% rise in crimes against property. In the 1970s, Amin instituted public executions for thieves, a practice which was given some publicity in Britain and seen to emphasise the barbarity of the regime. Yet in Uganda itself it was not unpopular but seen rather as one of the more positive aspects of Amin's programme of discipline and control.

Durkheim argued that societies create 'crime' as a way of establishing the moral boundaries of the community, with prosecutions serving to 'concentrate the upright consciousness'. From this perspective crime is an inevitable product of social order and prosecution serves to unite people by dramatising their common fears and common abhorrence for the forms of behaviour displayed. One of the most influential studies from this Durkheimian perspective is Erikson's (1966) study of three crime waves in a New England Protestant community between 1636 and 1692. He provides us with an account of how each crime wave dramatised the conflicts within the community and acted to redefine the operative principles upon which it was based. Each of the three religious heresies – the Antinomian, the Quaker and witchcraft craze – challenged the constitution of the community and its interpretation of Biblical lore and, in being persecuted, allowed for the reformulation of the dominant vision just as it underscored its legitimacy. However, scholars from the Marxist tradition have argued that the evidence suggests that it was power struggles rather than crises of community morality which precipitated each crime wave. Such crime waves, then, did not contribute to 'social solidarity' but served to eliminate rival power centres and reassert the legitimacy of the ruling elite (Chambliss and Seidman, 1982).

The question of whether the perception of increasing crime serves community or sectional interests is difficult to decide in the abstract for the appeal to community values is a form of symbolic capital which can be used in many ways. In Bugisu, the fear of the thief and the witch was certainly an issue which allowed for community mobilisation in a way that nothing else did. And, from the mid-1960s onwards, vigilante groups began to be formed throughout Bugisu in response to this fear and as a way of counteracting its threat. The nature of their popular appeal can be judged from this following extract from a speech made by a vigilante leader who had come to initiate a group in a nearby area:

We are the vigilantes and we are trying to bring law and order into this area. In our area we hear few alarms raised now because there is no trouble. But I have been told that you are still disturbed by thieves and witches. Where we live there are no longer any thieves and people can leave their houses without worry. We leave everything around – cows, goats, clothes – and when we return they are still there. But you are still suffering. Look at that person over there whom they have bewitched! He is going to die! And that one over there! Is there anyone here who is not afraid for his life? We have come but none of these sick people have called us. We have only come because we want there to be peace everywhere. So those who say they are fearful of their own lives or those of their friends, raise your hands and tell us of the witches and thieves.

It was in the name of *lukoosi* that the vigilantes stated their cause. In their hands it became an ideology which stressed discipline and control, with force needed to counter force. The earlier names of these groups indicated the 'emergency' aspects of the situation. Indeed the earliest models of organisation seem to have come from the army. Many Gisu had had army experience in the King's African Rifles during the Second World War. The vigilantes also appear to have seen their role as analogous to the use of the army to quell civil disturbances. The first groups chose names for themselves such as *Bamajonisi* – from the English word 'emergency'; *Bajooni* – from 'Johnny', a soldier; *Portola* – patrol. Others appeared to mimic the professional security organisations, taking over from the employment of individual watchmen, which were already operating in large cities such as Nairobi and which offered a full protection service for businesses and private householders. Thus one found the groups referred to as 'Bugisu Security Council' and 'Night Security'. However, the names that were to become most widely used after 1967 were 'Bugisu government' and more especially *Banalukoosi* – agents of order/peace. The vigilantes were clearly aligning themselves with the objectives of government, co-opting as they did so the ideology of *lukoosi*.

Side by side with the vigilantes and also aligned with *lukoosi*, another movement was also gaining rapidly in popularity, that of the drinking companies. These were essentially voluntary associations, which developed over time into forms of rotating credit organisation. However, their main purpose was to provide a safe venue for the drinking of beer and again they regarded themselves as representing a 'Gisu government'. In this the two associations had complementary aims, setting out in different ways to reconstitute effective sanctions over behaviour. While the drinking companies set out to fortify neighbourly sociability during the day, the vigilantes sought to counter the hostile forces which rose against the community at night.

This chapter sets out to offer a brief description of the genesis and *modus vivendi* of the two forms of organisation. The next chapter will consider some of the wider issues that relate to their emergence at this particular historical juncture. Then we will consider how far they might be considered as a response to the vacuum of power at the local level created by the erosion of the established structures of governmental authority.

THE DRINKING COMPANIES

For the neighbouring Teso, Karp (1980b) points to the essential ambivalence of beer-drinking as an occasion which combines an ideal of commensality, an 'unencumbered sociability', with fears of sorcery and poisoning which point to the inability of people to achieve it. For the Gisu in the mid-1960s, the risk element had clearly got out of hand. No man of course drank wittingly with his enemies, and because of this, who a man did or did not drink with was an apt way of talking about social relationships. But such a safeguard, in itself, was plainly insufficient, for the Gisu believe that one's worst enemies dissemble their intentions. The din and confusion of a typical beer party, where between ten and fifty men and women might be crowded together in often only a single dark room, gave ample opportunity, it was felt, for the planning of an ambush or slipping poison into a neighbour's drinking-tube.

It was such dangers that the drinking companies sought to minimise both by having a hand-picked membership and by imposing strict rules over behaviour at their parties. Each member paid a joining fee of 1s or 2s and at first members took it in turns to brew beer for each other freely. Such groups were based on extremely small neighbourhood areas with a membership of between ten and fifteen men, although since wives and visitors were allowed the number of people actually drinking was often double this. The earliest groups often formed around small co-residential cores of agnates or age mates but once they had been established it was rare for any particular tie to dominate in the membership. For example, in one group which started in 1966 called 'Tumbu' after a small stretch of a river nearby, ten of the thirteen founding members were from a single lineage segment. Two years later only ten of the twenty-four members came from the lineage as a whole.

These groups almost certainly originated in Busoba in Central Bugisu and it appears that they had been experimented with for some time before they became generally accepted. Tumbu, for example, had been inaugurated unsuccessfully as early as 1964 and only reconstituted in 1966 following the precedent set by a group which had been operating successfully since the previous year. In 1967 these groups suddenly became very popular and the density of such groups in Busoba averaged ten to twelve to the square mile. Although women attended the drinking the membership was predominantly male. The exceptions were some 'old peoples' groups', which tended to recruit equally from both sexes. The number of groups also tended to remain large, a feature dictated in part by the combination of parochial marriage patterns and the mother-in-law avoidance rules which prevented affines of adjacent generations and opposite sex drinking together. For this reason, too, fathers and sons often preferred to drink with different companies.

The proliferation of groups was paralleled by the speed of innovation in the organisation of the groups. The first officials chosen were a duplication of those found in the co-operative societies which marketed the valuable coffee and cotton cash crops and whose name too, *lituuli* (pl. *kamatuuli*), which means simply 'group', the drinking companies adopted for themselves. A chairman and vice-chairman were elected and so too was a secretary/auditor who kept the books and wrote down the minutes of the meetings. The titles of the officials were usually in English though sometimes Lugisu equivalents were used and in some cases new terms coined, which were direct translations from English. Thus 'chairman' was translated as *umuxulu uwe citsolongo*, 'head of stools'. Most groups adopted the expedient of electing a separate treasurer. The division of responsibility between the treasurer and the secretary was impressed as a necessity because of the widespread embezzlement by the single official of the co-operative societies. At this time, however, the funds handled by these groups were very small, consisting only of the membership fees. The other and most important official while the drinking was actually in progress was the individual entrusted with keeping order in the group.

The 'discipline' was the most important and indeed the prime reason for forming the groups. The main rule was a ban on all talking without the express permission of the *asikari* (policeman), and even then all conversation had to be directed to the whole company. In other words no one was to make a noise, talk out of turn, or even worse, whisper secretly to his neighbour. Nor was more than one person at a time allowed to leave the room in case they took that opportunity for conspiring together. The *asikari* reigned supreme in another sense also, for only he was allowed to reprimand another. Any offence against the 'discipline' was punishable by the *asikari* who could confiscate the man's beer-tube and and place it in his 'prison', or for repeated infractions send the man home. With regard to the *asikari*'s prison most groups adopted the same procedure. A string was tied across the room with a number of loops attached. At one end a man could tie up his tube if he wished to leave the room, safe in the knowledge that no one could secretly place poison in it while he was gone. The other end was marked by a red flower or sometimes by a red Sportsman cigarette packet and this was the *asikari*'s prison.

There were also economic factors which made the Gisu more receptive to these groups. Although Tumbu and many of the earlier groups had started on a non-monetary basis, by 1968 most had adopted the rotating system of beer-brewing as a way of making a lump sum of money for each member in turn. The price of beer was then set differently in each group but it was usually between 3s and 5s, way above the normal price of 1s paid for drinking. Under this system an outlay of 20s on millet could easily bring in about 100s, enough to cover most men's taxes. Many companies started a loan system from their communal funds at the same time.

The beer party provided the obvious vehicle for the introduction of a rotating credit association among the Gisu. It had always been the main way in which money was circulated in the community, providing a way in which a man or occasionally a woman might raise a relatively large sum of money quickly. However, before the drinking companies few people had been able to regularly attract large numbers of people to their house and thus it was an activity that was really profitable only for the few. Now the drinking associations guaranteed the same number of participants at each member's brewing.

The use of these associations to raise the lump sum necessary for tax undoubtedly contributed to their growth in the cotton-producing areas of Bugisu. In 1965, the poor price for cotton of 40c per pound discouraged many men from planting the crop. In 1966 the cotton acreages fell by half and the drinking companies provided an alternative way of raising tax money. In turn the growth of the drinking companies may well in fact have discouraged men further from planting cotton, for by 1968 acreages were only a quarter of those of 1965, and there had been a corresponding increase in the amount of millet and maize planted. At higher altitudes arabica coffee still remained a profitable crop and it is perhaps significant that drinking companies had not developed in these areas by 1969. Rather, they flourished in the seven southern sub-counties of Busoba, Bukhiende, Busiu, Bugobero, Butiru and Bubutu. These seven sub-counties together grew 51.4% of the cotton crop but only 7.2% of the Gisu coffee crop.

There is a considerable literature on the economic role of rotating credit associations and summaries of this are provided by Geertz (1962), Ardener (1964) and Kerri (1976). In his classic article, Geertz describes them as a 'middle-rung' in the development process, 'a device by means of which traditionalistic forms of social relationship are mobilised so as to fulfil non-traditionalistic economic functions' (1962: 242). As a way in which commercialism could be grafted on to traditional ethics and patterns of co-operation, Geertz sees the direction of change to lie in the evolution of more specialised economic institutions. The Gisu drinking companies do not neatly fit into such a developmental process. After thirty years' experience with cash-cropping, money had become the usual means of exchange and payment for both goods and services in the community and interest was charged on loans. Under these circumstances it seems that rotating credit associations were used not so much to facilitate commerce but to reconstitute traditional values through their capacity to formalise simple structures of reciprocity. Thus the financial aspects were used both as an incentive to membership and as a sanction against default. A fixed membership, a regular obligation, and a commitment based on the fact of delayed return created a basis for the development of trust and goodwill with far-reaching effects. With a time-lag of about a year before the system of rotating benefits had completed its round these groups now had considerable powers over their membership. Expulsion might result in considerable financial loss. Thus one can argue that these Gisu groups became not more narrowly economic but more generally social.

Indeed, once co-operation was established, self-interest and common-interest harmonised, and the authority of group discipline acknowledged in this one activity, the formal organisation of the drinking companies became the medium for many experiments in mutual welfare schemes. There was an interest in innovation almost for its own sake and many groups had by 1967 a special official whose duty it was to visit as many other associations as possible to glean ideas. This official was usually known as the 'one with knowledge' or more enigmatically, the 'C.I.D.' Co-operative effort and progressive change was emphasised by the names these groups chose for themselves. Most group names were in two parts, the first a locational reference and the second a 'rousing' qualifier, a qualifier which also shows the influence of the recently formed Uganda Peoples' Congress youth groups in the area and again illustrates the extent to which the drinking companies identified with government policies and initiatives. Thus Tumbu changed its name about a year after it formed to 'Tumbu Wake Up', and other groups called on each other to 'work hard', 'pull together', 'mix together', 'help themselves', 'walk carefully', 'be determined' and 'remember each other'.

At the same time, many groups elected a judge and two assessors on the model of the former Native Courts, and a system of fines was developed not only for offences occurring during the drinking parties but also for others outside the discipline of the beer party. Many groups formulated specific rules of good behaviour which were written down and had to be signed by members on joining. Leaving the meeting with anger, beating a wife when drunk, being abusive to another member and other flagrant forms of disrespect which threatened peaceful relationships in the vicinity, then became punishable by companies.

The question as to why the beer party served as the particular vehicle for the demonstration of discipline and control demands further consideration. As a mode of social interaction, Gisu beer-drinking highlights the need for self-control despite the disinhibiting effects of alcohol. Indeed, one might go as far as to say that in this society where violent responses are a recognised and feared possibility in a man, it assumes the nature of a test; the way in which the essential constitution of the person, that which is hidden in the heart, can be judged. In talking to Gisu about beer-drinking a recurrent theme was the fear of self-exposure. Thus some men who avoided beer parties explained this as a coherent strategy where the thing to be feared was not the violence of others but their own violent reactions when drunk. Such men could not join drinking companies. It can thus be said of Gisu drinking companies, as Weber (1948) has argued for Protestant sects, that membership acted as a certification of moral standing. One may go further and see how they allowed for the continual monitoring and testing of moral calibre, effectively defining the community of righteous citizens. In this, their membership firmly contrasted with the targets of vigilante group actions, the witches and thieves; those who were deemed unable to exercise control over their violent and hostile impulses.

THE VIGILANTES

It is possible that there were many isolated groups acting as precursors to the vigilantes. The killing of both witches and thieves had commonly been by *ad hoc* groups and it is possible that some of these had more than ephemeral significance. But the vigilantes were more than just groups who killed witches and thieves, for their main strength lay in the nightly patrols they organised to protect their areas from such 'night prowlers'. Those found walking at night were arrested and often punished, while an elaborate series of prohibitions was imposed over the whole community to make the detection of these felons easier. They also held public trials where the accused were given the choice of confession or death. It is important to note here that no magical means were used to establish the identity of such people, rather their identity was the subject of consensus. At the trials confession was usually followed by taking an oath on the Bible. These oaths were often in set form, a thief, for example, swearing:

I will never again touch people's things,
Not their chickens, nor their clothes, nor their crops,
If I do let me be killed.

Punishment was not, however, left to any supernatural agency, for the vigilantes remained as watch-dogs. Concerning the executions performed by these groups, it was said – and there is confirmatory evidence from the court files – that warning letters were often sent to the victim informing him of the hour and place of his death.

A homicide case coming before the District Court shows that a vigilante-type group was operating in Bufumbo, on the borders of North and Central Bugisu, as early as January 1965. Popular belief had it, however, that the movement was inspired in the following month after a tour of the then Constitutional Head of Bugisu District, the Umuinga, to North Bugisu. Everywhere he went, so the story goes, the area was attacked by thieves and eventually in exasperation the Umuinga, addressing a public meeting, exhorted the people to do something about the problem. He was taken literally and groups of vigilantes began to be formed.

By March such groups were said to have been widespread in North Bugisu, especially in the sub-counties of Buyobo, Busulani and Buhugu, a fact which is supported by the police statistics and court records. The quick action of the police seems to have brought these first groups to a speedy halt, but not before other groups following their example were reported to be acting in many other areas of Bugisu. These proved harder to eradicate completely and their activities continued sporadically in Central and South Bugisu during 1965 and 1966. The following year saw a resurgence of the movement on a wider footing, more universally accepted by Gisu villagers. The groups established at this time continued to operate despite the danger of arrest from police patrols – the same group often reforming after serving a prison sentence – certainly until the end of 1969, when Bugisu was, with the surrounding districts to which the movement later spread, declared a Disturbed Area by the government.

When I first arrived in Busoba in October 1965, I was told of such groups and the pros and cons were being widely discussed. It seemed at this time as though the movement was in disrepute among more moderate opinion in the area. The leaders and chiefs of Busoba, while strongly in favour of the summary execution of witches and thieves, were notably lukewarm to the idea and often referred to such groups as *kondos*, a term used widely in Uganda to refer to armed robbers. They pointed out that the movement caused more trouble than it did good, the same attitude as taken by the police. It should be noted here, however, that from the highest to the lowest political circles in Uganda one of the preoccupations of the day was the rising crime rate. In Parliament, a new bill to make robbery a capital offence was being discussed and was passed in February of the following year. The implications of this bill were a focus of interest in the village. Would this now mean that the killing of thieves would in all circumstances be counted as justifiable homicide and subject to no penalty? There were a number of MPs in favour of this. While most people quickly pointed out the abuse such a law would bring there was nevertheless a feeling that in the future thief killing might be treated even more leniently.

Yet vigilante groups did not form in Busoba at this time and most people seemed to be extremely wary of the organisation, pointing to what had happened in other areas where groups had formed. In the neighbouring sub-county of Busiu, for example, there were small groups acting under the title '99' – probably a derivation from the emergency telephone number 999 – who were not only killing thieves but also seemed to be operating a flourishing protection racket. These particular groups were said to be dominated by the young – particularly by school-leavers who could not find work yet would not demean themselves with agricultural labour. The groups were thus dominated by the type of man to whom the Gisu attributed thefts and whom, it was felt, were unlikely to be motivated by the well-being of the community at large. For them, it was said, the vigilantes just provided a source of income and the only qualification for membership was the possession of certain small $3s$ axes. In one area of North Bugisu the movement had had radical overtones with action said to be directed also at the chiefs and richer members of the community. One of the regulations passed by all vigilante groups was a rule that nobody was to walk around after nightfall, or 7.00 p.m. However, these groups had more elaborate prohibitions, with no lights allowed on after 8.00 p.m. – especially if this was an electric light – and no radios playing after 10.00 p.m. Ignoring such regulations provided grounds for punishing a number of teachers, rich traders and chiefs, usually by beating. The crops of some chiefs were also slashed to the ground in this area.

The incipient revolutionary aspects of the vigilantes in this area, the home ground of a well-known opposition MP, did not develop in the other areas to which the movement later spread. Two main factors seem to have counteracted the tendency to outright subversion against the chiefs. One was the prior or simultaneous evolution of the drinking companies with their more accommodating ideology and the other was that the vigilante groups were often taken under the wing of the chiefs themselves. I have no evidence that the local chiefs ever took an active part in the patrols but the leaders of vigilante groups were very often their sons or brothers and in some cases the men they used as unpaid assistants.

It is perhaps not difficult to see why the chiefs gave their support to the movement at this time. The dramatic loss of the chiefs' judicial powers has been described in chapter 8, a loss felt particularly at the lowest levels, where the number of chiefs had also been effectively cut in half. Further, the chiefs had always had an uneasy relationship with the police stationed in Mbale because of their obligation to arrest offenders against the penal code. Yet many of these offences, including some types of murder, are not considered culpable in the village. The chiefs' powers of arrest put them in a special quandary with the advent of the vigilantes. The Gisu saw their movements as an alternative to the police and on this issue the attitude of the chiefs was necessarily more akin to that of their fellow villagers. Whereas direct co-operation with the police against the vigilantes could only serve to further weaken the chiefs' standing in the rural areas, and indeed lay them open to personal vengeance, by co-operating with the vigilantes they could both forestall lynch-law and use their own powers of arrest to better effect. Thus, in some areas, the vigilante groups took the thieves they had arrested to the chiefs who, in turn, took them to the police. The chiefs thus gained kudos both from the police and their people and buttressed their own authority by gaining influence over a clandestine police force which operated with the support of the people.

At this point I turn again to the neighbourhood of Busoba to describe the introduction of a vigilante organisation in 1968 in an area where drinking companies were already established. Here there were many people with misgivings about the wisdom of setting up a vigilante group, although there were in 1968 many such groups operating in the surrounding areas. Yet there were also many equally anxious to form one, some because of their own personal misfortunes and others to extend the organisation already created by the drinking companies. Those who believed themselves bewitched or were particularly vulnerable to theft fell into the first category. An example is Watuleke, one of the most industrious cultivators in the area despite his club foot, and the only one to drain the swamp land to grow vegetables and sugar cane. It was the sugar cane which caused him the most trouble for he had to spend hours hidden in a tree each day guarding it from thieves. Wamumali, on the other hand, had both reasons. He was already the chairman of a drinking company and the foremost voice in favour of vigilante groups, pointing to the fact that the courts could no longer be relied on to protect people. The previous year Wamumali and a group of men from this area had been involved in a court case which became a byword throughout Bugisu. The trouble began when one of Wamumali's cows was stolen, and for two days Wamumali and his friends combed the surrounding countryside looking for the thieves who were eventually traced to a neighbouring parish. The group arrested the two thieves and took them together with the evidence (the hide of the cow and the remains of the meat) to the sub-county court. They registered the case of theft but the thieves bribed the magistrate and, in the event, Wamumali and his associates were tried for assault and imprisoned for three months. On their release, the sub-county chief advised that they should press a charge of wrongful arrest but Wamumali, with one feels considerable justification, declared such action futile.

One week in September 1968, a small group of men from the area, including Wamumali, met with the leaders of a vigilante gang operating about four miles away to discuss plans and organisation. At this first meeting they summoned four people to come for trial. All but one of these ran away. This man, Maboni (see case 2) admitted to having 'long ago' stolen a bunch of plantains from his father's brother, but claimed that he had now changed his ways and did not steal. He was made to swear to this and was evidently believed, for he was given the job of protecting everyone's plantains with a mandate to beat anyone found picking them after 11.00 a.m. The measure adopted for the other suspects was to send letters to the vigilante groups operating in the areas to which they had fled, asking them to enforce the return of the culprits to face the charges at a public trial a week later.

At this particular trial it was made compulsory for all to attend, and my assistant counted over 400 people. In all, some five accusations of witchcraft were made, of which only one was accepted, and four of theft, all of which were upheld. The first man accused was Xangaka, an obvious first culprit since he was blamed for almost everything that went missing in his vicinage. He was a man of about thirty and his crimes were considered so serious that even the parish chief had made him sign a paper the year before to the effect that if he ever stole again, anyone might kill him. The case against Xangaka was presented as follows. First an elder, Natiko spoke up:

Natiko: I am in a very bad way at home because somebody keeps stealing my things. One day my chickens were stolen, another day my saucepans which I had left out to dry. Someone just found them and took them away.
Leader of vigilantes: Do you know who stole them?
Natiko: I know him. It was Xangaka.
L of v: Did you catch him at it?
Natiko: No, but he is always stealing things.
L of v: Xangaka, is it true that you are a thief?
Xangaka: No, I have never stolen anything.
L of v: Has that old man been talking without any evidence then?
Xangaka: Yes, I have never picked up anything belonging to him. Has he actually caught me stealing?
L of v: Old man, have you any witnesses?
Natiko: Yes, my wife herself.

The wife was not present so Natiko was sent to fetch her. When she arrived, however, she shook so much with fear that her evidence was impossible to understand. As evidence was now being offered by other people it was decided to dispense with her testimony. Watuleke, whose fields adjoined one plot cultivated by Xangaka, now spoke up.

Watuleke: Xangaka has also stolen my chickens. One he killed and then threw into my neighbour's compound. Another he buried in the field where he was digging and my dog unearthed it.
L of v: How do you know that they were both stolen by Xangaka?
Watuleke: Because each time he digs in that field chickens are stolen.

Xangaka again denied the charges but the vigilantes ordered that he should be tied up in sacks until he saw fit to confess. One sack was pulled over his head and another over his feet, both being tied at the waist. He was left to wander around like this in the sun, stumbling over bushes and rocks, and accompanied by a member of the vigilantes whose job it was to advise speedy confession. He returned after about half an hour, and was addressed by the leader of the vigilantes, thus: 'Xangaka, now will you tell us about those chickens you stole? We have brought you here so that you can pay for them. Death is also there, which is better? How many chickens did you steal and from whom?'

Xangaka then admitted to stealing three chickens, was ordered to compensate the owners and additionally fined 5s (about the cost of a single fowl). He was then made to swear never to steal again on pain of death.

Two of the other men accused of theft had reputations similar to Xangaka, but the fourth was a young boy for whom the vigilantes recommended a more severe penalty. This boy had stolen a window frame from a school house. The night-watchman, blamed by his employers for the faulty performance of his duties, 'wandered around', as the Gisu say 'quietly', without anyone being aware of his intentions, until he found the frame in the boy's hut. He then brought the charge up before the vigilantes. The vigilantes had the boy tied up for an hour in sacks as 'punishment' and when he was brought back they suggested that he should be killed outright for he had begun to steal 'before time'. Stealing before a youth is circumcised is regarded as peculiarly deviant and the vigilantes considered that he would undoubtedly get worse as he grew older and would in addition teach his friends bad ways. However, the elders of the area remonstrated, and the boy in the end was made just to forswear theft.

Of the witches accused, three were women but only one, who had attracted many previous accusations, was tied up in sacks and made to swear to desist from witchcraft. In addition two men accused their brothers of bewitching them. In both cases the accusation was specific and arose out of interminable land disputes between the brothers concerned. The vigilantes evidently had no desire to interfere in this kind of dispute and refused to consider the cases. Their interest quite clearly was in those who had already gained infamy as witches and thieves and whose guilt was the subject of consensus. Thus they could stand for 'community interests' and rely upon the widest possible basis of public support.

In many respects the trial described here is reminiscent of those reported by Purvis (1909) for the first decade of this century, a time when they were the norm rather than the exception. Although the vigilantes resuscitated communal indictment in the first instance it did not prove a popular innovation, and no further trials of this nature were held in the area. Many people complained both before and after the trial of its undesirability, mainly on the grounds that people were afraid to accuse others in an open forum. Their faith in the power of the vigilantes was not so great that it overcame the fear of personal retaliation that public accusation was seen to invite. Nevertheless, the vigilantes' judicial role was not rejected out of hand, for they were called upon to hold inquests in the houses of individuals in much the same way as the chiefs and headmen had done before them. The vigilantes promised far more than the chiefs and headmen; not only the ultimate sanction of death but judgements which could be backed up by other activities in the community context.

In the weeks following the trial described, patrols were organised nightly and every man was expected to take his turn and help. During this time several men were beaten or made to stand naked in streams all night, but no one was murdered (indeed in the two years following, while I was still in the area, only one man was definitely killed by these vigilantes). A month or so after the trial, patrols became more intermittent, partly through fear of police action, but more importantly as the membership of the vigilante gang became more selective as the movement was adapted to local circumstances.

In this area the vigilantes became closely connected with the drinking companies, firstly in terms of their membership. In one square mile of Busoba where the development of drinking companies has already been described there were approximately four vigilante gangs operating between 1968 and 1970. Of the four leaders, three were chairmen of different drinking companies and the other a 'judge'. The other main officials of the vigilante groups – the 'majors' and *asikaris* – often also held equivalent posts in the drinking companies. Secondly, and partly because of this duplication, the activities of the drinking companies and vigilantes were not only co-ordinated but the vigilantes subscribed to the ideology of *lukoosi* which the drinking companies in their different way had fostered.

By 1969, both organisations had extended their activities into many spheres of social life, and both were seen as manifestly successful. While many drinking companies prided themselves on the fact that all their members had paid their taxes early in the year, the demonstrable mark of a good citizen, one heard stories of vigilante groups which held feasts to celebrate the freedom of their area from witchcraft and theft. A sidelight is thrown on this by the Police Annual Report for 1968 which attributes the unprecedented spate of burglaries in Mbale, the administrative town for the area, to the influx of thieves fleeing from justice in the rural areas. In other respects, too, the associations acted in parallel. In Busoba, the drinking companies talked about floating special funds to help out neighbours in need while the vigilantes insisted in their own way that people fulfilled their neighbourly obligations. For example, at one funeral I attended, the dead man's drinking company and not, as traditionally, his lineage arranged the normal collection of monetary gifts to help towards the funeral expenses. The vigilantes, however, undertook to provide the plantains necessary for the mourning feasts by the simple expedient of leaving nothing to neighbourly generosity but going out as a group to cut down a suitable contribution from everyone.

As has been described, both movements then were associated with the formulation of a positive ideology which gave some assurance that people had control over their own fate, at least in so far as to this amounted to control over each other. Theirs was a two-pronged attack on the problem, and it reflects the polarisation of the community into the reputable and disreputable, the citizen and the degenerate. The drinking companies set out to establish rules of conduct in the community of responsive and responsible men. As argued, the rotating credit association here provided the incentive and framework for such commitment. This was the world in which trust was possible and behaviour could be rendered predictable. The emphasis was on self-control and obedience to explicit rules of conduct: compliance could be tested and monitored. At the same time the rules were developed and justified as explicit strategies to avert danger. Thus, for example, the multiplicity of office-holders, which might be said to reflect the claims to parity of men in an essentially egalitarian framework, was always talked about in terms of the need for a clear-cut division of responsibilities to avoid dispute and strife. The vigilantes, on the other hand, mobilised against those who were conceived of as unredeemable, beyond control. If they could not be changed their negative actions could be countered only by direct coercion and death.

The idiom the vigilantes used was paragovernmental, appropriate indeed for a movement which envisaged itself as setting up a specifically 'Gisu government'. Yet while the vigilantes saw themselves as a direct alternative to the Ugandan state apparatus in the rural areas, the movement was not primarily seditious in origin or design. This was no revolt against the legitimacy of the state as such but rather a statement of its impotence; its failure to provide for personal security in the rural areas. Thus, while some of the vigilante groups formed at this time had more radical objectives and directly challenged the power of the chiefs, most groups did not. On the contrary they effectively co-opted the legitimacy of the state by linking their aims to those of the government: to ideas of order and the necessity for conformity to regulations, and by working in informal alliance with the local chiefs of the administrative structure. The ideology they propagated was that of *lukoosi*, order and respect. Thus the challenge the movement offered was not so much directed outwards against the legitimacy of the state but inwards towards the community. These groups emerged in a dominant mood of self-criticism.

NOTE

1   Yet, while *kondos* are as much a subject for popular fear in Bugisu as elsewhere, very little of the killing – at least of that which reaches the courts – appears to be of this type. Indeed, there were only two cases where thieves killed at the same time as they robbed and in both cases the robbery seemed somewhat incidental. In a further seven cases thieves turned and killed someone who was trying to apprehend them.

11

MAFIAS IN AFRICA

There has been much concern with the nature of peasant protest in modern Africa. On the one hand, there has been a debate, conducted in largely theoretical terms, on whether peasants can recognise their common class-interest and be mobilised in revolution against the forces of the neo-colonialist state. On the other hand, a great turmoil of religious movements has been documented, of Christian independent churches, nativistic religions, millenarian movements and witch-finding cults. A dominant mode of analysis here has been to see these after Worsley (1957) in political evolutionary terms, as precursors to more conventional political or revolutionary movements. Van Binsbergen (1981) has recently challenged this view by arguing that 'peasant' religious movements are not primarily directed outwards, against the state, but concentrate instead on reviving the rural community. In conventional terms they are reformist rather than revolutionary, offering ideologies which enable people to make sense of their experiences and establish rules of appropriate conduct in a world over which they may have little real control. The assertion of control is central to the argument here but I am talking of very different kinds of movement, modest in their objectives and pragmatic in form. For while the dramatic flourish of religious reconstructions has been salient in Africa, it is important to register the fact that other responses are also found. The idiom of the Gisu movements hinges on the specifics of Gisu culture, on their indigenous ideologies of social relationship, but they also developed in an historical situation which suggests more general preconditions for their formation.

In detailing the development of vigilantes and drinking companies in Bugisu an analogy with the mafia in nineteenth-century Sicily became salient. In part, this relates to the nature and scale of the organisations, reflecting the parochialism of a rural peasant base, but it also relates to certain similarities in the political situation in which they emerged. Hobsbawm writes of mafias that they are 'an institutionalized system of law outside the official law. In extreme cases they may amount to a virtual parallel or subsidiary system of law and power to that of the official rulers' (1959: 5–6). To some extent a parallel system might be said to exist in all remote rural communities under state control. What distinguishes mafia organisations, in these broad terms, is rule through a series of secret or unofficial gangs who use violence to assert their control. Further, Hobsbawm relates their emergence to anarchic conditions. The Sicilian mafia, it is argued, emerged to control a situation of lawlessness, in the vacuum of power created by the abolition of feudalism, the impact of capitalism and the ineffectualness of a foreign state.

The relevance of this line of reasoning to Bugisu in the mid- to late-1960s may be summarised briefly. Firstly, as already mentioned, the situation was perceived as one of lawlessness, evidenced both in increasing rates of crime and lack of effective authority in the rural areas. Further, not only had the state effectively withdrawn in the sense of not providing effective low-level administration but the consolidation of state power had increasingly left the peasant out on a limb, away from the locus of decision-making. One argument here is that, lacking effective leverage on government, self-help and self-reform became the only viable options. In so doing, like the Sicilian mafia, the drinking companies and vigilantes in Bugisu provided an effective mediating ground, bridging the gaps that had developed between the government on the one hand and the community on the other (Blok, 1974).

The statistics on crime, supporting the perception of violent lawlessness, form a necessary backdrop to these movements. The homicide statistics for the region have been discussed earlier and the level here is indicative of the rise in reported crime more generally. The police figures for the area show a steady rise in the number of offences against the penal code, with an increase of 322% from 1961 to 1968. A rise in the number of offences against the person (from murder to common assault) forms the most notable component of this increase. Yet while violent crime was a recognisable problem in Bugisu, a concern with 'law and order' was not confined to this area. It was seen to be a problem more generally in Uganda. Nor does it appear that Bugisu was the only area in Uganda to adopt the expedient of vigilante groups and drinking companies. Both spread out from Bugisu into the surrounding areas of Bukedi, while vigilante-like groups also appear to have arisen spontaneously elsewhere. Newspaper reports suggest that they operated in Lango and Acholi, areas which, like Bugisu, had before the setting up of the colonial administration acephalous forms of political system.[1] Moreover, all these groups appeared at much the same time, from the mid-sixties onwards. The timing and distribution of these movements in turn suggest the relevance of wider political currents, in particular the political changes which accompanied independence in 1962.

THE POLITICAL CONTEXT

The 400,000 Gisu, outside the major cleavage of power in Uganda, played an inconspicuous part in the development of Uganda as a sovereign state. While events in Bugisu in the mid-fifties were influenced by what was happening elsewhere in Uganda, the Gisu contributed little to these nationalist currents. Opinion was late to mobilise in party-political terms; party labels were introduced for the first time in the 1961 general election and even then the seven independent candidates polled more than one-third of the votes. The Gisu returned one Democratic Party (DP) and one Uganda Peoples' Congress (UPC) member to the national assembly. Nor since independence have they either as a tribe or individually played anything but a minor role in national affairs. The Gisu have not been recruited into the army in any great numbers and the main national significance of the district lies in its valuable export crop of arabica coffee. The marketing of this crop has been an important issue in the district and brought the Gisu into confrontation with both colonial and post-colonial governments (Bunker, 1983, 1984, 1987). The aim of the following section, however, is to document the effects of the changes that accompanied independence on the relationship between the local community and executive in Bugisu. The complexity of the political issues precludes any but the most schematic of treatments in the present context.[2]

Constitutional changes which led up to and followed independence were rapid as a more elaborate framework for government was developed at both national and district levels. At the national level the political compromise which took Uganda into independence produced a patchwork constitution; Buganda had federal status, other kingdoms semi-federal status, and areas such as Bugisu with no claims to a centralised heritage, a district status. After independence, with the rise of Obote's government and the supremacy of the Uganda Peoples' Congress (UPC), a political priority became the creation of institutions which could wield these disparate units into a unitary state. As part of the attempt to break down locally-based allegiances, the relationship between the districts and the central government was transformed so that the greater control exerted from the centre was evident in all fields. The reform of the judiciary, creating a uniform system of courts and law for the whole of Uganda, was part of this process, the development of party politics in the District Councils another. In the space of a very few years the district autonomy established during the colonial era had largely vanished in areas such as Bugisu, as the functions of government previously residing in the chiefs and District Commissioner became separate and integrated with others on a national basis.

If the erosion of district autonomy was planned and executed in the interests of state power and national unity, the undermining of chiefly authority to the extent that it occurred in Bugisu was perhaps an unforeseen concomitant. The establishment of the colonial administrative system in Bugisu in the early years of the century consolidated what was undoubtedly a fluid political system in a very short period of time, giving greater coherence to the lineage framework just as it channelled loyalty to a chief with extensive powers to support his position. While indirect rule, as normally understood, was never characteristic of Bugisu, traditional values were here as elsewhere incorporated into the administrative structure. At the higher levels the administration represented a political integration which had never existed before but it also extended downwards to the locality where the chiefdoms became a focus for lineage identity, each clan and lineage demanding its own chief. These chiefs, while not traditional dignitaries but local government appointees, nevertheless had wide and autocratic powers. The chiefs were the tax-gatherers, represented their people on the chiefs' councils, which were the main medium for reform and innovation with regard to customary law, and ran their own courts with powers of both arrest and judgement. After an initial period of resistance it appears that the new rule of the chiefs became widely accepted. This system remained more or less unaltered in the period 1930 to 1956. Between 1956 and 1964, however, politicians replaced the chiefs in the councils and young professional magistrates replaced them in the courts. At the same time as their powers declined the number of chiefs in the rural areas also decreased when the parish of between 2,500 and 5,000 people replaced the village of about 700 people as the smallest administrative unit.

A space of ten years thus saw a transformation of authority patterns at the local level. With the demise of the chief as sole and all-purpose authority in the local areas, people were faced instead with a multiplicity of government agents working in the sub-counties, from councillors and magistrates to officials from both the local and national Departments of Health and Agriculture, whose work was not directly co-ordinated with that of the chiefs. One important effect of this was to undermine the channels of communication between the local people and those who governed and served them. The local chiefs' identification with the communities they served, as well as the necessity for them to gain the support of the people in order to carry out day-to-day administrative tasks, made them responsive to local pressure. The decrease in the number of chiefs to a large extent destroyed the close working relationship between chief and people that had been characteristic of the old village unit of the administration (La Fontaine, 1960a). While there was supposed to be informal consultation between chief and people within the parishes in the 1960s, the size of the parishes and the short periods of service (an average of only three years in a survey I conducted in 1969) largely precluded it.

Further, the new separate agencies of government were seen neither to represent community interests nor to allow, either directly or indirectly, the community any say in their programmes. This was particularly evident with regard to the courts. Under the old system of Native Courts, the chief had sat in judgement with the help of two local men as assessors. In the new Magistrates' Court, the single magistrate was never a local man and often not even Gisu. In such cases he had neither knowledge of the people nor knowledge of customary values and procedures. A similar story could be told with respect to the District Council, originally created in the 1950s to encourage the expression of political opinions and to make policy on behalf of the district. In the late 1950s, indeed, the Bugisu District Council had been a powerful medium for the expression of tribal nationalism reflecting, in part, a new-found tribal unity. After independence it was increasingly constrained by its direct relationship with the Uganda Peoples' Congress (UPC) and the National Executive. With efforts to protect customary practices discouraged, the Council largely confined its activities to the running of a few services on behalf of the district and setting the rate of taxation. It was notable chiefly for its lack of any important legislation or discussion of the major issues of concern within the district.

Yet it was rivalry between the chiefs and the councillors which was to have perhaps the most significant effect on the power and the prestige of the chieftainships. The formation of the first fully elected District Council in 1956 immediately produced a situation where the councillors, as 'popular representatives', sought to win influence from the chiefs in the rural areas. Under the model of 'British local government which was adopted in this case the councillor 'directs' the administration which employs the chiefs, but in the rural areas he has no right to interfere with their work and must submit to the authority of the lowliest of them. Not surprisingly, many found it difficult to accept such a limitation to their powers and the Council became a forum for complaints against the chiefs, and used what little leeway it had under the Local Administrations Act to regulate them. The most drastic steps were to abolish the village unit of the administration in 1961 and further outlaw the use of unofficial headmen in 1967.[3]

In 1961, the parish thus replaced the village as the smallest unit of the administration. Thereafter the parish chief was supported by only one official subordinate, still known as the 'village chief', though he no longer had responsibility for any particular areas and served instead as a general factotum to the parish chief. This move decreased the number of chiefs actually working in the rural areas (the parish and village chiefs) from one chief to approximately 700 people to one chief to over 2,000 people. Inevitably, the parish chief was forced to rely to a greater extent on unofficial headmen. These could not, however, be considered a direct substitute for the village chiefs; unpaid and little more than the personal assistants to the village chief, they were not backed by the administrative hierarchy to the same extent. The posts carried little of the prestige of the chieftainships and there was little competition for them. Further, the headmen came under repeated attacks from the Council chambers. In 1967, the Council was able to exploit the grievances against a few headmen who had misappropriated tax money as an excuse to 'abolish' them also.

At the local level, the disruption of established patterns of authority undoubtedly accentuated the lack of effective groupings capable of protecting individuals or acting as any check on interpersonal violence. In a very real way the state had withdrawn and the Gisu were faced with a truly Hobbesian dilemma. While at higher levels, lineage organisation provides a framework for political loyalties, particularly significant where it corresponds to administrative divisions, at lower levels this is not the case. Outside the fairly narrow span of the agnatic lineage, with a dispersed membership, a man's strongest loyalties are to his brothers-in-law, maternal kin and age mates. Such individual networks act as a medium for conveying news and ideas quickly from one end of Bugisu to the other, and for the more powerful to wield influence, but they do not act in themselves as a focus for communal obligation. Further, old patterns of co-operation, of ritual and fixed membership labour groups had for the most part died out early in the colonial era. Now, the village unit of the administration and with it the village chief no longer existed, leaving the large and often sprawling parish as the lowest administrative sub-division. The community, it appeared had literally fallen apart into its component households, each headed by a man who recognised no automatic authority beyond himself.

The mood in 1965/66, when I began fieldwork in Bugisu, was pessimistic, self-critical and even fatalistic. There were daily laments during the rains at the broken bridges which no one would undertake to repair. Fear of witchcraft, theft and violence flourished while self-help appeared as the only remedy available to the individual. The problem of what to do about a neighbour when he flouted all his obligations towards you came to the fore in the face of a distant police force, an alien judicial system and a chief whose powers had been curtailed and who had in any case work enough in collecting the taxes. *Lukoosi*, order, was seen to have broken down and, with it, self-respect. 'The Gisu are just a bad people' became the comment after every act of violence. Previously, I have discussed how violence is seen as a constituent part of male identity and the problems of control this is seen to pose. What I want to stress here is that the problem was realised in an acute form at this time and in terms that suggested that it was insoluble. This state of demoralisation is important to understanding the new movements because the challenge which they offered was aimed as much at themselves as at the administration. The movements promised self-reform, a factor which was not always well understood by the police and district administration.

That these movements developed in the face of what the Gisu saw, realistically, as impotence on the part of the legitimate agents of social control to provide for any security of life or property in the rural areas, is without doubt. Indeed, the first vigilante groups developed barely six months after the substitution of Magistrates' for Chiefs' Courts. However, at least as far as the rural chiefs were concerned, they did not act to further undermine their powers but tended rather to become associated with them. The attitude to the police was more ambivalent. The vigilantes were seen to pose a direct threat to public order and the police acted fairly vigorously to suppress them. However, the police were a somewhat marginal consideration as the rural areas were not policed on any regular basis. The police investigated only the more serious crimes committed in the rural area, even then usually delegating their powers to the local chiefs. Occasionally, in times of public unrest, a few would be stationed in the rural areas, but their impact was limited. They were widely held to be frightened of the villagers. Nevertheless vigilante groups operated in spite of rather than in direct opposition to the police. In a neighbouring area of Bukedi, the people of one sub-county drew up a list of about twenty-five witches and thieves and issued the police with an ultimatum to the effect that if they failed to take appropriate action within a month then the community would take its own steps. I heard of no such threats or attempts to elicit positive support made by groups in Bugisu itself. Rather, they set out simply to supply their own remedies for what they conceived of as essentially local problems.

WITCH-CLEANSING CULTS AND THE VIGILANTES

Given this political background we may now turn to consider the relationship of these Gisu movements to others in Africa which have likewise had the aim of eradicating witchcraft. The main features of witch-cleansing cults have been well-summarised by Willis (1970). Their ephemerality, their therapeutic aims and their reliance on medicines distinguish them from the Gisu vigilantes. Nevertheless, the existence of contemporaneous witch-cleansing cults in East Africa (Willis, 1968; Parkin, 1968; Abrahams, 1985) suggests both some interesting parallels and invites speculation as to why the Gisu movements took a different direction.

A link with emerging political party organisation and even the expectation of government support is a theme common to the witch-cleansing cults recorded in the immediate post-independence era. It was commented on by Willis (1968) for the Kamcape movement among the Fipa of Tanzania in 1963-64, and by Parkin (1968) for the anti-sorcery movement among the Mijikenda of Kenya in 1966. However, the form witch-hunting took among the Lango of Uganda in 1967, described by Abrahams (1985), offers a more direct comparison with the Gisu case. Among the Lango, it was widely believed to be a government-approved scheme and advocates of the movement wanted a 'Five-Year Anti-Sorcery Plan' as part of their contribution to the Five-Year Development Plan. Here, unlike Bugisu, it seems that the chiefs were used directly to arrest suspects and the court processes to arraign them. Abrahams reports that the prisons were full of suspected witches. Like the Gisu movement the use of physical violence and, in this case, judicial hearings distinguishes it from the usual pattern of witch-cleansing cults. The emphasis seems to have been less on therapy and more on punishment. Nevertheless, from the available evidence, the movement in Lango appears to have been short-lived.

A question which arises is how to interpret the claims to government sponsorship in the light of the ethnographers' feelings that these movements were in fact the subject of official embarrassment. Willis, the first to deal with this question, relates it in part to the polarisation of political interests at the village level between the older 'traditionalists' and the younger 'progressives', who were aligned in this immediate post-independence era with the new grass-roots political organisation of TANU. He tends to see the Kamcape cult as a ritual drama, which highlights the political divide, and which allows the younger men as the witch-finders to assert power by trouncing their elders as witches. But, by its nature, it is power only for the day and as the cult passes on, the elders resume their customary role as village leaders. Parkin has questioned the static implications of this analysis, pointing to the radical changes in the local power structures which were taking place at this time. Less than two years later, village development committees were to replace the headmen in Tanzania. He thus suggests that it might be more enlightening to see such movements as advertising such changes and thus, despite the transitory nature of the cults themselves, their political significance might be more far-reaching. In the context of competing power structures, he writes that 'these cults or movements constitute temporary stock markets of influence' (1968: 428).

A more general point can be made. Since Richards's (1935) discussion of the Bamucapi movement among the Bemba, to some extent all the literature on witch-cleansing cults has related their emergence to a situation where the established local authorities have had their powers curtailed and could no longer sustain their claims as protectors of their people against witchcraft. Yet, if the old order is discredited, it appears that the aspiring political leaders as yet lack sufficient institutional backing to provide a viable alternative. That this should take a new direction immediately following independence is not in itself surprising. One might possibly suggest that the vacuum of power created in such situations was more extreme in Bugisu than elsewhere, thus enabling a more pragmatic response. However, one may speculate that there are other reasons to do in part with the political culture of the area which make a witch-cleansing cult a less likely possibility here.

If one runs through the major preconditions suggested for such cults, one can note firstly that there are no historical parallels for such movements in the area. Bugisu lies well outside the geographical zones where such cults have been reported (Willis, 1970). Secondly, in relationship to Mary Douglas's (1963) thesis that the new magic is a response to the outlawing of the poison ordeal, providing an alternative technique of sorcery control, it can be noted that the Gisu traditionally do not appear to have used poison ordeals to detect sorcery or witchcraft. Thirdly, one might go on to argue that the dispersed settlement pattern of Bugisu would militate against them. Witch-cleansing cults would seem to depend upon a discrete and bounded community structure within which witches can be identified and rendered powerless while the rest of the community is protected by the administration of prophylactic potions. As has been described, the problem in Bugisu combined the need to create a community in the sense of reestablishing the personal boundaries of co-operation and trust with the need to cleanse it.

Further, the political experience the Gisu gained through the establishment of coffee co-operative societies might also be an important formative factor in the situation. After the Second World War the issue of coffee marketing became the major political issue in the district and, in the face of the successive government attempts at intervention, the main way in which political rights to self-determination and control were asserted in the area. Bunker (1983, 1984, 1987) argues that the economic power of the Gisu peasantry gave it leverage over policy and allowed for successful campaigns during the colonial era to control the marketing of the coffee cash crop through their own co-operative societies. Such campaigns did not only involve the demonstrable ability of local societies to manage the crop but led on occasion to violent forms of protest, of crop-slashing and physical intimidation. Self-help and the formation of special purpose groups were not therefore alien to the Gisu. Bunker has paid special attention to the mediating role played by the Gisu elites whose power bases, whether chiefs, civil servants, councillors or co-operative officials, were tied both to their own local communities and to the state. As such, they were responsive to local pressure and able to act at times as an effective buffer to state power in the interests of their people. The issue of land tenure described in chapter 4 is another example here.

Certainly, the submerged and inarticulate protest of cult seems largely to have passed Bugisu by. After the Second World War the nativistic movement Dini ya Misambwa ('religion of ancestral practices') did spread into Bugisu from neighbouring Bukusu in Kenya. Nevertheless, the movement appears to have been limited geographically and its popular support short-lived. While outbreaks occurred throughout the 1950s, the activities of the movement were largely confined to the clans in the mountains bordering Bukusu. Nor were the 1960s to see an upsurge of fundamentalist Christianity, again marked in Bukusu (see de Wolf, 1977), and the established churches appeared likewise to be losing rather than gaining adherents.

The presence of an effective political elite and the economic power of the peasantry may go some way towards explaining the particular forms of political mobilisation which caught the imagination of the people in colonial Bugisu. By the same token the loss of such power after independence undoubtedly influenced the direction taken by the new associations. The vigilantes and the drinking companies were initiatives taken primarily at the neighbourhood level, where there was little direct involvement, initially, of the political elite in the district. Nor were they taken up to become district-level campaigns along the lines of protest previously seen in the area. The limitations imposed on the local elites through Obote's strengthening of central control undoubtedly contributed to this. As argued, by the end of the decade, the old channels for the expression of protest and reform effectively no longer existed, a factor which became more evident with the growing hiatus between the dynamic of events on the wider political stage of the Ugandan state and the realities of peasant life.

CONCLUSION

At this point we may turn again to the analogy with mafia organisation. The political context for the emergence of the Gisu movements was the disruption of established administrative structures in the rural areas that accompanied the centrist tendencies of the Ugandan state under Obote. Mafias as Hobsbawm sees them are a rational, almost inevitable, response to a vacuum of power. By their nature, mafias are among the most obscure of social movements. Their rural base, the low level of their organisation and their illegal nature have combined to render them invisible. Yet, as Hobsbawm argues, the fact that we have little information on them belies their probable widespread distribution and social significance. The lack of documentation has led to the mafias of southern Italy becoming the type-examples but this should not blind us to the occurrence of analogous organisational structures elsewhere. Certainly, in the African context, the movements described here would seem to have more in common with mafia organisation than with more widely recorded witch-finding cults or voluntary associations with which they also invite comparison.[4] The particular focus, their mobilisation against the thief and the witch, is one aspect of these Gisu groups, relating to the way perceptions of danger were formalised and mediated through a complex interaction of cultural and economic forces. Beyond this, both can be seen as local forms of self-assertion, attempts – and successful ones – to establish a viable parallel apparatus of social control in the community. The dual elements of self-reform and evasive compliance made both the vigilantes and drinking companies genuinely popular in their appeal. Yet they remained essentially low-level organisations. While there was some attempt to link groups into a loose federations within any one area, such internal structuring was fairly ephemeral. Yet, through their membership and the combination of official support and connivance, they were linked to the overarching structures of government. Indeed, they could be said to straddle the divide, a foot in both the camps of community and officialdom.

Hobsbawm has stressed the opportunistic character of mafia organisations. He writes, 'They are, as it were, the meeting-places of all sorts of tendencies existing within their societies: the defence of the entire society against threats to its traditional way of life, the aspirations of the various classes within it, the personal ambitions and aspirations of individual energetic members' (1959:30). A consideration of the leadership of the Gisu groups underlines this aspect for it is clear that they gave scope for the assertion of new forms of power. Initially, those who were in the best position to exploit them were those with established influence as, for example, the chiefs and their unofficial assistants. There were, however, other and rival power centres in the rural areas, particularly those asociated with the co-operative movement and the district council. As the sixties progressed and Obote moved towards the establishment of a one-party state, local branches of the Ugandan Peoples' Congress were developed at the rural level and here the vigilante organisation could be used for more direct political ends. In the run-up to the elections for party constituency chairmen in 1969, it was widely reported that vigilante groups were used to intimidate and terrorise rival candidates. If the similarity with the popular image of the mafia here seems salient, the degree to which local leaders were becoming local strongmen in personal command of an armed gang was difficult to judge at the time. On the one hand, this development had direct continuities with the parochial, lineage-based nature of political mobili-sation that has been noted for both traditional and modern Bugisu. On the other, party involvement now seemed to presage the emergence of qualita-tively different forms of patronage as large sums of money became available through party sponsorship of development projects.

In the late 1960s, the direction in which such groups might develop was as unpredictable as future political trajectory of Uganda itself. Clearly, vigilante-type groups are capable of many uses and the rather accommodating nature of the early Gisu groups described here must be understood as a product of observation at the particular place and time. Hobsbawm considers that as social movements, mafias have limited objectives and limited potential for transformation. He writes that 'it is only in politically backward and powerless communities that brigands and mafiosi take the place of social movements' (1959: 42–3). Nor does he consider that they are capable of being transformed into modern mass movements, for insular and parochial, they keep the marks of their peasant base. Yet here perhaps there is call to be more positive for in uncertain political times their strength lies in this very factor.

In the increasingly arbitrary and violent times of Amin and the return of Obote, vigilante groups and drinking companies continued to operate in Bugisu. A brief return to Mbale in 1981 showed not only that the drinking companies had spread into the towns but that the life of the town was organised almost entirely around them. Inflation had long since ruled out the regular drinking of bottled beer and the old bars were now used as licensing premises for a cluster of drinking company shelters erected in the vicinity. In 1981, both inflation and the black-market (*magendo*) economy were at their height. The minimum wage still stood at 450*s* a month (until July), sugar was 600*s* per kilo and the rate of exchange for the Ugandan shilling was 600s. to £1 on the blackmarket compared to the official rate of 13.5*s* to £1. The drinking com-panies, based in the main around groups of workmates, provided not only for daily drinking but were an essential medium for the arrangement of *magendo* contracts, the only way urban dwellers could supplement their official wages to ensure subsistence. They were often referred to by the euphemism 'evening classes'. The establishment of trust, to be achieved only in such face-to-face groups, was perhaps not only essential for subsistence through *magendo* but for survival itself. As for the vigilantes, I was told that they formed the core of the peoples' militia organised in Bugisu in the 1980s to protect the rural areas against the incursions of the civil war.

NOTES

1   See further, Abrahams (1985).

2   For more detail, see Heald (1982b).

3   Many of the decisions of the Council bordered on illegality, hinging on the interpretation of the Local Administrations Act which defines the positions and powers of the chiefs as well as their relationship to the Council. For example, it was a statutory requirement that there be county, sub-county and parish chiefs but provisions allow for districts to dispense with village chiefs under certain conditions. In fact the abolition of the villages in Bugisu followed an economic crisis in 1960 in which the Council first refused to levy a realistic rate of tax and then attempted to balance the budget by a drastic reduction in all services and by cutting the salaries of the parish chiefs as a preliminary to dismissing them. These events led to a Commission of Enquiry into the affairs of the Council. The abolition of the village chiefs instead of the parish chiefs emerged as the compromise decision.

4   For dissenting views on this issue, see Abrahams (1985) and Austin (1986).

EPILOGUE

The perception of growing and uncontrollable violence in Bugisu arose at a particular historical juncture, a response to both old and new circumstance. On the one hand, the arguments of this book have seen the forms that it took as deeply embedded in Gisu social forms. Thus it has been argued that increasing land pressure was tending, as it probably always had so tended, to exacerbate intergenerational conflict and, given a particular understanding of human responses, this led to increasing fears of violence, witchcraft and theft. On the other hand, this 'endemic' feature – or, as Sahlins (1981) would put it, this 'structure of the long run' – of Gisu society was combined with the relatively sudden collapse of rural administrative machinery which exposed the tenuous basis of community life, a community which in many ways had managed to preserve an indigenous ideology of relationships based on the essential equality and autonomy of each man. In other words, a structure of underlying anarchy.

In the introduction it was argued that the dilemmas of Gisu society could usefully be seen in Hobbesian terms. Indeed, there are two ways in which this is so for while Hobbes uses the idea of the state of nature to be a basic dynamic which underlies all forms of political organisation, that is as a latent but permanent threat, he also regarded it as realisable condition. Both positions are relevant. Nevertheless, the arguments of this book are not that Gisu society represented some regression to an original 'state of nature'. Far from it, it was a complex product of a specific history, of a particular way in which Gisu society had responded to the exigencies of colonial domination and its later demise. Hobbes becomes relevant because although writing from a divergent historical tradition, he makes common cause with the Gisu concern with the problematics of civil peace in situations where the state is threatened or weakened.

The Hobbesian problem as a general hypothesis has a long genealogy in anthropological writing and it might thus be useful to review the main lines of argument here. It is clearly discernible in the work of Tylor (1871), Mauss (1925/1954) and Lévi-Strauss (1949/1969) and, in the same tradition, more recently it has been elaborated by Sahlins (1968) who uses it to map out the potentialities of 'tribal society'. To take a brief extract, he writes:

to speak of Warre, then, is to uncover by analysis tendencies ordinarily concealed by powerful impositions of the cultural system. Primitive anarchy is not the appearance of things. It is the unconscious of the system . . . so the objective organisation of tribal society may only be understood as the repressive transformation of an underlying anarchy. Many of the special patterns of tribal culture become meaningful precisely as defense mechanisms, as *negations of Warre*. (1968: 7–8)

It is here he places his discussion of the gift, of the extension of kinship ties, of religion and ritual. Indeed, all the institutions of the tribal and acephalous communities he sees as having peace built into them. They all create the systematic dependence upon people that forms 'society'; that is, creates a moral order. Yet, Sahlins, like Hobbes, sees this as an achievement, and perhaps one may underline the tenuousness of the situation.

What perhaps is surprising about Gisu social organisation is that although it does build 'peace', *lukoosi*, into its institutional forms, it does so in such a half-hearted way. A concept such as *lukoosi* posits an ultimate altruistic basis to community life, an ideal model of family living projected to the level of the community. This in itself, is not rare in Africa: indeed, it has been seen as the generality, with extended kinship structures being seen as diffusing a basic morality. Fortes (1969), for example, presents this in absolutist and universal terms, proposing that amity is the basic axiom in kinship: an altruism forged in the family and in basic universal experiences of parenthood. In Bugisu, by contrast, there is a sense in which conflict is built into the heart of the family, and this conflict is projected outwards so that kinship cannot be unequivocally associated with amity as Fortes has argued. Indeed, without authority, either secular or mystical, one could argue that there is little scope for the full development of ideologies based on the common weal.

Nevertheless, we are faced with a concept of kinship and an ideal of social living which is coded in terms of restraint. The respect which is *lukoosi* implies the acceptance of a restraint, of submission of the self to rules laid down as right and proper. From the fact that this submission of the self exists in Bugisu without any authority established by kinship arise some of the paradoxes as well as of the distinctive character of the Gisu moral universe. With restraint set against individualism, again and again in the course of this book, the theme of social control has merged with that of self-control, with the focus on the individual's management of self.

We may refer again here to the joking relationship, *bukulo*. From one point of view this may be interpreted after Sahlins as an explicit strategy for peace; a past mode of dispute settlement, a mechanism for turning a situation of enmity into one of amity. Yet, on another more existential level, it has been argued that it can be seen as a continual reminder of the presence of enmity in social life and speaks to the necessity for self-control, for the individual to subdue his anger. The locus of the battle, the dispositions towards peace (*lukoosi*) versus those of war (*lirima*), remain with the individual, in the heart of man.

This raises the more general question of how acephalous communities cope with fear and with the mechanisms of restraint in social life and here I talk of the Hobbesian threat not as a hypothetical but as a realised condition. This is a theme that has been in many ways central to social anthropology but the prevailing concern with order at an abstract level of structure, where all can ultimately be seen as self-regulating, has led to little emphasis on the experiential reality. The psychological dimensions have been little explored. Again, I have argued that this is what makes the Hobbesian model relevant for the Gisu; his concern with the basis of civil peace and his psychological atomism speaks directly to the problems posed by the kind of individual autonomy that the Gisu assert and to their consequent problems in reconciling this with a formulated desire for security.

Indeed what is important about the Hobbesian version of interest theory from this point of view is not that he presupposes that all men are involved in a relentless pursuit of their own self-interest but that the nature of social competition is coloured by fear. The basis for the equality of man with man lies in his capacity for mutual destruction. For Hobbes, secure social living depends on keeping man's passions in check; kept in check by making it reasonable to so do. He argues that in a condition of fear, nothing is reasonable except to strive for power since power alone can guarantee 'felicity', the ability to achieve one's ends in competition with other men. Here we do not need to follow Hobbes all the way, for where a state of fear reigns security can be secured not only by the 'pursuit of power after power', by battling first, but by withdrawal, as Sahlins has so cogently argued (1972). Translating this from the socio-spatial terms, the dispersion of people as pictured by Sahlins, to a psychological attitude, we may say that where there is minimal social control, the emphasis must also be on self-control and it is this aspect that has been underplayed in discussions of the Hobbesian dilemma. Yet, as has been said, this is the motif that runs throughout Gisu discussions of the problem. It is up to every man to control his 'anger', to avoid violent responses when in dispute, to refrain from vengeful impulses whether of theft or witchcraft or physical violence. And it is important to reiterate that this anger is not seen as an irrational emotional affect but as deeply tied to the motivational structures of the self. Indeed, *lirima* is part of the essential dispositions of manhood and linked to the ability to be determined and courageous in the face of death. Yet, in a very real way, this also and always implies self against others. The first time I heard the word it was translated into English for me as 'ambition', a word with strong derogatory overtones in Uganda at that time as it implied overweening ambition and ruthless self-interest. But again it must be stressed that this self-control lacked institutional supports. It was a pragmatic strategy for living, held by men in the face of their fear of others.

One possibility here is that this was not so much a preservation of an indigenous ideology but an exaggeration of it, an exaggeration made possible by the very imposition of colonial structures of authority, operating in a sense 'above' and 'outside' the structure of interpersonal interactions between fellow Gisu. Chanock (1985) has argued that the idea of 'custom' served to freeze the frame, masking the extensive transformations African social systems were undergoing in a response to colonial power, both political and economic. For example, 'to make "customary law", a jump had to be made from the facts of private vengeance and chiefly power to an ideal world of regular rules, fines, courts and penalties' (1985:137). This required collaboration between the British officials and local African elites, a collaboration which, as he demonstrates, was frequently based on opposed interests and misunderstandings. In the process, custom came to be the distinctive mark of ethnic identity, a process which disguised its non-traditionalist format, transformed as it was from a world where often there had been little regularity in its application or sanction to one where it was both codified in laws and subject to the regular enforcement of an authoritarian agency.

The way the Gisu think about the rules which they see as governing their life is still complex and many are tied to specific kinship and ancestry. I have argued in chapter 9 that the commitment to the idea of rules is not necessarily the mark of an authoritarian tradition but may be especially prominent in an egalitarian one where an orderly basis to social interaction can only be achieved by the assumption of absolute, taken-for-granted modes of behaviour and conduct. The etiquette of kinship is paradigmatic here. Yet the basic concept of *lukoosi* has undoubtedly been subject to revision and shifts of meaning. As has been indicated, *lukoosi* came to be identified with colonial structures of authority. It also became associated with a central tenet of Christianity, being the word used to translate the love or grace of God. Ultimately it was to be adapted yet again to the project the vigilante groups pursued. While this could be seen as a gradual accretion of meanings, a welding together of diverse philosophies, through their key principles of righteousness – law and order, Christian love, the attitude of generosity and respectful distance – perhaps one should be wary of seeing here the emergence of any unitary view. Such words, as Wittgenstein maintained, are essentially odd-job words; flexible as to usage, specific to context and purpose. In evoking *lukoosi*, people co-opt the most general principle of the 'good' and the 'legitimate' that the Gisu world holds out: in so doing, new models for action are created and go into the repertoire of the possible and the practicable. Nevertheless the means-to-ends relationship might well remain discrete, allowing for a multitude of possible combinations and recombinations.

With concepts such as *lirima* we might argue that the case is essentially different for this appears not as a goal, purpose or aim, but something which more profoundly shapes men's consciousness of themselves as moral agents, part of their very possibilities of being human. It is not available in quite the same way for intellectual bricolage. But this is not to say that it has remained unchanged and is an essentially 'uncontaminated' Gisu concept. Here we have to consider the wider dynamics of action and return to the question of the impact of colonial structures of authority. It seems fair to ask in this context how far the particular conditions of colonial peace acted to disengage the concept from that of warriorhood and make it a constitutional feature of manhood and Gisuhood. Did it in the process 'involute', the negative imagery which it implies being tolerable in conditions where there was an external regulatory system but one sufficiently distant that it could be disassociated from the interpersonal relations between Gisu and Gisu? If such questions know of no direct answer, it certainly seems possible that the impositions of colonial systems of authority allowed for a situation where the Gisu could maintain or even enhance an orientation to life at the community level that was fiercely egalitarian, and it was only with the withdrawal of this order that the negative consequences of agonistic competition became matters of concern.

Anthropologists are committed to explaining present structures in terms of the basic and specific tendencies of a given cultural system. Sahlins (1981, 1985), for example, talks of structures of the long run; Parkin (1978) of the unfolding of a cultural logic; Ardener (1970) of a template; Geertz (1963) of involution, whereby a culture elaborates an underlying dynamic. All have stressed the role of meaning. Yet if one stresses that culture consists of shared meanings which, by conditioning the actors' subjectivity, effectively determine the universe of action then culture becomes a closed system and lacks the capability of self-transformation (see Bloch, 1977). Change then becomes largely a matter of external influences and conjunctions. Older theories tended to envisage this process as a kind of ping-pong match between competing structures, where gains and losses could be easily attributable to each side until opposition gave way, as in American acculturation theory, or was maintained in an articulated opposition, as in some recent Marxist analyses. Sahlins (1981, 1985) gets around this conundrum by adopting a Parsonian position with respect to the dual character of symbols or structure. Symbols have meaning as part of a given cultural logic and also become contextualised in action as part of human projects. Meaning and purpose mutually shape each other and in situations of change where people accommodate to new challenges and situations, cultural structures get used to new ends and in the process incorporate new meanings. Culture thus is seen as an incorporating structure whereby the very process of reproduction may entail its own transformation.

Action against witches and thieves was undoubtedly a persistent feature of Gisu society, justified as it was in terms of the basic structures of personal motivation and morality. The response of the Gisu in mobilising against them is comprehensible in terms of the Gisu vision of people 'gone to the bad' and the motivational theory which justifies their killing. As elsewhere in Africa, it could be argued that this makes accusation a kind of litmus test for conflictual social change since these beliefs are central to the way moral issues are considered, tensions expressed and action taken. It may also be seen in standard sociological terms as a classic response to 'disorder'; the mobilisation against the deviant part of the struggle to impose a single and dominating vision on an intractable reality.

The symbolic role of crime emphasised by Durkheim (1938) leads to a consideration of values in terms of their polarities; good is pitted against evil so that the latter may be used to define the former. Criminality, then, appears as a social resource used to buttress the moral order, a well to be dipped in when crisis threatens. The processes by which people may become deviant then is of little moment to the social values they proclaim by default. This is true also of the interactionist school of thought, which puts the Durkheimian contention in a more modern idiom by arguing that criminality should be seen as an automatic consequence of rules and of the machinery used for prosecuting offenders. A rather different approach has been adopted here, for it is taken that the total social processes by which a person comes to be labelled deviant are intrinsic to the understanding of the uncompromising attitude adopted towards offenders and are indicative of the problems facing Gisu society. Here we might say that whereas good and evil may be seen as dialectical contrasts at the level of values, they are mutually implied in the course of life. By this, I not only mean that the achievement of any one vision of reality necessarily blocks out others, with the consequent problems of exclusion, marginality and deviance, but the achievement of the vision itself creates in the pragmatic course of life its own evil, distinctive to it.

As has been seen, accusations are rooted in domestic processes, in the battle over inheritance between juniors and seniors. In such a way they may also be linked to the external constraint of land and land pressure. Thus the fears of witchcraft and theft come to be representative of all the evil that men face from each other, the terms of the competition increasing in line with the conditions of increasing ecological stringency. The fact that it is the poor, the failures in life who are attributed with malevolent hostility towards others, leads to further considerations. Both the drinking companies and vigilantes in effect took the form of an alliance of the respectable against the unrespectable, the haves against the have-nots, a division which was tending to correspond to that of the landed against the landless. In a society where traditionally every man had access to land, they can therefore be seen as part of a process of rural social differentiation, of incipient class division. More directly, in a situation of intense land shortage, such action must also be seen as part of a process whereby the poor were being dispossessed, brutally faced with the alternatives of out-migration or death.

Yet this problem should not be seen as unique to Bugisu. Throughout Africa rural densities have been rising and men perforce have been leaving the land

and flocking in increasing numbers to the towns and other centres of employment. What is unspecified in most such accounts is the degree of 'push' and the degree of 'pull' in such migratory patterns. By and large the ethnography is lacking but the local dynamics in many African societies may well lead to patterns of effectively forced migration as in Bugisu. For example, in exploring a similar problem involving acute land shortage among the Chagga of Tanzania, Sally Moore interprets disputes and the ranking process contained within them as 'part of a desperate elimination contest in which the community must slough off members in order to survive' (1975:113). Again certain structurally-placed individuals are most at risk, in this case the middle sons, who are least favoured by the inheritance system. In commenting on the moral conflicts raised by this process she writes that some of the pain 'of rejecting a brother is ameliorated if he can be identified as a bad character who is at least partially to blame for his own plight, as a person who is morally inadequate' (1975:136). The fate of such men varies. Among the Chagga they are forced off the land to become the unskilled and often unemployed of the towns. Among the Gisu a similar process is discernible though, as is evident, a considerable proportion meet a violent end, becoming part of the rising crime statistics of East Africa.

Thus the witch and the thief were tangible targets for a community concerned to reform itself from within, but they may also be seen as symptomatic of the ills which assailed the community. And, in turn, the uncompromising attitude to poverty may be seen to rest on more general normative principles: the values placed on autonomous manhood and the basic achievements of the life course. Mary Douglas has written that 'the witch image is as effective as the idea of the community is strong' (1970:xxv). It might be worth thinking about the nature of this specific community. One could call it more an 'ideological' community than a social one: one defined more by its commitment to basic values and without strong social parameters. Nor is this totally unusual in East Africa. Parkin (1978) has contrasted the different political responses of the Kikuyu and Luo in modern Kenya and related each to a 'continuing paradigm of cultural logic' (1978: 307). In the first the lineage as the basis for political mobilisation has all but disappeared; in the second, it is as strong or even stronger than ever. Yet he demurs from calling the first a 'breakdown', for what constitutes lineage organisation is not uniform, it is an amalgam of tendencies. The Kikuyu have developed a far more individualistic pattern at the social level but, nevertheless, they have strong loyalties to the idea of themselves as a separate group, as Kikuyu. They mobilise not lineage against lineage, but rather in terms of the most general symbols of their common identity and common interest.

Gisu *imbalu* is certainly a generalised symbol of cultural distinctiveness and it is tempting to follow Parkin and see it likewise as having some kind of logical relationship to a non-segmentary system of descent. It unites all Gisu in an essentially undifferentiated way as subject to the same ancestral power. It also confirms and elevates the essential autonomy of each man: it gives it a value which makes it unassailable. To be a Gisu is to be such a man. The harshness of Gisu reactions to men who fail to live up to such an ideal is part of this pattern. In effect they must be proclaimed as deviants, lest the image of Gisu manhood itself come into question. Such reactions then may be seen as a way the Gisu preserve a cherished ideal of manhood at a time when increasing economic stringency is putting it under threat.

APPENDIX 1
THE HOMICIDE SURVEY

Extrapolations from case analysis, from the particular to the general, are often a problem for anthropological research. Even if the implications of a particular case seem solid in themselves, the single case may give no grounds for generalising the result. This was a particular problem for my research. I had, on the one hand, statistics which covered the district as a whole and, on the other, a mass of observations which were clearly located at a given point of time and in a small geographic region. What was the relationship between one set of data and the other? For, while local case analysis did not in itself tell the whole story nor, as discussed in chapter 2, did the District Court case records. While on some issues they could be used to confirm or reinforce the interpretation as, for example, on the male monopoly of violence and the age range of witches and thieves, the court case records did not contain the critical data on economic status that would allow me to be sure that the hunches I was inferring from case analysis in the local setting had wider relevance for patterns of Gisu murder.

Ideally, perhaps, case analysis alone could have given me the surety I wanted but even here I found that I had distinct sources of data and no 'natural' link. Thus, for example, after my first few months in the field, observation led me to suppose that the poor were at most risk of gaining reputations as 'troublemakers' and thus, by implication, in danger of being killed. But I had no cases where I knew the reputation of someone before he was killed. This was important, because collecting such information after a killing was to some extent suspect, since it involved collecting what could be seen as whole batteries of essentially *post hoc* rationales, as discussed with reference to the case of Wafaxale (case 11). Thus it was difficult to know whether the imputation of theft in such a case was really current prior to the murder or an a *posteriori* justification. Further, it was really only possible to investigate murders in any depth which occurred within a radius of about two miles from where I lived, for here I could use the kinship ties of my friends, make contacts and obtain information. In my first eighteen months in the field I had only come across five cases of murder in this area and I could not expect very many more cases in my second eighteen months.

Moreover, case analysis alone could not answer the question as to the relative economic position of the victims and accused in the population at large. Thus I was unsure both of the validity of my case analysis and of its generality. How far did impoverishment really underlie reputation and, in turn, murder? The homicide survey was designed to answer these questions and provide a way of testing whether the observations made on the basis of case analysis could be generalised more widely. The survey was concentrated in the three Central Bugisu sub-counties of Busoba, Bukhiende and Busiu. The plan was to take every case of homicide where it was believed a man had been killed occurring while I was in the field and up to six years before, and fill out a schedule for the victim, for the accused or suspects and for a reference group. At the planning stage most thought went into the selection of a reference group, and eventually it was decided to select these from among the neighbours of the victim, both to ease practical difficulties and to ensure that the samples were matched for ecological variability.

The reference group was selected by mapping an area around the house of the victim, usually up to a radius of between a quarter to half a mile, to include about thirty homesteads. Each adult man living there was then enumerated and six of these were chosen by the random number method. This method, though it does not produce a random sample of the male population, was found to have a number of distinct advantages. In the first place it gave me considerable information on the locality of the victim and usually, too, of the accused, as in the majority of cases they too lived within the mapped area. Moreover, once a good relationship had been established by my assistant in any area, there was then very little problem in gaining co-operation. Further, much of the information could be cross-checked with neighbours and often, too, with the local headman. For the victims, of course, the information had to be gathered in this way from kin and neighbours. Collecting genealogies also played a part in filling out many of the details which might otherwise be overlooked.

As it has methodological lessons for survey research in comparable situations in Africa, the reasons for not taking a random sample from the tax registers of the area should be indicated briefly. Firstly, there would have been the problem of locating the respondents, requiring extensive help from the local chiefs and inevitably giving the survey official overtones. Secondly, the area covered fell into distinct ecological zones where patterns of wealth might be expected to differ, and it was important that the reference group selected should match the victim/accused sample as closely as possible with respect to this factor. Thirdly, and most importantly, the tax registers could not be taken to give a 100% listing of the male population. There were legitimate exemptions from tax for the old, handicapped and sick and, in addition, there were also men who either managed to avoid being put on a register at all or who were registered in an area other than the one in which they were living. Using the registers would thus have resulted in a bias towards the 'settled' citizen who paid his taxes and excluded the poorest sections (of particular interest to this study) of the community who were, in one way or another, exempted.

The survey plan was reasonably successful though the full aims were not realised due to the constraint of time. The survey was begun in September 1967 and continued intermittently, as cases came up or when the pressure of other work allowed, through to the end of my period of fieldwork in May 1969. However, I had originally hoped that the sample of victims would reach 50 but I only managed to collect thirty-seven cases. In addition, this sample includes six attempted murders and one case of poisoning which was reported to the police as murder. Careful thought went into the inclusion of these seven cases. The Gisu tend to invoke the idea of murder after any serious beating, but the cases included are those where public opinion (in two cases supported by statements made to me by the accused) indicated that the intention had been to murder. All the victims suffered extensive physical injury and in three cases (a total of four victims) only the chance intervention of a third party, in one case a police patrol, would seem to have saved the man.

With regard to the suspects, those enumerated for statistical purposes were only those against whom there were strong grounds for suspicion and in addition were thought to be the actual killers, whether or not this had reached the formality of a police charge or was solely the opinion of neighbours. This figure does not therefore include those suspects who were thought to be merely implicated or even those whom in a few cases were thought to have instigated the murder. These additional suspects, however, are found in the listings at the end of this appendix which tabulates details on each case. The final sample thus consists of thirty-seven victims, fifty-eight accused and 174 men in the reference group. The reference group sample was unfortunately never completed for six cases due to lack of time, but, nevertheless, is large enough to provide an adequate base against which to assess any special characteristics of the victims and accused in homicide cases.

The small size of the victim sample does however preclude some of the objectives of the original survey. In particular, although the cases span the period from 1959 to 1969, there are insufficient numbers to see if there had been major changes in the pattern of murder occurring over this period. Moreover, the cross-tabulation of variables, although possible with this number, makes any conclusions based upon them tenuous and thus none are included in the following discussion. Rather, the cases have been categorised according to the dominant rationale given to the killings, i.e. witch-killing, thief-killing, killing by vigilante groups and the remainder bracketed together as miscellaneous, as in tables 15.8 and 15.9. Some of the categories clearly overlap but the following principles were used in allocating a case to a category. Firstly, the vigilante-killings include all the cases where I was reasonably certain that vigilante groups alone were responsible and thus the suspects could be regarded as members of such groups. In a number of other cases where the identity of the accused was unknown, vigilante activity was also rumoured, but these were classified elsewhere as either a thief- or witch-killing. The vigilante-killings and thief-killings overlap extensively as in the majority of cases the men killed by the vigilantes were reputed to be thieves. There were two exceptions to this: one victim was killed for being a troublemaker by shouting out curses, while another was killed while trying to protect his sister's son from a vigilante group (homicide surveys 21 and 24). The witch-killing category includes all cases where witchcraft was adduced as a reason for murder. Thus, overall, some twenty-three of the thirty-seven victims were attacked as witches or thieves and forty of the fifty-eight accused were suspects in these cases, ten of them being members of vigilante groups.

Overwhelmingly, the results of the survey support the hypothesis that the victims of homicide are likely to come from the poorer stratum of the community. Over half the victims (51.3%, table 15.2) were unmarried at the time of the survey, compared with only 23.8% of the reference group. In other respects they were also disadvantaged. While only 47% of the men of the reference group considered their landholdings to be smaller than the norm for their area, this percentage rises to 60% for the victims, with 12/37 being said to have no land at all (table 15.4). Nor did they as a group have any compensatory qualifications for earning a living such as education; twenty-seven had had none and only one had been to secondary school (table 15.5).

Although the victim sample is small, overall these correlations are highly significant and, if one looks at the breakdown by category given in table 15.8, then it is clear that the overall results are closely related to the large proportion of these victims killed as thieves or by vigilante groups. Of the seventeen victims in these categories, nine had no land, thirteen had no education and no less than fourteen were unmarried. Further, of these fourteen bachelors only three had ever been married and each of these had had a long period without a wife prior to his death (six, eleven and eighteen years respectively). This brings out forcefully that to be accused of theft is one aspect of the wifeless role in Bugisu. Further, table 15.3 shows that the proportion of unmarried men killed relative to the reference group increases with age. While, in terms of absolute numbers the highest proportion of bachelor victims occurs in the age group 17–30 as would be expected, older bachelors would appear to run a greater risk of being killed. in the age group 45–59 only 9% of the reference group are unmarried but of the twelve victims of this age, no less than five (41.7%) were unmarried. This again supports the inference from case analysis that the position of bachelors deteriorates with age and as the disparity between their position and that of their contemporaries becomes more marked. This correlation does not hold for victims over sixty and, while it is difficult to draw firm conclusions on the basis of such a small sample, nevertheless it does point to the operation of other factors in cases of witch-killing. Of the six cases where

Table 15.1 *Age*

	17–29	30–44	45–59	60+	Total
Victims	8 (21.6%)	13 (35.1%)	12 (32.4%)	4 (10.8%)	37 (100%)
Accused	18 (31.0%)	28 (48.24%)	9 (15.5%)	3 (5.2%)	58 (100%)
Reference group	47 (27.0%)	69 (39.65%)	34 (19.5%)	24 (13.8%)	174 (100%)

Table 15.2 *Marital status*

	Unmarried	1 wife: bridewealth partially paid	1 wife: full bridewealth paid	2 or more wives	Total
Victims	19 (51.35%)	2 (5.4%)	14 (37.8%)	2 (5.4%)	37 (100%)
Accused	20 (34.5%)	2 (3.45%)	32 (55.2%)	4 (6.9%)	58 (100%)
Reference group	38 (23.8%)	11 (6.3%)	105 (60.45%)	20 (11.5%)	174 (100%)

Table 15.3 *Proportion of bachelors by age*★

	17–29	30–44	45–59	60+	Total
Victims	7/8 (87.5%)	8/13 (61.5%)	5/12 (41.7%)	1/4 (25%)	21/37 (56.8%)
Accused	12/18 (66.7%)	8/29 (27.6%)	2/8 (25%)	0/3 (0%)	22/58 (37.9%)
Reference group	23/47 (49%)	17/69 (25%)	3/34 (9%)	6/24 (25%)	49/174 (28.2%)

Note: ★As the number of men who admitted not having paid the full amount of bridewealth was small they are included in the category of bachelors in this table.

Table 15.4 *Landholdings*

	None	Less than average	Average	More than average	Unknown	Total
Victims	12 (32.4%)	10 (27.0%)	11 (29.7%)	1 (2.7%)	3 (8.1%)	37 (100%)
Accused	16 (27.6%)	23 (39.6%)	15 (25.7%)	0 (0%)	4 (6.9%)	58 (100%)
Reference group	20 (11.5%)	61 (35.0%)	75 (42.95%)	12 (6.9%)	6 (3.6%)	174 (100%)

Table 15.5 *Education*

	None	*Primary*	*Secondary*	*Unknown*	*Total*
Victims	27 (73.0%)	8 (21.6%)	1 (2.7%)	1 (2.7%)	37 (100%)
Accused	38 (65.5%)	16 (27.6%)	3 (5.2%)	1 (1.7%)	58 (100%)
Reference group	92 (52.8%)	51 (29.3%)	30 (17.2%)	1 (0.6%)	174 (100%)

Table 15.6 *Number of members of lineage segment living within ½ mile of house*

	0–2	*3–6*	*7+*	*Total*
Victims	14 (37.8%)	9 (24.4%)	14 (37.8%)	37 (100%)
Accused	13 (22.5%)	18 (31%)	27 (46.5%)	58 (100%)
Reference group	44 (25.3%)	51 (29.3%)	79 (45.4%)	174 (100%)

Table 15.7 *Length of residence in area*

	Less than 1 yr	*1–5 yrs*	*6–10 yrs*	*11 or more yrs*	*Total*
Victims	8 (21.6%)	4 (10.8%)	0 (0%)	25 (67.5%)	37 (100%)
Accused	3 (5.2%)	6 (10.4%)	2 (3.85%)	47 (80.35%)	58 (100%)
Reference group	1 (0.6%)	7 (4%)	7 (4%)	159 (91.4%)	174 (100%)

Table 15.8 *Characteristics of victims by category*

	(1) Killed as witches	*(2)* Killed miscellaneous	*(3)* Killed by vigilantes	*(4)* Killed as thieves	*Total*
Numbers	6	14	6	11	37
(a) Age					
17–29		2		6	8
30–44		6	3	4	13
45–59	4	5	2	1	12
60+	2	1	1		4
(b) Unmarried	1	6	5	9	21
(c) No land	0	3	2	7	12
(d) No education	5	9	5	8	27
(e) Not more than 2 agnates in vicinity	3	6	0	5	14

Table 15.9 *Characteristics of accused by category*

	(1) Killed witches	*(2)* Killed miscellaneous	*(3)* Vigilantes	*(4)* Killed thieves	*Total*
Numbers	8	18	10	23	58*
(a) Age					
17–29	3	5	1	9	18
30–44	2	11	7	10	29
45–59	3	0	1	4	8
60 +	0	2	1	0	3
(b) Unmarried	5	9	2	7	23
(c) No land	4	5	1	7	17
(d) No education	2	15	8	14	39
(e) Not more than 2 agnates in vicinity	2	1	1	9	13

Note: *One accused is counted twice in this breakdown, as he was accused in a miscellaneous case (no. 10) and also member of a vigilante gang in another (no. 23).

the victims were accused of witchcraft, all were over forty-five years old, all but one was married and all had land.

While poverty as indicated by the lack of a wife and little land is most apparent with respect to those killed as thieves, it is also apparent with other categories of victim. It is noteworthy that only two victims could be regarded in any way as wealthy men. Both were polygamists and both were professional men, one a retired teacher and the other a young man who was the manager of a coffee-drying station (homicide surveys 16 and 19). These two cases stand out from the normal run on other criteria as well. While both were attacked by groups of men, in neither case was there any clear motive for the killing. Indeed, the killings were regarded as all but inexplicable; the men were not disliked by neighbours, nor were they known to have cause to fear any particular enemy. In both cases, rumour had it that the trouble lay in marital disputes, with one of the wives being thought to have possibly hired assassins to assuage her jealousy. However, in neither case were there any arrests, and implicating a wife – against whom no action was taken in either case – appeared very much as a kind of residual reason to be invoked when others were patently not applicable.

Turning to the accused, overall far fewer fell into the poorest segment of the population. In fact the accused sample fell into a position intermediate between that of the victims and that of the reference group on the criteria of wives, land and education, so that 34% were bachelors, 27% landless and 65% uneducated (tables 15.2, 15.4 and 15.5). The tabulation by category in table 15.9, however, suggests that those who kill thieves or belong to vigilante groups tend to be drawn from a more representative sample of the population, at least as regards economic factors, than other killers. Indeed, especially for the vigilante groups, it appears that membership is drawn from among the more 'respectable' citizens and of the ten men here only two were unmarried and one had no land. A very different picture emerges for the accused in miscellaneous and witch-killing cases and their characteristics most resemble those of the victims. Indeed, of the eight men said to have killed witches (table 15.9), five were unmarried and four had no land. This again gives support to the accusational dynamics outlined in chapter 5.

One other major pattern is apparent with respect to the overall contrast between victims and accused and that is the number who were relative strangers in the area in which they were living. As many as twelve (22.4%) of the victims had lived less than six years in the area where they were killed and some of these were described as forever wandering with no fixed abode (table 15.7). Since one can assume that such migration is as much forced as chosen, it again attests to their unpopularity. In addition it is likely to lead them to live in a new area where they have few close kinsmen, reinforcing their social marginality and leaving them isolated and more open to attack. Indeed, the victims in the sample did tend to have fewer agnates living in the immediate vicinity than appears usual, with fourteen (37.8%) having less than two (table 15.6). On this criterion the accused again appear very much more like the reference group, with only 22.5% having less than two agnates in the vicinity and 15.6% having lived in the area less than six years, though this latter percentage is considerably higher than that of the reference group of 4.6%.

The importance of the survey lies in the way it correlates what might have remained two discrete sets of data, namely interpersonal accusational patterns and actual killing. The results of the survey do indeed give confidence that one can extend the inferences made on the basis of case analysis and that patterns described in chapters have relevance for the overall pattern of Gisu murder. And, of greatest importance, since the survey links both the victims and to a lesser extent some categories of accused with those who are economically disadvantaged, it may be concluded that the increasing pressure on land in the district has been a contributory factor in the increasing rate of homicide.

KEY TO HOMICIDE SURVEY CASES

V – victim; A – accused; M – murder; AM – attempted murder; M/s – manslaughter; Acq. – acquitted; Arr.Q – arrested for questioning; withdrawn – charge withdrawn; disch. – case discharged; class. – classificatory; B – brother; F – father; FB – father's brother; FBS – father's brother's son; FF – father's father; FFZSS – father's father's sister's son's son; FZSS – father's sister's son's son; F-in-law – father-in-law; M – mother; MB – mother's brother; MBS – mother's brother's son; S – son; WFB – wife's father's brother; ZS – sister's son; * not believed to be a killer and not included as such in table 15

Homicide surveys 1–35

Case no.	Name of V	Age of V	Age of A	Relationship of V to A	Police charge	Area of residence	Distance between houses of A and V	Murder weapon	Date	Notes
Witch-killings										
1 Mutsonga (AM) case 3, 123–6		60	28	F	None	Soba	Same compound	Panga	10/65	Attacked in house at night, house burnt. A suspected father of cursing him.
2 Wanda		61	(1)31*	None	None	Soba	½ mile	Panga & strangula-tion	9/66	V a night-watchman killed while on duty. Involved in land dispute with A1 and his father A2. V moved his house away from A1 and A2 2 years previously. A1 accused him of being a night dancer, and V's brothers also suspected him of witchcraft and had migrated to Buganda. Hired killers, A5 and A6, suspected to have been involved together with A1 in 9.
			(2)74*	None	None		½ mile			
			(3)54*	WFB	None		100 yds.			
			(4)47*	FB	None		200 yds.			
			(5)51	None	None		½ mile			
			(6)57	Same lineage	None		200 yds.			
3 Wolubongo case 10, 180–1		65	(1)31	FB	Acq.	Siu	250 yds.	Spear	1/66	V and A1 and A2 drank together. V killed as returned home at night. V believed to be a curser.
			(2)35	FB	Acq.		250 yds.			
			(3)29*	M's lineage	None		50 yds.			
			(4)43*	M's lineage	None		100 yds.			
4 Watsala		71	51	None	Acq.	Siu	75 yds.	Spear	7/66	V's house set on fire and V killed as attempted to escape through window. V suspected of killing A's FB by witchcraft. Land dispute.

Case no.	Name of V	Age of V	Age of A	Relationship of V to A	Police charge	Area of residence	Distance between houses of A and V	Murder weapon	Date	Notes
5	Wamimbi	49	(1)24 (2)22	MB MB	Arr.Q Arr.Q	Soba	1 mile 1 mile	Unknown	4/68	V disappeared after visited by the 2 A. Body never found. 2 A believed V had cursed them. Believed hired killers or vigilantes also involved.
6	Wambalya	59	Unknown	Unknown	None	Sano	Unknown	Spear	6/66	Killed at night. Suspect believed to be one or more of his sons who believed he was cursing them with infertility.
Miscellaneous killings										
7	Wafaxale case 11, 185–96	41	(1)43 (2)39* (3)18* (4)61* (5)64* (6)58*	None B FFZSS FZSS ZS Same lineage	Arr.Q none Arr.Q Arr.Q Arr.Q Arr.Q	Soba	All within ½ mile	Panga	6/66	V ambushed after a beer party. Many suspects.
8	Wapuwa	40	44	B	Withdrawn	Soba	Adjacent	Panga	9/65	Fought after a beer party.
9	Ali (AM)	59	(1)31 (2)38 (3)29	None None None	3 yrs. 3 yrs. (escaped)	Soba	½ mile ½ mile ½ mile	Panga	7/67	V & 3 A's worked in butcher's shop. Ill-feeling over wages. 3 A's threatened to kill V, but neighbours kept watch and came to rescue.
10	Weyawo	59	29	F-in-law	Disch.	Kiende	150 yds.	Spear	6/66	V speared as came out to investigate noise in cattle-pen at night. A suspected as dispute over return of bridewealth.
11	Katenya case 5, 137–8	39	38	None	Acq.	Siu	250 yds.	Spear	12/60	House set on fire, V gave chase to arsonist and speared in plantation. Possible revenge murder.

Case no.	Name of V	Age of V	Age of A	Relationship of V to A	Police charge	Area of residence	Distance between houses of A and V	Murder weapon	Date	Notes
12 Muxama		26	(1)71 (2)68 (3)25*	S Class S B	Withdrawn Withdrawn None	Siu	Adjacent ½ mile Adjacent	Panga	2/68	V's body found in river.
13 Nambafu case 6, 160-1		18	18	FBS & age mate	M/s 18 mths.	Soba	50 yds.	Stick & strangulation	10/59	V's body found hanging on tree to make it look like suicide.
14 Wanumbi		65	33	F	M/s 5 yrs.	Kiende	Same compound	Stick	1/59	A asked V for some milk to drink, V refused saying he wished to sell it. A picked up stick and beat V. A reputation that 'kills for nothing'.
15 Masungu		53	18	None	Withdrawn	Kiende	100 yds.	Stick	7/68	Killed at local market, said to be a troublemaker. V a dependant of a man of the area, given shelter in return for removing his host's jigger fleas. Possibly some connection with case 30 as involved men of the same area and were within few months of each other.
16 Muleyi		54	Unknown	Unknown	None	Kiende	Unknown	Spear	3/60	House set on fire at night, V killed as tried to escape. V retired teacher. No known motive, but neighbours suspected wife of hiring killers.
17 Mandali		53	(1)43 (2)41 (3)44*	Class FF Class FF MB	None	Soba	400 yds. 400 yds. 700 yds.	Poison	9/68	V collapsed after drinking beer, believed poisoned by A1 and A2, on instigation of A3. V & A3 involved in land dispute; V wanted back the land he had previously sold to A3.

Case no.	Name of V	Age of V	Age of A	Relationship of V to A	Police charge	Area of residence	Distance between houses of A and V	Murder weapon	Date	Notes
18 Alabwa (AM)		36	(1)41 (2)26	None None	None	Soba	1 mile	Strangulation	4/69	V waylaid after beer party by 2A. V saved by passers-by. Possibly connected with no. 7.
19 Balayo (AM)		36	Unknown	Unknown	None	Sano	Unknown	Panga	8/67	Gang of men broke into house at night and left V for dead. 6 months before able to return to work as manager of coffee-drying station. No known motive; neighbours suspected one of his four wives of hiring killers.
20 Mukayi		41	(1)36 (2)43	None None	Withdrawn Withdrawn	Kiende	½ mile	Stick	1/63	Attacked during a beer-party brawl. V living in area as stranger.
Vigilante killings										
21 Calo		57	(1)38 (2)41 (3)40 (4)35 (5)40 (6)39	None None None None None None	M/s 18mths. M/s 18mths. Acq. Acq. Acq. Acq.	Soba	¾ mile	Knife	8/67	V gave sanctuary to his ZS who was being pursued by a vigilante gang who suspected him of stealing. Fight outside V's house; ZS escaped.
22 Palapande		33	Unknown	Unknown	None	Soba	Unknown	Panga	3/69	V a notorious thief who had only returned to his natal area the week before. Hearing of a plot to kill him, a local man called on the protection of the local vigilantes. Said vigilantes waited in plantation around the house and attacked 4 men as they tried to enter. All escaped, except V. Body never found.

Case no.	Name of V	Age of V	Age of A	Relationship of V to A	Police charge	Area of residence	Distance between houses of A and V	Murder weapon	Date	Notes
23 Sakulule		38	(1)65 (2)27 (3)45 (4)32	None None None None	Arr. Q Arr. Q Arr. Q None	Kiende	¾ mile ¾ mile ¾ mile ¾ mile	Unknown	1/68	Body never found. Said to have been killed by vigilantes as a thief. Disappeared after vigilantes took him out of a beer party.
24 Wanda (Cangi)		51	Unknown	Unknown	None	Kiende	Unknown	Panga	11/67	Said to have been killed by vigilantes for troublemaking, spreading scandal and shouting curses (tsilomo tse bumasala)
25 Musolwa		34	Unknown	Unknown	Unknown	Soba	Unknown	Unknown	8/69	V was convicted in no. 9, and suspected also of involvement in nos. 2 and 5 as hired killer. When released from prison was killed by vigilantes.
26 Wamusira		67	Unknown	Unknown	None	Sano	Unknown	Unknown	3/68	Killed in house at night by vigilante gang for theft.
Thief-killings 27 Mutsopa		29	36	MBS	M/s 2yrs.	Siu	1 mile	Stick	2/15	V reputed to be thief. Said that A invited V to drink at his house and presented V with the gift of a chicken as he was leaving. Then A raised the alarm and accused V of theft. V beated to death by crowd.
28 Mwayafu		24	(1)38 (2)20 (3)24 (4)26 (5)28	None MBS Lineage Lineage Lineage	All charged & sentenced M/s (judgement missing from court records)	Siu	1 mile 50yds. 100 yds. 200 yds. 100 yds.	Stick	9/67	V accused of theft.

Case no.	Name of V	Age of V	Age of A	Relationship of V to A	Police charge	Area of residence	Distance between houses of A and V	Murder weapon	Date	Notes
29	Kikuru	38	59	None	M/s 3mths.	Soba	½ mile	Spear	2/65	V a Kikuyu who worked as a driver for road contractors. A pleaded in court that found V stealing his cattle.
30	Wamulundi	55	(1)43 (2)37 (3)55 (4)45 (5)39 (6)39	None Lineage Lineage Lineage Lineage Lineage	With-drawn With-drawn With-drawn None None	Kiende	¼ mile ¼ mile ¼ mile ¼ mile ¼ mile	Stick	4/68	V attacked in market place at night, accused of stealing A1's sugar cane. V cut firewood to live as had no land.
31	(1) Wambi (2) Walyaula	40 30	(1)53 (2)44	None None	M/s 4mths. M/s 4mths.	Kiende	¾ mile	Stick	3/64	V1 lived with his MBS, V2. Party in search of stolen goat of A1 found the two serving goat meat to neighbours who had been helping to weed their millet. Arrested and beaten.
32	Wandulu	30	(1)22 (2)18	None None	M/s 4yrs.	Sano	Unknown	Stick	11/63	V stole radio of A1. A1 and his B, A2, chased and killed V.
33	Luboxa	30	Unknown	Unknown	M/s 3yrs.	Sano	Unknown	Stick	8/64	Killed when caught skinning a stolen cow.
34	Wabusiru	39	Unknown	Unknown	Unknown	Sano	Unknown	Panga	11/68	V well-known thief, killed in house at night by a group of men, possibly vigilantes.

Case no.	Name of V	Age of V	Age of A	Relationship of V to A	Police charge	Area of residence	Distance between houses of A and V	Murder weapon	Date	Notes
35	(1) Xauxa (AM)	21	(1)19	None	All A acq.	Soba	Within 1 mile	Sticks	9/67	A5 once friends with V, but fallen out over a debt. A5 associated with a vigilante group and called in his B, A1, and cousin, A6, and friends to deal with V1 as a thief. V2 also picked up as found wandering around at night. A5 told Vs would be taken to river and killed, but group intercepted by police.
	(2) Muxama (AM)	28	(2)40	None	of being		Within 1 mile			
			(3)37	None	armed at		Within 1 mile			
			(4)20	None	night and		Within 1 mile			
			(5)27	None	of assault		Within 1 mile			
			(6)27	None	causing		Within 1 mile			
					actual					
					bodily					
					harm					

GLOSSARY

liasa xuxwi-, to avenge
lo bu-, finger millet
loka xu-, to bewitch
   li/kama-, act of witchcraft
   loki bu-, witchcraft
lomo li/kama-, word
lomani umu/ba-, quarrelsome person
loosi, umu/ba-, old woman
losi bu-, witchcraft
luka mu/mi-, parish of the administrative system (Ganda)
lulu bu-, bitterness
lya xu-, to eat

makombe umu/ba-, ancestral ghost
   i-, home of the dead
mani ka-, strength
masala bu-, avoidance relationship
   umu/ba-, avoidance relative
maya ka-, troublemaking
mwoyo ku-, heart

ng'aa xu-, to play, joke
nje tsi-, deviance
nyala xu-, to be able
   bu-, ability/authority
   nyali bu-, ability/power

osa xuxwi-, to purify

rangisa xu-, to lead
rima li, anger
rola xu, to bewitch by
   rolo kama-, form of witchcraft

sa ci-, kindness/compassion
saala xu-, to give birth, produce
saale bu-, friendship
   umu/ba-, friend
saani umu-, fully mature man
sala xu-, to kill/slaughter
   i-, a cut
   kumu-, lethal medicine
samba xu-, to dance
sambwa umu/ba-, ancestral spirits
   kumu/kimi-, ancestral power
saza-, county of the administrative system (Ganda)
sera bu-, millet beer
simu ci/bi-, spirit shadow, life force
siro kumu/kimi-, avoidance
solana xu-, fight
soni bu-, avoidance relationship
   ba-, affines of opposite sex and alternate generation

tsi-, sexual fear/reticence
tamba xu, to be without, to be poor
   tambi umu/ba-, a poor man
   tambisa xu- to be a nuisance
   tambisi umu/ba-, trouble-maker
temu bu-, dangerousness
tongole bu-, village unit of the administration (Ganda)
tsuba xu-, to curse
   tsubi umu/ba-, curser
   tsubo ci-, cursing
tubuta xu-, to snatch from a joking partner
tumbafu xu-, to be confused, mixed-up
tuuli li/kama-, society/company

uli bu-, authority (Ganda)

wangala xu-, to come of age, last long, be brave
   wangafu umu-, brave man
were-, free, unincorporated spirit
wetsa xu-, search
weyani bu-, adultery

xafu (ingafu), cow
xala xu-, to cut
xomana xu-, to abuse
xonde ci-, hatred
xulu bu-, age/importance
   umu/ba-, elder
xwala xu-, to marry
   xwale bu-, marriage
   xwe bu-, bridewealth
xwingila xu-, to enter (circumcision)
xwonaka xu-, to spoil

KINSHIP TERMS

mayi, mother, i.e. kinswoman of senior generation (excepting father's sister) or married to kinsman of senior generation
papa, father, i.e. kinsman of senior generation (excepting mother's brother) or married to kinswomen of senior generation
umwana, child, i.e. junior kinsperson who calls speaker *mayi* or *papa*
kuka, grandfather, i.e., all kinsmen of the second ascending generation
kuxu, grandmother, i.e., all kinswomen of the second ascending generation
umwitsuxulu, grandchild, i.e. all kinspeople of the second descending generation
senge, father's sister, i.e., all women that father addresses as 'sister'
umwisengetsana, brother's child
xotsa, mother's brother, i.e., all men that mother addresses as 'brother'
umwiwana, sister's child
yaya, sibling of same sex
umukoko, (man speaking) sister, i.e. all kinswomen of the same generation excluding mother's sister's child
umusani, (woman speaking) brother, i.e. all kinsmen of the same generation excluding mother's sister's child

umusoni, mother's sister's child
mulamu, brother's wife, husband's brother's wife
masakwa, wife's sister's husband, parent of child's spouse
muxwasi, brother-in-law (man-speaking)

REFERENCES

Abrahams, R., 1985, 'A modern witch-hunt among the Lango of Uganda', *Cambridge Anthropology*, 10 (1): 32–44.

Abrahams, R. D. and Bauman, R., 1978, 'Ranges of festival behaviour', in B. Babcock (ed.), *The Reversible World*. Ithaca: Cornell University Press.

Apter, D., 1961, *The Political Kingdom in Uganda*. Princeton: University Press.

Apthorpe, R., 1967, 'Nsenga social ideas', *Mawazo*, 1: 23–30.

Ardener, E., 1970, 'Witchcraft, economics, and the continuity of belief ', in M. Douglas (ed.), *Witchcraft Confessions and Accusations*. London: Tavistock.

Ardener, S., 1964, 'The comparative study of rotating credit associations', *Journal of the Royal Anthropological Institute*, XCIV: 201–29.

Arendt, H., 1958, *The Human Condition*. Chicago: University Press.

Asad, T., 1987, 'On ritual and discipline in medieval Christian monasticism', *Economy and Society*, 16: 159–203.

Austin, R. A., 1986, 'Social bandits and other heroic criminals: western models of resistance and their relevance for Africa', in D. Crummey (ed.), *Banditry, Rebellions and Social Protest in Africa*. London: James Currey.

Barnes, J. A., 1967, 'The frequence of divorce', in A. L. Epstein (ed.), *The Craft of Social Anthropology*. London: Tavistock.

Beattie, J., 1970, 'On understanding ritual', in B. Wilson (ed.), *Rationality*. Oxford: Basil Blackwell.

Becker, H. S., 1963, *Outsiders*. New York: Collier-Macmillan.

Beidelman, T. O., 1963, 'Witchcraft in Ukaguru', in J. Middleton and E. H. Winter (eds.), *Witchcraft and Sorcery in East Africa*. London: Routledge and Kegan Paul.

——, 1966, 'Utani: some Kaguru notions of death, sexuality and affinity', *Southwestern Journal of Anthropology*, 22: 33–52.

Belshaw, D. G., Brock, B. and Wallace, I., 1966, *The Bugisu Coffee Industry: an economic and technical survey*. Report for International Bank for Reconstruction and Development.

Black-Michaud, J., 1975, *Cohesive Force: feud in the Mediterranean and the Middle East*. Oxford: Basil Blackwell.

Bloch, M., 1971, 'The moral and tactical meaning of kinship terms', *Man*, NS, 6: 79–87.

——, 1973, 'The long term and the short term: the economic and political significance of the morality of kinship', in J. Goody (ed.), *The Character of Kinship*. Cambridge: University Press.

——, 1977, 'The past and the present in the past', *Man*, NS, 12: 278–92.

Blok, A., 1974, *The Mafia of a Sicilian Village 1860–1960: a study of violent peasant entrepreneurs*. Oxford, Basil Blackwell.

Bohannan, L., 1952, 'A genealogical charter', Africa, 22: 301–15.

Bohannan, P. (ed.), 1960, *African Homicide and Suicide*. Princeton: University Press.

Bourdieu, P., 1965, 'The sentiment of honour in Kabyle society', in J. Peristiany (ed.), *Honour and Shame*. London: Wiedenfeld and Nicolson.

——, 1977, *Outline of a Theory of Practice*. Cambridge: University Press.

Brock, B., 1968, 'Land tenure and social change in Bugisu', *Nkanga, 4: Society and Social Change in Eastern Africa*.

Brown, G. 1968, 'The dialect situation in Bugisu', *Journal of African Languages*, 7, part 1: 58–67.

Bunker, S., 1983. 'Central–local struggles for bureaucratic control in Bugisu, Uganda', *American Ethnologist*, 10 (4): 749–69.

——, 1984, 'Ideologies of intervention: the Ugandan state and local organisations in Bugisu', *Africa*, 54 (3): 50–71.

——, 1987, *Peasants against the State*. Urbana and Chicago: University of Illinois Press.

Chambliss, W. and Seidman, R., 1971/82, *Law, Order and Power*. Massachusetts: Addison–Wesley.

Chanock, Martin, 1985, *Law, Custom and Social Order: the colonial experience in Malawi and Zambia*. Cambridge: University Press.

Christensen, J. B., 1963, 'Utani: joking, sexual licence and social obligation among the Kaguru', *American Anthropologist*, 65: 1314–27.

Cohen, S. (ed.), 1971, *Images of Deviance*. London: Penguin.

Colson, E., 1962, *The Plateau Tonga of Northern Rhodesia: social and religious studies*. Manchester: University Press.

Crick, M., 1976, *Explorations in Language and Meaning*. London: Malaby Press.

Doke, C. M., 1945, *Bantu: modern grammatical, phonetical and lexiographical studies since 1860*. London: Oxford University Press for the International African Institute.

Douglas, M., 1963, 'Techniques of sorcery control in Central Africa', in J. Middleton and E. H. Winter (eds.), *Witchcraft and Sorcery in East Africa*. London: Routledge and Kegan Paul.

——, 1966, *Purity and Danger*. London: Routledge and Kegan Paul.

——, 1967, 'Witch beliefs in Central Africa', *Africa*, 37: 72–80.

——, 1968, 'The social control of cognition: some factors in joke perception', *Man*, NS, 12: 154–65.

——, (ed.) 1970, *Witchcraft Confessions and Accusations*. London: Tavistock.

Durkheim, E., 1938, *The Rules of Sociological Method*. Chicago: University Press.

——, 1952, *Suicide: a study in sociology*. London: Routledge and Kegan Paul.

Erikson, K. T., 1962, 'Notes on the sociology of deviance', *Social Problems*, 9: 307–14.

——, 1966, *Wayward Puritans: a study in the sociology of deviance*. New York: John Wiley and Sons.

Evans-Pritchard, E. E., 1937, *Witchcraft, Oracles and Magic among the Azande of the Anglo-Egyptian Sudan*. Oxford: Clarendon Press.

——, 1940, *The Nuer*. Oxford: Clarendon Press.

——, 1965, *Theories of Primitive Religion*. Oxford: University Press.

Fadiman, J. A., 1982, *An Oral History of Tribal Warfare: the Meru of Mt. Kenya*. Ohio: University Press.

Fortes, M., 1945, *The Dynamics of Clanship among the Tallensi*. Oxford: University Press for the International African Institute.

——, 1953, 'The structure of unilineal descent groups', *American Anthropologist*, 55: 17–41.

——, 1959, *Oedipus and Job in West African Religion*. Cambridge: University Press.

——, 1961, 'Pietas in ancestor worship', *Journal of the Royal Anthropological Institute*, 91: 166–91.

——, 1965, 'Some reflections on ancestor worship in Africa', in M. Fortes and G. Dieterlen (eds.), *African Systems of Thought*. London: Oxford University Press.

——, 1966, 'Totem and taboo', *Proceedings of Royal Anthropoligical Institute*: 5–22.

——, 1969, *Kinship and the Social Order*. London: Routledge and Kegan Paul.

——, 1972. 'On the concept of the person among the Tallensi', in G. Dieterlen (ed.), *La Notion de la Personne en Afrique Noire*. Paris: Editions du Centre National de la Recherche Scientifique. Reprinted in Fortes (1987).

——, 1976, Introduction to W. H. Newell (ed.), *Ancestors*. The Hague: Mouton.

——, 1977, 'Custom and conscience in anthropological perspective', *International Review of Psychoanalysis*, 4: 127–54. Reprinted in Fortes (1987).

——, 1987, *Religion, Morality and the Person: essays on Tallensi religion*. Cambridge: University Press.

Freedman, J., 1977, 'Joking, affinity and the exchange of ritual services among the Kiga of Northern Ruanda: an essay on joking relationship theory', *Man*, NS, 12: 154–65.

Gayer, C., 1957, 'Report on land tenure in Bugisu', in Ministry of Land Tenure, *Land Tenure in Uganda*. Entebbe: Government Printer.

Geertz, C., 1962, 'The rotating credit association: a "middle-rung" in development', *Economic Development and Cultural Change*, 10: 241–63.

——, 1963, *Agricultural Involution. The processes of agricultural change in Indonesia*. Berkeley: University of California Press.

——, 1973, *The Interpretation of Cultures*. New York: Basic Books.

Gellner, E., 1969, *Saints of the Atlas*. London: Weidenfeld and Nicolson.

Giddens, A., 1976, *New Rules of Sociological Method*. London: Hutchinson.

——, 1979, *Central Problems in Social Theory*. London: Macmillan.

Gluckman, M., 1956, *Custom and Conflict in Africa*. Oxford: Basil Blackwell.

——, 1963, *Order and Rebellion in Tribal Africa*. London: Cohen.

Gray, Sir J., 1963, 'Kakungulu in Bukedi', *Uganda Journal*, 27: 46–7.

Greenblatt, S., 1982, 'Fithy rites', *Daedalus*, Summer: 1–16.

Griaule, M., 1948, 'L'alliance cathartique', *Africa*, 18: 242–58.

Gulliver, P. H., 1957, 'Joking relationships in Central Africa', *Man*, 57: 225.

Guthrie, M., 1948, *The Classification of the Bantu Languages*. London: Oxford University Press for the International African Institute.

Hailey, W. M. (Lord), 1950, *Native Administration in the British African Territories. Part I: East Africa*. London: HMSO.

Hallowell, A. I., 1955, 'The self and its behavioral environment', in *Culture and Experience*. Philadelphia: University Press.

Handelman, D., 1982, 'Reflexivity in festival and other cultural events', in M. Douglas (ed.), *Essays in the Sociology of Perception*, London: Routledge and Kegan Paul.

Heald, S., 1982a, 'The making of men: the relevance of vernacular psychology to the interpretation of a Gisu ritual', *Africa*, 52: 15–36.

——, 1982b, 'Chiefs and administrators in Bugisu', in A. F. Robertson (ed.), *Uganda's First Republic: chiefs, administrators and politicians, 1967–1971*. Cambridge: African Studies Centre.

——, 1986a, 'Witches and thieves: deviant motivations in Gisu society', *Man*, NS, 21 (1): 65–78.

——, 1986b, 'The ritual use of violence: circumcision among the Gisu of Uganda', in D. Riches (ed.), *The Anthropology of Violence*. Oxford: Basil Blackwell.

——, 1986c, 'Mafias in Africa: the rise of drinking companies and vigilante groups in Bugisu District, Uganda', *Africa*, 56: 446–67.

Henry, A. F. and Short, J. F., 1954, *Suicide and Homicide*. New York: The Free Press of Glencoe.

Hobbes, T., 1651/1968, *Leviathan*. Harmondsworth: Penguin.

Hobsbawm, E. J., 1959, *Primitive Rebels: studies in archaic forms of social movement in the 19th and 20th centuries*. Manchester: University Press.

Holy, L., 1979, 'The segmentary lineage structure and its existential status', in Holy (ed.), *Segmentary Lineage Systems Reconsidered*. Department of Social Anthropology, Queen's University of Belfast.

Howell, P. P., 1954, *A Manual of Nuer Law*. London: Oxford University Press for the International African Institute.

Howell, R. W., 1973, 'Teasing relationships', *Addison-Wesley Module in Anthropology*, 46.

Johnston, Sir H. H., 1902, *The Uganda Protectorate*, Vol. 2. London: Hutchinson.

——, 1919, *A Comparative Study of the Bantu and Semi-Bantu Languages*, Oxford: Clarendon Press.

Karp, I., 1978, 'New Guinea models in the African savannah', *Africa*, 48 (1): 1–16.

——, 1980a, Introduction to *Explorations in African Systems of Thought*, Bloomington: Indiana University Press.

——, 1980b, 'Beer drinking and social experience in an African society: an essay in formal sociology', in I. Karp and C. S. Bird (eds.), *Explorations in African Systems of Thought*. Bloomington: Indiana University Press.

Kennedy, J. G., 1970, 'Bonds of laughter among the Tarahumara Indians: towards the rethinking of joking relationship theory', in *The Social Anthropology of Latin America: essays in honor of Ralph Leon Beals*. Los Angeles: University of California. Latin American Studies Center.

Kenyatta, J., 1938, *Facing Mount Kenya*. London: Secker and Warburg.

Kerri, J. N., 1976, 'Studying voluntary associations as adaptive mechanisms: a review of anthropological perspectives', *Current Anthropology*, 17 (1): 25–47.

Kirk-Greene, A. H. M., 1980, 'The thin white line: the size of the British colonial service in Africa', *African Affairs*, 79, 25–44.

Kitsuse, J. I. and Cicourel, A. V., 1963, 'A note on the uses of official statistics', *Social Problems*, 11, 131–9.

Kuper, A., 1982, *Wives for Cattle: bridewealth and marriage in Southern Africa*. London: Routledge and Kegan Paul.

La Fontaine, J. S., 1957, 'The Social Organisation of the Gisu of Uganda with Special Reference to their Initiation Ceremonies', unpublished PhD thesis, Cambridge University.

——, 1959, *The Gisu of Uganda*, Ethnographic Survey of Africa. London: International African Institute.

——, 1960a 'The Gisu', in A. I. Richards (ed.), *East African Chiefs*. London: Faber and Faber for the East African Institute of Social Research.

——, 1960b, 'Homicide and suicide among the Gisu', in P. Bohannan (ed.), *African Homicide and Suicide*. Princeton: University Press.

——, 1962, 'Gisu marriage and affinal relationships', in M. Fortes (ed.), *Marriage in Tribal Societies*. Cambridge: University Press.

——, 1963, 'Witchcraft in Bugisu', in J. Middleton and E. H. Winter (eds.), *Witchcraft and Sorcery in East Africa*. London: Routledge and Kegan Paul.

——, 1967, 'Parricide in Bugisu: a study in intergenerational conflict', *Man*, NS, 2: 249–59.

——, 1969, 'Tribalism among the Gisu' in P. H. Gulliver (ed.), *Tradition and Transition in East Africa*. London: Routledge and Kegan Paul.

——, 1973, 'Descent in New Guinea: an Africanist view', in J. Goody (ed.), *The*

Character of Kinship. Cambridge: University Press.

——, 1977, 'The power of rights', *Man, NS*, 12: 421–37.

——, 1979, 'Land and the political community in Bugisu', in W. A. Shack and P. S. Cohen (eds.), *Politics in Leadership: a comparative perspective*. Oxford: Clarendon Press.

——, 1985, *Initiation*. Penguin Books.

Larner, C., 1984, *Witchcraft and Religion: the politics of popular belief*. Oxford: Basil Blackwell.

Lemert, E. M., 1967, *Human Deviance, Social Problems and Social Control*. Englewood Cliffs, New Jersey: Prentice Hall.

Levine, R. A. 1963, 'Witchcraft and sorcery in a Gusii community', in J. Middleton and E. H. Winter (eds.), *Witchcraft and Sorcery in East Africa*. London: Routledge and Kegan Paul.

——, 1984, 'Properties of culture: an ethnographic view', in R. A. Shweder and R. A. Levine (eds.), *Culture Theory: essays on mind, self and emotion*. Cambridge: University Press.

Lévi-Strauss, C., 1949 (reprinted 1969), *The Elementary Structures of Kinship*. London: Eyre and Spottiswoode.

Lienhardt, R. G., 1951, 'Some notions of witchcraft among the Dinka', *Africa*, 21: 303–18.

Low, D. A., 1973, *Lion Rampant: essays in the study of British imperialism*. London: Frank Cass.

Low, D. A., and Pratt, C., 1960, *Bugunda and British Overrule, 1900–1955*. London: Oxford University Press.

MacIntyre, A., 1981, *After Virtue: a study in moral theory*. London: Duckworth.

Marcus, G. E. and Fischer, M., 1986, *Anthropology as Cultural Critique*. Chicago: University Press.

Marwick, M., 1965, *Sorcery in its Social Setting*, Manchester: University Press.

Mauss, M., 1925 (reprinted 1954), *The Gift*. London: Cohen and West.

——, 1985, 'A category of the human mind: the notion of person; the notion of self' (translated by W. D. Halls), in M. Carrithers, S. Collins and S. Lukes (eds.), *The Category of the Person*. Cambridge: University Press.

Mayer, P., 1949, *The Lineage Principle in Gusii Society*. International African Institute, Memorandum no. 24.

Mazrui, A. A., 1970, 'Postlude: towards a theory of protest', in R. I. Rotberg and A. A. Mazrui (eds.), *Protest and Power in Black Africa*. New York: Oxford University Press.

Mbiti, J. S., 1969, *African Religions and Philosophy*. London: Heinemann.

Merton, R. K., 1957, *Social Theory and Social Structure*. New York: The Free Press of Glencoe.

Middleton, J., 1960, *Lugbara Religion: ritual and authority among an East African People*. London: Oxford University Press.

—— and Kershaw, G., 1965, *The Kikugu and Kamba of Kenya*. London: Oxford University Press for the International African Institute.

—— and Tait, D. (eds.), 1958, *Tribes Without Rulers*. London: Routledge and Kegan Paul.

Mitchell, J. C., 1956, *The Yao Village*, Manchester: University Press.

Moore, S. F., 1972, 'Legal liability and evolutionary interpretations: some aspects of strict liability, self-help and collective responsibility', in M. Gluckman (ed.), *The Allocation of Responsibility*. Manchester: University Press.

——, 1975, 'Selection for failure in a small social field: ritual concord and fraternal strife among the Chagga, Kilimanjaro, 1968–1969', in S. F. Moore and B. Meyerhoff (eds.), *Symbol and Politics in Communal Ideology*. Ithaca: Cornell University Press.

Moreau, R. E., 1944, 'Joking relationships in Tanganika', *Africa*, 14: 386–400.

Murphy, R., 1971, *The Dialectics of Social Life. Alarms and excursions in anthropological theory*. London: Allen and Unwin.

Ocaya-Lakidi, Dent, 1979, 'Manhood, warriorhood and sex in Eastern Africa', *Journal of Asian and African Studies, XII:* 134–65.

Parkin, D., 1968, 'Medicines and men of influence', *Man, NS, 3:* 424–39.

——, 1978, *The Cultural Definition of Political Response: lineal destiny among the Luo*. London and New York: Academic Press.

——, 1982, Introduction to *Semantic Anthropology*. London: Academic Press.

——, 1986, 'Towards an apprehension of fear', in D. L. Scruton (ed.), *Sociophobics: the anthropology of fear*. Boulder and London: Westview Press.

Pedler, F. J., 1940, 'Joking relationships in E. Africa', *Africa*, 13: 170–3.

Perryman, P. W., 1937, 'Native witchcraft', *Uganda Journal*, 4 (1): 7–27.

Peters, E., 1967, 'Some structural aspects of the feud among the camel-herding Bedouin of Cyrenaica', *Africa*, 37: 261–82.

——, 1975, Foreword in J. Black-Michaud, *Cohesive Force*. Oxford: Basil Blackwell.

Purvis, Rev. J. B., 1904, *A Grammar of the Lumasaba Language*. London: Society for the Propagation of the Gospel.

——, 1909, *Through Uganda to Mount Elgon*. London: T. Fisher Unwin.

Radcliffe-Brown, A. R., 1940a, 'On joking relationships', *Africa*, 13: 195–210. Reprinted in Radcliffe-Brown, 1952.

——, 1940b, Preface to E. E. Evans-Pritchard and M. Fortes (eds.), *African Political Systems*. Oxford: University Press for the International African Institute.

——, 1949, 'A further note on joking relationships', *Africa*, 19: 133–40. Reprinted in Radcliffe-Brown, 1952.

——, 1952, *Structure and Function in Primitive Society*. New York: The Free Press of Glencoe.

Read, K. E., 1955, 'Morality and the concept of the person among the Gahuku-Gama', *Oceania*, 25: 233–82.

Reynolds, Vernon, 1958, 'Joking relationships in Africa', letter to *Man*, 21: 29–30.

Richards, A. I., 1935, 'A modern movement of witch-finders'. *Africa*, 8 (4): 448–61.

——, 1937, 'Reciprocal clan relationships among the Bemba of N.E. Rhodesia', *Man*, 222: 188–93.

—— 1956, *Economic Development and Tribal Change*. Cambridge: Heffer.

Rigby, P., 1968, 'Joking relationships, kin categories and clanship among the Gogo', *Africa*, 38: 133–54.

Roberts, D. A., 1962, 'The sub-imperialism of the Ganda', *Journal of African History*, 3 (3), 435–50.

Roscoe, J., 1915, *The Northern Bantu*. Cambridge: University Press.

——, 1924, *The Bagesu and Other Tribes of the Uganda Protectorate: the Third Part of the Report of the Mackie Ethnological Expedition to Africa*. Cambridge: University Press.

Roy, J., 1984, *Hobbes and Freud*. Canadian Philosophical Monograph.

Sahlins, M., 1961, 'The segmentary lineage: an organization of predatory expansion', *American Anthropologist*, 63: 322–45.

——, 1968, *Tribesmen*. New Jersey: Prentice Hall.

——, 1972, *The Stone Age Economics*, London: Tavistock.

——, 1981, *Historical Metaphors and Mythical Realities*. Ann Arbor: University of Michigan Press.

——, 1985, *Islands of History*. Chicago: University Press.

Salzman, P. C., 1978, 'Does complementary opposition exist?', *American Anthropologist*, 80: 53–70.

Schacter, S. and Singer, J., 1962, 'Cognitive, social and physiological determinants of emotional state', *Psychological Review*, 69: 379–99.

Schapera, I., 1955, 'The sin of Cain', *Journal of the Royal Anthropological Institute*, 85, 33–43.

Scheffler, H. W., 1966, 'Ancestor worship in anthropology: or observations on descent and descent groups', *Current Anthropology*, 7: 541–51.

Sharman, A., 1969, ' "Joking" in Padhola: categorical relationships, choice and social control', *Man, NS*, 4: 103–17.

Shweder, R. A. and LeVine, R. A. (eds.), 1984, *Culture Theory: essays on mind, self and emotion*. Cambridge: University Press.

Siertsema, B., 1981, *Masaba Word List*. Musée Royal de l'Afrique Centrale, Archives d'anthropologie.

Southall, A. W., 1960, 'Homicide and suicide among the Alur', in P. Bohannan (ed.), *African Homicide and Suicide*. Princeton: University Press.

——, 1970, 'The illusion of tribe', *Journal of Asian and African Studies*, 5: 1–12, 28–50.

——, 1976, 'Nuer and Dinka are people: ecology, ethnicity and logical possibility', *Man, NS*, 11 (4): 463–91.

Stevens, P., 1978, 'Bachama joking categories: towards new perspectives in the study of joking relationships', *Journal of Anthropological Research*, 34: 47–71.

Strathern, A., 1973, 'Kinship, descent and locality: some New Guinea examples', in J. Goody (ed.), *The Character of Kinship*. Cambridge: University Press.

Strauss, J. H. and M. A., 1953, 'Suicide, homicide and social structure in Ceylon', *American Journal of Sociology*, 58, (5).

Taylor, I., Walton, P., and Young, J. (eds.), 1973, *The New Criminology: for a social theory of deviance*. London: Routledge and Kegan Paul.

Tempels, P., 1959, *Bantu Philosophy*. Paris: *Présence Africaine*.

Tew, M., 1951, 'A further note on funeral friendships', *Africa*, 21: 122–4.

Thomas, H. B., 1939, 'Capex Imperii – the story of Semei Kakunguru', *Uganda Journal*, 6: 125–36.

Turner, V. W., 1957, *Schism and Continuity in an African Society*. Manchester: University Press.

——, 1964, 'Witchcraft and sorcery: taxonomy versus dynamics', *Africa*, 34: 314–24.

——, 1969, 'Symbolization and patterning in the circumcision rites of two Bantu-speaking societies', in M. Douglas and P. Kaberry (eds.), *Man in Africa*. London: Tavistock.

Twaddle, M., 1966, 'The founding of Mbale', *Uganda Journal*, 27: 25–38.

——, 1969, 'Tribalism in Eastern Uganda', in P. Gulliver (ed.), *Tradition and Transition in East Africa*.London: Routledge and Kegan Paul.

Tylor, E. B., 1871, *Primitive Culture*. London.

Uganda Government (Official Reports) 1960, Uganda General Census, 1959, Vols. 1 and 11.

——, 1965, Report on Uganda Census of Agriculture 1963–64, Vols. 1, 11 and 111.

——, 1960–70 Uganda Statistical Abstracts.

——, 1967, *Uganda Atlas* (2nd edition).

Van Binsbergen, Wim. M. J., 1981, *Religious Change in Zambia, Exploratory Studies*. London: Kegan Paul International.

Vincent, J., 1982, *Teso in Transformation: the political economy of peasant and class in Eastern Africa*. University of California.

Von Hentig, H., 1948, *The Criminal and his Victim*. New Haven: Yale University Press.

Wagner, G., 1940, 'The political organisation of the Bantu of Kavirondo', in E. E. Evans-Pritchard and M. Fortes (eds.), *African Political Systems*. London: Oxford University Press for the International African Institute.

——, 1970, *The Bantu of Western Kenya*. Vol. 1. London: Oxford University Press.

Wallace, I. R., Belshaw, D. G. R. and Brock, B., 1973, *The Bagisu Coffee Industry: an economic and technical report*. Makerere Institute of Social Research.

Weber, M., 1948, 'The protestant sects and the spirit of capitalism', in H. H. Garth and C. W. Mills (eds.), *From Max Weber: essays in sociology*. London: Routledge and Kegan Paul.

Were, G. S., 1977–78, 'The historical origins of circumcision among the Bamasaba', *Transafrican Journal of History*, 6 and 7: 129–41.

——, 1982, 'The Bagisu and their past: some notes on their legends about creation, the origins of death, the economy of their ancestors and the phenomenon of Kintu', *Transafrican Journal of History*, 11, 184–95.

Willis, R. G., 1968. 'Kamcape: an anti-sorcery movement in south-west Tanzania', *Africa*, 38 (1): 1–15.

——, 1970, 'Instant millennium: the sociology of African witch-cleansing cults', in M. Douglas (ed.), *Witchcraft Confessions and Accusations*. London: Tavistock.

Wilson, M., 1957, 'Joking relationships in Central Africa', letter to *Man*, 140: 111–12.

Wolf, Jan de, 1977, *Differentialism and Integration in Western Kenya*. The Hague: Mouton.

Wolfgang, M. E., 1958, *Patterns in Criminal Homicide*. New York: University of Pennsylvania Press.

Worsley, P. M., 1957, *The Trumpet Shall Sound: a study of 'cargo' cults in Melanesia*. London: MacGibbon and Kee.

Zahan, D., 1970, *The Religion, Spirituality, and Thought of Traditional Africa*. Chicago and London: University of Chicago Press.

INDEX